A History of Motors and Motoring 1901~1902~1903

Volume two

Edited by Michael Frostick

ISBN 085429 216 0

FOULIS

Haynes

Acknowledgements

The Editor and Publishers would like to express their gratitude to the National Motor Museum at Beaulieu for assistance without which this series could not have come into being. Particular thanks are due to Lord Montagu for placing the library at their disposal and to Mr Eric Bellamy, the librarian, for much specialised assistance. Thanks are also due to Mr Michael Ware the Curator and to the photographic department. They would also like to thank the editor and publishers of many motoring magazines who have offered their co-operation.

Introduction – about this volume

After about seventy-five years of life, the Motor Car, the Automobile - call it what you will - has suddenly developed a 'history'. Old cars have become museum pieces of great value, books and catalogues are becoming rare, and many magazines priceless. All this because not only are historians naturally interested; but because many ordinary motorists, and their families, are also fascinated to know how it all started. The Ford that came before their Ford, the Austin before their Austin, the road before their road.

Though many painstaking and excellent books have been written on specialised subjects, there is really no better way to know what went on than to study the contemporary magazines which told the story as it happened. They give not only the facts, but the attitude of the motorist and towards the motorist of that time. A year by year account of how the rich man's hobby grew into everyman's transport.

Unhappily the search, up to now, has been difficult, for not even the library of the National Motor Museum has everything (though it has more than most) and Public Libraries, understandably, have little to offer. A complete "run" of either the *Autocar* or the *Motor* should it ever appear at an auction would fetch well in excess of £5000. The sole aim of this series, therefore, is to provide, an exact reproduction, a digest of the contemporary magazines from which, at modest cost, anyone interested can follow the story as it was originally told - an opportunity that has never previously existed.

Some criticism was levelled at the first volume on the grounds that the page headings from the original articles had been removed, and therefore those enthusiasts who wanted not only the information, but the chapter-and-verse as well, felt thwarted. The removal of the page headings was done deliberately as it was felt that in the end, the book looked nicer; but bowing to public demand, we are happy to include the information this time. However, still mindful that the book needs to stand on its own feet we have not felt bound to stick to an absolute date order.

Introduction to Volume Two

We like to think that our present rate of technical development is astonishing; but in fact it pales into insignificance beside the strides that motoring made in the first few years of its life. By the turn of the century cars had become a lot less of an adventure, they had become more readily available, and much more reliable; and although still unpopular with the horse-brigade had been accepted, even in England, as something that was with us for keeps.

Three things dominate the period covered by this volume. The wild inter-city races - including the beginnings of the Gordon Bennett cup races, which went on to give birth to the Grands Prix. The formation, particularly in these Islands, of restricting legislation; and the development of many firms whose names have but recently gone from the scene and whose products achieved world wide popularity in the apogee of private motoring between the wars.

The book opens with the death of Queen Victoria - a passing felt by the nation in a way we can no longer really understand; but which is reflected even in the motoring press so that it makes an important, if sombre, beginning.

Commercial vehicles and motor cycles are much in evidence, and not only widen the scope of our story but give us an insight into the spreading influence of the internal combustion engine. In our first volume, people were still frightened by the thought of an engine inside which explosions took place; but by now those engines had become commonplace, although the snags of over-popularity which were to emerge after the second world war had not even been dreamt of.

There are signs that the military were waking up to the possibility of using cars as weapons of war, although it needed the Kaiser's assault to bring them to do anything about it. But at least Mr. Simms was on the warpath of a successful sale.

In the private sector there was now a wide choice of cars, and garages were springing up. The Doctor's Coupe made its first appearance and names such as Mercedes and Benz (although not yet joined) were as prominent as the British Daimler, Packard, Napier, Wolseley, Vauxhall and all. The game had started in earnest.

Of all the games, the inter-city races were the most exciting: the Paris-Bordeaux and the Paris-Vienna and then, of course, the ill-fated Paris-Madrid which brought it all to a sad, but perhaps timely, end. Mixed up with all this were the Gordon Bennett races, run for a cup given by an American Newspaper proprietor by the name of James Gordon Bennett - no less a person, in fact, than the man who had sent Stanley after Livingstone. At first these races were incorporated in the town-to-town events, but later became separated, to carry the flag of motor racing on until the French launched the first Grand Prix.

The regulations were somewhat curious but the enthusiasm unbounded - particularly on a national level. To counter these jingoistic events there were a number of much smaller and much merrier happenings: hill-climbing, speed trials and even motoring events lasting a whole week, were much in favour with the ordinary enthusiast - and you were more or less an enthusiast by definition as soon as you bought a car.

Across the Atlantic it was much the same story, with speed and endurance runs becoming popular, and as we can see even getting themselves reported in the British press.

France, if anywhere, could lay claim to being the most motor minded of countries, with definitive road signs already in use and a fine big motor show to round off our present volume.

Legislation was being enacted everywhere to control the car and the motorist was already getting a bad name. The debates went on, speed traps and number plates were in the air and the cartoonists were already at work on the maniac motorist. Someone went out to prove that the horse wasn't as safe as all that, and the "dreaded side-slip" became something that had to be contended with long before the invention of skid-schools.

Technical development was steady, rather than astonishing, but the greatest advances were in simplicity of use, reliability (touring became a reasonable possibility even on the continent) and silence. Speed was sought by a few and the makers of lights and tyres struggled to keep up. The sunrise of popular motoring was still a long way off; but the grey dawn was taking a hold on the sky and the early birds were having the time of their lives.

Lastly the journals from which our story is gathered were proliferating. *The Autocar* (which had begun to give up hope of convincing everyone that that was what a car should be called) was joined by *The Motor* - only that distinguished journal was in fact called *Motor Cycling and Motoring*. *The Automotor Journal* (the Yellow Book) went on giving perhaps the best technical descriptions of the time, and the field was widened and enhanced by Lord Montagu's Journal *Car Illustrated*. Although some extracts from it have been included here we can hardly do it justice, for it was as much a social journal as a motoring one - full of stately homes (none of them open to the public) and their stately owners, some of whom, particularly the ladies, looked more than a little on the fierce side. The motor Car was established and the Edwardian splendours only just round the corner.

Contents

THE AUTOCAR

A Journal published in the interests of the mechanically propelled road carriage.

EDITED BY HENRY STURMEY.

No. 274. Vol. VI.] SATURDAY, JANUARY 26TH, 1901. [Price 3D.

THE AUTOCAR.

EDITORIAL OFFICES :
19, HERTFORD STREET, COVENTRY.

PUBLISHING OFFICES :
3, ST. BRIDE STREET, LUDGATE CIRCUS, LONDON, E.C.

THE NATION'S LOSS.

All automobilists from the King downwards in common with the entire British Empire are mourning the death of Queen Victoria. It is superfluous for us to dwell here upon the loss which the nation has sustained, and every journal in the land and beyond the seas is already, and no doubt will be for many a day to come, sounding the well-deserved praises of the great lady who has gone. At the same time we think one of her many great qualities may possibly be overlooked, and to this we may well refer. It is necessary to remember that our departed ruler belonged really to a former generation; yet she adapted herself without exhibiting the least sign of prejudice to all the mechanical and scientific advances which have made the Victorian era the most remarkable of any epoch in the history of the world's progress. It is only necessary to think for a moment of the methods of locomotion which were in vogue in 1837 and those of which the Queen availed herself almost up to the last to see what a singularly unprejudiced mind her's was. The only vestige of reluctance to avail herself of modern methods was the way in which she continued to travel by road for some years after the railways had become a part of national life. For this personal preference no one can blame her, as it is perfectly certain that the road equipages at her disposal were far pleasanter than the early railway coaches, and as Sovereign she surely had the right of adopting that mode of travel which she most enjoyed. If she then preferred the road she never opposed the railway. This aspect of her grand character should be studied by all those small-minded persons who would stifle everything that is new simply because it is not mellowed with age. In what regard would Victoria the Good have been held had she shown a tithe of such narrow-minded opposition to the mechanical advances which took place during her glorious and beneficent reign?

CONTENTS.

COLONIAL AND FOREIGN EDITION.

IN ADDITION TO THE USUAL EDITION OF "THE AUTOCAR," A SPECIAL THIN EDITION IS PUBLISHED EACH WEEK FOR CIRCULATION ABROAD. THIS THIN ISSUE CAN ONLY BE OBTAINED BY DIRECT SUBSCRIPTION. THE ENGLISH AND FOREIGN RATES WILL BE FOUND ON THE LAST PAGE. ORDERS WITH REMITTANCE SHOULD BE ADDRESSED "THE AUTOCAR," COVENTRY.

Notes.

A SATISFACTORY RECORD.

Despite many demonstrations to the contrary, so many people insist in regarding the autocar as an unpracticable vehicle, that the following extract from a letter which we have received from Mr. P. Brown, of Caldy Manor, West Kirby, will not be without interest. We may say that the machine referred to is a six horse-power Parisian Daimler. "During the last six months the car has covered 4,427 miles, an average of 170 miles per week, and in all weathers and over some very bad roads too, and never, with the exception of a few punctures, had any trouble with engine or any part of car. It has been a grand success, and is a great credit to the makers, the Daimler Motor Co., Ltd., of Coventry. The cost for all petrol, lubricating oil, grease, and methylated spirits used works out at ¾d. per mile."

THE 4½ H.P. DURYEA CAR.

There was a time when the performance of a certain Duryea car between London and Brighton, particularly with regard to the exact hour of its arrival at London-super-Mare, aroused a good deal of interest in this car, and provoked a stream of what the correspondents of the sporting press refer to as "paper talk." Since then Duryea cars have been little heard of in this country, but now that one is to be seen at Friswell's, 48, Holborn Viaduct, the curiosity of automobilists generally is certain to be aroused. By the embodied elevation we give of it, it will be seen to be a smart-looking vehicle with a suggestion of Benz *carosserie* about it, and, in fact, it is altogether a carefully-considered, well-designed, and beautifully-finished vehicle. Reference to the plan shows the two-cylinder engine to be set beneath the seat on the right of the car. The cylinders are each 4in. bore, and the stroke of the pistons is 4¼in. Mr. Friswell tells us that the engine gives six and a quarter horse-power on the brake, with 870 revolutions per minute. The toothed gear, which is always in mesh, and drives only when one of two cone clutches are thrown in, gives two speeds forward (eight miles and twenty-two miles) and one reverse. The ignition is by dynamo, which, as can be seen by plan, is driven off the fly-wheel by a belt, accumulators being carried for starting purposes only. All control is concentrated on the one lever seen at the left-hand side, and by which not only are the clutches thrown in and out, but the mixture feed

to the cylinders is choked, or the electric current interrupted.

The steering is effected by the handle seen in the centre of the car, the standard being set close up to the seat to allow the knee rugs to be comfortably arranged. To our mind that is the sole recommendation of such a system. At first sight the engine gear, etc., appear very ungetatable, but this is not really so, for the body of the car is held in position on the frame by catches only, and is lifted right off with the greatest ease, exposing everything at once. Mr. Friswell was good enough to run the engine for our benefit, and although the explosions are not balanced as in the Turrell car, there is but little vibration, and when the car is standing the engine can be made to run very slowly indeed by the choking of the induction already referred to. The ignition cannot be variously timed. Altogether, this specimen of American automobile building is well worth inspection.

A CONVERTED BICYCLE.

The accompanying illustration shows an ordinary safety bicycle fitted with the motor parts which can now be supplied by the London Autocar Co.,

of 182, Gray's Inn Road, W.C. The motor, which is secured to the bottom tube by means of an aluminium casting, forming part of the crank chamber, is 2 3-16in. bore and 2⅜in. stroke, nominally about one horse-power. The carburetter and battery are contained in one case. The commutator has a contact maker on the Aster principle, i.e., a simple make and break, no trembler. The sparking coil (not shown) is carried on the back stays behind the saddle.

* * *

Messrs. Carless, Capel. and Leonard, Hope Chemical Works, Hackney Wick, N.E., have issued a new edition of their little book on "Petrol: What it is, where it may be obtained, and other information to autocarists." The booklet contains all necessary information for the safe storage of petrol, and the rules of the railway companies for its conveyance. It also gives particulars of the firm's special lubricating oils and greases for motors. The list of agents has been revised to date, over one hundred fresh names having been added. The firm advise us that they will be pleased to forward a copy to anyone applying for same.

* * *

The autocar appears to have become quite a permanent feature in Algeria. At Mustapha the representative of a French autocar firm has just opened a large garage, and is also devoting attention to the question of automobile waggons for the transport of goods over Algerian roads.

THE FIRST SUCCESSFUL PNEUMATIC-TYRED OMNIBUS.

A Most Interesting Trial.

By Echaudé.

A Composite (first and second class) Omnibus.

On its return to the works from the grand manœuvres, where it had been scouring the country with the foreign military *attachés*, the new De Dion-Bouton steam omnibus was to take the writer on a trip in order that a special report might be penned for the benefit of readers of *The Autocar*.

The telephone had announced its arrival at Puteaux, and a *rendezvous* was fixed for the morrow at 3 p.m.

Mr. Hugh Wegulin and Mr. Charles Rush, of London, who were visiting Paris, accompanied me, as they were also desirous of having an opportunity of testing the capabilities of this latest pattern steam omnibus.

One of the principal features is that it is fitted with four and a half inch Michelin pneumatic tyres.

This is, of course, a great stride along the path of progress, as no pneumatic tyres have hitherto been able to successfully support enormous weights. The new omnibus has been considerably reduced in weight, the present one only weighing, empty, without fuel or water, 2,200 kilogs. (about 2 tons 400 lbs.), but still a great weight for pneumatics.

The motor is twenty horse-power, the casing is all made in aluminium, and the engine complete only weighs 450 kilogs. (about 900 lbs.) Sufficient water is carried to drive twenty miles without a stop, and a supply of coke for sixty-two miles. The average speed on give-and-take roads is from twelve to eighteen miles an hour, but on the top gear " all out " on a level road the speed will often surpass twenty-five miles per hour.

We steamed out of the Puteaux Works about 3.40 p.m. *en route* for St. Germain. The first im-

pression of this omnibus, running on pneumatic tyres, to one who has been accustomed to the broad iron-shod wheels, which are so noisy, grinding over gravel and *pavé*, makes the comparison decidedly peculiar, as not only did we glide noiselessly over the rough *pavé* to Suresnes, but the speed was sensational, especially when the long hill up towards the Fort Mont Valérien was taken at a good twelve miles per hour.

We hardly felt at ease as we speedily wound down the deep sloping hill towards Rueil, and it must be admitted going at full speed there was a nasty roll at the extreme end of the 'bus, which was caused by a side sway on the big tyres.

We were rather unhappy going over twenty miles an hour down hill in an omnibus weighing over two tons. especially Mr. Hugh Wegulin, who stated candidly that he would much rather be at the helm of his sixteen horse-power racing Panhard and travelling at twice the speed than risking his life in the hands of even an expert French driver.

It is a fact that all autocarists are like " fishes out of water " anywhere but at the steering-wheel when on a strange car. One gets a fit of fidgets when speed is tempted, especially in traffic. Here you have uncomfortable twitches on your seat, and occasional mechanical snatches at the steering-wheel. Really, the only satisfactory seat is when you are driving and steering : then you feel at ease.

After we had got to Rueil the road twists round through Chatou. Vesinet, and Pecq, to avoid the horrible *pavé* on the Route Nationale to St. Germain, consequently this part of the ride was virtually an uninterrupted crawl. Personally, I was anxious to

One of the latest patterns.

get on a straight road, in order that the maximum speed could be obtained, which was whispered to me to be about forty kiloms. per hour. We now commenced to run up the long stiff hill to St. Germain, which is one of the steepest gradients to be found in the *banlieue* of Paris. The driver changed his speed to the lowest before negotiating this hill, when we steamed up in splendid style, much to the surprise of a party of foreign Paris exhibitionists visiting St. Germain, who were walking the hill to relieve their hay motors, drawing a large *char-à-banc*. We shut off steam at the Pavillon Henri IV. to enjoy the usual five o'clock tea, which we ordered to be served on the terrace. What a mag-

A waggon which was awarded a gold medal at the Paris Exhibition.

Pneumatic-tyred De Dion Omnibus.

nificent panorama from the Pavillon Henri IV.—almost equal to Florence! Unfortunately, the sky was not as blue as in sunny Italy, and black clouds were overhead threatening rain, but the western breeze swept them away, and occasionally the sun glanced upon the lovely view, showing it off to its best advantage, diversified as it was by the light brown, green, and varied tints of early autumn. Thirteen miles away, as the crow flies, the tip of the Eiffel Tower peeps just above the distant hills to remind one of the gigantic exhibition, which was still drawing all Europe like an enormous magnet.

The River Seine winds its way throughout the country down in the valley below. And the beautiful scene from the terrace makes one regret to have to leave it so soon. Tea being over, and the evening quickly drawing to a close, we had to think of getting back. My desire, however, for speed led me to ask the driver if he could take the road through the forest of St. Germain to the Croix de Noailles, as here a fine stretch of road lends itself to the all-out system. The fact was our mechanician as well as his companion, who was none other than the stoker, were anxious to give us a "feeler" along the forest road, as they had given a fresh feed of water to the reservoir tank, and the needle of the pressure gauge showed past the red arrow, indicating full steam up!

We soon left St. Germain in the rear, and came upon the field of action.

Now the road was quite straight for several miles, and our stoker was busily poking up his coke fire, getting ready for the fray, whilst the mechani-

cian kept a keen look out ahead in order to profit by a clear course. Once past a pair of thoroughbred steeds, drawing a light waggonette, we began to feel the humming noise of the gear underneath our feet, and the engine was now working at its best. We were travelling, and no mistake! The trees appeared to be falling like the wings of a big fan on each side, and the dust was raised in one cloud far behind us. We were now going at fully forty kiloms. an hour, which was very unusual for an omnibus to hold eight persons in addition to the driver and stoker. On coming near to the Croix de Noailles we swerved round a nasty bend at a somewhat excessive pace, and the roll from the tyres and the skid upon the dust gave us the sensation of a bad side-slip, making us hold on tightly to the opposite cushions.

We now slowed down considerably, and made our way to Maisons Lafitte to get on the road back to Paris. We caught up with the sporting fraternity just coming off the course, and the road was crowded with cabs, carriages, char-à-bancs, and autocars, but we steamed among or by them with perfect ease.

Our homeward journey through Houilles and Bezons was, however, very slow. At Colombes we had to light up our big acetylene lamps, and then we steamed up to the Porte Maillot, after a novel experience in the first pneumatic-tyred omnibus, which was decidedly interesting, not to say sensational. Undoubtedly, this pattern omnibus would be eminently suitable for England, whilst for the colonies it would be an incalculable boon for assistance to mankind and the relief of animal labour. The

The vehicle built for the use of the **Queen** Regent and the Infant King of Spain.

machine emits little or no steam, and it is virtually noiseless, especially with the wheels fitted with pneumatic tyres.   Of course, De Dion-Bouton et Cie. make the same omnibus fitted with iron-shod wooden wheels, weighing about two and a half tons to carry twelve passengers that would come within English and colonial requirements.

Messrs. De Dion-Bouton et Cie. are now making several patterns of twenty, twenty-eight, and thirty-six horse-power engines fitted to either omnibus, waggon, or lorry.

The Brigata Ferrerieri del Genie, or in other terms the military engineers of Italy at Turin, have this year made some interesting experiments with a De Dion-Bouton fifty horse-power waggon. The results are quite difficult to believe.   Not content with climbing up the steep mountain roads in pouring rain, leading over the Mont Cenis, with a load of four tons in the lorry, they pulled up another four tons in a trailing waggon.

This identical fifty horse-power waggon has just been loaded with four tons, and has drawn twenty-seven tons up a never-ending slop of four per cent.

Several important companies have been formed in Spain at La Coruna, Santiago, Pamplona, and Valladolid, among the principal being the *Sociedad Espanola de Automoviles Segovie à la Granja*, and part of their route passes the royal residence, con-

sequently a special omnibus has been made bearing the royal arms of Spain, and it has been placed at the disposal of the Queen Regent and the infant King when it might suit their Majesties' pleasure to utilise it.

Over fifty omnibuses have been delivered to Spain alone, whilst others have been sent to Bolivar, America, Italy, and Austria. Some of the French colonies, Algiers, Tunis, and Madagascar, have also got some steam omnibuses running and giving every satisfaction.

Where railways are few and far between there is not the slightest doubt but that this mode of transport is the most practical and economical, whilst speed is another important feature, and certainly not the least to be forgotten.

Messrs. De Dion-Bouton et Cie. have been awarded gold medals for the light and heavy weight competitions recently held in connection with the Paris Exhibition; also for their small "voiturette" delivery van (petrol motor), omnibus (steam), and waggon (steam).   The problem of steam as the *beau ideal* automobile motive power for heavy weights is practically solved for all industrial and agricultural purposes. It now only remains for the manufacturers to continue to introduce improvements to render their vehicles still more practicable in order to make their use universal.

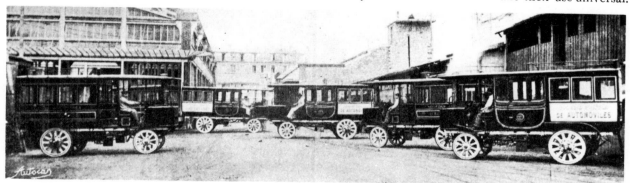

Some steam 'buses ready for despatch to Spain.

THE BOYER LIGHT CARRIAGE.

This is a light car which attracted a good deal of attention at the late French Exhibition as embodying most, if not all, of the points desired in this description of car. The tonneau portion of the body is readily dismounted by simply unscrewing four bolts, and the car is ready for a *tour à deux* with rear storage for travelling impedimenta. Indeed, the frame of the Boyer is so made that it will take any desired form of body. De Dion, Aster, Buchet, or Meteor motors can be, and are, fitted. Whichever engine is selected, provision is made for carrying same in the front of the frame beneath the bonnet in as strong and as rigid a manner as possible. These engines being water-cooled, a circulating pump, driven by means of a leather-rimmed friction wheel on the spindle, pressing against the motor fly-wheel, is fitted. A radiator with radiating flanges enters into the cooling system, and is carried right forward below and between the front springs. The tank is carried in rear of the vehicle, and can be seen in both elevation and plan. All the joints in the water-circulation system likely to suffer from vibration are made of special rubber piping. The tank will contain five and a half gallons of water, which, owing to the rapid circulation brought about by the pump, is sufficient without replenishment for about three hundred miles.

The drive from the motorshaft is taken by a friction clutch thrown in and out by a pedal on footboard in the usual way, the clutchshaft communicating with a train of gear similar to that known as the Panhard gear, giving three forward speeds and one reverse, this gear being controlled by a lever set at the right side of the driver. The gear is contained in dustproof gear case, and runs in oil. The speeds obtained by means of the gear with the motor running at 1,800 revolutions per minute range from 6.2 miles per hour upwards. An infinite variation of the three speeds is, of course, obtainable by means of the advance and the retard of the ignition. All bearings are ball bearings. Worm and block steering is fitted, a wheel being carried on top of steering pillar. Below this on appropriate sectors are found the sparking and throttle levers, conveniently to hand. In addition to the clutch pedal already referred to, the footboard boasts another pedal which actuates a powerful band brake surrounding the differential gear box, the depression of this pedal also taking out the clutch. Again on the right, and with pawl working in a ratchet segment, is a lever applying band brakes on the hubs of the driving wheels. The lubrication of all parts of the motor and gear is arranged for by means of tubular leads and an oil pump and tank holding two quarts of oil, the two latter attached to the dashboard. The petrol tank is also similarly carried, and has a capacity of two and a half gallons. The weight of the Boyer light car varies from seven hundredweight to eight and a half hundredweight, according to the style of body

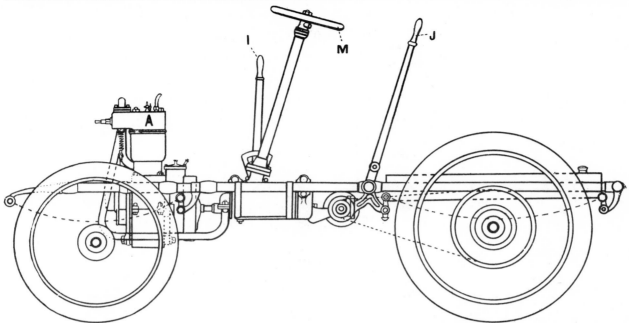

chosen. The wheels are of the artillery description fitted with pneumatic tyres, 26in. by 2½in. steerers and 30in. by 3in. drivers.

The following references to the lettering on elevation and plan will make the foregoing description plain :

A. Motor.
B. Cone clutch.
C. Change speed gearing in case.
D. Bevel gear case.
D¹. Water tank.
E. Countershaft.
F. Countershaft chain pinions.
G. Chain rings on driving wheels.
H. Band brake on differential gear.
I. Change speed lever and quadrant.

J. Lever of double band brake on rear wheel hubs.
K. Float feed.
L. Carburetter.
M. Steering wheel.
N. Silencer.

The agents for the Boyer are the British and Colonial Motor Car Co., Ltd., 38, Snow Hill, E.C. An additional interest is attached to the machine from the fact that the particular one which we show at the head of this article is the identical vehicle which was driven without a breakdown from Paris to Barcelona. As will be recollected from the recent report, this at the best of times trying journey was accomplished under extremely severe conditions, both as to roads and weather.

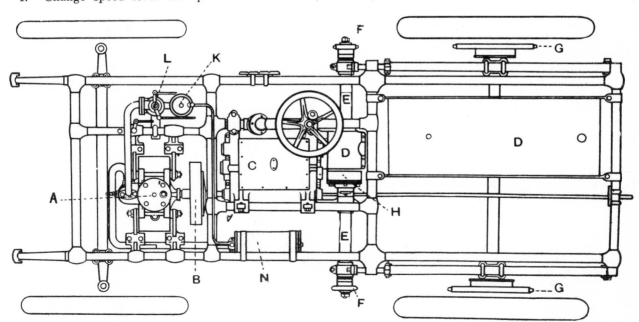

A VENERABLE MOTOR CYCLIST.

The above illustration portrays Mr. P. Norgate, of Guist Hall, Dereham, Norfolk, about to start for a ride on his Ariel quadricycle with his mother, who is in her ninety-first year, on the front seat. It shows that the delights of automobilism are not confined to the younger generation, but that they may be shared even by those who have long since passed the allotted span. The picture also speaks volumes for the ease and smoothness of running of a good quad carefully driven, and shows it will not disturb the sensibilities of so aged a lady, as, we are informed, Mrs. Norgate thoroughly enjoys an occasional run on the little four-wheeler.

A COMPARISON.
By J. E. HUTTON, A.I.E.E., ETC.

In a great many things automobile we have copied the French. We have adopted most of their common expressions, such as "automobile," "garage," "mécanicien," "chauffeur," etc., but why have we not gone a little further and copied some of the very valuable results of their years of experience.

Take, for instance, petrol. The very "essence" of the automobile. In France you can buy it anywhere and everywhere—indeed, we once came to a building rejoicing in the name of "restaurant," where we could obtain "essence" but no beer! In France the petrol is put up in very convenient five-litre cans, with a screwed stopper which bears a *seal*, which has to be broken before the contents can be emptied. And what is the result? In France you get the most lively, gassy, sparkling liquid instead of the flabby stuff, often full of water, that is drawn from a forty-gallon wood cask, or spilt out of an absurd ten-gallon drum, with an opening like a cess-pool. Certainly, the cans now used by Pratt (Anglo-American Oil Co.) are a great improvement over the ridiculous drums we so frequently see.

Then, again, the lubricating oil. In France it seems well nigh perfect, and is sealed up, like the petrol, in convenient small cans, instead of the useless great ones used by the English manufacturers. And what stuff you can get in England! Often we have seen valves glued tight with a substance resembling treacle; in France, never. The French oil is a perfect golden colour, and as clear as the petrol. It is put up in convenient one and two-litre cans, provided with a useful neck for pouring.

And tyres! The less said about them the better. We have read lately that we are to have French tyres in England now, but at English prices. The average English chauffeur takes an hour to mend a small puncture on a 90 mm. tyre. In France you take out the air-chamber, mend it, and put it on again in fifteen to twenty minutes; or, better still, put in a new tube and mend the other at leisure. Then, again, in France you carry spare tubes in convenient water-proof bags filled with chalk. In England, if you are particular, you will carry them in an old sack, newspaper, or, better still, mixed up with oilcans and tools. We once saw an Englishman wiping his greasy hands on a spare tube!

In conclusion, do let us wake up. Begin where the French are now, instead of always being two years behind, as we are in everything.

THE AUTOMOTOR

AND

HORSELESS VEHICLE JOURNAL

A RECORD AND REVIEW OF APPLIED AUTOMATIC LOCOMOTION.

Circulates amongst Makers and Users of Motor Cars, Cycles, etc., in the United Kingdom, the Colonies and the Continent.

VOL. V. NO. 50.   NOVEMBER 16TH, 1900.   PRICE SIXPENCE.

CONTENTS.

MOTOR BICYCLES.

THE casual observer cannot but be struck by the fact that although the riders of ordinary bicycles far exceed tricyclists in number, yet a motor bicycle is seldom seen amongst the swarm of motor tricycles that now travel upon the roads. The absence of the motor bicycle is indeed patent to all. We have often heard it said that there is no demand for such a machine, that any cycle fitted with a motor must be able to stand upright anywhere by itself, and that a bicycle is essentially a machine which is required for muscular exercise. Whether these statements are correct or not does not concern us at present. They do not seem to us to be accountable, however, for the absence of such machines. One has only to experience the sensation of a long run on even a heavy and complicated motor bicycle in order to be satisfied that a great demand would arise if a cheap and reliable machine of this kind were available. The advantages of the single track, of the more perfect steering, and of the reduced width of machine are by no means small, and are in themselves sufficient to command purchasers. From the practical standpoint the one drawback is their liability to skid on greasy roads. From the manufacturer's point of view the chief difficulty lies in their design. The question of skidding is possibly not so serious as has been represented; it may be that some of the early clumsy machines suffered unduly from

this tendency, or it may be that the inexperience of the riders led to such results. With a well-designed motor bicycle there does not appear to be any inherent reason why side slips should occur more readily than with an ordinary machine, but it is obvious that the rider should maintain as rigid a grip of the frame in order that he can resist any such tendencies when they arise.

The design of these machines is anything but easy, in consequence of the narrow and limited space available, and in consequence, too, of the high speed of the motor relatively to the driving wheel. The difficulties, due to these and many other important considerations, are probably most forcibly demonstrated by an examination of the many motor bicycles which have already been made. In these machines we find the motor placed in almost every conceivable position, we find belt, chain, friction, and toothed gearing, and we have either the front wheel, the back wheel, or the crank-pin driven by the motor.

Amongst more recent motor bicycles those which we illustrate herewith are of interest. Some of the outline drawings are from the *Motor Age*.

The Werner Motor Bicycle (Fig. 1) is possibly better known in this country than any other cycle of this kind. The motor is fitted with an air-cooled cylinder of 2½ inches bore by 3½ inches stroke. The fly wheels are now enclosed in the crank-chamber, but were, in the earlier models, placed outside. The motor is secured to the steering tube of the machine and to the double forks; it drives the front wheel by means of a leather band passing over pulleys on each. The right hand fork is bent so as to allow the pulley rim, which is attached by four arms to the rim of the wheel, to clear it. The pulley rims have a V section. A small exhaust box is fitted to the exhaust pipe near the motor. The carburettor, battery, and spark coil are attached to the upper members of the frame. The bicycle itself does not differ in general respects from an ordinary machine. The Motor Manufacturing Company (Limited) are selling these cycles in England.

The Ducommun Bicycle (Fig. 2) is very similar, as regards the position of the motor, to the Werner. It is, however, an entirely different arrangement; the motor is fixed to the frame of the cycle, and it drives the rear wheel by means of a crossed band. Two of these machines, made at Mülhausen, were exhibited at the Paris Exhibition, the one fitted with tube ignition, and the other with electric. The exhaust box is fixed to the frame, near the bottom bracket, and the carburettor is suspended from the top tube. From the point of comparison with the Werner cycle, it will be seen that advantages, as regards connections, accrue from the attachment of the motor to the main frame, but that the driving belt is liable to come into contact with the driver's leg. The greatest difference between these machines is that the weight of the motor acts in an entirely different manner when turning round a corner.

The Centenari Cycle (Fig. 3) does not differ largely from the Ducommun, but an intermediate counter-shaft is fitted to the frame,

FIG. 1.—The Werner Motor Bicycle.

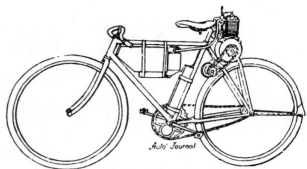

FIG. 5.—The Boulevard Motor Bicycle.

FIG. 2.—The Ducommun Motor Bicycle.

FIG. 6.—The Orient Motor Bicycle.

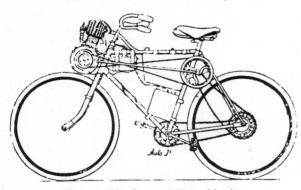

FIG. 3.—The Centenari Motor Bicycle.

FIG. 7.—The Republic Motor Bicycle.

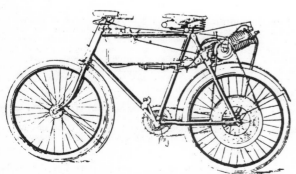

FIG. 4.—The Centaure Motor Bicycle.

FIG. 8.—The Marsh Motor Bicycle.

FIG. 9.—The Steffey Motor Bicycle.

FIG. 13.—The Chapelle and Chevallier Motor bicycle.

FIG. 10.—The Constantin Motor Bicycle.

FIG. 14.—The Compact Motor Bicycle.

FIG. 11.—The Shaw Motor Bicycle.

FIG. 17.—The Compact Motor Bicycle.

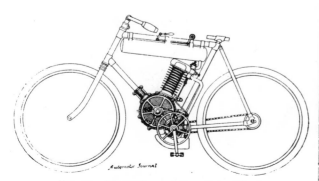

FIG. 12.—The Bluhm and Baur Motor Bicycle.

FIG. 18.—The Delin Motor Bicycle.

THE CHAPELLE MOTOR BICYCLE.

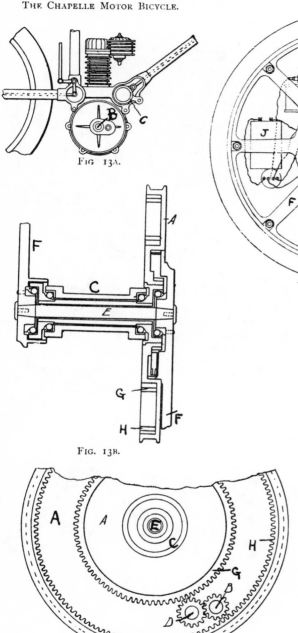

FIG. 13A.

FIG. 13B.

FIG. 13C.

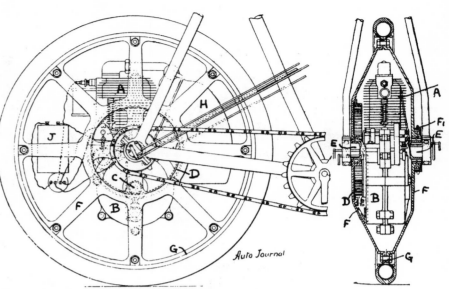

FIGS. 15 and 16.—The Compact Motor Wheel.

at their outer surfaces. The crank chamber, B, the air-cooled cylinder, A, the carburettor and oil tank, H, and a Simms magneto machine, J (Fig. 14), are all rigidly connected to one another and are held stationary inside the revolving castings, F, by the trunnions. (In Fig. 15 a battery and coil are shown at J, but a magneto has replaced these in practice.) The crank-shaft, C, is fitted with a pinion which gears with an internally toothed ring, D, fixed to the left hand casting, F. The motor drives the road wheel through this gearing, the ratio of which is about 7 to 1. A chain wheel, F_1, on the right hand casting, F, provides for the usual free wheel drive from the pedals. In the machine as built one regulating lever only is provided, and this is connected with a hand lever on the left handle bar ; the lever on the right is connected to a rim brake on

the front wheel. The regulating lever passes through the left hand trunnion, E, and is connected both to a valve controlling the explosive mixture, and to a compression-relieving device. The shape of the aluminium castings, F, allows of access between the spokes to the various parts of the mechanism, but for a thorough inspection of the motor it is necessary to remove the pneumatic tyre and dismantle the whole wheel. The spokes serve to maintain a continuous circulation of cool air round the cylinder when the machine is travelling. The design of this machine (Fig. 17) has many good features ; its weakest points are apparently the dusty position of the motor and the side strains which are imposed upon the ball bearings and the aluminium cage.

The Delin Motor Bicycle (Fig. 18) is of an entirely different type to any of those above described. It can only be driven by the motor, and no pedals are fitted. The motor is placed with its shaft parallel to the frame, and it is fixed to a forked lower tube, which is carried by a curved tube from the head, and which forms the rear wheel forks. A pair of bevel wheels transmits the power from a long counter-shaft to the back wheel. The petrol tank is fixed to the top tube, and a float-feed carburettor is placed near the air-cooled cylinder of the vertical motor. Foot rests are provided. The absence of the usual means of propelling a bicycle has rendered this machine comparatively simple, but it is doubtful whether the difficulties of starting and the entire reliance on the motor are compensated for sufficiently in this way.

The Holley Motor Bicycle (Fig. 19) is another machine in which no provision is made for muscular propulsion. In this cycle the motor is

FIG. 19.—The Holley Motor Bicycle.

placed on the right hand side of the bottom bracket, and its fly-wheel on the left side ; the shaft passes through the bracket and drives the rear wheel by means of a chain. The exhaust pipe and box are clearly seen in the drawing. The weight of this cycle is about 60 lbs., and its motor alone weighs some 28 lbs. For starting the machine, the rider pushes it along the road until the motor starts working, he then jumps on. The motor develops about 1¾-h.p., and its speed is regulated in the usual manner.

Dufaux's Bicycle Motor (Fig. 20) is another form of attachment for a bicycle ; this is known in France as the " Motosacoche."

FIG. 20.—Dufaux's Motor Cycle.

Dufaux fils." The propelling mechanism is fitted in a triangular tubular framework, as shown ; it fits into the usual diamond frame of a bicycle. The mechanism can be secured in place upon any ordinary

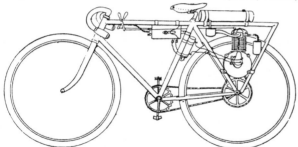

FIG. 21.—Dr. Clark's Motor Attachment.

machine by means of special straps. The width of the attachment is less than 3¼ inches, and it does not therefore interfere with the ordinary use of the cycle. The motor develops 1¼-h.p. at 1,200 revs. per minute. The extra weight involved is about 30 lbs. A belt, running over a jockey pulley, transmits the power to the rear wheel.

DR. CLARK'S (of Utica, N.Y., U.S.A.) attachment for an ordinary bicycle is shown in Fig. 21. The triangular frame over the rear wheel is held in place by clamps ; it carries the motor. A chain wheel is fixed on the left hand side of the rear wheel, and this is driven by a chain wheel on the motor shaft.

THE BELLAN AND CAMUS CARBURETTOR.

THIS carburettor is designed with the object of automatically regulating the richness of the explosive mixture according to the speed of the engine, so that more cool air, in proportion to warm mixture, is admitted as the speed increases. Fig. 1 is a general view, Fig. 2 a

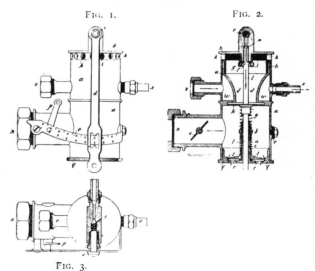

FIG. 1.   FIG. 2.

FIG. 3.

section, and Fig. 3 is a plan view, with the petrol valve in section. The upper part of the carburettor, which is jacketed, w, with exhaust gases, is fitted with a petrol admission valve, c (Fig. 3), and air holes, h. The feed of the petrol into the passage, m, is regulated by the lever, d, and the valve, c, e being a graduated scale. The passage of the petrol into the body of the carburettor is controlled by a valve, f, on the rod, l, and by the spring, y, on this rod. The rod, l, carries a grooved disc, k, which obstructs the passage of the oil and air to the lower part of the carburettor, and to the inlet valve of the engine, through the pipe, n. At every suction stroke of the engine the action of the air on the plate, k, causes the valve, f, to be opened ; the petrol is then vaporised and mixed with the air as it passes over and round this disc. At the bottom of the carburettor are auxiliary air holes, r, which are normally closed by a plate, t, under the action of the comparatively strong spring, u ; this spring is said to be twice the strength of the spring, y, and it therefore only allows the plate, t, to be lifted when the suction of the engine is sufficient. A throttle valve, o, is placed in the pipe, n, and is regulated by the lever, p.

The weakest point in this carburettor appears to us to be in the double regulation of the petrol, and in the large capacity of the space between the two valves.

ANOTHER RUDDER PROPELLER.—The new-comer is not electrical, it is actuated by an oil motor weighing about 90 lbs., fixed upon a light frame, and carrying a horizontal shaft with a screw propeller ; the total weight of the apparatus is about 165 lbs. This arrangement is the invention of M. Levavasseur, and was, according to the *Velo*, tested at Vincennes in September. The motor develops 3-h.p., and can impart a speed of nine miles per hour to a boat carrying eight passengers.

THE AUTOMOTOR
AND
HORSELESS VEHICLE JOURNAL

A RECORD AND REVIEW OF APPLIED AUTOMATIC LOCOMOTION.

Circulates amongst Makers and Users of Motor Cars, Cycles, etc., in the United Kingdom, the Colonies and the Continent.

VOL. V. NO. 53. FEBRUARY 15TH, 1901. PRICE SIXPENCE.

CONTENTS.

MOTOR BICYCLES.—II.

In a recent issue we gave a description of a large number of motor bicycles, and we then commented upon their comparative absence upon the roads, and upon the great diversity of design which is so peculiarly noticeable in them. Since that time we have been forcibly impressed with the almost universal interest created by our article, and we have therefore been induced to add to our already lengthy list of bicycles, and to review the whole subject at greater length.

We deal with the more general aspects of this subject in another part of this issue, and we therefore restrict ourselves here to the further description of actual machines which have already been made or designed. That motor bicycles do not date back very far is not to be wondered at, for it is only comparatively recently that the ordinary bicycle has assumed a form which is in any sense suitable for the application of mechanical propulsion. Most of the first machines were fitted with motors which drove the rear wheel direct, without the intervention of any transmission gearing, but of this type only one design was ever made on any large scale, and it proved a commercial failure. In many of these earliest forms the motor consisted of cylinders which were placed on each side of the rear wheel, and which were connected to cranks at each end of the back axle; in others, revolving cylinders were fixed to the wheel, and they were connected to a fixed crank on the stationary back axle. The first motor bicycle which was actually placed on the market was that of two German engineers, Messrs. Wolfmüller and Geisenhof, and it was manufactured both in Germany and also in France.

The Wolfmüller Bicycle is shown in Figs. 1 and 2, and will be only too well remembered by those who ever rode it. It is hardly a practicable model, but it undoubtedly possesses an interest for those who are studying the subject, and it has certainly afforded a fair amount of useful data upon which to work. The framework of this machine consists of four horizontal interconnected tubes, and four similarly-arranged inclined tubes. Each of these two parts is rigid enough in itself, but as they are connected together at an angle with each other, and as there is no connecting stay from the front head to the saddle pillar, the complete frame proved to be so far from rigid that the bicycle earned the name of "the buck-jumper." The motor consists of two parallel and adjacent cylinders, A, A, which are fixed within the horizontal portion of the frame, and which face the rear wheel. The two trunk pistons, which reciprocate in unison with each other, are connected by rods, l, l^1, to cranks, g, g^1, on the back axle; the connecting rods are fitted with ball joints in the pistons, and with ball bearings on the crank pins, in such a manner that the rods are free to move in the oblique direction necessitated by the relative positions of the cylinders and the crank pins. In order to assist the motor in overcoming the negative work of the compression strokes, strong rubber springs (Fig. 2) are attached to the end of the connecting rods and pass to fixed points on the frame. A valve box, fitted with two atmospheric inlet valves and two mechanically-operated exhaust valves, is bolted upon the upper side of the combustion chamber, and a pair of ignition tubes, E, also lead into this chamber. The exhaust valves, and in some machines timing valves for the ignition, are operated alternately by a reciprocating rod, m, and an ingenious throw-over mechanism which connects it alternately with each of the valve-opening levers, W. The rod, m, is operated by a cam, e, on the rear wheel, which displaces the roller, r, against the action of a spring. The rear wheel is built of solid discs, and is sufficiently heavy to form a fly-wheel under ordinary conditions; it is fitted with a pneumatic tyre. The motor cylinders are water-jacketed, and are connected, through the tubes forming the frame, with a water tank, G, which also forms a mud guard for the rear wheel. A large petrol tank and carburettor, K, lies inside the front portion of the frame. A separate tank was generally used for feeding the lamps, D, and a special air supply and chimney was fitted to them in such a way that the air entered a box, M, before passing down one of the frame tubes, and that the hot gases passed out of this box, M, after passing up the other front tube; the object of this arrangement was to prevent the lamps from being affected by vibration or by external air currents. The whole control of the machine was effected by varying the combustible mixture passing to the motor; this was regulated by the screw adjustment, e^0, on the right handle bar, S^2. It will be noticed that no means are provided for propelling this bicycle in the usual way, and that the only way to start the machine is

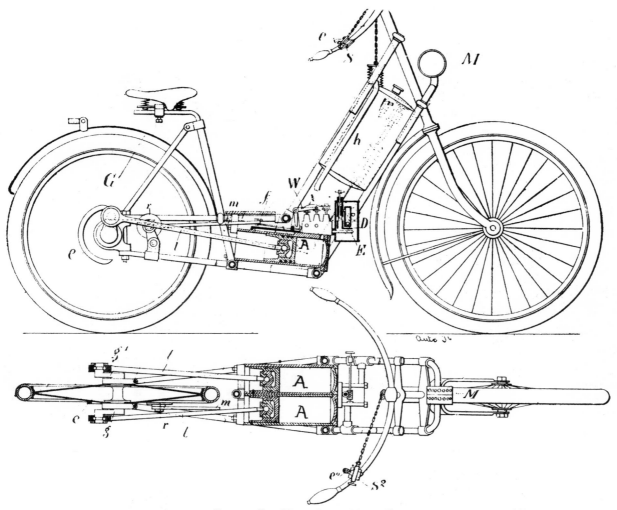

FIG. 1.—THE WOLFMÜLLER MOTOR BICYCLE.

to push it along the road until the motor begins to work ; as soon as this happens the rider has to take a flying leap into the saddle. In practice it was found that its management was far from easy ; its great weight, the tendency to pre-ignition when starting, and the jerky motion already referred to rendered it unsuitable for general use. At high speeds, however—and it is capable of travelling at a speed of nearly 30 miles an hour—these disadvantages are almost inappreciable. Foot-rests are fixed at each side of the cylinders, as seen in Fig. 2, and these give the rider a good grip of the machine. Practical experience with this bicycle has shown that it is wonderfully free from skidding, and that an experienced rider can maintain very thorough control over it. In some cases electric ignition was substituted for the hot tubes, but with both devices the ignition period was constant, and the range of speed was consequently somewhat limited ; this led to miss-fires at high speeds and to back-fires when starting or running slowly—on a really greasy road it was impossible to start at all without assistance.

Major Holden's Bicycle (Fig. 3) is the only modern motor bicycle which we have seen in which the engine drives the rear wheel direct. It is also one of the only machines in which the usually accepted form of ordinary bicycle has been departed from and in which original design has been aimed at throughout. The front part of this machine is practically that of the "geared ordinary" or "Crypto," in which the rider propels the front wheel. The frame is lengthened behind the saddle to make room for a special form of motor, and the motor forms

a part of the frame and is placed as low down as possible. The rear wheel is smaller than usual. The motor consists of two cylinders which are placed side by side horizontally. Each cylinder contains two pistons, one of which reciprocates in each end of its cylinder. All four pistons are connected together, those in the same cylinder by means of a common piston rod and the two piston rods by means of a common crosshead. The crosshead passes through slots in the sides of the cylinders, and is connected to cranks on the rear wheel by means of outside connecting rods. The cylinders are closed at their ends, and are provided with admission and exhaust valves. By this arrangement the motor practically has four cylinders and, as they work alternately (on the Otto cycle), the rear wheel receives two impulses at each revolution. The exhaust valves are operated by means of an ingenious device which converts the reciprocating motion of the crosshead into a half-speed rotary movement of the exhaust cams. Electric ignition is used and is so fitted that it can be switched on and off from one of the handle bars. A carburettor and petrol tank are secured inside the front angle of the frame, and the supply of the explosive mixture to the motor is regulated by a lever on the handle bars. In this machine very careful consideration for details is evident throughout, and the practical results obtained with it appear to be very satisfactory. It will be noticed that the weight has been kept low down, and that the rider can easily reach the ground with his feet. Foot-rests are placed on each side of the motor, and it is only intended that he should use the pedals either when starting or when ascending a very steep hill. The machine is fitted with an arrangement by which the valves can be held open when it is desired

Fig. 2.—The Wolfmüller Motor Bicycle.

Fig. 3.—Major Holden's Motor Bicycle.

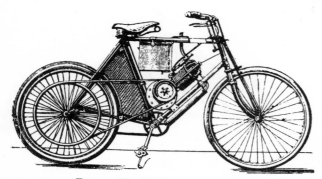

Fig. 4.—The Parfaite Motor Bicycle.

Fig. 5.—The Minerva Motor Bicycle.

Fig. 6.—The Pernoo Motor Cycle.

Fig. 7.—The Labre Motor Bicycle.

Fig. 8.—The P.T Motor Bicycle.

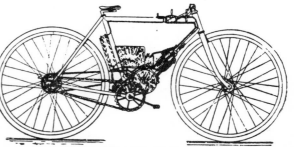

Fig. 9.—The P.T. Motor Bicycle.

FIG. 10.—The Banker Motor Bicycle.

FIG. 11.—The Landru Motor Bicycle.

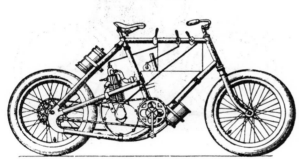

FIG. 12.—The Regas Motor Bicycle.

FIG. 13.—The Thomas Motor Bicycle.

FIG. 14.—The Thomas Motor Bicycle.

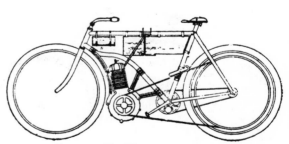

FIG. 15.—The Thomas Motor Bicycle.

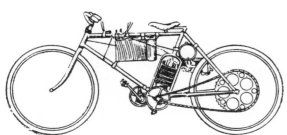

FIG. 16.—The Holley Motor Bicycle.

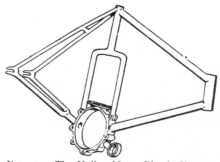

FIG. 17.—The Holley Motor Bicycle Frame.

FIG. 18.—The Ridel Motor Bicycle.

FIG. 19.—The Hertschmann Motor Bicycle.

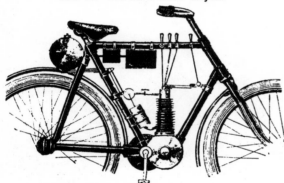

FIG. 20.—The Omega Motor Bicycle.

FIG. 21.—" Le Progrès " Motor Bicycle

FIG. 22.—The Baines Motor Bicycle.

FIG. 23.—The Lawson Motor Bicycle.

FIG. 24.—The Humber Motor Bicycle.

FIG. 26.—The Humber Electric Motor Tandem.

to relieve the functions of the pistons. The motor is enclosed in an aluminium casing.

The Parfaite Bicycle (Fig. 4) is fitted with a small air-cooled high-speed motor, which is attached to the front inclined member of the frame of an ordinary type of bicycle, and the exhaust box is fixed on the underside of the same tube. A pulley on the half-speed shaft drives the rear wheel by means of a belt, and the ordinary chain-wheel foot drive, with free wheel, is provided on the other side of the machine. The mixture is carried from the carburettor to the motor through the tubes forming part of the frame. Levers for regulating the electric ignition and the explosive mixture are fitted upon the handle-bars, and a compression-relieving device is also supplied. The motor develops about 1½-b.h.p. when the bicycle is travelling at 20 miles an hour, and the complete machine weighs about 90 lbs.

The Minerva Bicycle (Fig. 5) is of the "converted" type, in which the propelling mechanism is intended to be attachable to almost any ordinary bicycle. The motor is of the usual high speed air-cooled form and can be attached in the position shown (Fig. 5) by means of four bolts. The carburettor, petrol tank, and ignition apparatus are contained in a box which can be suspended from the top member of the frame, and the usual controlling levers are also fixed upon this tube. A metal driving rim is provided with clips which enable it to be fastened to the spokes of the rear wheel, and a belt connects this rim with a pulley on the crank-shaft of the motor. The weight of the driving gear is about 40 lbs.

The Pernoo Bicycle (Fig. 6) differs considerably from the majority of cycles now on the market. The chief peculiarity of this machine is the position of the motor, which is placed at the extreme rear and is supported by double forks about the back wheel. In this case again a belt is used to transmit the power from a pulley on the motor-shaft to a rim about the rear wheel. The carburettor is fixed behind the central tube of the frame, and it is connected with the admission valve by a long pipe. The battery and the induction coil are fixed to the upper tube of the frame, and long rods are used for operating the compression cock and the ignition device on the motor. This bicycle has met with a good deal of success in France; its weight is about 100 lbs.

The Labre and Lamaudière Bicycle (Fig. 7) is considered one of the best designed French machines hitherto placed on the market.

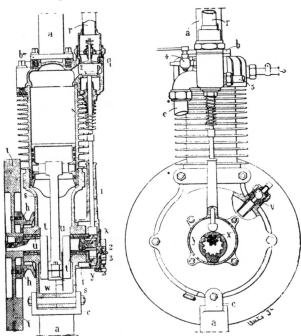

FIG. 7A.—The Labre Motor.

The motor (Fig. 7A) is specially constructed for its purpose and is not only very narrow but is so made that it forms a part of the central upright member of the frame. It is of the air-cooled type but differs in several respects from those of other makers. The exhaust valve, z, is actuated by a cam, y, which is caused to revolve at one-half the motor speed by means of 12 internal teeth which mesh with a six-toothed pinion, x, on the motor shaft; the cam revolves eccentrically to the crank-shaft, and is carried by a bearing surface on its inner face, and by a short shaft, 2, in an aluminium casing, 1. An external fly-wheel, i, is fixed to the crank-shaft, and the driving pulley, h, is placed between it and the crank chamber. A splasher, w, is carried by the connecting rod, and it serves to throw the oil in the crank chamber into the cylinder; a valve, v, is provided in order to prevent pressure in the crank chamber forcing the oil through the main bearings. The aluminium crank chamber is made in two parts, and the cylinder is screwed into its upper end. The cylinder head is bolted in place by three bolts, and the motor is secured in the frame, a, by the bolts seen in Fig. 7A. The cylinder bore is 55 mm. and the stroke 65 mm.; the motor weighs about 18 lbs. complete, the fly-wheel weighs 9 lbs. At a speed of 2,000 revs. per minute the power developed is about 1½-h.p. Electric ignition with timing gear is fitted, the contact making and breaking cam is connected to the exhaust cam. A carburettor, of the surface type, and the battery are attached to the top tube while the induction coil is placed behind the saddle. The power is transmitted from the motor to the back wheel by means of a belt which passes over an adjustable jockey pulley. The machine is fitted with the usual chain gear for enabling the rider to start and to assist the motor when desired. The complete bicycle weighs about 75 lbs., of which about 50 lbs. is carried by the rear wheel.

The P.T. Motor Bicycles (Figs. 8 and 9) are fitted with a motor which is capable of developing 1-b.h.p. at 1,000 revs. per minute. It weighs about 20 lbs., and is 12½ inches high by 6 inches diameter by 4 inches wide. The exhaust valve and the electric ignition device are operated by a special half-speed motion which renders unnecessary the use of a separate cam-shaft. Compact carburettors and exhaust quieteners are made for these machines, and the all-round reduction of size and weight has been carefully considered in the propelling mechanism. In both forms shown the motor drives an intermediate reduced-speed-gear shaft by toothed wheels, and the power is then transmitted by a chain to the rear wheel. In Fig. 8 the motor is carried in the central tube of the frame, and in Fig. 9 it is placed in the inclined tube leading from the bottom bracket to the steering head. The usual pedal drive is still retained and is not interfered with by the above mechanism.

The Banker Bicycle (Fig. 10) only differs in general respects from the Marsh cycle, previously described, in a few minor respects. The chain drive from the motor to the rear wheel is on the same side of the machine as the foot-propelling gear. The motor develops 1¼-h.p. and weighs 19 lbs.; it is 3¾ inches wide over all. The complete machine weighs 56 lbs.

The Landru Bicycle (Fig. 11) is provided with a frame of special shape to accommodate the motor in the position shown. Unlike the majority of cycles, the motor drives the ordinary crank-shaft by a chain, and the power is then taken to the rear wheel by a single chain which is used both for the motor power and for the work done by the rider. The effect of this arrangement would appear to be that the rider can only use the pedals when the machine is travelling very slowly. The carburettor and induction coil are attached to the upper part of the frame, and the battery is placed between the motor and the bottom bracket. In this design the weight is kept low, and a larger percentage of it appears to be thrown on the front wheel.

The Regas Motor Bicycle (Fig. 12) is another machine in which the frame is specially designed for the reception of the motor, and in which the weight is kept low down. The motor is connected by a driving chain to the rear wheel, and on the other side of the wheel a chain passes in the usual way to the foot gear. The driving wheel is held at the junction of three forks.

Three forms of the **Thomas Motor Bicycles** are shown in Figs. 13, 14, and 15. In two of these the motor is fixed inside the ordinary diamond frame, and lies upon the tube connecting the steering head with the bottom bracket. The motor in the first case drives an intermediate pair of wheels (mounted on the tube carrying the seat pillar) by means of a chain, and the power is then transmitted by a belt to the rear wheel. In the second machine a friction wheel, carried by a pivoted arm on the central tube, is driven by a belt, and can be brought into contact with the tyre of the rear wheel. These machines have a special bed securely bolted to the frame and extending the whole length of the supporting tube, and the motor is fixed both to this bed and, by stays, to the upper and the central tubes. The positions of the carburettor, battery, and coil are indicated in the drawing. In Fig. 15 a larger motor is used, and this is held low down below a specially constructed frame, in which the inclined tube is curved upwards and is utilised to hold two downwardly projecting supports; these supporting arms are bolted to the crank chamber. The motor drives the rear wheel by a belt; a jockey pulley on the seat pillar tube enables the belt to be tightened. The motors are of the air-cooled type, and all their running parts are made of tool steel. The bearings, which are of phosphor bronze, are rendered oil-tight by means of a packing ring, so that the two-to-one spur wheels can run in oil. They are made in two sizes for bicycle propulsion; the $1\frac{1}{2}$-h.p. motor is 12 inches high, and $2\frac{7}{8}$ inches wide, weighing 20 lbs.; the $2\frac{1}{4}$-h.p. machine is 18 inches by $3\frac{1}{4}$ inches, and weighs 50 lbs.

The Holley Motor Bicycle (Fig. 16) is, in its latest form, fitted with pedals for the rider's use. In the earlier machine made by the same firm no provision of this kind was made (*see* p. 53). From many points of view the arrangement employed is good, and the result is a motor bicycle fitted with auxiliary foot-power rather than an ordinary man-propelled cycle fitted with a motor. The construction of the frame is clearly shown in Fig. 17, and it will be noticed that the bottom bracket forms the central portion of a motor crank chamber, and that the tube leading from it to the seat pillar is forked so as to allow an air-cooled cylinder to be fixed in the necessary position. A separate hanger is attached forward of the bottom bracket, and the ordinary pedal drive is carried by it. The motor drives the rear wheel by means of a chain; it develops about $1\frac{3}{4}$-h.p., and weighs some 28 lbs. The complete cycle weighs about 74 lbs. The position of the cranks and pedals necessitates a greater length of wheel base, and it seems evident also that the saddle requires to be further forward relatively to the seat pillar than usual; the effect of this is to throw a greater proportion of weight upon the front wheel.

The Ridel Bicycle (Fig. 18) can hardly be regarded as a suitable design even for use in the coldest weather. The motor is fixed immediately behind the saddle, and it drives the rear wheel by a belt. In the motor itself we have to look for the only interesting feature of the machine. It has an air-cooled cylinder, which is fitted to an aluminium crank chamber in the usual way, but instead of a connecting rod the piston drives the crank-shaft by a slotted extension, in which the brasses of the crank-pin slide; this extension of the piston itself slides in guides formed by the walls of the crank chamber. The motor develops about $1\frac{1}{4}$-h.p., and the bicycle weighs about 75 lbs.

The Hertschmann Bicycle (Fig. 19) is not unlike the Holley machine in general principles, but the motor consists of two cylinders which are placed on either side of the tube leading from the bottom bracket to the steering head. The power of the motor is about $\frac{2}{3}$-h.p., and the cylinders are kept cool by wind funnels which are directed forward from them. In the drawing tube ignition is shown and the carburettor, tanks, &c., are omitted.

The Omega Bicycle (Fig. 20) is designed upon lines in which a special frame is used, and in which toothed gearing only is employed for driving the rear wheel. The motor drives the pedal shaft by spur wheels, and the other gearing resembles that of the "acatène" ordinary bicycle.

"Le Progrès" Bicycle (Fig. 21) is fitted with a motor of $1\frac{1}{4}$-h.p., which drives the back wheel by means of a belt. In this bicycle the rear forks are lengthened, and the motor is fixed low down between the bottom bracket and the back wheel. A round belt is used for transmitting the power from the motor to a rim on the driving wheel. The exhaust box is fixed beneath the tube leading up to the steering head, and the petrol tank is suspended from the upper tube of the frame. The usual regulating levers are provided.

The Baines Bicycle (Fig. 22) is one of the latest English productions in which the motor entirely replaces any means of foot propulsion. The motor is fixed in the position which is usually occupied by the bottom bracket. The frame is built low, and the weight is also kept low down. The tubes leading to the motor are forked and are thus secured to the crank chamber. The tube leading upwards to the seat pillar is utilised as an exhaust chamber. The whole frame is of stronger construction than in ordinary cycle practice and the front forks are stiffened in the manner shown. Double ball bearings are fitted to the back wheel. The motor drives an intermediate wheel from which the power is transmitted by a chain to the rear wheel, and a friction clutch is provided in such a way that rocking foot-rests throw it into or out of engagement as required. The motor fitted is of the $1\frac{3}{4}$-h.p. De Dion type, but has been altered in several respects in order to reduce its width. The battery, coil, and carburettor are carried between the motor and the front wheel; the petrol tank is suspended from the upper tube. As this is one of the first attempts to place a purely power-propelled bicycle upon the market, we shall watch its progress with interest, and shall hope to deal with it in greater detail after having given it a practical trial.

The Lawson Motor Bicycle, shown in Fig. 23, is the only machine amongst those we have dealt with in which the motor is placed alongside the driving wheel. In this bicycle it is the front wheel which is driven, but Mr. Lawson has hitherto built machines in which a somewhat similar device has been applied to the rear wheels. The forks are strengthened by additional stays, as shown, and the motor is fixed to these in such a way that its crank-shaft passes through the centre of the front wheel hub and carries a fly-wheel on its further end. An epicyclic train of gearing connects the crank-shaft with the driving wheel. The remainder of the bicycle does not differ from usual practice.

The Humber Bicycle (Fig. 24) is chiefly noticeable in consequence of the very long wheel-base. Some of these machines were built in 1896, after experiments had been made with various other designs. In one of the earlier designs the motor was mounted on a cantilever frame behind the rear wheel, but it was found that the weight in this position was too great, especially with the usual short wheel-base. The cycle shown in the drawing gave very good results, and was a very pleasant and fast machine on dry roads, besides showing the advantage of its long wheel-base on wet roads. The form of the framework is clearly shown in the drawing; it is applicable for the use of ladies. The motor, of the De Dion pattern, is fixed just in front of the rear wheel, and it drives that wheel by means of a chain. The carburettor, battery, and petrol tank are carried forward of the motor, in the frame. The bottom bracket is fitted with an eccentric bearing for enabling the long chain to be tightened. Both chains are on the same side of the rear wheel. In practice one found that riding with "hands off" was wonderfully easy, and that the tendency to skid was by no means great.

The Hampden Bicycle Motor (Fig. 25) is another attempt at making the crank chamber a part of the cycle frame itself. A pinion

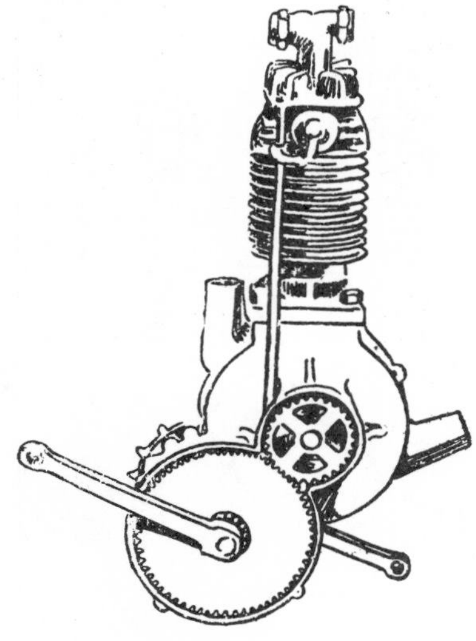

FIG. 25.—The Hampden Bicycle Motor.

on the motor shaft drives a spur wheel, which is mounted freely about the foot-driven axle, at half its own speed, and this spur wheel is connected by chain wheels and a chain to the left-hand side of the rear

THE QUEEN'S AUTOCAR.

The Queen's electric carriage is a victoriette seated for two persons. It is upholstered in dark green morocco, with folding hood of polished grain leather, lined with dark green cloth. The side panels are, as will be seen from the illustration, very gracefully curved, and the front dash is also curved, and of patent leather, as on the wings.

The colour of the car panelling is rose madder lake, the remainder of the body being black, picked out with deep red lines.

The carriage has 28in. bicycle pattern wheels, with 3in. pneumatics, and weighs, together with the battery, about 12 cwt.

The capacity of the battery is forty miles on the one charge, and a speed of twenty miles an hour can be attained.

We understand that Her Majesty is in the habit of driving the vehicle herself, and is delighted with the ease and simplicity of control and manipulation.

The carriage was supplied to H.M. by the City and Suburban Electric Carriage Co., of 6, Denman Street, Piccadilly Circus, who also have a number of orders in hand from members of the nobility of both sexes.

The depot of the company is very central, and consists of a new building of seven floors, having a total area of 19,000 square feet, with accommodation for over a hundred carriages. The firm not only supply the carriages, but undertake for a fixed sum per annum to keep them in full going order, charge batteries, and, if desired to do so, they also send out a driver with each car. All the owner has to do when he or she wants the electromobile is to telephone to Denman Street, and in a few minutes it will arrive ready for work in the charge of a competent driver.

An autocarist, finding at his hotel that his accumulators had given out, sent them by boots to be recharged, with the instruction that they must be sent home promptly at eight a.m. next day. Boots fulfilled his duties, and on receiving back the accumulators, burst into the smoking room with the ejaculation: "Sorry to intrude, gents, but had to bring in this gent's 'hincubators,' they aint safe outside."

Lord Roberts paid an unexpected visit to rural Essex last week. He travelled with other officers by special train from Fenchurch Street to Pitsea Junction, where an autocar met the Commander-in-Chief and his staff and rapidly whirled them away in the direction of Epping. The visit had been kept as private as possible, but the countryside somehow got a hint of it, and Earl Roberts was heartily cheered as he left the station in the car.

THE SIMMS MILITARY MOTOR.

While not a few others have been indulging in flights of imagination, aided by a competent artist, Mr. F. R. Simms has been hard at work, and we have from time to time referred to what he was doing in the way of military motors since he exhibited his first one, a motor quad with a Maxim in place of a front passenger, at the Richmond Show in June, 1899. The first of the series of motor war machines which he has designed, and is building for Messrs. Vickers, Sons, and Maxim, Ltd., to come through is the small armoured car for the protection and inspection of railways, which we illustrate here.

The duties of this handy little machine in time of peace are the inspection of the permanent way, the carrying of despatches, and the piloting of military or ordinary trains. In case of war, the Simms war car is intended for the protection of railway lines, and to keep up a continuous communication.

The war machine is not intended to dispense with the armoured trains; on the contrary, it is to assist the latter in their operations, but doing independent and scouting work. The Simms war machines of the rail type being armour plated, and carrying a one pounder Maxim gun, as well as a small machine gun, are intended to be employed in larger numbers, each forming, so to speak, a little self-contained fort, ready to start at a moment's notice, and capable of a speed up to thirty miles an hour. Each of the Simms war machines is constructed to be manned by one officer and two or three men, and it is thought possible that a railway line extending over 500 miles could easily and efficiently be held by twenty-five of these machines, or one hundred officers and men, i.e., each war car having an area of twenty miles. One thousand miles of line could thus be held by fifty of these cars, or about two hundred men, as compared with at least five figures of men, which would otherwise be required, and at much less risk of life and property. By frequent inspection or continuous scouting, it would almost seem impossible that any serious damage could be done to any portion of the line. The extremely small target which this little war car offers, especially when in motion, while being impervious to small arms, causes the risk of damage by heavier fire to be very small. Further, all the machinery is practically within two feet of the ground, and protected by a strong belt of armour.

The car itself is constructed throughout of channel steel, and is made absolutely rigid to withstand severe shocks and strains when running at high speeds, caused by sharp curves, or very sudden stoppages or starting. The car frame is further supported by spiral springs in ordinary railway pattern horn plate boxes. The axles are of great strength, and made of Bessemer steel. All the wheels run on roller bearings. The car is propelled by a seven horse-power Simms water-cooled motor, fitted with the Simms-Bosch magneto-electric ignition and timing gear, which, independently of the speed-changing gear, allows the car to be run at any speed up to its maximum.

The motor is entirely automatic in action, as it is fitted with a constant level float feed and the special system of ignition referred to. Four gallons of water suffice for cooling the engine on a journey of eight hours. The lubrication is also entirely automatic. The weight of the motor, inclusive of magneto machine, timing gear, float feed, and vaporiser, but exclusive of flywheel, is 82 lbs.

The engine is coupled to a three-speed gear of Panhard type, contained in an aluminium dustproof and oil-tight box, by means of a Champion friction clutch. The power is transmitted to the driving wheels by a countershaft, extending through the gear box, carrying a pinion connected by a stout Brampton chain to the sprocket wheel keyed to the driving axle. The three-speed gear, which runs in an oil bath, also contains a reverse, by which the direction of the car may be reversed at the like speeds. All the machinery is underneath the foot-boards, so as to render all the space available for the men and stores. The motor, gear, and car are all

operated by one man, there only being two levers to attend to, besides the brake levers (foot and hand). Three powerful brakes are provided, capable of bringing the vehicle to a dead stop within five yards, when travelling at full speed. The speeds are eight, sixteen, and twenty-four miles an hour, capable of being accelerated to thirty miles per hour. The normal speed of the engine is 1,200 revolutions per minute, which may be reduced to as low as 250, or increased to 2,000 by means of the timing gear, thus enabling independent control of the speed of the car. The armour is constructed in two parts—the under and upper part—the latter being of a crinoline shape. The under part of the armour protecting the machinery is constructed of heavy Vickers nickel steel plates, and is fixed to the main frame of the vehicle by means of special bolts provided with rubber buffers, to prevent undue noise or vibration. The upper part of the armour is of a fine curvature

and bullet-proof. A step is provided for easily getting in and out of the vehicle. Owing to great care in the design and construction having been used, the car runs practically silently and without vibration, thus permitting accurate aim, even whilst travelling at a high speed. Sufficient room has been allowed for about 40,000 rounds for the ordinary machine gun, of .303 type, and the oil tanks contain sufficient fuel for two hundred miles. The car is so arranged that at night a searchlight may be worked in connection with the engine. There is also sufficient space allowed for sleeping accommodation for three men, a kind of tent protection being easily rigged up over the car. The car in question has been designed and constructed for normal gauge, and the outside dimensions are as follows: 7ft. long × 5ft. 6in. wide × 4ft. high. The total weight of the vehicle, complete with armour, is 28 cwt.

A most successful trial was recently run between Sharnell Street and Port Victoria. Mr. Simms also has a much larger war car for road purposes in hand for Messrs. Vickers, Sons, and Maxim, Ltd., measuring 28ft. over all, with a beam of 8ft. This car is also entirely armour-plated, and is further equipped with two rams—one fore and aft—two turrets, and two guns, and is capable of running on very rough surfaces.

This car has also been successfully completed, and we hope shortly to have the pleasure of witnessing its road trials.

A SPARKING PLUG ATTACHMENT FOR BENZ ENGINES.

The accompanying illustration will convey clearly to owners and users of Benz cars the means by which Mr. F. F. Wellington, of St. George's Square, Regent's Park, N.W., makes it possible for them to employ one of his well-known sparking plugs in connection with a Benz engine. The brass flange, which has a central tapped hole to take the sparking plug, is permanently secured to the cylinder by the usual studs and nuts, while the plug is easily removed for inspection or replacement.  Benz engine drivers will, we are sure, welcome this simple fitting, which looks like saving them much loss of time whenever sparking plug troubles may occur.

The Right Hon. A. J. Balfour recently placed an order with Messrs. Panhard and Levassor for a seven horse-power light carriage.

* * *

Major E. H. Smith, of Arundel House, Wednesbury, informs us that for the convenience of automobilists passing that way he will keep a stock of petrol.

THE DAWSON CAR.

As we intimated in our brief account of the Canterbury-London run made by us a fortnight since on this car, we are now able to give reproductions of two excellent diagrams, which, as to fig. 3, show the general arrangement of the vehicle and its driving mechanism, and, as to fig. 4, the simple but ingenious change speed chain gear which provides four speeds either forward or reverse.

With regard to the Dawson motor, which exhibits so many points of interest, it was most fully described, as well as illustrated, in our issue of 11th November, 1899, but we deem it advisable now that the car is completed and on view, and on trial in London, to reproduce the drawings and briefly recapitulate the special features of the engine.

Fig. 1 shows an elevation of the engine; and diagrams 1, 2, and 3 (fig. 2) the slide valve box and slide valve by which it is permitted to the lower piston 11 (fig. 1) to pump air into the air reservoir No. 5 (fig. 3), or to be driven as a compressed air engine by the air under pressure in the reservoir, or to pump air into the outer atmosphere through a check valve, which can be regulated to any desired pressure.

It will be enough here to add that by means of the mechanical arrangements (illustrated in figs. 1 and 2), simply controllable by the driver without quitting his seat, the engine can be started forward or reverse, the air pressure in the air reservoir 5 (fig. 3) being employed for this purpose, the air valves being set as in diagram 1 (fig. 2). When the air cylinder is required to charge air reservoir, the air valves are set as in diagram 2. The third and most efficient duty performed by this auxiliary, though contained, air engine is the scavenging of the combustion cylinder at the bottom of each exhaust stroke, and the injection of pure air at pressure at the bottom of each charging stroke of the piston 10 (fig. 1). For a more detailed description of the Dawson motor we must refer our readers to our issue of 11th November, 1899, already mentioned.

In fig. 4 we have a simply comprehensible diagram of the Dawson four-speed chain gear, which is now illustrated for the first time. The operation of this gear can be better followed if a running description, rather than a tabular reference, be given. On the engineshaft 1 is carried a friction clutch 2, which engages at will with the male porton on flywheel 2a. The loose sleeve on which the female portion of the clutch is mounted, and which runs free on the engineshaft, carries a chain pinion 3. The spring 4 holds the female portion of the clutch up to its work when the engine is driving. On the countershaft 6 is mounted the chain sprocket 5, driven at a suitable ratio by roller chain from chain pinion 3. This portion of the gear is enclosed in a separate gear case not shown. At the opposite end of the countershaft is a clutch box 7, free to slide endwise on a feather on the countershaft. Jaws upon either end of this sleeve may be engaged with clutches 8 and 9, forming part of clutch sleeves 8' and 13, upon which are mounted chain pinions 12, 14, and 15 respectively. The clutch sleeve 7 is caused to engage with clutches 8 or 9 at will by means of rod 10 and bell crank 11. Clutch sleeve 8' with pinion 12 and clutch 8 are free to rotate upon countershaft when disengaged from clutch box 7. Clutch 9, pinion 14, and pinion 15 are whole with clutch sleeve 13, which is also free to rotate upon countershaft 6 when disengaged from clutch box 7. Pinions 9 and 15 are thus rigidly connected with each other.

Upon the driving axle 27 is mounted a sleeve 16

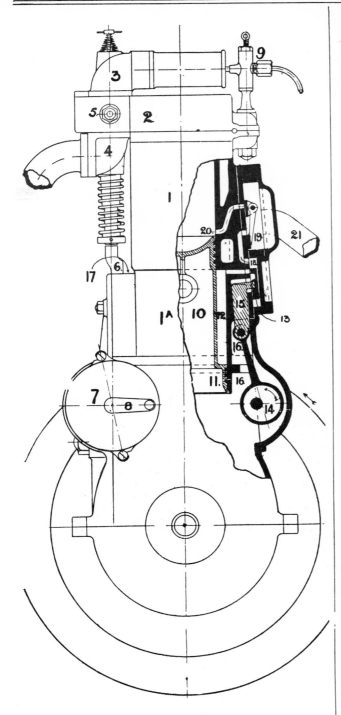

Fig. 1.

1. Motor explosion cylinder.
1a. Air cylinder.
2. Compression chamber and valve box.
3. Induction valve box.
4. Exhaust valve.
5. Sparking plug.
6. Exhaust valve rod.
7 and 8. Commutator and distributer (now replaced by 18, fig. 3)
9. Petrol feed device.
10. Petrol piston.
11. Air piston.
12. Air space for air driving, or pumped.

13. Air engine slide valve box and valve
14. Eccentric actuating air valve.
15. Valve rod.
16. Air way to crank chamber.
17. Air exit.
18. Air port communicating with.
19. Augmenting valve box.
20. Augmenting port into combustion cylinder, which is opened at the end of each outstroke of piston 10.
21. Air main to air reservoir.
22. Valve to cover port 18. (Diagrams 1, 2, and 3.)
23. Valve to cover port 20. (Diagrams 1, 2, and 3)

carrying a precisely similar arrangement of gear to that on the countershaft 6, except that the relative positions of clutch boxes 9 and 8 are reversed. Sleeve 16 on driving axle is rigidly connected to the differential gear box 17, and when rotated carries round the usual bevel pinion frame thereof, thus driving the two parts 27 and 28 of the divided driving axle. To part 27 of the divided axle is attached the near side road driving wheel, while the tubular portion 28 of the driving axle carries the off-side wheel. The axle 27 passes right through the tubular axle 28, and so enables the whole structure to be locked up by means of a nut and washer on

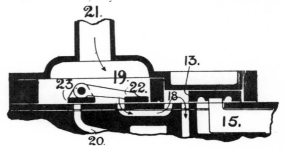

Diagram 1.   Starting and normal working position.

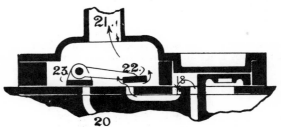

Diagram 2.   Charging air reservoir.

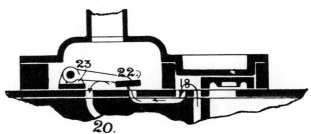

Diagram 3.   Augmenting charge in combustion chamber.
Fig. 2.

the outside of the off driving wheel. This arrangement of chain gearing enables four speeds to be obtained from three chains, at the same time affording a range of speeds difficult to acquire otherwise without the employment of abnormally small pinions and large sprockets. The ratios of pinions to sprockets may be arranged in any suitable manner, but in the vehicle at present under review the following ratios are employed:

Pinion.	Sprocket.	Ratio.
3	5	$2/7$
12	26	$1/2$
14	25	$1/1$
15	23	$1/4$

The four speeds are:

Fourth speed or highest.—Clutch box 7 engages with clutch 9, while clutch-box 18 engages clutch

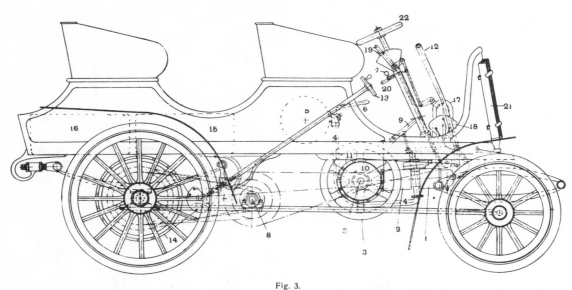

Fig. 3.

1. Motor explosion cylinder.	7. Reversing lever.
2. Air cylinder.	8. Countershaft.
3. Engine or crankshaft.	9. Pedal-actuating friction clutch
3a. Flywheel.	(10) and band brake (11).
4. Air main pipe.	10. Friction clutch.
5. Air reservoir.	11. Band brake applied by pedal (9).
6. Starting lever.	12. Change speed lever.

13. Hand wheel controlling main	18. Secondary current distributer
band brakes on road driving	or commutator (shown with-
wheels (double acting) (14).	out case).
14. Band brakes on road driving	19. Ignition timing lever.
wheels (double acting).	20. Lever giving (a) control of air
15. Petrol tank.	brake or (b) increased power.
16. Water tank.	21. Radiator.
17. Magnet (shown without case).	22. Steering wheel.

19. Pinion 14 therefore drives sprocket 25, and the rear axle rotates at same speed as countershaft, which revolves twice to seven revolutions of engineshaft.

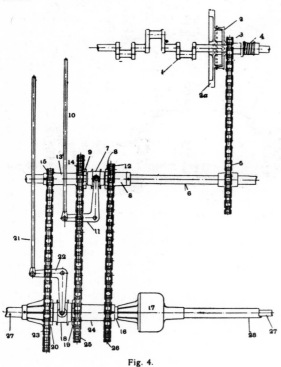

Fig. 4.

Third speed.—Clutch box 7 engages clutch 8, while clutch box 18 remains in engagement with clutch 19. Then pinion 12 drives sprocket 26, and driving axle rotates at half-speed of countershaft.

Second speed.—Clutch boxes 7 and 18 are crossed over clutch box 7, engaging with clutch 9, and clutch box 18 with clutch 20. Then pinion 15 drives sprocket 23, and driving axle rotates quarter speed of countershaft.

First speed.—Clutch box 7 engages with clutch 8, clutch box 18 remaining in engagement with clutch 20. Then pinion 12 drives sprocket 26 at half speed of countershaft, the drive passing through sleeve 24 and sprocket 25 to equal pinion 14, which thus also rotates at half speed of countershaft, then through sleeve 13 to pinion 15, and back to sprocket 23, which is clutched by clutch box 18 to sleeve 16, and being so fast to bevel pinion frame of differential gear box 17, rotates driving axle at one-eighth speed of countershaft.

Thus the four speeds have a ratio of one, half, quarter, and one-eighth to speed of countershaft, which is two to seven of engineshaft.

Both clutches may be manipulated by a single lever, one movement sufficing for each change of speed. We shall describe the Dawson system of ignition in another issue.

———◆◆◆———

As a mark of their pleasure at the honour lately conferred upon M. Bouton by the fact of his having been made a Chevalier of the Legion of Honour, the workmen of the great firm of Messrs. De Dion and Bouton lately subscribed for, and presented to the mechanical head of the house, a handsome cross studded with brilliants. After congratulatory speeches from the oldest foreman and the Comte de Dion, the cross was pinned upon M. Bouton's breast by the oldest workman in the factory. We congratulate M. Bouton on the honour done him, and both the Count and his partner upon the evident good feeling now existing between them and their workpeople.

A VISIT TO THE PANHARD WORKS.

The body fitting shop

The works of the famous French firm of Messrs. Panhard and Levassor have hitherto been a sealed book to British pressmen, so the special representative of *The Autocar* lost no time in journeying to Paris directly the *entrée* was courteously afforded him. He went with considerable expectations and no little respect for a firm whose name has so long been famous in the autocar world, and he was not disappointed in what he saw. In fact, he left with his previous high opinions of the leading French firm intensified. He has no intention of describing what he saw in detail, but merely intends to give an idea of the general impression produced from a run round the factory. It should also be understood that he is fully aware that the processes of manufacture he briefly describes are used in many other autocar factories. It is true he was shown some original methods, but as they were confided to him for his private edification alone he cannot honourably refer to them here.

The works are quite a town in themselves, cut off from the outside world, and from the very first glimpse of them the visitor is impressed with their oneness, their order, and the signs of some great but invisible controlling hand. To the right of the entrance gate are the offices, to the left the residence of Commander Krebs, and stretching before one, as far as the eye can conveniently carry, is a broad, well-surfaced road, with lofty workshops bordering it on either side. A few cars are standing on the road, dwarfed almost into voiturettes by the breadth of the highway; workmen are passing from one shop to another, but there is

No Hurrying, No Confusion,

hardly any sound—one might almost suppose they were idle works, and would leave with that impression if the interiors of the shops were not inspected. But, once inside, how different was the impression created!—a whirl of machinery, a regiment of men. There were 850 of them at work on the winter's day that we visited the establishment. Nearly all, as in our own autocar shops at home, were adult workmen, the merest sprinkling of boys, and no female labour being employed. We are conducted into the

machine shop, in which 350 lathes, polishing and planing machines are working away as fast as the labyrinth of overhead revolving shafting and belts can drive them. Men quietly feed the machines with steel bars, or remove the finished work, whilst the heaps of long strips of metal cut to waste by the lathes ever mounts higher and higher, and we found ourselves wandering away into a mental calculation as to how many carts it would take to remove all.

The exact size of this shop we do not know; it is, however, the largest and most impressive in the whole series. We entered in the middle, and, looking right or left, the end of the shop could not be clearly distinguished through the vistas of shafting and belting. One-half is devoted to machining parts for the motor proper, the other to machining parts for the gears and repairing tools.

The Machine Tools

in use are all modern and the best money can secure. They are mostly French—indeed, largely made by Messrs. Panhard and Levassor themselves—but America and Germany are also represented.

Here was a machine sawing through a piece of steel 6in. thick, and doing it very quickly, without any fuss. There was a flywheel for some big car being cut out of a solid block of steel, and near our attention was attracted to a heavy planing machine that was facing great aluminium castings.

One of the most fascinating processes to watch was the gradual creation of a crankshaft. The crankshaft arrives in the shop a massive block of steel, too heavy for a man to move. It is sawn, turned, and machined, and all its bearings polished and cut true to themselves and to one another—a very difficult and nice piece of work that has to be seen to be appreciated. Great care is taken to ensure accuracy, and Panhard and Levassor do not profess to turn out a crankshaft for a large car

In Less than Four Weeks.

Some of the gear cutters in the gear department of this shop are on a big scale, as can be imagined by those who are familiar with Panhard cars. The way the pattern gear wheels were racked on each

1. Looking down the main street between the workshops towards the entrance gates. Wood maturing on right of roadway.   **2.** A part of the great machine shop. This view gives rather an inadequate idea of the actual size of the building.   **3.** Tool shop where the tools and machine tools are manufactured. **4.** The erecting and fitting shop.

machine that could produce them was one of the many little things we noted as illustrative of the

One of the stores. A storekeeper at work.

military order and system everywhere apparent in these model works. Before leaving this shop we had one last long look at the mass of work being produced, and when we reflected what would be accomplished in that day, and that the same was being done on six days of every week of the year, we realised, as we had perhaps never done before, the extent of the motor industry in France.

We next visited the forge, where three powerful steam hammers were being supplied with work from eight forges, men bringing the glowing metal from the hearths by means of sling tongs. Here the frames for the cars are welded together, and all the other details of construction that belong to the blacksmith's art are carried on.

The Engines

themselves having been finished are taken to the testing shop, where they are bolted on what might be described as skeleton cars, with all the usual levers and lubricating feeds fitted, and with a drum added to take the brake band for the brake horse-power test. They are put through their trials, which are, of course, searching and complete.

Every engine has to register under this brake test a greater horse-power than will be eventually claimed for it, and it does not leave this shop until it does so

register, all necessary alterations and adjustments being there carried out. Over a dozen engines were thus being treated when we visited this shop, from a comparatively small eight horse-power up to a big engine, twenty-four horse-power or more, for a racing car. In the care and thoroughness so obvious in the work of this testing shop, the visitor had a broad hint to one of the reasons why the firm occupy the high position in the motor manufacturing world that they enjoy. From this Hall of Judgment we were conducted across the broad street already alluded to —noticing on our way the stacks of castings standing in the open (a bit of bad practice) ready for the machines—to the store-rooms, where parts finished

A bay in the pattern shop.

and in the rough are kept ready. The place was so quiet, so clean and orderly, and the various parts were so neatly stored in nests of pigeon-holes, that it was more like entering some museum than a store to feed a busy factory.

The Storekeepers,

too, by their quiet and courteous manner, gave colour to this fancy, and we were told they were a superior class of men, as they were responsible for parts and fittings that represented many thousands of pounds, and in many cases were quite portable.

The motor testing shop.

Stacked all around were cranks by the hundred, aluminium cases by the score, wooden wheels by the pile, "Loyal" radiators enough to cool Parliament on an Irish night, castings, valves, springs, brakes, tyres, piston rings, and, in short, something of everything, and plenty of everything that go to complete that vehicle of many parts—an autocar.

The sweet scent of wood, and the sound of steam saws, and the swish of many carpenters' planes, told us we were approaching the shop where the woodwork was done even before we actually entered the building. Like all the shops at these fine works, one was at first impressed with the size, secondly with the order and almost military system, and lastly with the character and quantity of the work being turned out. Where does it all go to? one constantly asks, and it is difficult for an Englishman, with his small home-formed ideas of the extent of the motor industry, to provide the answer to his own query.

In this shop they were making wooden wheels from well-seasoned wood of French growth. We saw the timber yard afterwards where the wood in the tree and sawn up was maturing. The spokes were being shaped by a machine invented and made on the premises—indeed, every single machine used in this shop had the same origin. Twenty carpenters' benches were being used, we noticed, the work chiefly in hand at the hour of our visit being wheels, body fittings, and patterns for the foundry. The fitting-shop is another large place. We had the curiosity to ask the actual dimensions, and our courteous conductor went away to get the exact figures. They worked out in English at 167ft. long, 155ft. broad. To this shop comes the frame, naked and unadorned, and here the channel steel is fitted in with wood, the engine hauled up by chains suspended from the roof, and fitted in its appointed place on the frame, the gearing, wheels, steering all fitted, so that it will be appreciated that this is a very animated shop indeed, as well as one of the most interesting, for here the motor car first assumes shape, and many parts can be conveniently studied that are not so easy of inspection after the body is once fitted on. We counted

Eighty-seven Engines

of various horse-power on the floor of this shop waiting their turn to be hoisted by the chains and dropped down upon the frames that they were destined to give life and movement to. In another corner were rows of heavy machinery unused, waiting until wanted to take the place of a worn machine. Every one of these was made entirely on the premises.

One of the oldest shops in the works is now used for body fitting, and is interesting because of the great variety of patterns of bodies fitted. When we were conducted over the shop forty-three frames were having their bodies fitted on, and hardly two were quite alike. The selection included such dissimilar vehicles as a twelve horse-power brougham

A part of the great machine shop.

for the King of the Belgians, with very big pneumatic tyres (120 mm.), evidently intended to be equal to ignoring the worst of even Belgian roads; a twenty-four horse-power racing car that may be a starter in the Gordon-Bennett race; a huge omnibus for military purposes; and a motor car to run on rails in Algiers. All the speed cars had electric ignition, as well as the usual Panhard tube, and we were informed that before long every Panhard car would be sent out provided with both forms of ignition. From this department the cars are sent on to the finishing shop, where they receive their final artistic touches previous to being despatched. Here we found

Fourteen Motor Vehicles

just on the point of leaving the works, and we were particularly taken with a very smart brougham finished in black and green, with red lines, the motor of which was so cleverly hidden away that it could easily be mistaken for an electric vehicle intended for short trips only.

This account of the Panhard works does not aspire to be technical or exhaustive, but mention must be made of the important department where most of the machine tools used in the shops are manufactured. As many of these tools are very heavy, the machinery to make them has to be proportionately large, and specially impressive in this particular is a huge planing machine. A travelling crane lifts the massive tools from one part of the shop to the other, and we watched the operation of swinging away a big metal saw that had just been completed. The engine that drives all the machinery throughout the works has a 23ft. 4in. flywheel, and develops five hundred horse-power. The engine and its room are as spic and span as on a warship.

When a Car is Completely Finished,

it is tested for three days before being allowed to leave for its owner. During this period of probation the cars stand in a garage, and are taken out one after the other for runs into the country, fourteen expert drivers being employed solely for this purpose. There were waiting their turn for a spin when we walked through the garage, two twelve horse-power *char-à-bancs*, one being intended for England; one six horse-power omnibus, to carry six people; one waggonette, eight horse-power, and another twelve horse-power; one phaeton, six horse-power, and another with a spider seat; one twelve horse-power, four-seated car, to the special design of an English gentleman, very handsomely finished; one tonneau, six horse-power, and three eight horse-power. We give the list in full, as again showing how great is the variety of motor vehicles that come through these works.

To go over such extensive and well-appointed works as these was a great pleasure, but it also induced regret that British engineers should have been so long kept out of their inheritance by their folly in allowing the laws of their country to stifle an industry which would have provided work for thousands of them, and which will yet do so, but years later than would have been the case if the roads of free England had been free to autocars as were those of France ten or more years ago. It must not be imagined that we despair of the English industry; far from it, as there are firms at home turning out work which is at least equal to that of Panhard and Levassor, but there is no firm comparable with it for magnitude. The home industry is making great strides, but it is at present little and good. It ought to have been, and might have been but for shortsightedness, what it will be—great and good.

The engine room and 500 h.p. main engine.

Now that King Edward VII.—*vide* daily press—has been placed in some risk owing to an uneducated horse shying at an autocar, surely an Equine Education Bill should at once be brought forward for the establishment of a little gentle compulsion.

* * *

Mr. J. Ernest Hutton, who recently described his run from Northallerton to Cannes, has had a most pleasing return trip from Nice to Paris on his twelve horse-power Panhard. He drove from Nice to Paris, a distance of 1,100 kiloms., in two and a half days, and from Paris to Boulogne in six hours. We hear he has sold this twelve horse-power Panhard to Mr. Frank Lazenby, and has ordered a still later pattern for delivery the first week in May.

* * *

Last week we referred briefly to the proposed motor service to be started between Enniscrone and Ballina. We omitted to mention that the towns are eight miles apart, and that two roads are available, the road by the river being considered the prettier. One of the promoters has made rather a good suggestion to the effect that till the local cattle become used to the cars, they (the cars) should always take one road, so that those who had nerves themselves, or imagined their horses similarly afflicted, could make a point of keeping on the other road. The Ballina Co. would like to receive prices for motor sundries, etc., and if addressed to Messrs. Timlins, Ballina, these will reach the right quarter.

Will any dealer in Kilmarnock or Clyr who supplies petrol kindly advise Mr. E. J. Thompson, Glen Tower, Great Western Road, Glasgow, to that effect? Or if any of our readers have purchased petrol in either of these places, they will oblige us and Mr. Thompson by giving him the address.

* * *

Mr. Guy Lewin, of the Kingston Motor Co., Kingston-on-Thames, mentions as a good proof of the increasing reliability of autocars that whilst a large number passed his premises during the holidays he had no call for repairs or adjustments. There is undoubtedly something in this theory, although we think he will agree with us that the change is partly due to the fact that owners know their machines better, as a number of the so-called "troubles" are due entirely to lack of acquaintance with the machine, or to absolute neglect and carelessness. This reminds us that the Kingston Motor Co. always have a stock of accumulators fully charged, besides a big supply of petrol and the best-known brands of lubricating oils. They also have a pit over which the car can be driven straight from the road, and storage for from twenty to twenty-five cars, and to complete the up-to-date arrangements of the firm they are prepared always to send a mechanic at any hour of the day or night on receipt of a wire. They also supply drivers when required, and, in addition to their cars, are starting a motor launch on the river hard by.

THE FIRST OF THE CUP CARS.

Our illustration is made from a photograph which was secured under rather bad conditions of the first of the fifty horse-power Napier cars to come through for the Gordon-Bennett international autocar race, which takes place in France on May 29th. Little idea of its size, and of course no idea of its power, can be gleaned from the illustration, but reference to the photograph of the engine which we published on February 16th will give some idea as to the dimensions of the motor compared with the more ordinary powers, and we may say that, although the engine is nominally of fifty horse-power, it gives off seventy on the brake. The engine itself, which at full power runs at eight hundred revolutions per minute, only weighs 10 lbs. per brake horse-power, and the complete car, engine, and all weigh about 48 lbs. per brake horse-power. Perhaps the most noticeable feature of the car, apart from its gigantic "engine room," is the fact that the chain sprockets on the countershaft are obviously larger than those upon the rear road wheels. This at once strikes the observer, as it is so different from the diminutive countershaft sprockets that the eye has become accustomed to. So far as the transmission is concerned, it is practically the same as in the ordinary Napier cars, but of course enlarged proportionately to the power it has to carry. The car throughout is from the designs of Mr. Napier, and practically every part of it except the tyres, chains, and a few small parts of the ignition apparatus have been built by the Napier Motor Company, and it will be driven by Mr. S. F. Edge in the great race. It should be clearly understood that the machine is built for the Gordon-Bennett race, and not as a touring car for use on English roads. It is calculated to be at least equal to the speeds of the crack express trains, and its performances in the race will be followed by all sporting automobilists.

HUMOURS OF AUTOCARING IN SWITZERLAND.

La Suisse Sportive, a Swiss contemporary, thus describes the "pleasures" of motoring in Switzerland: "You come from Paris, and wish to take a promenade in our hospitable Switzerland. Your route takes you through Geneva, Lausanne, Berne, Lucerne, Zurich, Basle, and so on. You stop in places of all kinds and conditions to eat, and spend your money, you buy oil, benzine, tools, and accessories, and you are under the impression that all this is permissible without any further ado. However, you err! Do not forget that the Swiss or Helvetian Confederacy is composed of twenty-five states, and that the twenty-five Governments of these twenty-five states may lawfully impose taxes upon you. Whether you pass through the various territories without a stoppage, or whether you, impressed by the delightful scenery, are prompted by the legitimate desire to pause a few hours to fully enjoy the grand surroundings, you must, in the first place, pay a visit to the mayor or district magistrate of the parish in question, and there have the kindness to pay the special tax imposed upon high-class luxuries. And then do not fear. Progress in the twentieth century goes ahead with rapid strides—in fact, is much more rapid than your wretched machines. You will experience very soon, much before you have crossed the frontiers of the twenty-five states, that you must undergo just as many examinations as there are cantons, that you will be forced to purchase in each canton a new shield bearing your number in the cantonal colours. And the modes of informing the world of your presence do not overlook them! Deep-voiced horns, shrill-sounding horns, cow-bells, trumpets, bag-pipes (specially for Ury, Schwyz, and Unterwald), different decoy whistles or bird calls, which imitate the cry of the eagle or the song of the swan, etc. A conscientious tourist must have a van driving ahead of him in which he can place his twenty-five certificates confirming his driving ability, his twenty-five number plates, fifty lamps with glasses of various colours, twenty-five instruments for signalling purposes, and his twenty-five times forty marks (£2) in ready cash—that is, altogether, the trifling sum of a thousand marks (or £50) for the twenty-five taxes. Should, for instance, three hundred automobilists visit Switzerland, they would add, besides their other expenses, which indirectly benefit each state, nearly three hundred thousand marks (or £15,000) to the incomes of these twenty-five states. And who now dares to say we Swiss are not cute enough to thoroughly skin the foreigners."

THE PARIS-BORDEAUX RACE.

The winner of the Paris-Bordeaux Race (M. Fournier) on the "20" h.p. Mors.

The classic race between Paris and Bordeaux is practically a history of progress in the automobile industry, since it is in this great event that we are able to see the new developments in motors and carriages, and the rivalry of new firms who take advantage of this exceptional opportunity to prove what their vehicles are capable of doing. Nothing is more eloquent of the marvellous advance of the industry than a comparison between the race of 1895, when Levassor astonished the world by driving a four horse-power car between Paris and the capital of the Gironde in a little more than twenty-two hours, and the race on Wednesday of last week, when a twenty horse-power Mors reduced this time to six hours, and covered the 327½ miles (527 kiloms. 650) at the average speed of 53.3 miles (85 kiloms. 85) an hour. Six years ago the racing car was fitted with a motor of six horse-power, but last week there were several vehicles of twenty-eight nominal horse-power, while in one or two cases they were said to have sixty or seventy horse-power. We say that these powers are nominal, because they merely represent a type of carriage, and are by no means the actual power developed. Makers are rarely disposed to take the public into their confidence over the details of these special racing machines. The indicated power of the vehicles is kept a secret, but it may safely be said that a car entered as twenty-four horse-power is capable of giving considerably more. Even accepting the figures stated, the increasing of the motive power four-fold in five years is a remarkable achievement, the more so as the weight of the cars has not even been doubled in the same period. Whether this rate of progress can be continued much further is a question that can only be solved by the forthcoming races. The competitions have already shown makers how to get the best out of their motors, and it is at a moment when they are anxious to settle an interesting problem in weight and speed that an attempt has been made in some quarters to suppress racing altogether. The success of the Paris-Bordeaux event has evidently brought these people round to see the error of their ways, for the newspapers which have been the most uncompromising in their anti-racing crusade are actually admitting that if proper precautions are taken, a race, after all, may be both interesting and instructive.

The Gordon-Bennett Cup.

To a certain extent, it may be said that the open race was merely intended to be a pendant to the Gordon-Bennett cup competition, but as it turned out, the cup had to pale its ineffectual fires before the open race. If the cup competition had been run off separately, as was the case last year, it would have been an utter fiasco. At first it seemed as if this international triangular match were going to be one of the biggest events of the year. Both England and Germany had entered vehicles, and after the brilliant performances of the Mercedes cars at Nice there was every promise of the competition with the new French fliers proving of absorbing interest. But unfortunately the owners of the Mercedes vehicles withdrew on the ground that the Automobile Club of Germany made their selection too late to enable the cars to be ready in time, and neither Benz nor Canello-Dürkopp would take their place. At the last moment Tischbein entered a vehicle, which, however, could not be got off in time for the race; and then Mr. W. K. Thorn, president of the Automobile Club Bearnais, offered to place his Mercedes at the disposal of Tischbein if the French carriage body could be replaced by one of German manufacture. They went all over Paris in search of this body, but no carriage-builder had one on hand. Then among the English Napiers, the Hon. C. S. Rolls and Count Zbrowski declared forfeit, and the only one to turn up was Mr. S. F. Edge. The English representative drove

A flashlight photograph taken at the start of the 50 h.p. Napier, with Mr. Edge at the helm. More than one well-known face will be noticed in the background.

his car from Boulogne to Paris, and had so much trouble with his English tyres that he saw it was useless trying to go to Bordeaux unless he could get fresh ones. As this was not possible in the time, he replaced them with French tyres, which, of course, disqualified him for the cup competition, and he decided upon starting in the open race. As the Napier arrived at the premises of the Automobile Club, where it had to undergo the process of marking, it attracted a vast amount of attention, and there is no doubt that it created a strong impression among the Frenchmen by its powerful lines. It looked heavier and bigger than the French vehicles, partly due to the fact that it has not such a low centre of gravity as the new cars. If, as was stated, the Napier developed seventy or seventy-five horse-power, it was by far the most powerful of the competing vehicles, for though the new Mors was at first said to be fitted with engines of this force, it was entered as twenty-eight horse-power, and it may therefore be supposed to give something like thirty-five horse-power. All the foreign competitors having scratched, the cup race became a run over for the French vehicles, but even then things did not go smoothly, as there was trouble between Charron and Girardot and the makers whose vehicles they were to drive. Fortunately, matters were satisfactorily arranged, and Charron and Girardot, on their new twenty-four horse-power Panhards, and Levegh, on his twenty-eight horse-power Mors, turned up at the start.

The Fête de Nuit.

The vehicles were to be sent off at 3.30 in the morning, and to pass away the still small hours a fête was organised at the Chalets du Cycle in the Bois de Boulogne, where all the automobilists who had not gone down to Bordeaux were present. And then there was a nocturnal procession up the Suresnes hill to Saint Cloud. The sight was an extremely picturesque one, as hundreds of cyclists with their coloured lanterns kept prudently to the side of the road, while the big cars flashed their headlights up the hill. On arriving at the starting-place beyond Saint Cloud, we found the road to Versailles in possession of the gendarmes, and a squadron of cavalry guarded the approaches, though why they were there is a mystery that is yet unsolved. The autocars lined up on each side of the road according to their numbers, and photographers flashed magnesium light to get views of the competing vehicles. Still another light leaped out of the darkness through one of the spectators coming to the assistance of Fournier with a match while he was filling up the petrol tank. The spirit caught fire, and it was only by Fournier's presence of mind that the flame was prevented from reaching the tank. The gendarmes were busy seeing if the papers of the competitors were in order. The officials had a lively time of it during this operation. Some of the chauffeurs, including Levegh and Gilles Hourgières, had not brought their certificates, and the police insisted that they should not start, but as the result of an interview with the Prefect the objection was over-ruled, though two competitors had to turn disconsolately homewards. A lot of time was wasted over these formalities, and it was not until four o'clock that the start was given to the cup vehicles. Charron was sent off first amid cheers, but he had not gone many yards up the first hill when he stopped and hurriedly arranged something, and then resumed his journey. Two minutes afterwards the word was given to the favourite, Levegh, who simply flew up the hill with his powerful Mors car, and after a similar interval Girardot was sent off, and made an equally favourable impression by the way in which he tackled the gradient. The departure of the cup triumvirate was followed by an interval

A FRENCH ARTIST'S IMPRESSON OF THE RACE AND ITS ACCOMPANYING SIROCCO.

SAINT-CLOUD. — Allez !

VERSAILLES (7 kil.). — Cochon, va !

CHARTRES (79 kil.). — Comment c'est-y Dieu permis !...

CHATEAUDUN (124 kil.). — Polisson !... Paltoquet !... Chenapan !...

VENDOME (163 kil.). — Sacré bougre de chameau !...

TOURS (250 kil.). — Miséricorde divine !...

CHATELLERAULT (289 kil.). — Brigand d'Paris !... Assassin !...

POITIERS (321 kil.). — Satan !... Anarchiste !...

ANGOULÈME (431 kil.). — La vache !...

556 kil. — Enthousiasme.

557e kil. — Bordeaux, onnn !

Reproduced from "Le Journal," "Paris-Bordeaux (impressions de route)," by Caran d'Ache.

of eleven minutes. At 4.15 S. F. Edge, the first competitor in the open race, received the word, and the Napier car jumped forward and climbed the hill at a speed which considerably opened the eyes of the public. The others were sent off every two minutes. Giraud on his light Panhard carriage, Voigt on a twenty-four horse-power Panhard, André Axt on a twenty horse-power Panhard, Gilles Hourgières on one of the new twenty-eight horse-power Mors, Fournier on a twenty horse-power Mors, De Caters also on a Mors, were started in that order, and then followed the other big cars, light carriages, voiturettes, and motor cycles in the order of entry, the total number sent off being sixty-three.

The Race.

As at all the towns along the route, Versailles was neutralised; that is to say, the vehicles were not allowed to exceed the legal limit of speed, and they were given a quarter of an hour to pass through the town, this, of course, being deducted from the total time. Levegh had already passed Charron, who began to have trouble with his valves, and just outside Versailles he stopped about twenty minutes to adjust them. On leaving the town, the competitors were started at the bottom of a very steep hill, which was naturally not to the liking of the motor cyclists with their eight horse-power motors, as a sharp turning just here did not allow of their tackling the

43

M. Charron on his Panhard cup defender (reproduced from a flashlight photograph taken at the start).

hill by getting up speed on the level. Baron de Turckheim on his De Dietrich got stuck on the hill, and one of the competitors in a light carriage began to experience the glorious uncertainty of pneumatic tyres, while the motor cyclist Osmont met with a painful accident through a stone flying up and smashing his glasses, when a piece of glass entered his eye. This was removed and the eye bandaged, and he continued his journey. At Limours, Levegh was still leading two minutes ahead of Girardot, but Edge had been passed by Voigt and Giraud, and then followed Hourgieres, Charron, and Fournier. The last-named improved his position up to Chartres, and got in front of Edge, while Charron was constantly stopping on account of his valves, and he again lost a lot of time on leaving the town. One of the light Hanzer carriages came

to grief through the bursting of a tyre, which caused the vehicle to turn right round and smash the two off side wheels, and the two occupants were thrown out, but sustained no injury. Thiéry also had trouble with the valves of his Decauville motor. Altogether fifty-five vehicles passed through Chartres in the official time. On nearing Châteaurenault the little De Boisse three-wheeled vehicle ran into the gate of a level crossing which was closed, and was so far damaged as to compel the driver to give up the race. Levegh and Girardot were fighting out a grand battle, and the Panhard representative seemed to be gaining on the Mors vehicle up to Chateaudun —124 kiloms.—but the most remarkable thing was the driving of Fournier, who was now leading in the open race, and was only three minutes behind Girardot. Voigt was close up, but he found it a disadvantage in having only three changes of speed, while the others had four. André Axt followed eighteen minutes afterwards, with Edge and Girardot at his heels. Charron was eighth, and Maurice Farman ninth. Edge lost his position through stopping fifteen minutes at Chateaudun. Another accident, due to a level crossing, occurred to a Godard-Demarest light carriage, which arrived just as the gate was closing, and in the collision the driver was thrown out with considerable force, and was so far injured that he had to be attended by a doctor. Girardot, who had been getting marvellous speed out of his Panhard, now began to have trouble with his friction clutch, and he reached Vendôme—163 kiloms.— twenty minutes after Levegh, who arrived there at 6h. 27m. Fournier was only three minutes behind

Levegh's " 28 " h.p. Mors.

Girardot, and then came Voigt, Gilles Hourgières, André Axt, Maurice Farman, Giraud, and Edge. Charron found that it was hopeless to continue when he had to stop every few miles to see to his valves, and he gave up the race. The first motor

The Gendarme checking the papers (a flashlight picture).

cyclist (Teste) reached Vendôme at 7h. 34m. The weather was hot and heavy and the roads thick with dust, which rose in dense clouds as the autocars sped along at fifty and sixty miles an hour. Levegh was going strongly, and reached Tours—220 kiloms.—at 7h. 19m., and Fournier, who arrived twenty minutes afterwards, had actually beaten him by three minutes. Voigt was third. Girardot stopped to fix up his friction clutch. He was already hopelessly out of it for the cup, and was philosophically letting the Mors vehicle increase its lead. After Girardot came Maurice Farman, André Axt, and Edge, and the motor cyclist Teste. Gilles Hourgières, who was expected to do great things with his new Mors, lost a lot of time through tyre punctures. The situation of the leaders remained unchanged up to Saint Maure—254 kiloms.—except that Edge had

M. Rudeaux on the Darracq, the seventh in the light vehicle class. Net time, 11h. 49m. 58s.

retreated to the rear and Girardot had fallen a long way behind, but a few miles further on an accident happened to the Mors cup vehicle, which struck a gulley across the road with so much force that the forepart of the car was smashed. It is supposed

that the cause of this is the curved axle, which brings the motor case down to within a few inches of the road, and is very liable to be caught by an obstruction. Fournier now went ahead, but when about a couple of hours afterwards Girardot, whose bad luck is proverbial, saw Levegh's Mors stranded by the wayside, Fate for once in a way smiled upon him. Fournier reached Chatellerault at 8h. 37m., followed thirteen minutes afterwards by Voigt, while Maurice Farman was third, André Axt fourth, and Giraud fifth. Despite the sweltering heat, enormous crowds of people waited for hours along the route to see the autocars pass, and special precautions had to be taken to prevent spectators from crossing the road until the cloud of dust that rose up after the passage of each vehicle had cleared away. Couché-Verac — 356 kiloms. — was reached by Fournier at 9h. 58m., preceding Voigt by twenty-four minutes. Maurice Farman passed through at 10h. 45m., André Axt at 11h. 4m., and Giraud at 11h. 12m. Pinson, Teste, Girardot, Osmont, and Gleizes followed in that order, and then came S. F. Edge, who reached the town at 12h. 4m. Close at

Starting a Renault voiturette.

his heels was Gilles Hourgières, who had picked up Levegh and his companion. He was constantly puncturing his tyres, and had given up all hopes of finishing in the first flight. There was no change in the positions of the leaders up to Ruffec—388 kiloms.—which was reached by Fournier at 10h. 25m., half-an-hour in front of Voigt, and an interval of twenty-one minutes separated Voigt from Maurice Farman. The sun was hot and stifling as the first lot passed through Ruffec, but in the afternoon a violent thunderstorm burst over the district and thoroughly soaked those unfortunate competitors who were still behind. Many of them gave up the race from this cause. Voigt punctured a tyre, and only arrived at Angoulême—431 kiloms.—nine minutes in front of Maurice Farman, and Pinson also had a similar misfortune. S. F. Edge did not get to Angoulême until after two o'clock, and as he went through without stopping at the control he was obviously no longer racing. Up to Barbezieux—465 kiloms.—Maurice Farman was able to pass Voigt for the second place, but Fournier was still increasing his lead, and got to Barbezieux forty-nine minutes before Farman. Fournier now had matters all his own way, and steadily augmented his advance, while Maurice Farman was improving his advantage on Voigt, who had up till now been going wonderfully well. On leaving Libourne, the motor cyclist Gleizes had a serious accident through trying to light a cigarette when travelling full speed. On letting go the handle-bar, the machine went off at a tangent, and the unfortunate rider was badly knocked about. He remained unconscious for four hours. Interest in the race, which had been growing all along the course, culminated in enthusiasm at Bordeaux, where Fournier got a magnificent reception as he arrived at Pavillons at 1h. 9m. 45s., his net time for the full distance of 327½ miles (527 kiloms. 650) being 6h. 11m. 44s., which is equal to an average of 53.3 miles (85 kiloms. 85) an hour. Maurice Farman finished nearly an hour afterwards, followed after an interval of five minutes by Voigt. Then there was a pause of thirty-three minutes until Axt completed his long journey in good style, and Giraud had a great success with the splendid performance of his light Panhard carriage. His average was 39.7 miles (64 kiloms.) an hour. The only cup arrival, Girardot, finished eighth, his average being

The Béconnais, fourth in the light vehicle class
Time, 10h. 41m. 25⅞s.

37 miles (59 kiloms. 509) an hour. The four Renault voiturettes ran with remarkable regularity, and finished close together, the winning car in this category, driven by M. L. Renault, making an average of 36.16 miles (58 kiloms. 244) an hour. The De Dion-Bouton machines took the first five places in the motor cycle class, and the average speed of the winner (Teste) was 40.7 miles (65 kiloms. 600) an hour. Altogether, thirty-six vehicles reached Bordeaux before the control was closed.

The results of the different categories are as follow: Gordon-Bennett cup race—Girardot, twenty-four horse-power Panhard, 8h. 51m. 59s. Paris-Bordeaux race—Cars weighing more than 650 kilogs.: Henri Fournier, twenty horse-power Mors, 6h. 11m. 44s.; Maurice Farman, twenty-four horse-power Panhard, 6h. 41m. 1s.; Voigt, twenty-four horse-power Panhard, 7h. 16m. 11s.; Pinson, twenty-four horse-power Panhard, 7h. 46m. 51s.; André Axt, twenty horse-power Panhard, 7h. 47m. 17s.; Gilles Hourgières, twenty-eight horse-power Mors, 8h. 37m. 39s.; Henry Farman, Panhard, 8h. 53m.; De Crawhez, Panhard, 8h. 55m. 34s.; Berteaux, Panhard, 11h. 10m.; Léon Lefebvre, Bolide, 11h.

53m. Light carriages of 400 to 650 kilogs.: Giraud, Panhard, 8h. 9m. 48s.; Baras, twenty-eight horse-power Darracq, 8h. 42m. 52s.; Edmond, twenty-eight horse-power Darracq, 10h. 25m.; Béconnais, Béconnais carriage, 10h. 41m. 25s.; Théry, Decauville, 11h. 11m.; Sanz, Boyer, 11h. 12m.; Rudeaux,

The 28 h.p. Mors, which finished ninth. Driven by M. Gilles Hourgières.

Darracq, 11h. 49m.; Ulhman, Decauville, 12h. 18m.; Filtz, Turgan et Foy, 13h. 57m.; Chabrières, Decauville, 14h. 5m. Voiturettes of 250 to 400 kilogs.: L. Renault, Renault Frères, 9h. 32m. 27s.; M. Renault, Renault Frères, 9h. 40m. 14s.; Oury, Renault Frères, 9h. 46m. 50s.; Grüs, Renault Frères, 9h. 52m.; Lot, Liberia, 16h. 4m. Motor cycles: Teste, De Dion, 8h. 1m.; Osmont, De Dion, 8h. 3m.; Bardeaux, De Dion, 8h. 54m.; Collignon, De Dion, 9h. 11m.; Bardin, De Dion, 10h. 30m.; Gasté, Liberator, 10h. 32m.; Holley, De Dion, 10h. 33m.; Cormier, De Dion, 11h. 34m.; Rivierre, Werner bicycle, 12h. 30m.; Bucquet, Werner bicycle, 12h. 47m.

M. Teste, the first motor cyclist to arrive, on his two-cylinder 8 h.p. De Dion, with new spring front forks.

THE FINISH OF THE CUP AND THE PARIS-BORDEAUX RACE.

On the off chance that an English car might start in, and the still more remote chance might win, the Gordon-Bennett cup race, we resolved to be

HALF-A-DOZEN EARLY ARRIVALS AT BORDEAUX.

M. Axt, fourth, 20 h.p. Panhard (1900 Cup Model).
The sixth arrival (fourth in heavy car class), M. Pinson on 24 h.p. Panhard, three speeds.
The second man, M. Maurice Farman, on 20 h.p. Mors.

M. Voigt (third) on 24 h.p. Panhard, three speeds.
The fifth arrival (first light carriage, and consequently conqueror of several big cars), M. Giraud on Panhard light carriage.
The eighth arrival (winner of Gordon-Bennett cup), M. Girardot, 24 h.p. Panhard, four speeds.

represented at both ends of the course by members of our staff, and the writer, who journeyed as far afield as the finish, considers that a few words in supplement to the brief telegram last week may be of interest. We crossed on Whit-Monday in company with Mr. Worby-Beaumont, who could not deny himself the pleasure of witnessing the start, and after calling at the handsome quarters of the A.C. of France, and subsequently at the Hotel Brighton, where the majority of the A.C.G.B. party were staying, and where we found Mr. Mark Mayhew and the Hon. C. S. Rolls, we learnt that the French clubmen had shown most sporting feeling towards the English car, and had unofficially informed those most nearly interested that the car would be started, timed, and checked, although she would, so far as the race itself went, obviously be disqualified before she moved. The conditions of the race laid down definitely that every part of a competing vehicle must be built in the country by it represented, and the use of foreign tyres of course crabbed the deal. The above arrangement was all that the English club or the owner or makers of the car could desire, and it was felt by the whole English party present that the French club had met them in their difficulties in a particularly handsome and generous manner. If the English car had won, well the fact that she ran on Michelin tyres would 47 not have militated in the smallest degree against the renown and glory that would have been hers, and it is only by bearing this in mind that the sporting action of the Automobile Club of France can be thoroughly appreciated.   Upon reaching Bordeaux we found Messrs. A. C. Harmsworth, Alfred Bird, and Max Pemberton, the well-known novelist, whose brilliant lately-concluded story "Pro Patria" is still fresh in everyone's mind.   These three gentlemen had driven down from Paris, as to Messrs. Harmsworth and Bird in the former's new twelve horse-power Serpollet steam car, and as to the author of "Footsteps of a Throne" in Mr. Harmsworth's twelve horse-power Panhard, driven by Engineer Lancaster, than whom a better exists not. Colonel Crompton and Claude Crompton swelled the party later, having cycled from Paris.

Mr. Harmsworth was good enough to take us out to the finishing point about two and a half to three miles from the city at a crossing of ways called Les Quatres Pavillons, 345.89 miles from the starting point at Saint Cloud, in his Serpollet, and though three miles is little enough to have of so entrancing a vehicle, it was enough to convince us that that car is quite the most luxurious road travelling vehicle in which we have yet ridden.   Owing to the absurdly optimistic prophecies of *Le Vélo* and *L'Auto Vélo*, we ran out over the horridly-paved Bastide Bridge, and the full mile of tram-lined *pavé* beyond, and climbed the hills out to the Quatre Pavillons so as to be there before ten o'clock.   As the flying Fournier never arrived until nine minutes past one, the three odd hours were made to pass as well as might be by watching and criticising the automobiles which went speeding outwards towards Libourne in order to take up favourable positions. Verily we believe every car in Bordeaux was requisitioned for the finish of this great event, for they swept by in battalions and clouds of dust.   In the intervals enquiries were made as to what was known anent the progress of the race, and occasional telephone messages to the house of M. Journu, of the Automobile Club Bordelaise, which was hard by, were made known.   First we heard that Fournier and his Mors were leading well at Chatellerault, 166 miles away, having passed Levegh, and that Girardot, the ultimate cup winner, had smashed his clutch at Chartres.   Later came the news that Fournier was leading the next man Voigt at Ruffec, 101 miles away, by twenty-five minutes, and that lots of punctures, owing to nails on the roads, had been suffered by many competitors.   The time wore slowly on in the great heat and dust, until another message came through to the effect that Fournier had left Libourne, fifteen miles away.   Then the crowd, which made up in enthusiasm what it lacked in numbers, braced themselves with the expectation of excitement.   The minutes passed almost in silence, so tense had the feeling become.   Even the *camelots* ceased to cry *Le Vélo*, and like all the rest strained their eyes upon the brow of the hill over which the petrolic Jehu speeding towards them must come.   Suddenly a cry went up from the high bank on the right, *Le voila!* and at the top of the narrowed way between the poplar tops as they descended the reverse side of the slope were seen to be blotted out as with a cloud.   The cloud, as it appeared, surged over the top of the hill, descended with awful rapidity, and whirled towards

us.   It showed a black eye, which every instant increased in size.   The eye was the Mors, whose wildly whirring engine was now distinctly audible Machine, men, and cloud, which blotted out all behind, rushed up the winning slope, and amid the wild cries of all who witnessed, completed the most remarkable automobile run yet accomplished.   Over an hour and a half elapsed before the second man was in, and the same wild scene of welcome was enacted, though in lesser degree with each arrival. The following table gives these as they occurred, also the average speed per hour throughout the journey:

CLASS 4.—Cars weighing 12¾ cwts. and over.

			Nett time. H. M. S.	Miles per hour.
50 h.p. Mors	... ...	Fournier...	6 7 44	equal 53·51
40 h.p. Panhard Levassor	...	Farman ...	6 37 15	„ 49·95
„ „ „	...	Voigt ...	7 12 11	„ 45·54
„ „ „	...	Pinson ...	7 42 51	„ 42·51
„ „ „	...	Axt ...	7 43 17	„ 42·38
„ „ „	...	Hourgières ...	8 39 39	„ 37·87
„ „ „	...	De Crawhez	8 51 34	„ 37·02
„ „ „	...	Farman ...	9 27 50	„ 34·65
„ „ „	...	De Berteaux	11 6 39	„ 29·50
„ „ „	...	Lefebvre	11 38 50	„ 28·10

CLASS 3.—Cars weighing from 7¾ cwts. to 12¾ cwts.

			Nett time. H. M. S.	Miles per hour.
Panhard-Levassor	...	Giraud ...	8 21 48	equal 39 21
Darracq	... ...	Baras ...	8 38 5	„ 37·98
„	... ...	Edmond ..	10 21 4	„ 31·68
Béconnais	... ...	Béconnais ...	10 37 25	„ 30·87
?	... ...	Sauz ...	11 6 26	„ 29·53
Decauville	... ...	Théry ...	11 7 42	„ 29·47
Darracq	... ...	Rudeaux ...	11 45 58	„ 27·87
„	... ...	Ullmann ...	12 12 20	„ 26·87
„	... ...	Filitz ...	13 53 59	„ 23·59
Decauville	... ...	Chabrière ...	14 1 4	„ 23·39

CLASS 2.—Cars from 4½ cwts. to 7¾ cwts.

			Nett time. H. M. S.	Miles per hour.
Renault	... ...	L. Renault	9 28 27	equal 34 62
„	... ...	M. Renault	9 36 14	„ 34 15
„	... ...	Oury ...	10 40 50	„ 30 71
„	... ...	Grus ...	10 50 41	„ 30 25
Lot	... ...	G. Lot ...	15 51 4	„ 20 69

CLASS 1.

			Nett time. H. M. S.	Miles per hour.
De Dion-Bouton Tricycle	...	Teste ...	7 57 0	equal 42·38
„ „ „	...	Osmond ...	7 59 27	„ 41·04
„ „ „	...	Collignon	9 5 33	„ 35·89

Seven other tricycles came through at various intervals, the last being Buquet, who occupied 13h. 43m. 10s.

The average mileages of the first seven arrivals will be found to be less than those we cabled from Bordeaux, but at that time we were not in possession of the total distance neutralised by the controls, and the times given us by the timekeeper were less 2h. 37m. the time of neutralisation.   The distance so neutralised was seventeen and a quarter miles, which accounts for the reduction of the averages previously given.   Although Messrs. Harmsworth, Bird, and Pemberton were members of the A.C.G.B. and I., and Mr. Bird was actually nominated as one of the judges by the French club. while Colonel Crompton represented the British War Office Committee, they received very scant courtesy at the hands of the local clubmen.   Mr. Bird at least might, we think, have been offered something more than the hospitality of the road, wherein he remained throughout the day.   It was only after meeting with our old friend M. Paul Rousseau, the director of *Le Vélo*, that we obtained access to the timekeeper, and were able to get the particulars always freely offered to representatives of the press.

The little party of the six English returned to Paris on the following day per the Paris rapide, which occupied 1h. 26m. 16s. more in making the journey than had Fournier on the previous day.

SOME IMPRESSIONS OF THE PARIS-BORDEAUX RACE.

At the Tours Controle.

BY H. O. DUNCAN.

Charron (Panhard).   Levegh (Mors).

Giradot (Panhard)   SNAP SHOTS AT 70 MILES AN HOUR.   Voigt (Panhard).

The snap shots were taken by Mr. H. Austin (who kindly placed them at our disposal) at a spot about thirty miles from the start. Owing to the early hour (4 30 a.m.), the light was poor for "express" work. Mr. Austin estimates that each machine passed him at about seventy miles an hour.

Having inspected the most interesting cars in the yard of the Automobile Club, at the Place de la Concorde, on Tuesday morning, during the operation of official stamping, which was almost as good as seeing the start at early dawn on Wednesday, I decided to leave by the Rapide from the Gare d'Orleans for Tours.

It would not then be necessary to pass the night in festivity at the Chalet du Cycle, and—all the cars would probably start satisfactorily, but how many would arrive at Tours, a distance of 210 kiloms. from Paris? There a fair portion of the road would be covered. I should have the advantage of enjoying my usual night's rest, and by being up betimes should be able to see the first car arrive.

Part of my programme was not successful, as that "quiet night's rest" at Tours turned out a complete fraud, what with the heat and mosquitoes, together with the noise in the yard of the Hotel du Faisan, and the paved street passing before it, which is the main road from Paris to Bordeaux, was simply swarming with cars, and my peaceful slumbers were continually disturbed by the hooting of horns, the rattle and noise of motors of various horse-power being like a field battery of Gatling guns. I gave up all hope of sleep, when Jarrott and Harvey Ducros obtained admittance to the hotel yard with a sixteen horse-power Panhard, having driven through the night to Tours, and whilst probably negotiating for bedrooms—the house being full—they left their car throbbing and cutting out, which evidently roused the whole of the inmates, as it was bitterly alluded to at the early morning breakfast table.

Having engaged overnight a horse-drawn vehicle to be outside at 6 a.m., I found my companion *de route* in the person of Cecil Edge, who had procured a bottle of champagne and some sponge cakes for S. F. Apparently he had obtained the latter after some little trouble, having given the 49 literal translation of the words *gâteaux d'éponge*.

Messrs. Cecil Edge, Jarrott, and Harvey Ducros were on the spot to look after the British interest in the Coupe Gordon-Bennett, represented by the seventy horse power Napier car, piloted by S. F. Edge, with Napier himself on board.

The Controle Arrangements.

As we approached our destination we passed a batch of military marching towards the selected spot, where the cars were to stop, in order to assist the local gendarmes in keeping the public back.

Every arrangement possible was spendidly carried out at the controle to facilitate the safe passage of the cars through the crowd. About 300 yards up the road an official wearing a yellow brassard held a yellow flag in one hand and a brass horn in the other. The latter was sounded to announce to the controle the arrival of a car, and the flag was dropped as a signal for the driver to slow up for controle.

Tours was neutralised. Twenty-five minutes were allowed for each competitor to go slowly through the town to the re-starting controle, preceded by a cyclist wearing a blue brassard, who carried the official time on paper of the arrival of the car, so that the departure controle should give the start at the exact time.

At the arrival and departure controles heaps of cans of petrol and lubricating oil, tyres, and other parts were guarded by the representatives of various competing cars, and everything imaginable was in readiness, so that not a second should be lost out of the twenty-five minutes allowed.

The early morning sun began to make its power felt, and the full-leafed linden trees that lined each side of the route were a blessing and a boon thoroughly appreciated not only by the peasant crowd which had assembled, but also by the unacclimatised Britishers, and Harvey Ducros indulged in " forty winks " in our carriage drawn up in the shade, which was about the total rest obtained during forty-eight hours by any of our party.

Having satisfied ourselves that everything was in order and quite ready for the arrival of the Napier, we adjourned to the only available shady hotel, outside which we could partake of some *café au lait*.

It was now past seven o'clock, and we were wondering the cause of the apparent lateness as compared with our estimation and calculation of speed for the likely time of arrival. Personally, I anticipated the victory of Levegh, and expected him first in at Tours. We talked makes, and I backed my opinion, to the tune of twenty francs, that a Mors would come in first at Tours, although Charron on a Panhard had started from Paris first. My bet was accepted by Jarrott and Cecil Edge, as we were out for sport.

Hardly had we got the cup of *café au lait* to our lips when the sound of the blowing of a horn was heard, and instantly the hitherto patient crowd became one mass of excited humanity, rushing in all directions on to the road, or towards the controle, only to be pushed back by the soldiers and gendarmes on duty to keep the road clear for the throbbing monsters to pass.

The First Arrival.

" Levegh " came upon my ears from the distance, and in a few more seconds, exactly at 7.19, No. 4 pulled up quietly at the controle, and quite unconcerned Levegh took off his goggles and enquired the time allowed for neutralisation.

I was somewhat surprised to see the small amount of dust on Levegh's car, but this was accounted for by his not having anyone driving ahead of him. When Levegh left for the departure controle we quite expected a whole procession of cars to come in closely following each other, but fully twenty minutes elapsed before another was signalled by the horn from the official with the yellow flag. I said to Jarrott, " I should not be surprised to see Fournier on another Mors come in." This appeared impossible considering that he was No. 18, and each competitor had started at two minutes' intervals. However, Fournier was the next to arrive, and pulled up at the controle at 7.40. He appeared much more excited than his stable companion. I shook hands with him, and told him that " Levegh was only twenty minutes

The start at 4 a.m.

ahead." He replied: " I shall soon be with him," evidently having confidence in the speed of his car.

We had returned to our *café au lait*, but impossible to partake of it, as the sound of the horn sent us running again in all directions.

Voigt (partner in the well-known French firm, Charron, Girardot, and Voigt) arrived at 7.47, being the first of the Panhard competitors, No. 13.

He said to me in perfect English : " My machine is not fast enough!" After which he got away through the town. We began to wonder where the Napier was, and I decided to ask the next driver coming in if he had any news of S. F. At 7.53 Girardot came up, the second arrival qualified for the Gordon-Bennett cup, on his dark-blue car, No. 7, and stopped at the controle just before me.

Again shaking hands, I said: " Have you seen the Napier anywhere on the road?" "Oh, yes," he replied, " Edge is not competing in the cup, as he was disqualified at the start, owing to his car being fitted with foreign tyres. He started in the Paris-Bordeaux race, and left after me."

Here we had some news of the Napier, and hope still reigned supreme among the Britishers.

Every minute our watches were out to see how long the first car had got ahead, as we now advanced from the controle upon the road, where we could get a glimpse upon the horizon at the commencement of the long avenue of linden trees. A big car presently appeared, and the yellow official's horn was welcome to our ears. We said, "Here's the Napier!" But, alas! it was a false alarm. The car contained two dusty looking tourists, who evidently were not competitors, but were simply bent on seeing the race. They appeared amused at the dropping of the yellow flag to a car numberless.

Clouds of dust in the distance was a sure token of a racing car, and again the cry rang from our little crowd, "This looks like the Napier!" But Maurice Farman swept past us in his Panhard No. 3.

Too Slow or too Fast!

Again I interviewed these old friends at the controle, and on seeing me Maurice saluted in English by saying, "It is awful! My car is too fast!"

The Napier in the Rue Royale.

This left me wondering who was right about the Panhards. Voigt said his car was too slow, and now Farman said his was too fast. The latter's performance in the whole race would certainly prove he was on a fast car. It was 8.12 when Farman arrived, and three minutes after Axt, driving another Panhard, No. 14, came up, making four machines of this make, well up in the race.

A second after the horn announced another car, and the cry was, "Still they come." Looking round from the controle to see who was next, I yelled out to my friends, "This time it's the Napier, and no mistake!" And S. F. Edge and Napier calmly pulled up at the controle, whilst their red car, No. 3, was simply besieged by Britishers; some were occupied in handing up an enormous funnel, through which others emptied twenty litre cans of Stelline. Napier was busy lubricating. Cecil Edge fed S. F. on sponge cakes and champagne. I got half suffocated from the exhaust, having taken up a bad position at the back of the car in the attempt to empty a can of

petrol down that big funnel. I gave up this job, and then had a talk with S. F., who appeared quite satisfied with his position, being seventh in at Tours, and right amongst some of the best.

Supposing the Napier had been competing in the Gordon-Bennett cup, it was not at all badly placed at this period of the race, considering Edge had started on the two-minutes interval principle, and after Girardot, who held No. 7.

Several minutes' stoppage—twenty or thirty, I believe—had been indulged in somewhere between Paris and Chartres by the Napier. An independent friend of mine had taken the time over a long stretch of road slightly down hill, where he could easily distinguish a kilom. stone in the distance from the one where he stood. Fournier had covered the kilom. at one hundred an hour, whilst Edge did it at one hundred and ten an hour, so undoubtedly the Napier is a fast car. Unfortunately, however, it was not out on the French roads early or often enough to be in proper readiness for the contest. Returning again to the controle, I saw the Napier away loaded at the back with Jarrott and Cecil Edge, S. F. and Napier in their seats, whilst Harvey Ducros stood on the step, and they disappeared down the town to the departure controle, where the remaining petrol had been placed, so that the reservoir tank could be filled that was calculated to last to Bordeaux.

The First Light Car.

At 8.20 Giraud, on a twelve horse-power light Panhard car, No. 12, came in, and the contrast between the comparative gigantic seventy horse-power Napier and the small light twelve horse-power car struck me immensely, and I was much interested in Giraud's very smart-looking light car, the first to arrive to be classed under this category. This race struck me as a battle between lightness and weight, and the question arose, "Would continually-increased horse-power motors be necessary if the weight of the car were kept down to a minimum, and would the speed be forthcoming under such conditions without risking breakdowns?"

The contrast became all the more vivid when I saw Teste riding in splendidly at 8.36 on a De Dion-Bouton racing tricycle, No. 25.

A smart officer belonging to the gendarme corps, who was keeping charge over the controle, saw I was personally known to all the racing divisions, and between the acts we had several chats together. A peculiar thing, he was also very much impressed after the big racing cars had passed with Giraud's light car, also with the small motor tricycle, and he casually remarked: "Croyez-vous que c'est nécessaire que les voitures soient si lourdes pour obtenir la vitesse de one hundred à l'heure?"

He was above the average gendarme that young officer at Tours.

Pinson then arrived on Panhard No. 30 at 8.47; Gleizes on a De Dion-Bouton tricycle, No. 27, at 8.55; and Osmont mounted likewise at 9.5. The latter told me he had had an accident near Vendôme whilst he was leaning over, out of the wind; and owing to a shock from his front wheel going over a stone, he was jerked forward, and one of the glasses of his goggles came in contact with his handle-bar and smashed his left eye-glass, which

51

necessitated his stopping at a chemist's at Vendôme to get some pieces of glass taken out of his eye, which was exceedingly painful. You may imagine what his position might have been.

Those Magnificent Straight Roads.

I now had quite enough of seeing the various cars arriving up to the controle, and therefore found my horse to drive several kiloms. out upon the road to witness the cars pass on their speedy

Leaving the Automobile Club de France after marking the cars.

way. On my way out I got off the road to the side to let Baras pass on his Darracq light car; also Gilles Hourgières on his Panhard. Finally, I took up a position about five kiloms. out of the town just on the top of a gradual rise, and from where I could see the road before me for miles as straight as an arrow. Oh, these magnificent roads! How they are unknown in England to the man who has never left the "tight little island." How they are misunderstood by the daily newspaper scribes who pen stupid leading articles against the speed of motor cars.

Imagine a lovely road about ten yards wide, cut for hundreds of miles straight across country lined on each side by beautiful linden, poplar, or chestnut trees to ensure a shady walk, ride, or drive to peasants and any such travellers. The question of speed over roads of this description has never been realised one second by those who are ignorant of the pleasures of motor driving, as at present, on the majority of automobiles, when right in the country, upon the roads in question, you can drive all out and still feel you are virtually "crawling," so that if you had at your disposal a car with several extra speeds you would always be running at the highest without feeling inconvenienced, or inconveniencing others. On the contrary, no one can imagine how safe and how practical it is to drive at forty miles an hour and more over French roads in a suitable car of first-class make. I realised this, as I saw more than twenty more competitors rush past, and all who recognised me gave me a friendly salute—"Bonjour!" In my little four and a half horse-power De Dion-Bouton voiturette I felt the sensation of wanting more speed over those ideal roads. As for accidents, if small towns and villages are respected as they should be on ordinary occasions, the French roads are made specially for autocaring,

as the surface is simply splendid, and there being no hedgerows to veil the view in front or at turns, you can drive along in safety and ease.

Having nearly got burned up with the terrific heat, I resolved to return to the Hotel du Faisan for *déjeuner* and take the first train back to Paris, having thoroughly enjoyed the race, what I saw of it, and obtained what I desired—an intimate acquaintance with the various makes of cars—and having, above all, seen for myself how the Napier behaved itself.

The Fliers Out for Practice Spins.

It will be interesting to mention that I had been touring on my De Dion-Bouton voiturette along the valley of the Loire, accompanied by my wife, during Saturday, Sunday, and Monday of the Whitsuntide holidays. At Amboise, situated on the riverside of the Loire and upon the old Bordeaux-Paris route, upon which the cycling road contests were celebrated in the Mills, Holbein, and S. F. Edge days, I met Levegh on his racing car. We saw a motor car approaching us for several kiloms. ahead, along the road bending round the river, and we remarked the amount of dust left behind, as though a train of gunpowder had been laid along the middle of the road over a distance of two miles, and exploding along the whole line at sixty miles an hour, leaving its trail of smoke behind!

I thought it wise to draw up on the grassy side of the road to allow the car to go by, but principally to avoid riding through a horrible cloud of dust lasting several minutes.

I saluted Levegh as he shot past me. I recognised his cramped position; his mouth and moustache were also familiar, although he was buried behind his goggles, and had a cap tightly drawn upon his head.

From a previous conversation with Levegh, I knew he would be over the roads, and he was only working his car and getting more acquainted with

The Napier in the Place de la Concorde.

it, besides getting to know every inch of the road. Fournier, accompanied by his *mécanicien*, was also out daily, and I met him also about fifty miles from Paris on my outward trip by way of Orléans, Blois, and Tours. Again, on my return journey towards Paris, between Vendôme and Chateaudun, in the open country miles from any village, when I was about to repair a puncture under some trees in the shade, I heard in the distant hills the regular throbbing of a big motor car, and before getting to work I waited for it to pass. When it came in sight I saw at once it was a racing monster travelling over the lovely straight road at top speed. Within fifty yards I recognised Fournier, and by all the wildest shouts and signs possible bade him stop. He did so, coming back on the reverse gear to the place where I was stranded.

Immediately he learned of my *panne* he asked his *mécanicien* to change the air-tube for a spare one I had with me.

The business-like way that *mécanicien* went about getting the cover off with his glove-covered hands made me appreciate thoroughly his smartness, considering I had previously experienced three successive punctures and changes.

In ten minutes my tyre was blown up and the pump placed away, and we were ready to enjoy fresh fields and pastures new.

Fournier told me he thought he and Levegh stood a splendid chance, as he said, "The Panhards are excellent machines, but they are not moving fast enough for us!"

We were somewhat astonished to hear Fournier say to his *mécanicien*, "Now look sharp, as I have an appointment at seven for dinner at l'Espérance," the well-known Parisian *café*, it being about 4.30 p.m., and we were about 160 kiloms. from the capital.

This left me on the roadside in a dreamy mood, as I mechanically glanced at my watch, thinking nothing was impossible with such powerful, speedy monsters. I also realised what magnificent assistance it was to have such a smart *mécanicien* on a racing car who had probably several years' practical experience in driving and in the Mors and other motor workshops. One must be no fool to change an inner air tube in a few minutes on a big racing car, and especially when, with the speed, the tyres are so hot that the air tubes have to be taken out with rags in order not to blister one's fingers! It is a well-known fact that with excessive speed the tyres get so hot as to virtually melt.

The Lincolnshire Automobile Club is pardonably proud of the fact that the autocar which won the Paris-Bordeaux race is the property of one of its vice-presidents, Capt. F. J. Laycock, of Wiseton Hall. Henri Fournier, who drove the winning car, is Capt. Laycock's driver.

* *· *

A1 of the Liverpool trials, the Milnes one and a half ton lorry, is now in the hands of the Liverpool Corporation, City Engineer's Department, and is being fitted up as an experimental high speed water cart. On Monday A2, the sister Milne machine, ran from the G.P.O., Liverpool, at 4.30 with the mail to Southport, accompanied by the postmaster of Liverpool (Mr. F. Salisbury), who represented the post-office at the recent trials. Mr. Shrapnell-Smith on his Ariel quad, with Mr. Rosenheim on the front, accompanied the postmaster on the trial trip. The machine ran throughout without a hitch, and arrived at Southport three minutes ahead of booked time. The road was very bad.

A TRADE MEETING.
The Exhibition Question.

The trade meeting called to consider the question of exhibitions, and adjourned from 21st May, met on Tuesday evening last at the Automobile Club. The meeting consisted of about fifty representatives of manufacturers and agents of whole cars, parts makers and accessories makers being barred. The chair was occupied by Mr. Roger Wallace, K.C., and the following resolutions were proposed and passed without dissent:

Proposed by Mr. W. D. Astell (New Orleans Motor Co.)—"That the manufacturers and agents here represented recognise that the Automobile Club held the first purely automobile exhibition in this country; has been, and is, the recognised authority to hold trials of motor vehicles, and to give certificates in connection therewith; and has rendered, and is rendering, invaluable services to the automobile movement in this country. They, therefore, consider the Automobile Club is the proper authority to supervise exhibitions in this country, and seek that the club should continue that supervision."

Proposed by Sir Ed. Jenkinson (Daimler Co.)—"That the manufacturers and agents here represented are of opinion that there should be one exhibition only of automobiles in or within twenty miles of London per year."

Proposed by Mr. C. Friswell (Friswell, Ltd.) "That there shall be only one exhibition per annum, that it shall be under the same management as the recent exhibition, that it shall be at the Agricultural Hall at the same time approximately as the recent exhibition, and under control of the Automobile Club."

Proposed by Mr. J. J. Mann (Marshall and Co.)—"That a circular letter be written by the Automobile Club to all manufacturers of motor cars requesting each to sign a declaration that he will not exhibit at any other exhibition within twenty miles of Charing Cross. This agreement to hold good until the end of 1903."

Proposed by Mr. Henry Sturmey—"That the Automobile Club shall have the right to decline space at their exhibitions to all who have not signed such an agreement and have exhibited elsewhere."

Proposed by Mr. Shrapnell-Smith—"That the Automobile Club withholds its patronage from motor-car exhibitions held in other parts of the country than within twenty miles of Charing Cross, unless under the auspices of local club centres."

It will be seen that the general result of the meeting is to secure what it is believed all the trade desire, viz., that they shall not be put to the great expenses involved by unnecessary and too frequent exhibition. The arrangement only holds good until the conclusion of the club's exhibition in 1903, that is to say, for about twenty-two months.

The committee of the Automobile Club will shortly issue for signature by the trade the letter referred to.

Mr. J. I. Thornycroft, F.R.S., M.I.C.E., who accompanied the heavy car trials on his new Panhard voiturette, will one day this week be honoured by the Glasgow University with the degree of LL.D. *in honoris causa.*

FIG. 1.—The Wolseley 10-h.p. Car.

THE "WOLSELEY" 10-h.p. MOTOR CAR.

WE give in the accompanying drawing (Figs. 2 and 3), a detailed elevation and plan, the general appearance being seen in Fig. 1, of the 10-h.p. car of the Wolseley Tool and Motor Car Company, Birmingham, which ran so successfully throughout the Glasgow trials. This car has now been awarded a gold medal by the Judges, the 6-h.p. car receiving a like recognition of its all-round excellence.

This vehicle is constructed, broadly speaking, on the same lines as that described in THE AUTOMOTOR JOURNAL, Vol. IV., pp. 452-453, but contains several important modifications in detail. The engine, E, is of the double cylinder horizontal type, with pistons coupled to cranks at 180° The most important features have already been pointed out in connection with the photograph on p. 369, Vol. V., of THE AUTOMOTOR JOURNAL.

One of the chief characteristics of the Wolseley engine is that each of the cylinder ends consists of a jacketed piece containing the admission and exhaust valves, which can be removed separately from the engine. The ignition plug for each cylinder passes horizontally through the jacketed ends. All the joints throughout the motor are ground, so as to avoid the necessity of packing, and a subsidiary feature, but one of considerable importance in prolonging the running life of a motor, is to be found in the ample surface allowance given to the bearings throughout. The ignition is on the high tension principle, induction coils and accumulators being employed in the ordinary way. The contact breakers are worked from the ends of the half-speed shaft of the engine, and are situated in a small light box, which is adapted to be rocked so as to enable the instant of ignition to be accelerated or retarded. Fibre blocks are used to secure the wires running into the box or casing to the contact breakers, and the box itself is made both water and dust proof.

Dealing now with the transmission mechanism, the power is first applied through the cone friction clutch, C, and Renold's chain gear AB., to the countershaft, D, of the charge speed gear. This shaft carries the sliding sleeve on which are mounted the spur pinions of the gear, these being engaged by side contact with fixed spur wheels on the differential cross shaft, FF., the final transmission to the road wheels being by chain gears, KK.

The sliding sleeve of the change gear is under control of the hand lever, L, which operates the striker in the gear box by means of the sector, M, and pinion, N, on the striker spindle, *n*.

The countershaft band brake, R, and the clutch, C, are controlled by pedals, V, and the road wheel brakes, T, are operated by the ever, U.

The radiator, S, which with its end pillars, W, constitutes the water tank, is neatly arranged to surround the bonnet covering the engine. The water circulation is maintained by a pump driven by gear from one end of the half-speed shaft of the engine. The petrol tank, P, is mounted on the front of the dashboard within the bonnet, the sparking plugs being, as already described, at the front end of the cylinders, and easy of access.

The system of steering control through a bevel and worm gearing has been fully described in THE AUTOMOTOR JOURNAL, Vol. IV., p. 453. The brakes on this car are designed to hold both for forward and backward movement, but in the event of the car running back, or when it is left standing upon a hill, the sprag, Z, may be lowered by dropping the catch, *a*.

The road wheels are of equal diameter, front and back, and have 90 mm. pneumatic tyres. The carriage body is of the Tonneau type, to seat four persons, and neatly designed and finished.

Altogether this vehicle is a very high class piece of engineering work; designed on the liberal lines which the great French races have proved to be most advantageous in a motor vehicle, and constructed with that regard for the smallest details which has brought English engineering work into such deservedly high repute.

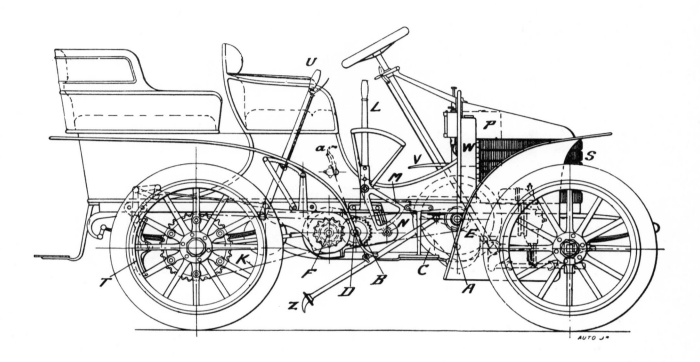

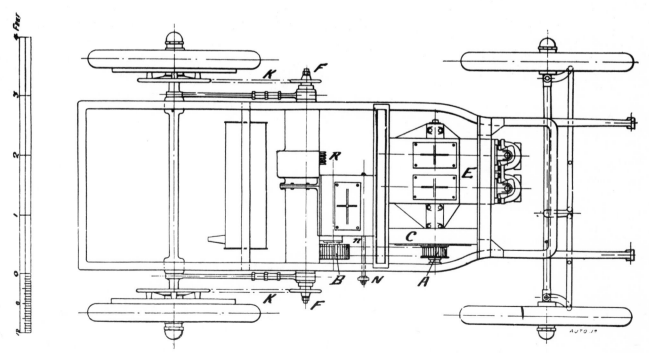

Figs. 2 and 3.— The 10-h.p. Wolseley Car—Elevation and Plan.

Flashes.

The hill-climbing trials of the Midland Automobile Club, which were to take place at Gorcutt Hill, between Birmingham and Alcester, on Tuesday next, the 27th inst., have been postponed till after the Glasgow trials, as so many members of the club are at present away on their holidays, and it is felt that a representative entry will scarcely be obtained till after the "big event."

* * *

The Mitchell is the name of a new motor bicycle of American construction which is being introduced into this country by Messrs. Davis Allen and Co., of Singer Street, Tabernacle Street, London, E.C. The motor is of 1¾ h.p., running at 1,800 revolutions. It is supported above the lower cross tube of the frame, and drives the rear wheel by means of a strap. The frame is specially strengthened for the work it has to do. The weight of the machine complete is 104 lbs. Over 150 of them are said to be already in use in the United States.

* * *

Mr. D. Citroen, of 45, Holborn Viaduct, E.C., informs us that he, having acquired the sole selling rights of the Minerva motor for this country and the colonies, wishes to rectify an impression which appears to have got abroad that cycle manufacturers are at liberty to fix motors other than the Minerva in the position covered by the Minerva patent. He states that no infringement will be tolerated, and that the idea seems to have originated from the use of expressions such as "fitted with a motor of the Minerva type," which are occasionally met with in published letters.

* * *

We have received a copy of their new motor sundries list from Messrs. Bransom, Kent, and Co., Ltd., of 332, Goswell Road, E.C. The firm tell us they make a point of keeping everything listed in stock, and the list is a very varied one, commencing with all the best known makes of accumulators and dry cells, contact breakers, and electrical fittings generally, and continuing with illustrations and prices of motor parts of all kinds, and after dealing with a very full line of accessories of every description concluding with an illustration and particulars of the firm's Royal George motor bicycle, which machine is driven by a Minerva motor.

* * *

The Renault, if only by its performance in the Paris-Bordeaux race, established itself as a remarkably fast and reliable voiturette, but it is interesting to those less ambitious for speed to know that the standard machine is giving every satisfaction with private owners. We have gathered from several of the latter that they are more than pleased with the behaviour of their machines, and only this week we were shown a letter by the Roadway Autocar Co., the British agents for the Renault, from a doctor in the North of England. He is using the machine for his practice daily, and he says that all his horses are out to grass and for sale. This is interesting, as it so happens that he lives in a very hilly district, and he states that most of the hills can be taken on second speed, which is much quicker than any of his horses could trot them.

Mr. M. G. Lacroix, B.Sc., mechanical engineer, and manager of Messrs. F. Mitchell and Co., motor-car specialists, Victoria Works, Longley Road, Tooting Junction, writes informing us that he has been touring, and has had no opportunity of reading *The Autocar* for some weeks. We gather from his somewhat incoherent communication that he refers to a paragraph in our issue of July 13th (page 39), which notes the appearance of a series of articles in *The English Mechanic* by Mr. Hyler White on "How to Build a Steam Carriage," and to Mr. White's reply to our criticism (*The Autocar*, July 20th, page 70). Mr. Lacroix takes some kind of exception to Mr. White's ideas, and concludes with the following offer, which practically amounts to a challenge: "To give Mr. White a chance to prove his real value, I am prepared to pay him £200 if he will build one E.M. car after his own specification."

* * *

In reference to a recent paragraph in *The Autocar*, Messrs. Rubery and Co., of Darlaston, who have so long been known in the autocar world in connection with motor-car frames, write us pointing out that they have been supplying the British motor builders with "castle" nuts for the last four years or more. This being so, we think it is only right that they should be credited in the matter. We may add, for the benefit of our readers who do not understand the term "castle nut," that such nuts are like the ordinary nut, but with six or more vertical projections above the face of the nut; that is to say, the nut is somewhat similar to a deep nut with six saw cuts on its face. These nuts can be locked with a split pin with the utmost ease, and with exactly the right amount of screwing home, as the pin would, of course, engage with any two of the six slots, and it is no trouble to get it in, as it used to be with the old drilled nut, which only gave one position circumferentially and vertically for the split pin.

* * *

A very interesting piece of work has just been successfully accomplished by Mr. Boundy, of Kendal. In connection with his business, he wanted a car for carrying heavy loads of masonry, and five years ago he set about building himself such a machine. The van is driven by a 9 h.p. motor. It has a three-speed gear, giving a maximum speed of twelve miles an hour, and being fitted up for the conveyance of passengers instead of masonry affords ample accommodation for ten. The work has been a labour of love with Mr. Boundy, and it is only in his leisure time that it has progressed. He has obtained all his parts, such as the engine, gears, axles, and radiator, from different prominent houses in the trade. He has fitted them together, and, of course, made many of the simpler parts himself. We hear that his car has already made its trial trip from Kendal to Dalton and back, some sixty miles, and that it successfully scaled Lindale Brow into the bargain. The idea of an amateur attempting to assemble a car seems to have created the utmost amusement in the county, and Mr. Boundy has been the object of a considerable amount of chaff, but now that his car is running well, his fellow townsmen are speaking proudly of local enterprise. We hope to illustrate and describe the van before long.

Major's Reading Motor and Cycle Depot has lately been enlarged to meet the demands of increased business.

* * *

A letter of sympathy was sent by the Lincolnshire Automobile Club to Capt. Laycock, who is a vice-president of the club.

* * *

General French seems fully alive to the value of the autocar in South Africa, as he is adapting it, together with cycles, to railways for swift patrol work.

* * *

A very noticeable figure seen frequently in an automobile on the country roads round about Maidenhead is that of Sir Francis Laking, the King's physician.

* * *

Mr. W. H. Kingsbury, of 61, Bath Street, Glasgow, is arranging to have a stock of motor accessories, lubricating oils, etc., on hand during the Glasgow trials.

* * *

The police in the Leake and Wrangle districts of East Lincolnshire have taken to hiding for the capture of autocarists who drive through from Nottingham *viâ* Boston to Skegness.

* * *

It is said that the King, when autocaring, frequently wears the customary "goggles" with gauze sides, and a cap with flaps to protect the ears. On one or two occasions His Majesty has donned the costume complete, with waterproof pilot coat.

* * *

A friend of ours to whom we gave a sample of Collan oil, which is a specially prepared leather preservative, speaks quite enthusiastically of the preparation, and tells us that he feels sure it has saved him from purchasing two new belts. Its use has improved the grip and bite of the belts enormously. Collan oil is made by T. Olsen, of Stockholm, Chr. Hanson, whose address is given as "Collan Oil Co., London," being his British representative. We fancy users of belt-driven cars will thank us for drawing their attention to this preparation.

* * *

Mr. Henry Mulliner, of Messrs. Mulliner and Co., 28, Brook Street, W., has patented and made a very neat and handy dustproof cap suitable for the universal joints of small voiturettes of the De Dion type. He tells us he had it in use the whole of the summer, and found it very satisfactory, both waterproof and dustproof. The device consists of a strong leather washer, which is contained in a light metal case that clips on to the axle and fits up snugly against the joint, so that, instead of the unsightly and ineffective leather cups or wrappings with which the axles have hitherto been disfigured, we get a neat plated disc, which is not only smart-looking, but really efficient as a protection of the *cardans*. Further, and this is no small point, there is no difficulty whatever in attaching or removing the protector, as the leather washer is split radially, but the joint in it is held together by a small steel spring. Then the metal case in which it is contained is also split, and fastened by a couple of light spring latches. It is an extremely neat and handy little fitting, and will, we are sure, be welcomed by many De Dionists.

We are informed by Mr. W. H. Bamber, the works manager, in regard to Mr. W. Hemingway's appointment at the Daimler Co.'s works at Coventry, that Mr. Hemingway is taking charge of the drawing office, and that all other departments are in the same hands as before.

* * *

The manufacture of motor bicycles has been taken up by Mr. T. Ratcliffe, of the Reliable Cycle and Motor Works, Frinton-on-Sea, Essex. Minerva motors and fittings are employed, and the general arrangement followed is similar to that adopted in the Minerva and Excelsior machines.

* * *

Mr. Boundy, of Kendal, tells us that should any automobilists in the Lake district require any small repairs done to their machines he can inform them of a good man. He has no interest in any engineering firm in the locality, but he has seen some of the work done by one or two so-called experts in the district.

* * *

Dr. Gatling is reported to have invented a motor plough, which he asserts will accomplish as great a revolution on the farm as his gun did on the battlefield. The great inventor makes the startling claim that his plough, under the guidance of one man, will break the surface of a thirty-one acre field in a single day.

* * *

It was announced some time ago that the Panhard and Levassor Co. had acquired the French rights in the Auto-sparker system of dynamo ignition, introduced by the Motsinger Co., of Pendleton, Ind., U.S.A. We now learn that the Motor Mfg. Co., Ltd., have acquired the British and Colonial rights in the same device, and will shortly be fitting it to all their vehicles.

* * *

One day last week Mr. W. L. Duck, accompanied by his wife, drove his Ariel quad a distance of 230 miles inside twelve hours. He tells us he did not have to make the slightest adjustment, and altogether it was quite the most enjoyable run he has ever had. Up to the present we have not heard of so long a run being accomplished by a quad inside half a day.

* * *

In reflecting upon the remarkable escape of M. Santos-Dumont, in which it would appear that the intrepid aeronaut well nigh set gravity in defiance, it is perhaps well to remember that had he not hooked his belt to the basket or car on his balloon he would unquestionably have been dashed out of it when it fell, as he could not have maintained his horizontal position without the support of the belt and hook.

* * *

Last week we said that the cause of the accident to the twenty-four horse-power Panhard driven by Capt. Laycock was not known, even to the four occupants of the car. We now learn from the gallant captain himself that an examination of the car by his head motor man shows that the cone in the ball race of one of the hind wheels had smashed, leading to the jamming of the wheel, and the skidding of the car into the hedge. We are very pleased to learn that the injured ones are making excellent progress.

THE TILBURSTOWE HILL CLIMB.

Mr. C. Jarrott on the 16 h.p. Panhard, his 10 h.p. De Dion Spider on the right. Mr. C. W. Brown's 3½ h.p. Pieper on the left.

The English Motor Club, in promoting this particularly interesting contest for the second time, were favoured both with splendid weather and a big entry. Forty-seven vehicles were down upon the programme, and of these thirty-seven essayed the climb, and thirty-six successfully passed the time-keeper at the summit. The single failure, from what cause has not transpired, was A. T. Westlake, on a one horse-power Bluhm motor bicycle. The arrangements made by Mr. Baily and his committee were excellent in every way, the competition passing off without a hitch of any kind. The fixture attracted a very large crowd of sightseers, who journeyed to the picturesque little Surrey village of Godstone both per automobile and bicycle. The total length of the climb from the bridge at the foot of Tilburstowe Hill to the summit is 1,214 yards, which, so far as grades go, is divided as follows:

408 yards of 1 in 17, 333 yards of 1 in 13, 175 yards of 1 in 11.9, 38 yards of 1 in 11.5, and 260 yards of 1 in 87. It will thus be seen that the slope does not compare in severity or length with that lately employed by the Automobile Club, viz., Dashwood Hill, but it is, nevertheless, a fairly severe test, and its various changes of gradient test the skill and judgment of drivers in changing speeds.

The greatest interest was very naturally felt in the fifty horse-power Napier, which on Saturday made its first public appearance in this country. To mount such a rise at a speed of thirty-seven and threequarter miles per hour suggests the big Napier as probably the fastest hill-climbing automobile yet built, although, of course, no means exist at present of comparing its performances up such slopes with those of cars built across the Channel.

A 16 h.p. Panhard.

Mrs. Kennard starting 2¾ h.p. De Dion, with Whippet trailer

The 50 h.p. Napier in full blast.

Looking up the road after the passage of a fast car.

The difference in the times of Mr. Mayhew's twenty horse-power and Mr. Jarrott's sixteen horse-power Panhards is wider than would seem to be warranted by the difference of four horse-power, but the fact that Mr. Jarrott was badly interfered with on the 1 in 11 section by an old lady who selected the very moment of his passing to rush across the road must be taken into consideration. He had to use both brakes to avoid a catastrophe, and to this his comparatively bad time may be ascribed. The motor cycles of Classes 1 and 2 were all assisted by the employment of the pedals, as were also those in Classes 3 and 4.

Mr. M. Egerton's 12 h.p. Darracq.

The Locomobiles showed up well in Class 5, scoring the first three cars up, but it is, of course, recognised that steam cars are suited by a competition of this kind. The different performances of the vehicles engaged can best be gathered by a study of the following tabulated results, to which, in the case of the first three cars in each class, we have appended the approximate speed in miles per hour at which they mounted the hill. The surface was in excellent condition from top to bottom, and the course was admirably kept by members and friends of the club who acted as marshals. The officials were: Judge, A. J. Wilson, E.M.C.,

Mr. J. H. Gladding's 9 h.p. Napier.

Mr. Harvey Du Cros, jun., on his 16 h.p. Panhard.

Back view of Mr. Mark Mayhew's 20 h.p. Panhard.

A.C.G.B.I.; timekeepers, F. T. Bidlake and Harry J. Swindley *(The Autocar)*; and hon. sec., F. W. Baily. After the competition, many members and competitors dined together at the Clayton Arms, Godstone, Mr. Mark Mayhew, L.C.C., being in the chair.

TABULAR SUMMARY OF THE PERFORMANCES OF THE MACHINES ON TILBURSTOWE HILL.

	Handicap for Class.	Handicap for Total Entries. M.	S.	Actual Time. M.	S.	Handicap Time. M.	S.	Speed Miles per Hour.
Class 1.—Motor Bicycles.								
1.—J. Leonard, $1\frac{1}{2}$ h.p. Werner (2) ..	Scratch	0	42	2	$2\frac{2}{5}$	2	$2\frac{2}{5}$	21·02
2.—H. J. Lamb, $1\frac{1}{2}$ h.p. ,, (1) ..	20 secs.	1	2	2	$6\frac{4}{5}$	1	$46\frac{4}{5}$	20·35
3.—T. H. Tessier, $1\frac{1}{2}$ h.p. ,, (3) ..	Scratch	0	42	2	$7\frac{2}{5}$	2	$7\frac{2}{5}$	20·19
Class 2.—Tricycles up to 3 h.p.								
1.—M. Moyle, 3 h.p. De Dion	Scratch	0	20	1	$44\frac{4}{5}$	1	$44\frac{4}{5}$	24·66
2.—F. Flutter, $2\frac{3}{4}$ h.p. De Dion (1) ..	15 secs.	0	35	1	45	1	30	24·42
3.—T. Parrish, ,, ,, (2) ..	,,		,,	1	46	1	31	24·19
4.—R. Dennis, $2\frac{3}{4}$ h.p. Speed King (3)	,,		,,	1	$52\frac{2}{5}$	1	$37\frac{2}{5}$	
5.—T. L. Spencer, $2\frac{3}{4}$ h.p. Motor Manufacturing Co.	,,		,,	2	$21\frac{3}{5}$	2	$6\frac{3}{5}$	
6—W. J. Westfield, $1\frac{3}{4}$ h.p. De Dion	50 secs.	1	10	2	$32\frac{2}{5}$	1	$42\frac{2}{5}$	
7.—L. Jones, $1\frac{3}{4}$ h.p. Clement De Dion	,,		,,	3	$37\frac{2}{5}$	2	$47\frac{2}{5}$	
Class 3.—Tricycles above 3 h.p								
1.—T. Maltby, jun., 5 h.p. De Dion (1)	10 secs.	Scratch		1	$40\frac{3}{5}$	1	$30\frac{3}{5}$	25·65
2.—C. Jarrott, 8 h.p. De Dion (2)	Scratch	,,		1	$42\frac{2}{5}$	1	$42\frac{2}{5}$	25·14
Class 4.								
1.—Mrs. Kennard, $2\frac{3}{4}$ h.p. De Dion, with Whippet trailer (two persons)	25 secs.	1	30	4	49	4	24	8·87
Class 5.—Cars up to 7 h.p.								
1.—A. Ginder, $5\frac{1}{2}$ h.p. Locomobile ..	Scratch	0	20	1	$46\frac{3}{5}$	1	$46\frac{3}{5}$	24·00
2.—T. J. Morse, ,, ,,	,,		,,	2	$12\frac{1}{5}$	2	$12\frac{1}{5}$	19·43
3.—W. M. Letts, ,, ,,	,,		,,	2	$25\frac{2}{5}$	2	$25\frac{2}{5}$	17·69
4.—A. E. Crowdy, 6 h.p. Darracq ..	40 secs.	1	0	2	$37\frac{1}{5}$	1	$57\frac{1}{5}$	
5.—E. J. Stevens, $5\frac{1}{2}$ h.p. Locomobile	Scratch	0	20	2	$40\frac{1}{5}$	2	$40\frac{1}{5}$	
6.—S. D. Begbie, 5 h.p. Century	10 secs.	0	30	2	$40\frac{2}{5}$	2	$30\frac{2}{5}$	
7.—S. T. Hone, $4\frac{1}{2}$ h.p. De Dion	2m. 10s.	2	30	3	13	1	3	
8.—C. K. Gregson, $3\frac{1}{2}$ h.p. De Dion ..	3m 35s.	3	55	3	$18\frac{2}{5}$	0	$16\frac{3}{5}$	
9.—A. W. Heard, 5 h.p. Century	10 secs.	0	30	3	$24\frac{4}{5}$	3	$14\frac{4}{5}$	
10.—H. Johnson, 5 h.p. Peugeot	2m. 10s.	2	30	5	$18\frac{4}{5}$	3	$8\frac{4}{5}$	
11.—G. H. Smith, $4\frac{1}{2}$ h.p. Empress ..	,,		,,	5	$52\frac{4}{5}$	3	$42\frac{4}{5}$	
12.—C. W. Brown, $3\frac{1}{2}$ h.p. Pieper	3m. 45s.	4	5	5	$54\frac{4}{5}$	2	$9\frac{4}{5}$	
13.—E. Midgley, $5\frac{1}{2}$ h.p. Gladiator, four persons	2m. 30s.	2	50	6	$22\frac{2}{5}$	3	52	
Class 6.—Cars up to 9 h.p.								
1.—J. H. Gladding, 9 h.p. Napier, four persons	45 secs.	2	15	3	$32\frac{2}{5}$	2	$47\frac{2}{5}$	12·00
2.—Motor Car Co., $8\frac{1}{2}$ h.p. Motor Car Co., two persons	Scratch	0	35	4	34	4	34	9·36
Class 7.—Cars up to 16 h.p.								
1.—C. Jarrott, 10 h.p. De Dion Spider	Scratch	0	35	1	$37\frac{1}{5}$	1	$37\frac{1}{5}$	26·38
2.—C. Jarrott, 16 h.p. Panhard	15 secs.	0	50	1	$52\frac{2}{5}$	1	$37\frac{2}{5}$	22·90
3.—H. Du Cros, jun., 16 h p. Panhard	,,		,,	2	3	1	48	20·80
4.—M. Egerton, 12 h p. Darracq	Scratch	0	35	2	$34\frac{1}{5}$	2	$34\frac{1}{5}$	
5.—Jack Lawson, 8 h.p. Panhard	40 secs.	1	15	2	$50\frac{3}{5}$	2	$10\frac{3}{5}$	
Class 8.—Large Cars above 16 h.p.								
1.—S. F. Edge, 50 h.p. Napier., two persons	Scratch	Scratch		1	$7\frac{4}{5}$	1	$7\frac{4}{5}$	37·72
2.—Mark Mayhew, 20 h.p. Panhard, two persons	15 secs.	0	15	1	27	1	12	29·48

Result of Handicap for Total Entries.

	Handicap Times. M.	S.
1.—C. K. Gregson, $3\frac{1}{2}$ h.p. De Dion	0	$36\frac{3}{5}$
2.—S. T. Hone, $4\frac{1}{2}$ h.p. De Dion ..	0	43
3.—C. Jarrott, 10 h.p. De Dion Spider	1	$2\frac{1}{5}$
4.—C. Jarrott, 16 h.p. Panhard ..	1	$2\frac{2}{5}$
5.—H. J. Lamb, $1\frac{1}{2}$ h.p. Werner Bicycle	1	$4\frac{4}{5}$
6.—S. F. Edge, 50 h.p. Napier ..	1	$7\frac{4}{5}$

Result of Total Entries.

	M.	S.		
1.—S. F. Edge, 50 h.p Napier ..	1	$7\frac{4}{5}$	= 37·72	miles per hour.
2.—Mark Mayhew, 20 h.p. Panhard	1	12	= 29·48	,, ,,
3.—C. Jarrott, 10 h.p. De Dion Spider	1	$37\frac{1}{5}$	= 26·38	,, ,,
4.—T. Maltby, 5 h.p. De Dion Tricycle	1	$40\frac{3}{5}$	= 25 65	,, ,,
5.—C. Jarrott, 8 h.p. De Dion Tricycle	1	$42\frac{2}{5}$	= 25·14	,, ,,
6.—M. Moyle, 3 h.p. De Dion Tricycle	1	$44\frac{4}{5}$	= 24·66	,, ,,
7.—F. Flutter, $2\frac{3}{4}$ h.p. De Dion Tricycle	1	45	= 24·42	,, ,,
8.—T. Parrish, $2\frac{3}{4}$ h.p. De Dion Tricycle	1	46	= 24·19	,, ,,
9.—A. Ginder, $5\frac{1}{2}$ h.p. Locomobile ..	1	$46\frac{3}{5}$	= 24·00	,, ,,
10. { C. Jarrott, 16 h.p. Panhard	1	$52\frac{2}{5}$	= 22·90	,, ,,
10. { R. Dennis, $2\frac{3}{4}$ h.p. Speed King Tricycle ..	1	$52\frac{2}{5}$	= 22·90	,, ,,

THE FIFTY HORSE-POWER NAPIER.

WORLD'S RECORDS BY AN ENGLISH CAR.

By HARRY J. SWINDLEY.

It is hard on English manufacturers that they cannot test the machines their brains and hands have developed on English roads, but are obliged to betake themselves and the vehicles across the Channel to the more hospitable and reasonable shores of France, if they really desire to try their cars high. Because of such a desire I found myself in Paris last week-end, bidden thither by Mr. S. F. Edge for the purpose of clocking the speed of the fifty horse-power Napier over a selected distance on some suitable road as near Paris as might be.

As soon as I learnt what was desired, I wrote my good friend M. Paul Rousseau, the Directeur-Administrateur of *Le Vélo*, who is always in such matters a very present help in trouble, and asked him to tell me where ten miles of straight, good, level, and desolate road might be come at. He replied that there existed from eighteen to twenty kiloms. of such road between Orleans and Vierzon, which length was of excellent surface, of good width, and destitute of even a house, to say nothing of a village, for the entire length. As matters shaped afterwards, we did not go there. I would we had, but I quote M. Rousseau in the event of any reader of *The Autocar* wishing to know of such a stretch of highway.

The Napier crossed by Folkestone and Boulogne, very much the best way too, if I may judge by Mr. Edge's story, and that of Mr. Alf. C. Harmsworth's well-known expert, Lancaster, from whom at Dieppe I had a doleful account of the trouble and worry he had been at in getting Mr. Harmsworth's Serpollet and his twelve horse-power Panhard across from Newhaven to Dieppe on Thursday night. But this, by the way, and merely to suggest to English automobilists visiting France with their automobiles that Folkestone-Boulogne is the route they should adopt.

Arriving at Victoria on Friday morning, I was astonished and pleased to find Mr. A. C. Harmsworth and Mr. Harold Harmsworth and two friends, Mr. Beeton and Mr. Dubbs, *en route* for Dieppe to join the two cars already referred to. Mr. Harmsworth, after learning the purpose of my trip, most kindly suggested that I should travel as far as Rouen on the Serpollet. "You can sit on the front seat with Lancaster, and see how she's driven; you'll like that," said he! I accepted instantly, for to sit alongside Lancaster on any car, watch him drive, and lure him on to talk shop is an education for most of us.

Both vehicles were in waiting on the quay when we landed, and our embarkation thereon was watched by a large and interested crowd of Dieppois, who had been told that the cars belonged to Milor Harmsworth, *un Anglais très, tres riche,* who was going to take part in the Paris-Berlin race.

The forward canopy of the Serpollet was piled up with so much luggage that she quite "wore a top-heavy look," and garnered a profuse crop of leaves and twigs from the overhanging trees before she fetched the Norman capital.

Her human freight included Mr. Harold Harmsworth, Mr. Beeton, Lancaster, myself, and Lancaster's understudy, who balanced himself throughout the run in a marvellous manner on the forward near side mudguard. Mr. Alfred Harmsworth drove his twelve horse-power Panhard, with Mr. Dubbs at his side, another *mécanicien* in the place appointed for *mécaniciens*, and his valet, shoulder deep in baggage in the tonneau.

Once loaded up, we were quickly under weigh, taking the left-hand road out of Dieppe, for the purpose of touching at Arques, and getting a look at the grand ruins of the old castle there, which are well worth a visit. The twelve horse-power Panhard quickly took the lead, for the Serpollet, having shown me at Bordeaux how excellently she could perform, chose upon this occasion to behave in exactly the opposite manner. For the reason that the condenser was somewhat choked, she would not steam on the hills, and as we accidentally turned right at Arques and climbed out of the valley of

the Arques river, back to the old main road, Lancaster and I put in a powerful amount of pumping. To aid the driver in this stimulating amusement, a second mid-footboard pump lever has been fitted, and even with that addition both driver and his seat companion get ample satisfaction if the car chooses to sulk. Our friends, taking their ease behind, derived the most intense satisfaction from our exertions, for at times we almost rowed the car up the hills, and they cheered us with reminders of the appetite we were stimulating and the generally wholesome effect of violent exercise on the human frame. Having driven about ten miles, most of it uphill, and most of it glued to those pump levers, we found ourselves back on the main Rouen road, about seven kiloms. from Dieppe, and obliged perforce to take to the very highway we had desired to avoid.

From my experience of Friday afternoon, I have come to the conclusion that, with his auxiliary pump, his three gauges, his pedals, gear lever, and oil tank pump, to look after, the driver of a big Serpollet has plenty to occupy his attention, even when everything is going well, but when things are a bit awry, well—then that driver's life becomes an exceedingly busy one. We pulled up once to see whether dirt in the automatic pump was at the bottom of the trouble, but that was not the solution, so, finding that we were short of water, we backed into a farmhouse some two hundred yards off the road for the purpose of filling up. We were soon on the road again, and with a modicum of pumping and a short halt at Tôtes to drink cider and look at the quaint old kitchen of the Hotel du Cygne, we reached Rouen and the Hotel d'Angleterre (where the twelve horse-power had landed Mr. Harmsworth an hour before) in time for dinner. After dinner I left my genial host and his party, and proceeded by train to Paris, where, at the Hotel Brighton, which most comfortable house is becoming quite the rendezvous there for English automobilists, I found the Hon. C. S. Rolls, his henchman Claud Crompton, and S. F. Edge awaiting my arrival. Rolls and Crompton were much pleased with the running of the former's Mors car, which is duly entered amongst the fliers for the big race, and spoke with some seriousness of single kiloms. peeled off in 35s., which meaneth in the vernacular 63.87 miles per hour. The morrow was the day appointed for the *poinconnage* of the fliers at the Automobile Club, and it was arranged that, so soon as Edge had got his papers and the "big demon," as the clubmen call the Napier, over there, had been duly ear-marked, we should leave for Chartres, between which city and Paris Edge opined there was a stretch of road straight and long enough for his purpose. After the usual delay and some trouble with the *douaniers* —when is there not trouble with *douaniers?*—we were *en route*, and snorting angrily (yes, that is the exact description of the Napier's exhaust) up the Champs Elysées. I was agreeably surprised to note with Edge at the wheel how really handy the big car was in traffic, which is the more remarkable having regard to the fact that her first speed sparked up is twenty-five miles per hour. Speeding before clearing the environs of Paris was, of course, quite out of the question, but Edge just let her out up a long and steepish hill beyond Suresnes, and here I got my first impression of the Napier's contempt for inclination. She took this ascent at not a fraction under forty miles per hour, and that on her third speed. "There's no speed road until we pass Ablis," said Edge, but as we were then wiping off kiloms. in 48s. apiece, which is a shade over forty-six miles per hour, I awaited the coming speed piece with some interest.

When Ablis had been left behind, and the road stretched away straight as a dart for something like ten kiloms., I got my first real taste of speed driving, beside which my previous experiences on sixteen and twenty horse-power cars in this country paled into the merest insignificance. Kiloms. were reeled off in 42s. to 45s., or fifty-three to fifty-four miles per hour, and still Edge called it crawling. But better was yet to come, for after St. Cheron is passed the road falls gradually towards Chartres, and here the big car began to get among the thirties. I was snapping odd kiloms. somewhat carelessly, for with mudguards on and three up I had no thought of the actual trial, and made her cover one kilom. in 31s. dead, but as it was clocked in a haphazard kind of way I should not care to put it forward as official. This works out at seventy-two miles per hour, and if she was not doing that she was very near it. By the shrieking and howling of the wind in one's ears, we might have been doing a hundred, and, withal, her engine beating rhythmically and sweetly, as though the job were wholly to its fancy. After dinner at the Hotel du Grand Monarque, where the automobilist is most warmly welcomed, hospitably entertained, and his car housed free, lubricating and petrol tanks were replenished, and the engine carefully gone over in preparation for the morrow.

We were on the Bordeaux road at 3 a.m. next day, making for what, according to our host, was a desolate eighteen kiloms. south of Thivars, but this turned out to be quite a village-fringed stretch, and it looked as if we should have to stay the night again in Chartres and try north once more in the morning. At about two in the afternoon, however, we found the road between the eighty-third and seventy-fifth kiloms. stones from Paris quite deserted, and we resolved upon making the test run there and then. Let me say at once that the portion selected was by no means an ideal stretch, the finishing point being considerably above the level of the start. Having measured off the necessary number of odd yards to make five miles, for, alas! we could not get the full ten, we made ready by detaching the big wing mudguards and the heavy Bleriot lamp. The *mécanicien* was stationed at the point measured off, and the car was run back about two kiloms. to get up steam. Even then, though on a falling grade, Edge had barely got in his fourth before the moment came to start the chronometer, and it may be truly said that it was not before the eighty-second kilom. stone was reached that the car was going all out. But then she was "Awa! True beat, full power," and only those who sat on her, he with knit brows and pursed lips who bent low over the steering wheel, and the other sitting on the footboard and crouching behind the dashboard, watch in hand, realised how she was "awa," and what the full power of her engine really meant. From the eighty-third to the eighty-fourth, a fair give and take bit, I put my second watch on for the flying kilometre, and looking so soon as the stone

had fled past saw that the chronograph showed 32 2-5s. (sixty-nine miles per hour), 1 4-5s. better than Jenatzy's "Jamais-Contente" time, and 3 2-5s. better than the kilometre of Serpollet accomplished during the Nice week this year. A kilometre farther on the road dips down to, and up from, the valley of a little steam, rising more than it falls, and it was here on the lower portion of the drop that the speed of the good car was at its zenith. The air screamed past the ears in wild shrieks, and the trees and bushes lining the road flashed by like light. I think I am quite within the truth when I say that we travelled at least twenty-five per cent. faster here than on the flying kilometre, and if this is a correct estimate our speed at this point was eighty-six and a quarter miles per hour on the common road. It produced its effect even upon the iron-nerved, imperturbable Edge, for bending down he yelled in my ear—otherwise the wild rush of the wind would have hurled his words away—"It's pretty fast here!" The biggish rise up hardly seemed to stop here at all, but it steadied her, and thence to the seventy-fifth kilometre the speed felt low by comparison with that wild downward rush. The full five miles was accomplished in 4m. 44 3-5s., an average of 35 2-5s., which equals 66.93 miles per hour.

Before the full trial Mr. Edge ran the car a trip over the course with the *mécanicien* on board, and I went two kiloms. down the road to see her pass at the bottom of the slope, where she was at the top nick. Words altogether fail; I cannot pretend to a verbal description of the effect of the "big demon" as she hurtled by, more like a projectile from a big gun than a self-propelled vehicle steered and controlled by a human hand. She grew from the appearance of a little truck on four wheels as she came over the top of the hill to a shrieking monster as she whirled by. The air forced from her path hit me hard in the face and chest, stones, sticks, and leaves fled after in her vortex, a great cloud of dust rose up instantly and cloaked her from view, and only remained the dust cloud, the beat of her engine, and the maddened snort of her exhaust dying away in the distance to tell that she had passed. So soon as the dust cleared, one could see her attendant cloud blotting out the perspective between the trees until she whirled up out of the little valley and disappeared over the hill. I had time to sit down and ponder the fact that the next time she passed that point in the same sort of hurry I, and not the *mécanicien*, would be on board.

Our return journey to Paris at forty-five miles per hour was mere crawling comparatively—indeed, at that pace the Napier strikes one as safe as a house. The dainty pleasure-seekers home returning from the Bois down the Champs Elysées did not seem at all to appreciate the presence of the big car among them as Edge deftly edged her through the traffic on her way to her well-earned rest at Kriegers in the Rue Ponthien. And so we left her. Whatever may be her fate in the Paris-Berlin race, and owing to the frequent *controles* (some only divided from each other by stretches of eleven to fifteen kiloms.) and bad roads we do not fancy her chance, there remains no doubt that England and Napier can, up to the present at all events, claim to have turned out the fastest automobile yet put upon the road.

THE NEW YORK-BUFFALO ENDURANCE CONTEST.

Waiting for the start. The scene in the street at the side of the Automobile Club Buildings, New York.

The five-hundred miles run of the eighty-one self-propelled vehicles, which began at New York on Monday, Sept. 9th, and was scheduled to finish at Buffalo on Saturday, Sept. 14th, was concluded on Friday, Sept. 13th, at Rochester, something like sixty-five miles short of Buffalo, the original destination, because of the most lamentable death of our assassinated President McKinley.   After being shot by the Anarchist Czolgosz in the Temple of Music at the Buffalo Pan-American Exposition, President McKinley had rallied, and his recovery was thought assured ; his subsequent relapse and swiftly following death were wholly unexpected, and the consequent shock paralysed the United States during the following week, putting an end to both business and sports.

The 30 h.p. Panhard, driven by D. W. Bishop, spurting over the summit of Nelson Hill. Weight of vehicle complete with fuel and accessories 2,800 lbs.

Under these extraordinary and most painful circumstances, the run of the automobiles into Buffalo, where the murdered President lay dead, was not to be thought of, and it was officially ended at Rochester on Friday night, where the forty-one survivors of the eighty-one starters from New York five days before were notified of the termination of their arduous labours.

The weather was fair for the first two days, and very wet and stormy for the last three days, and the roads were wretched throughout.

The end of the first day's run, Monday's, was at Poughkeepsie, where the following list of forty-two vehicles appeared before 6 p.m.:

B4.	8 h.p. Haynes-Apperson.
B5.	8½ h.p. Haynes-Apperson.
D64.	Orient motor bicycle.
B80.	4½ h.p. Mark VIII. Columbia Runabout.
B81.	7 h.p. U.S. Long Distance Runabout.
A73.	5 h.p. De Dion-Bouton motorette.
A74.	8 h.p. De Dion-Bouton motorette.
A75.	De Dion-Bouton motorette.
A72.	5 h.p. De Dion-Bouton motorette.
B39.	4½ h.p. Locomobile.
B86.	American Bicycle Co.'s hydrocar.
A37.	3½ h.p. Locomobile.
C55.	30 h.p. Panhard.
B13.	6 h.p. White Sewing Machine Co.'s Stanhope.
B12.	6 h.p. White Sewing Machine Co.'s Stanhope.
A45.	Grout Bros.' open Stanhope.
A11.	6 h.p. White Sewing Machine Co.'s Runabout.
B35.	6 h.p. Foster's touring waggon.
B14.	6 h.p. White Sewing Machine Co.'s Stanhope.
B70.	6 h.p. Foster's touring waggon.
C31.	9 h.p. Automobile Co.'s phaeton.
B32.	12 h.p. Winton semi-racer.

A38.   3½ h.p. Locomobile.
C1.   16 h.p. Robinson touring car.
A36.   3½ h.p. Locomobile.
B52.   12 h.p. Searchmont touring car.
A47.   3½ h.p. Locomobile.
B21.   6½ h.p. American Bicycle Co.'s Stanhope.
B54.   6 h.p.   Stearn's Runabout.
A8.   2½ h.p. G.N. Pierce Runabout.
A63.   8 h.p.   Duryea phaeton.
B78.   4½ h.p. Mark VIII. Columbia.
C18.   9 h.p.   Holyoke phaeton.
B34.   7 h.p.   St. Louis carriage.
C79.   16 h.p. Packard.
C56.   14 h.p. Packard, Model C.
B26.   12 h.p. Winton semi-racer.
B15.   6½ h.p. Overman Runabout.
B16.   6½ h.p. Overman Runabout.
C24.   12 h.p. Packard, Model C.
C23.   12 h.p. Packard, Model C.
C61.   12 h.p. Packard, Model C.

At the closing of the control, 9.30 p.m., seventy-five survivors out of the eighty-one starters had arrived. For distances, classifications, and descriptions of vehicles, the reader may consult the previously published *Autocar* article descriptive of the New York-Buffalo run (see page 317 *et seq.*)

The second day's run, Poughkeepsie to Albany, was made in fair weather over abominable roads, one might fairly say no roads at all, merely waggon tracks in the natural soil, in many places abundantly bestrewn with loose stones and small boulders, and nowhere paved or macadamised, except some short stretches in the villages. Sixty-four survivors reached Albany before 9 p.m., and four came in later.

The third stage, Wednesday, Sept. 11th, Albany to Herkimer, with mid-day control at Fonda, began with sixty-eight starters, the latest taking the road at 10 a.m. There had been rain overnight, and the mud roads were even more villainous than those run over on Tuesday, and there was a heavy rain in the afternoon. A vast amount of skidding resulted from these conditions, in spite of slow speeds and

One of the five "Gasomobiles"—the 9 h p. (petrol) phaeton (weight 2,330 lbs), driven by Alex. Fischer.

rope-wound wheels, and some serious breakdowns followed the inebriated lurches of the waggons in every direction except that intended by their un-happy drivers, drenched to the skin, covered with mud, plagued with all manner of ignition troubles from wet wires and tremblers, and running at their slowest through inches of slippery mud. Here, in this very heavy and most trying stretch, the light steam machines with their small weight, continuous torque, and independence of spark vagaries, showed up surprisingly well, coming to the front in a wholly unexpected and hitherto unprecedented manner. Fortunately, the broken and bent axles, the tail-turning, brake failures, and tyre shedding—one waggon suffered the simultaneous loss of both rear tyres—caused no serious injury to life or limb, though the drivers, in many cases flung headlong from their waggons to the earth, were the recipients of numberless painful bruises. Finally, at the end of what may safely be described as one of the most heroic efforts at automobile driving ever made, fifty-one vehicles reached Herkimer before the control closed at 9.40 p.m.

The fourth stage, Herkimer to Syracuse, 65.1 miles, was run on Thursday, fifty-six vehicles leaving Herkimer before 10 a.m. Rain began at 8.45 a.m., and the roads were simply horrible. Many serious accidents occurred during this day's run, but no one was very much hurt.

The run of the fifth day, Friday, Syracuse to Rochester, 87.2 miles, began with fifty starters, the last leaving Syracuse at 9.40 a.m. The heavy rains of the two days before had washed pretty much all the mud and soil off the face of the primitive roads, exposing the gravel and boulders, for all the world like the dry bed of a watercourse in many long stretches,

The 12 h.p semi-racing Winton, with D. B. McGregor and Vice-president A. C. Bostwick on board.   Weight 1,850 lbs.

and often traversed by gullies washed out by the torrents of Wednesday and Thursday. Of the fifty starters in this day's run, forty-three reached Lyons, mid-day control, and thirty-eight left before control closed at 3.40 p.m., and thirty-nine vehicles reached the Rochester control before 9.45 p.m. This day was full of blood-stirring episodes and serious breakages, again with no great personal damage to the drivers. One Winton vehicle lost a wheel and part of an axle—small wonder where a ton waggon is carried on inch diameter axles. A White light steam waggon buckled a rear wheel, and one De Dion stripped the teeth from a gear, and there were many, many other mishaps. In all, forty-one vehicles reached Rochester, cylinder-fired motors and steam motors showing up at the finish in about the same proportions as at the New York start, five days before.

Here follows the list of survivors:

ARRIVALS AT ROCHESTER, SEPTEMBER 13TH.
Control opened at 3.45 p.m., closed 10.30 p.m.

Order.	Time of Day.	Class and Number.	Driver.	Make of Vehicle.
1	3.45	C 55	D. W. Bishop	Panhard
2	4.07	C 23	J. W. Packard	Packard
3	4.15	A 47	C. A. Benjamin	Locomobile
4	4.20	B 5	Edgar-Apperson	Haynes-Apperson
5	4.32	C 24	William Hatcher	Packard
6	4.46	B 80	E. B. Pettengill	Columbia
7	4.47	B 12	O. S. Southworth	White
8	4.53	B 78	J. Seligman	Columbia
9	4.59	B 70	F. R Densmore	Foster
10	4.59	C 31	Albert T. Otto	Gasomobile
11	5.01	B 35	S. D. Waldron	Foster
12	5.04	B 13	M. Hughes	White
13	5.08	B 86	M. H. Winters	Hydrocar
14	5.09	A 11	R. H. White	White
15	5.09	B 4	Elmer Apperson	Haynes-Apperson
16	5.17	B 28	O. K. Raymond	Lane
17	5.20	C 2	A. R. Shattuck	Panhard
18	5.23	B 32	Percy Owen	Winton
19	5.24	C 77	Alexander Fischer	Gasomobile
20	5.30	B 14	P. H. Deming	White
21	5.31	C 79	Dr. T. J. Martin	Packard
22	5.50	A 37	J. A. Mitchell	Locomobile
23	5.51	A 72	J. Louvegnez	De Dion
24	6.05	A 8	P. P. Pierce	Pierce
25	6.22	C 1	J. T. Robinson	Robinson
26	6.30	C 30	S. D. Ripley	Gasomobile
27	6.36	B 34	J. L. French	St. Louis
28	7.08	B 81	F. E. Lewis, 2d.	U.S. Long Distance
29	7.29	C 65	C. R. Woodin	Century
30	7.34	A 82	F. H. Fowler	Knox
31	7.37	A 75	C. J. Field	De Dion
32	7.47	A 6	H. Burhans	Duryea
33	7.48	A 38	G. A. Knowles	Locomobile
34	7.54	C 56	A. L. McMurtry	Packard
35	8.24	C 18	C. R. Greuter	Holyoke
36	8.45	C 59	W. H. Owen	Gasomobile
37	9.16	B 27	L. S. Clarke	Autocar
38	9.19	B 22	Alexander Dow	Winton
39	9.25	C 20	H. Curtis	Toledo
40	9.39	B 39	J. W. Clark	Locomobile
41	9.45	C 61	J. M. Satterfield	Packard

Mr. D. W. Bishop, on his big Panhard, led through the whole run. Haynes-Apperson, Foster, Locomobile, White, Packard, and Duryea waggons are said to have run steadily and well and with slight repairs through the whole distance. I have, as yet, no authentic story of the run of any one machine. I have at hand as I write a medley of fairy tales, some manifestly fiction, some seemingly solid fact, and all of a more or less thrilling sort, and none worth the space required for telling for two reasons: First, there was no attention whatever paid to the twelve miles per hour maximum speed rule of the contest; it was go as you please from the start, and the devil take the hindmost, or the man in front if his pursuer could overtake him. There was a hill-climbing contest at Nelson's Hill, a quite sufficiently stiff grade half a mile long, but the records at hand are not such as to be of any particular value. The second and over-shadowing cause of the complete worthlessness of all the records of this run is the fact that no one (save the drivers themselves) knows what really happened to the individual machines. There was no disinterested club official or appointee aboard each vehicle to chronicle actual happenings. The day's runs were short, with a long night between, which, it is asserted, was filled by the special mechanics or factory employees sent out by each maker in bringing their machines into starting form any time before 10 a.m. next day. It is said that one concern had no less than twelve special mechanics on the route, leaving one control by train as soon as possible after the start of their own waggons, and reaching the next long before their own waggons, and working diligently until the next start; and it is asserted that many of the manufacturers had complete lists of repairs at each control, and that in one case a new boiler was substituted, and in another case a pair of entirely new engines replaced the ones which started from New York. Another concern had a machine shop on wheels in the run, supplied with duplicates of every part of their vehicles except the waggon body.

Manifestly, the lighter and more readily repaired machines, constructed with interchangeable parts, could go on for any length of time under such extraordinary repair and replacement conditions, and hence the whole record is clouded and besmirched beyond the possibility of serious engineering consideration.

The list of survivors, read in connection with the list of original starters, will give the technical reader all the accurate information he is ever likely to obtain of this most remarkably ill-conducted contest.

It may be said that, according to the tales told, possibly true and possibly false, the wheel-steered machines suffered more from faults of direction than the lever steered machines, and that the double-tube tyres went through better than the single-tube tyres, this excellence being due to the distressing manner in which the light, single-tube, projecting, thin steel wheel rims were crumpled and banged out of shape by the boulders in the roads, and that these same boulders played havoc with wire-wheel spokes, but did not seriously damage the wooden-wheel spokes.

I am promised logs of this voyage from drivers I know to be intentionally truthful, and should I obtain anything which seems to me to be reliable I shall forward it to The Autocar.

More than this not even those who followed the contest foot by foot and mile by mile can give, since none of these saw more than a very small part of the happenings of this absurdly uninstructive event.

Had each waggon carried a wholly disinterested historian the narratives of hair-raising adventure and exhausting physical effort by them given would have made the New York-Buffalo run as highly instructive and valuable as it is now wholly barren of valuable teachings.

Five motor bicycles started from New York on Monday morning: No. 9—Thomas Motor Bicycle Co., of Buffalo; 1 h.p.; weight, 90 lbs. No. 64—Orient Motor Bicycle, Waltham, Mass.; 2¼ h.p.; weight, 200 lbs. No. 67—Indian Motor Bicycle, Hendee Co., Springfield, Mass.; 1¾ h.p.; weight, 100 lbs. No. 88—Regas Vehicle Co., Rochester, N.Y.; 2¼ h.p.; weight, 160 lbs. No. 89—Same

The president of the American Automobile Club on his 12 h.p. (2,550 lbs.) Panhard.

makers; 1½ h.p.; weight, 110 lbs. Of these motor bicycles Nos. 64 and 88 reached the Albany control, end of second stage, within the control hours. At the start, leaving Albany, Nos. 9, 64, and 88 were inside of control time. The heavens opened, and the floods came, and only No. 9, the Thomas motor bicycle, was on hand in control leaving time at Fonda, Wednesday noon. The roads were either running rivers or quagmires, and the unlucky motor bicyclists rode when they could find high side-paths, and tramped through the mud pushing their machines when there were no side paths to be found. None of them reached Herkimer in time to obtain a control record.

Leaving Herkimer, however, Nos. 9 and 64, Thomas and Orient, were within hours, and both reached Syracuse in control time. Leaving Syracuse, No. 64 only has a record, and none of the lot appear in the control list of arrivals at Rochester.

It is a wonderful thing that any of the little two-wheelers ran through the mud and rain of Thursday. It was, indeed, a feat of pluck and muscular endurance, not to be even thought of without admiration and shuddering respect.

To reverse the shield, and show the silver side for a moment, in the bright rays of Monday morning's sun at New York, and the sombre mourning twilight of Friday night at Rochester, it may be truly said that the actual starting of so large a field of automobiles, many of them really sound, substantial, well-built autocars, and all but four of strictly American design and construction, and by many different makers, marked a vast stride of practical advance in American motor

waggon theory and practice. Hitherto it has been the rule in American automobile events to have a crowd of entries and a miserably small showing of actual starters. In this run nearly all the entries were also starters, and more than half of them ran to Rochester, over as wretched stretches of roadways as can be found in any civilised country. The vehicles were not from any one centre; they came from Boston in the east to St. Louis, 1,200 miles or so to the westward, thus showing that the automobile virus has penetrated so deeply into our most widely separated manufacturing centres that it can never be eradicated. The autocar must go, and the horse must go; the autocar from the factory to the road, and the horse from the streets and roads to the farm, until the time when some one of the "clever devils" makes a farm motor waggon that can take heavy loads to market, and can also plough and sow and reap—a by no means absurd or impossible combination. Then the horse must go once more—this time to his final sphere of usefulness, in the lands of the hippophagi, where the frankfurter is a valued comestible.

HUGH DOLNAR.

New York, September 23rd.

"The Autocar" vehicle which won the cup for cars between 1,000 and 2,000 lbs. in weight in the Nelson hill-climbing contest. Weight, 1,200 lbs. H.P., 8.

A NOVEL ADVERTISEMENT.

The illustrations we publish are made from a couple of photographs kindly placed at our disposal by Mr. F. M. Maynard. They show the method of advertising adopted by a firm noted for their aggressive announcements. The actual jug stands 7ft. 8in. high independently of the car, and it is 3ft. 6in. in diameter at its widest part. It is made of aluminium, but the label is a sheet of glass suitably curved and decorated. The driver is accommodated inside the giant jug, and, of course, as the label is transparent, he is able to see tolerably well where he is going. It will be noticed that the two lamps on the front are also miniature jugs in outline. The engine is a 4½ h.p. De Dion, and the De Dion transmission is also used. The jug and special carriagework were supplied by the Grosse Berliner Motor Wagen Gesellschaft.

* * *

La France Automobile, of 28th ult., comments very severely upon certain features of the late Glasgow trials. The option on Whistlefield is construed into an attempt to favour English as against French made cars, particularly as regards the De Dion and Bouton voiturette. Much also is made of the depot incident, which led to the disqualification of the Panhard car driven by Mr. Harvey Ducros, this being advanced as nothing more or less than an attempt to favour the English cars. Those who are well acquainted with the facts, of course, will smile at such an allegation, but both with regard to the regrettable Whistlefield option and the carage incident above-mentioned, we think the A.C. committee should cause a letter of protest to be addressed to our French contemporary.

The Houk Automobile Co., Ltd., has been formed with a capital of £10,000 to carry on in the United Kingdom or elsewhere the business of cycle, carriage, motor car, and general manufacturers.

* * *

A reader who has had a long trial of the E.I.C. plug says, in answer to our enquiry of last week, that the points of this plug are not always near enough. He has had one plug in use for about 1,700 miles, but the points have worked apart of late, and he has had to take it out. He found that the spark was a good one when driving with little gas, but it would not jump under the compression of full gas. In this way he had trouble when starting. The spark gap can easily be adjusted.

THE PACKARD SINGLE CYLINDER MOTOR WAGGON.

The Packard car.　Miss Grace Fuson, an expert driver, at the wheel.

Mr. Packard, of Ohio, feeling a desire to enter the ranks of practical automobile users too strong to be resisted, and taking a favourable view of the Benz single-cylinder driven system, went to Mr. Winton, of Cleveland, Ohio, for a waggon, and explained to him that while he regarded the Winton as a most admirable creation, there were yet some details in which he wished his prospective vehicle to embody certan more or less novel ideas of Mr. Packard's own. Mr. Winton, who is English born, replied with all the suave consideration of a true British manufacturer to the effect that the Winton waggon as it stood was the ripened and perfected product of many years of lofty thought, aided by mechanical skill of the highest grade, and could not be improved in any detail, and that if Mr. Packard wanted any of his own cats and dogs worked into a waggon, he had better build it himself, as he, Winton, would not stultify himself by any departure whatever from his own incontestably superior productions.

Mr. Packard thanked Mr. Winton cordially for his disinterested and far-seeing suggestions, and proceeded to construct a heavy waggon with a single-cylinder motor, which now, having been under construction little more than a year, and there having been produced for sale but few more than a hundred vehicles all told, has yet gained for itself a most enviable reputation, its users without exception being its staunch friends, many of them not hesitating to assert that the Packard is the very best single-cylinder driven vehicle which has yet appeared.

Mr. Packard writes me that he is making extensive detail improvements in his carriage, and is increasing his plant as fast as he can, and will soon be able to have waggons in stock, he hopes, although at present he is much behind his cash orders. The Packard factory is at Warren, Ohio, U.S.A., and the New York office, managed by the firm of Adams and McMurtry, is at 114, Fifth Avenue.

Since the circumstances in connection with the rapid rise of the Packard waggon into public favour give much interest to this new vehicle, I have prepared the following full description of its mechanical details. As I am aware that an account of the experiences of Samuel Rushmore, a well-known manufacturer of electric work and acetylene searchlights in Jersey City, N.J., in driving a Packard from New York to Buffalo, has been sent for publication in *The Autocar*, I feel sure that what I have to offer will be of interest to many readers.

At the outset, Mr. Packard fully understood and recognised the fact that the single-cylinder driven motor must have weight, or mass, far in excess of the demands of actual working strains, to take up the violent thrust of the widely-separated working strokes of the motor. Whitney, originator of the present type of Stanley steam waggon, represented by the Locomobile, Mobile, and, in fact, almost all Amercan steam waggons, made his first vehicle to weigh only 650 lbs.; he gradually increased his weights, leaving his motor unchanged, to about 1,000 or 1,100 lbs., and was thoroughly satisfied

Plan of Packard frame with body removed.

that this weight of about 1,000 lbs. for a two-passenger waggon was the best for American roads.

Stanley, quite to the contrary, assumed that every pound of non-paying load which could be spared should be spared, and the two-passenger waggons which the Stanley Brothers are now building at Newton, Mass., weigh only about 500 lbs. each empty. Both the Whitney and Stanley waggons had the same type of motor, a pair of small double-acting steam cylinders, and hence gave what may be called a constant torque on the drivingshaft and wheels. With this type of motor the only possible gain from mere added mass of the waggon is in making it "stay down on the road better," as Whitney phrased it. That is to say, weight makes the waggon bounce about less on a rough road than it would if it were lighter. On smooth roads, like those about Newton, where Stanley Brothers drive, weight added after the waggon is heavy enough to carry its full load is incontestably a blunder, because it costs fuel to move every pound of the waggon weight, and added weight of waggon frame means added load to be carried by the axles and tyres, which must be made larger and stronger and more costly, to meet the needless burdens imposed by needless weight.

With the single-cylinder fired motor, all this is changed. The waggon must run by momentum, not impulse, three-fourths of the time, and in the working one-fourth of the time the

motor must give out a comparatively enormous propelling impulse. Packard uses a cylinder 6in. in diameter, and the "kick" which it gives a waggon when it works cannot be absorbed by any weight of flywheel, which can be well used, but must go into the mass of the whole fabric, which must be heavy enough to absorb the violent shock at slow speeds to avoid giving great discomfort to the riders.

Packard's weight of 2,005 pounds for an empty two-passenger waggon having thirty-six circular inches of motor piston area, is not a pound too heavy for the comfort of the passengers.

The general appearance of the Packard waggon model C is well shown at the head of this article, with Miss Grace Fuson, of New York, as driver.

The general scheme of the Packard is to provide a very substantial tubular running gear, the two-reach members being connected to both front and rear axles by globe joints, as fully shown in detail engravings. This tubular frame takes the springs, and the springs carry an angle iron frame of ample strength, to which all of the running motor parts are secured, thus giving a reliable motor support. The body is carried above the motor frame, and can be removed by taking out four screws, and uncoupling a few minor connections, almost the entire mechanism being carried on the angle iron frame. The plan and oblique views of the Packard with the body removed show the general arrangement of the principal parts very clearly. Lever steering was first used, but is now wisely abandoned in favour of the wheel, tangent screw and worm gear, as the waggon is altogether too heavy to be easily handled by lever steering. Radius rods are jointed to the running gear and the tops of the springs both lengthwise and crosswise to resist stopping and starting strains.

The Packard Model C cylinder is 6in. by 6½in., the wire spoke wheels have 4in. pneumatic tyres, 34in. diameter, front and rear alike. These tyres are made by the Hartford, Diamond, Goodrich Co., weigh 34 lbs. each, and cost $36 each.

The wheel gauge is 56in. The wheelbase was at first 75in., but is now changed to 84in.

Oblique view of Packard frame with body removed.

The water jacket is of corrugated sheet copper. The expected compression maximum is 80 lbs., and the maximum motor speed is 850 revolutions per minute. The ignition is jump spark, with dry cell batteries, coil, and trembler, the spark time of occurrence and the spark time duration being governor controlled, as described later. The transmission gear is of the epicyclic spur gear order, figs. 10 and 11 (p. 659). This gear is changed by a substantial hand lever in front, so as to give two forward speeds and a reverse, and also to handle the regular brake, which is a steel band lined with brass blocks. An emergency brake, possibly old, but new to me, is as follows: The rear wheel rims are recurved to the inside, thus forming an internal groove, and to this groove a lever hung brake shoe with a curved face is fitted. This brake is operated by a treadle on the footboard, with wire cable transmission both ways, and will check the waggon so long as the wheels can turn, no matter whether the motor transmission gear is, or is not, operative. This is highly important. No waggon or bicycle should ever be used which is not provided with a brake of ample power in both directions always ready for use, no matter what else gives way. Going forward, this emergency treadle brake has to be held to its work. Going backward, the centres are so located that the brake is self-tightening, and hence forms a most efficient "sprag" to prevent a down hill backward runaway.

The starting crank is applied at the right side of the waggon. Of course, with a 6in. piston and 80 lbs. compression, a compression release is required when cranking for a start. This release takes the form of a cock tapped into the cylinder, and so located as to give only one and a half inches compression travel of piston, making easy starting possible with a hand crank only seven or eight inches long. The starting is very certain. The detail illustration showing the cushion flap lifted will give an idea of the arrangement of the compression release rocker and regulating devices.

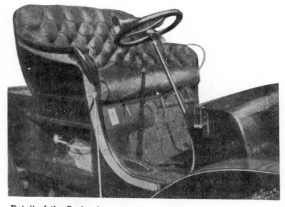

Detail of the Packard, seat cushion flap raised, showing the compression relief rocker, the carburetter and fuel regulation, the electric switch push buttons, the vertical gear controlling lever, and the emergency brake treadle. The photograph is from Mr. Rushmore's Packard waggon, which is fitted with one of Rushmore's powerful acetylene searchlights, the ray direction being adjusted by the small vertical rocker with a little handle at the top, fastened to the seat arm, as clearly shown in the engraving.

The foregoing will give the reader an understanding of the leading features of Packard's general ar-

rangement of driving and controlling elements. The great length of this article and the number of illustrations needed to give a fair description, the Packard and Hatcher U.S. patents forbid a fully detailed description.

The Mechanism.

The Packard automobile is built under the following U.S. patents, probably also patented in England, although of this I am not sure:

No. 667,792, February 12th, 1901. J. W. Packard, igniting device. This mechanism is designed to effect three distinct results—(1) to give the spark

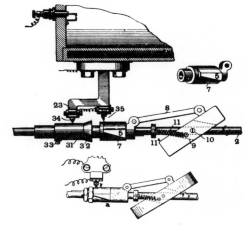

Fig 1.

a constant time duration regardless of the revolutions per minute of the motorshaft, (2) to make the spark occur earlier as the motor runs faster, and (3) to stop the production of the spark altogether when the motor reaches a predetermined speed. Enough of the drawings with this patent are given in figs. 1 and 2 to show the simple means by which the highly important ends sought are gained.

The horizontal shaft 2 is driven rapidly from the motorshaft, top toward observer, and carries three elements—first, to right a governor of the simplest form, consisting of a pierced block 9 pivoted to the shaft 2 by the screw 10, so as to swing on the shaft 2, by which this single governor element is pierced. This governor element is in practice made of a single rough grey iron casting, and is held when at rest top to extreme right by means of a spring collar 11a, to which one end of the spring 11 is hooked, the other end being hooked to the governing element 9, opposite side to a link eye integral with the governor element, from which eye a link 8 extends to the left, where the link is pivoted to a cam 7 splined to slide on the shaft 2. As the speed of shaft 2 increases, the governor element tends to assume a position at right angles to shaft 2, against the influence of the spring 11. The cam 7 carries one wedged shape cam 5, the leaving side of the cam being parallel to the axis of shaft 2, and the meeting side of toe 5 being inclined to said axis, so that as the cam is moved by the governor to the left the face of the cam becomes wider with reference to a fixed point.

Cam 7 has a hub extending to the left, on which a sleeve 31 is adjustably secured by the screw 33. The right end of sleeve 31 is formed in a cone larger than the sleeve. The cam 5 operates a V roller 35, and the sleeve cone 32 operates a V roller 34; lifting the roller 35 (see fig. 2) makes a contact between the terminals 27, 28, and establishes the spark, which continues as long as the roller is held up by the wedge-shaped cam toe face 5, so that the faster the motor runs, the larger the

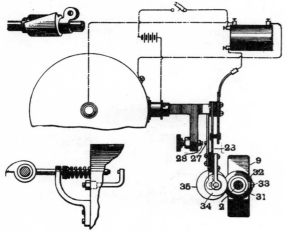

Fig. 2.

arc of cam revolution affecting the roller position, this resulting from a proper taper of the face of toe 5, giving equal times of spark duration for any speed of motorshaft revolution. When the cam and cylinder 31 are moved a sufficient distance to the left by the governor action, the cone 32 lifts the roller 34, and deprives the terminal 27 of its electric current, hence no change ignition takes place, and the motor speed cannot be more augmented.

In practice Packard omits the sleeve 31, roller 34, and related parts, using the simpler construction shown in the lower figure of fig. 1, and causing the stopping of the spark by pushing the cam toe 5 on the cam body 7 and a to the left so far that the spark roller drops off the cam toe, and thus prevents the making of a spark.

The correct reasoning as to essentials of waggon

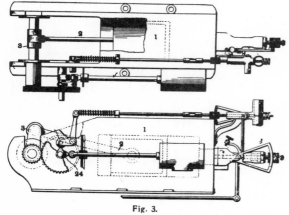

Fig. 3.

motor performance, and the extreme certainty, simplicity, and cheapness of the mechanical elements employed to effect these motor performance essentials reflect the highest credit on their originator, and this spark regulation alone, if Mr. Packard had

originated nothing else in waggon motors, would entitle his work to profound respect.

The spark is the chief faulty point in waggon motors as now made, and this equalisation of spark duration time and the provision of elements by which the maximum speed of the motor may be

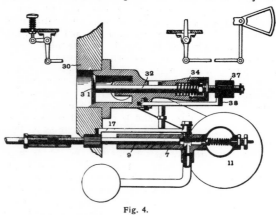

Fig. 4.

adjustably fixed are highly important steps towards certainty of motor performance.

Packard's U.S. patent 667,792 carries nine claims —the first two as follows :

(1.) An igniting device for hydrocarbon engines comprising, in combination, a sparking circuit, a circuit closer, a governor, and means, controlled by the governor, for causing the circuit closer to produce a spark of constant duration at different speeds of the engine, for the purpose set forth.

Fig. 5.

(2.) An igniting device for hydrocarbon engines, comprising, in combination, a sparking circuit, a circuit closer, a rotating shaft, a cam arranged to rotate with and slide on said shaft, said cam having an operative face constructed to control the circuit closer so as to produce a spark of constant duration as the speed of the engine varies, a governor driven by the engine, and connections between said governor and said cam whereby the cam is moved longitudinally of the shaft as the speed increases or decreases, for the purpose set forth.

U.S. patent 667,902, February 12th, 1901, to W.

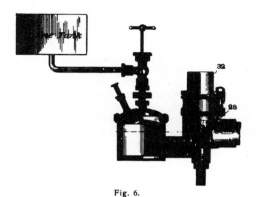

Fig. 6.

A. Hatcher, speed regulator for explosive motors, is as follows :

See figs. 3 and 4; 1 is the cylinder, 2 the rod, 3 the crank, and 24 the second motion shaft of the motor, from which the variable stroke plunger 9, working in the fuel pump barrel 7, is made to deliver the liquid fuel in variable quantities to the mixing chamber 11, the virtual length of the screw-threaded plunger 9 being changed by means of the pinion 37 and the hand-operated toothed segment 38 From the mixer 11 the air and fuel charge goes to the motor cylinder through the valve 31, fixed in the cylinder head 30, this admission valve

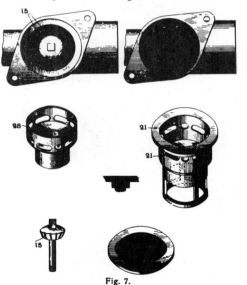

Fig. 7.

being operated by the piston suction against the influence of the spring 34, and the lift of the valve 31 being limited by the long pinion 37, threaded on the stem 32 of the valve 31, pinion 37 being operated by the hand-actuated toothed segment 38 so as to advance or retreat on the valve stem 32, and thus regulate the lift of the charge admission valve 31, and so vary the volume of the cylinder charge drawn from the mixing chamber 11 by the

piston suction. Connection is made between segments 17 and 37, so that their individual actions are made adjustably interdependent.

By these means Hatcher first measures an adjustably fixed bulk of liquid fuel into the mixing chamber, and next draws an adjustably fixed quantity of this mixture into the cylinder during the charging stroke. This mechanism necessitates an unknown residue in the mixing chamber, and hence is not ideal. It is, however, undoubtedly available for excellent average results, the result of fuel diminution or augmentation being merely spread over several strokes of the motor, instead of being clean cut for each individual motor charge.

The first three claims of this patent are as follows :

(1.) In a hydrocarbon engine for motor vehicles, the combination with a cylinder and mixing

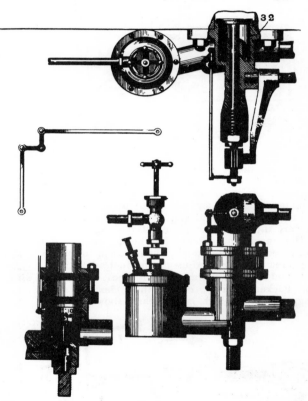

Fig. 8.

chamber, of a pump discharging into the mixing chamber and having a measuring chamber for the fluid, a valve for controlling the admission of mixture to the cylinder, a stop for limiting the movement of the valve, and means, controllable at will, for simultaneously varying the capacity of the pump measuring chamber, and the position of said stop relative to its valve to vary the speed and power of the engine.

(2.) In a hydrocarbon engine for motor vehicles, the combination with a cylinder and mixing chamber, of a pump discharging into the mixing chamber, a valve controlling the admission of mixture to the cylinder, a stop mounted on and movable longitudinally of the stem of said valve to regulate the extent of movement thereof, and

73

means, controllable at will, for simultaneously varying the volume of the charge of fluid delivered by the pump to the mixing chamber and moving said stop longitudinally of the valve stem, whereby the amount of fluid admitted to the mixing chamber is properly proportioned to the amount of mixture admitted to the cylinder.

(3.) In a hydrocarbon engine for motor vehicles, the combination with a cylinder and mixer, of a pump discharging into the mixer and having a longitudinally extensible piston, a valve controlling

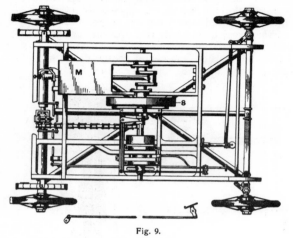

Fig. 9.

the admission of mixture to the cylinder, a stop connected with the valve for limiting its opening movement, and means, controllable at will, for simultaneously varying the length of the pump piston and adjusting said stop relatively to the valve, to vary the speed and power of the engine.

Here again the practice has been changed from the patented form, a wedge being used, instead of the screw shown for adjusting the fuel admission.

Patent 667,909, February 12th, 1901, to Hatcher and Packard jointly, covers their flexible motor waggon frame, which is so clearly shown in fig. 5

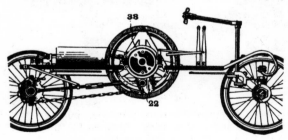

Fig. 10.

as to need no description. This patent carries five claims, of which the first is as follows:

1. In a motor vehicle frame the combination of the front and rear axles, two reach bars extending from the front axle to the rear axle, and connected to both axles by universal joints, and two diagonal braces each connected rigidly to an intermediate portion of a reach-bar at one end, and connected by a universal joint to an intermediate portion of the rear axle at its other end.

By this construction Hatcher and Packard secure a strong, substantial frame, which is a necessity for

American roads, and also that perfect flexibility, which is an imperative requisite where a waggon is to be used on uneven road surfaces.

The manner in which Hatcher and Packard attacked the carburetter ogre, which up to date devours all, both great and small, is fully shown in figs. 6, 7, and 8, illustrating the specifications of U.S. patent 667,910, February 12th, 1901, to Hatcher and Packard jointly. The specification says:

"The operation of the invention above described is as follows: The gasoline stands at the level of the line x, just at the base of the openings 15, and the air valve normally stands in its closed position, cutting off all communication with the air inlet pipe. At stated intervals suction is created in the pipe 32 in the usual manner, the effect of which is to draw into the mixing chamber a charge of gasoline, which is sprayed in through the openings 15, and to simultaneously raise the air valve and permit a charge of air to enter at the inner edge of the flange 28, the air and oil coming into intimate contact, and being carried up into the mixer together. When the engine is taking light charges of the mixture,

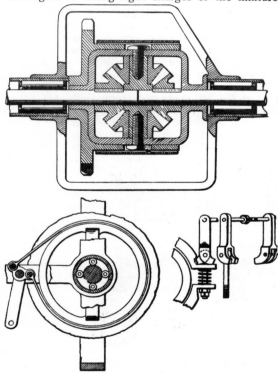

Fig. 11.

the air valve is raised but slightly, and the openings 21 are not uncovered. When, however, the draft upon the mixture is stronger, the air valve is raised sufficiently to uncover more or less of the openings 21, so that air may enter through said openings, as well as through the central opening of flange 28. The air valve falls back to its seat, and closes all the air inlets after each charge of mixture is drawn into the cylinder. We have found an apparatus constructed as above to regulate automatically the charges of air and hydrocarbon in a very satisfactory manner."

The word "satisfactory" is well qualified by the

word "very." Experts well know that every car-buretter must be manipulated by a wise driver to make it work under varying atmospheric conditions in a "very" satisfactory manner, and the readers of *The Autocar* are also well aware that I, personally, expect the carburetter in all its forms, moods, and tenses to wholly disappear in the final automobile; indeed, I have the very strongest reasons for believ-ing that the day is close at hand when it will be well known that the carburetter is a mistake.

The Hatcher-Packard carburetter carries five claims :

The general arrangement of the driving elements of the Packard waggon is covered by U.S. patent to Hatcher alone. This patent has five sheets of illus-trations, which are partly reproduced in figs. 9, 10, 11, and 12, which are so clear as to need no special text for experts in motor waggon construction. The specification says :

"The power shaft 7 is driven by a suitable motor M, preferably a hydrocarbon engine. Upon one end of the power shaft is a flywheel 8, and in line with the power shaft is a countershaft 9, the ends of said shafts being close together. Referring to fig. 12, 10 indicates a frame or spider, which is fast upon countershaft 9. The shaft and frame are supported, as shown, by the bearing 11. The spider 10 has a series of lugs 2, which are integral with and in the same circle with lugs 13 upon the flywheel 8. Through the lugs 2 and 13 passes a circular rod 14, surrounded by spiral springs 15, which springs keep the lugs 2 centrally located between lugs 13. The arrangement of lugs and springs forms a yielding connection between the motor and the driving wheels, which prevents strains in the machinery due to suddenly starting the motor or applying the brakes and also due to inequalities in the roadway. To pre-vent undue strain upon the springs 15, the flywheel is also provided with intermediate fixed lugs, against which the lugs 2 abut when there is an extreme strain upon the motor.

"Turning freely on the countershaft 9 is a part 17, which is provided with a power-transmitting gear 18, two internal gears 19 and 20, and a braking surface 21, all of which parts are either integral or securely fastened together. The driving gear 18 intermeshes with a gear 22, from which power is transmitted to the driving wheels through devices which will be herinafter described.

"A slow backward movement is imparted to the driving gear by means of a gear 23 (see figure 12), which is keyed upon the shaft, and intermediate gears 24, which mesh with the gears 23 and 20. The gears 24 are carried upon the studs 25 upon disc 26, which is free to revolve upon the shaft 9. Surround-ing the disc 26 are brake shoes 27, which may be applied to stop the rotation of said disc, as will be hereinafter described. When the disc 26 is stopped, power is positively transmitted from the gear 23 through the gears 24 and 20 to the gears 18 and 22, giving the vehicle a backward movement.

"Integral with the disc 26 is a flange 28, within which are shoes 29 of an expanding clutch. As shown, the clutch shoes 29 are expanded by means of screws 30, arms 31, links 32, sliding collar 33, and means for moving the collar, which will be re-ferred to hereinafter. When the clutch shoes 29 are rendered operative, the disc 26 and its pinions are carried around positively with the shaft 9, and

the pinions 24 lock the gear 23 to the internal gear 20. The driving gear 18 is thus rotated with the speed of the driving shaft 7, and the countershaft 9, giving the vehicle a high speed forward.

"A low speed forward is given to the vehicle by means of a gear 34, fixed on the shaft 9, and two pairs of intermediate gears 35, mounted on studs 36, which are carried by a disc 37 loose upon the shaft 9. The disc 37 may be held stationary by brake shoes 38, and when so held the integral gear 19 and the driving gear 18 will be slowly rotated forward, thus cutting down the speed and increasing pull upon the driving wheels for the purpose of climbing hills and overcoming other resistances."

This patent carries twelve specific claims, which need no quotation.

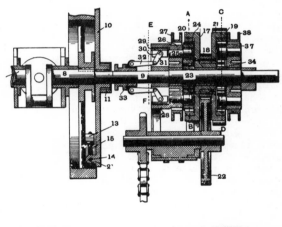

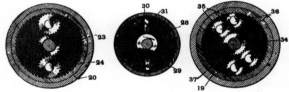

Section on A B of Fig. 12. Section on E F of Fig. 12. Section on C D of Fig. 12.

The introduction of the heavy coiled springs be-tween the motorshafts and the transmission elements is an excellent feature. Such springs have long been used in heavy machinery drives between the motorshaft and the first driven element, and have always been found highly conducive to smooth run-ning and long life of the parts. So far as I know, the present is the first example of such use of inter-posed springs in a motor waggon in the States, though no novelty in Great Britain.

HUGH DOLNAR.

New York, U.S.A., October 14th.

———— ◆ ————

French opinion and feeling are gradually swinging once more towards the automobilist. The authori-ties are raising the seven miles per hour ordinance for the roads through the Bois de Boulogne, save at such times as the park is crowded. On all other occasions automobiles may be driven at a reason-able pace so long as same does not approach a dangerous speed.

IS AN AUTOCAR SAFE IN A THUNDERSTORM?

By Sidney F. Walker, M.I.E.E., M.I.M.E., etc.

In the writer's opinion the answer to this question is that the autocar is safe in the same sense that a railway train is safe to the ordinary traveller. We know that out of the millions of men and women travelling by train day by day, for long and short distances, only a very small number of accidents occur. In fact, railway men claim that a train is one of the safest places. And we know also that if a signalman at an important junction loses his head but for a single instant hundreds of lives may be sacrificed in consequence. In the same way the writer suggests the chances of an autocar being struck by lightning are very small, yet he would not like to say that such a vehicle cannot be struck. A consideration of the conditions involved will make this clear, though it must be distinctly understood that, while the advance of electrical knowledge generally has given electrical engineers a better insight into the ways of discharges of lightning than they have ever possessed, there is no branch of the subject upon which less is known. And the reason is that while the pressures, the voltages that are being used by electrical engineers in their various work, are getting higher and higher, and with each advance in the pressure a clearer and clearer knowledge of the phenomena of lightning, and of all high tension phenomena, is being obtained, no experimenter has yet approached anywhere near the pressures that exist in the case of thunderstorms. The highest pressures that have been used so far in experimental or unpractical work are those used by Signor Tesla in his classical experiments of ten years ago and those used with Röntgen ray apparatus. Neither of these exceeded 100,000 volts, while the pressures which must exist between a highly charged thundercloud, and the body into which it discharges, may be many millions of volts; and the full significance of this fact will be appreciated when it is remembered that the mischief a lightning or other high tension electrical discharge is capable of doing varies as the square of the pressure existing between the charged body and that to which it discharges.

The question is further complicated by the fact that the protection of any building or other object from a lightning discharge is largely a geological one, and it depends very largely indeed on the components of which the earth's crust is made up at the point of discharge. Again, it must be remembered that in all cases of very high and very low figures, whether in connection with temperature, with electrical tension, with chemical, or with any other physical action, as the higher and the lower figures are reached, different phenomena peculiar to the high and low figures develop. And, once again, it must also be remembered that electricity when confined, whether passing along a conductor or when in what is known as the static condition, in which it is compartively quiescent on a conductor, has two methods of relieving the tension, viz., by leakage through the confining envelope, and by sparking through—that is to say, by violent rupture—and both of these methods are going on during the whole time that the phenomena we know as lightning are in operation or preparing.

What a Thundercloud is.

And now as to the actual *modus operandi*. A thundercloud is a body of water vapour which has acquired a charge of electricity. How it has acquired it does not matter, but it is more than probable that it is acquired partly in the process of formation of the vapour, and partly by friction between the cloud and the surrounding atmosphere. The water vapour, of which the cloud consists, is an aggregation of particles of water vapour which have come closer together than the vapour in the surrounding atmosphere, and much closer together than the vapour contained in the atmosphere when there are no clouds about. The highly charged cloud will do what all bodies charged with energy do, whatever its form, and especially where the energy exists at high pressure, namely, try to share its load with other bodies. In part it will succeed by actual leakage to the vapour held in the surrounding atmosphere, and to the gases of the atmosphere itself, and if the tension attained is not very high, as atmospheric tensions go, or time is given, the whole charge will be dissipated in this manner. Probably there is an enormous amount of electrical action going on in the atmosphere of which we know nothing, because the tensions, the pressures, never reach the point at which they become dangerous. Even when the very high tensions are reached, the silent discharge by leakage in various forms is still going on, and at a greater rate than with lower tensions; but when a thunderstorm occurs, with the attendant lightning discharges, it is either because the pressure increases faster than the leakage can relieve it, or because the other conditions, the movements of the clouds and of the earth itself, lead to conditions favourable to violent discharge. And violent discharge will take place whenever there exists sufficient pressure between any portion of the charged cloud and some object on the other side of its enclosing envelope, to enable it to break through. The same thing occurs frequently with cables that are used for distributing current for electric light and power in towns. There is a certain pressure which will break through the insulating envelope of the cable, and when this pressure exists a spark passes, doing a considerable amount of damage. As the cable gets older, and as the material of which its insulating envelope is composed deteriorates, this sparking pressure decreases. Also the conditions of the electrical supply service vary, so that under certain conditions a very much higher pressure may exist between the inside and the outside of a cable than in others, and it has often occurred that a pressure has been produced much greater than the engineers had provided for, and then the cable breaks down. With a thundercloud, the insulating envelope is the surrounding atmosphere, and the other side of the cable, the other side of the circuit, is the earth's crust beneath. If, and whenever, a sufficient pressure exists between any part of the cloud and any part of the earth's crust, a discharge will take place between the two, with usually attendant damage.

A Geological Problem.

And now comes in the geological portion of the problem. The discharge will only take place between the cloud and a conducting mass upon or in the earth's crust of such a capacity that it can receive a portion of the charge the cloud wants to get rid of. Metals in the earth's crust such as iron pipes, metals on the surface such as railway metals, engines and their accessories, minerals and water in the earth's crust, such as seams of coal, veins of metal ores, water-bearing strata or ground overlying strata which does not allow the water which falls in the form of rain to get away—all form excellent conductors to which the charged cloud will deliver a portion of its charge if it can do so: that is to say, if there is sufficient pressure between the cloud and any point on the earth's surface by or through which the charge can get to the conductor it is to distribute itself over. The cloud would rarely discharge to a mass of very hard rock, for instance; yet it might do so if the rock was in its path to a conductor that would receive a large portion of its charge, and if sufficient pressure existed between the cloud and the conductor in the earth to enable it to force its way through the rock. On the other hand, the discharge often passes by paths which are apparently very unlikely ones, such as through the head and body of a cow or a sheep standing in the middle of a field, the reason being that beneath the animal that was struck was a conductor that would receive the charge, and that the necessary pressure existed between the cloud and the hidden conductor to bring the animal into account. Again, any object which by its position or its nature lessens the sparking distance between the two conductors, the cloud and the conductor on the earth's surface, becomes itself in danger, because it will form part of the path of discharge, and will receive a current or a series of currents, and be exposed to a pressure that it is unable to stand. This again is equivalent to the case where a very minute piece of metal is embedded in the insulating envelope of a cable. The presence of this minute piece of metal would very considerably reduce the sparking distance between the inner and outer conductor, and when the discharge took place it would probably pass by way of the piece of metal, which would be completely destroyed. Such an object, with reference to a discharge from a thundercloud, is a tree, especially one in which the roots spread out to a considerable distance from the trunk, and in which the branches are also well leaved and spread out. If the soil below the tree is one that naturally bears water, or if it is one that may bear water temporarily owing to the presence below it of a strata which will not allow the water to pass, but which extends for a good distance round, the tree assists the discharge by reducing the sparking distance, and is often, though not always, wrecked itself, owing to its having to accommodate the rush of a large quantity of energy through it. A tall chimney, with its soot lining, leading to boilers, engines, pipes, etc., is another case in which the sparking distance is reduced by its presence.

Another Phenomenon.

And then we come to another phenomenon in connection with the passage of high tension discharges of electricity. Everyone will be familiar with the experiment that is always shown in elementary electricity classes, viz., that in which a gold leaf electroscope or a pith ball electroscope is exposed to the action of a charged body, and the gold leaves or the pith balls are seen to diverge, owing to the presence of the charged body having driven the electricity of the same name as itself away from itself down into the leaves or the pith balls.

And exactly the same thing happens when a charged cloud passes over the earth's surface, the electricity of the same name as that of the charge upon the cloud being driven away into the earth, if it can get there. The ability to drive the charge into the earth depends, with a given pressure in the cloud, approximately upon the conducting power of the object exposed to the inductive action, as it is called, of the charged cloud. If the objects below the cloud are all bad conductors, say very hard rocks which harbour very little water and no minerals, very little induction can take place. If, on the other hand, the object is a conductor, such as the lining of a chimney, and it is leading to objects which are in good conductive connection with the objects which make up the conductive power of the earth's crust, then induction takes place freely, and the inductive action very largely increases the pressure available for sparking across the intervening envelope. Hence the objects that are likely to be struck are those which themselves, being conductors, lower the sparking distance, and being also in conductive connection with a large mass of conductive matter in the earth's crust open the way for inductive action, and so increase the pressure available for sparking.

How to Keep an Autocar Safe.

How does the autocar come in here? It falls into the first category, since it contains a comparatively large mass of metal, but by itself it could not take, and would not invite, the discharge of a cloud such as would be dangerous. It would invite such a discharge, and would probably be wrecked by the discharge, if it formed part of the discharge path to a conducting mass below. Such a conducting mass would be the wet ground of a large level field, under which a bed of clay existed, so that the wet could not get away. A path like this might also be formed in certain special cases on a wet road, but they would be rare. For safety, then, in a thunderstorm the autocar should keep right out in the open and on the hardest bit of road that can be found in the neighbourhood. The driver can hardly know the geology of the neighbourhood, but if he happens to know anything of it he would be wise to get off any ground overlying clay, if the ground is undrained so that it can hold the damp. Probably the middle of a good hard road, well kept with hard stones, will be best, and it is probable that there will be few automobiles struck under those conditions. The rubber tyres will probably make very little difference to the discharge, as the thickness, which represents the distance, by the way, the lightning flash has to come, is very small, and in addition they will be very wet, and the skin of water will form a very fair conductor to the high tension current. An autocar or a bicycle under a tree forms part of the path to the conductor on or in the earth's crust, and accommodates a share of the discharge, with usually disastrous results. It assists to invite the discharge, and has to take more than it can accommodate without damage. It should be remembered that any electrical discharge, even a low tension electrical current, has mechanical properties, which consist in driving the substance of the matter it is passing through in the way it is going itself, and that this property is very much accentuated in the very high tensions met with in lightning discharges. This will account for the great damage done by lightning.

THE SMALL MERCEDES CAR.

The first of these vehicles to appear in this country has been imported by the Motor Traction Co., of 77, Walnut Tree Walk, Kennington, S.E. The 6 h.p. engine is a two-cylinder motor with crankshaft set transversely, water-cooled with water-jackets over combustion chambers, around valve chambers, and throughout stroke of pistons. The well-known Cannstatt form of multi-tubular water-cooler is in front of motor bonnet, with induced draught caused through tubes by the rotation of a fan immediately in rear of the tank, driven by bevel-gearing off the half-time shaft. The crank chamber and four change speed gear box are one, and the drive is conveyed from the countershaft by two chains to an intermediate shaft set above the rear axle. This intermediate shaft is furnished with a pinion at either end, and these pinions meshing each with an internally-toothed spur wheel on road axle the drive is thereby conveyed to the road wheels. The engine is fitted with centrifugal governor acting on the induction, and capable of control from the footboard. Handle-bar steering with upright pillar is fitted, and the gears are struck by a lever set on the steering column below the bar. The manner in which the gear lever is moved to obtain the desired speed is novel, simple, and certain, but not possible of clear description without a diagram. A very heavy fly-wheel, as may be seen from the engine illustration,

is used. The carburetter is conveniently placed beneath footboard, and it is rendered possible to agitate the float without trouble. The petrol tank, which is of considerable capacity, is carried on the front of the dashboard within the motor bonnet. The car shown us at the Motor Traction Co.'s works was finished in and upholstered white, with an ample hood of the same colour. The wheels are of the artillery type, and are shod with large rectangular-section solid rubber tyres, which afford most comfortable and easy running. The engine, which is nominally of 6 h.p., is stated to be capable of working up to 8 h.p.

We are asked to mention that Mr. F. Russell Skinner's address is 9, Weatherby Terrace, South Kensington, as he is continually receiving communications after some delay, owing to their being sent to the wrong address.

* * *

The first chapter of Mr. H. G. Wells's recently published "Anticipations" discusses the probable development of locomotion — the railway train giving place for passengers to autocars, which, of course, are to be swiftly driven over the "Eadhamite" roads evolved by the author-prophet in an earlier work.

THE 7 H.P. BENZ CAR.

This vehicle, the latest 7 h.p. two-cylinder Benz, will be remembered by participants in the Southsea run, when it was driven by Mr. A. Cornell, cf Tonbridge. It ran through exceedingly well, and its turn of speed was somewhat a revelation to a good many. The car was driven out from Cosham to Exeter with only one stop to tighten key in sprocket pinion. The cylinders are placed tandem fashion facing each other, and this construction, with the careful balancing of the engine, gives very smooth running. An enclosed aluminium crank chamber is provided, and the lubrication is automatic. The first drive from the engineshaft is by a wide belt to the countershaft in the change speed and reverse gear box, the gearshaft driving by chains to rings on driving wheels. The gear gives three speeds forward and a reverse. There are three driving pedals. One for the reverse;. the second one, when half way down, releases the belt and disconnects the car from the engine, whilst full pressure brings down the band brakes on driving wheels. The third pedal applies the countershaft brake, and is very handy in traffic for pulling up quickly. In addition to the three positive speeds afforded by the gearing, suitable variation can be obtained by the gas throttle or quantity lever, which is conveniently placed to the left-hand on the steering column. We have not tried this carriage ourselves, but Mr. Cornell tells

us that the smoothness of running is very marked. This he attributes to the good balancing of the engine and the belt drive. The steering is of the broken axle or Ackerman type, the water circulation is maintained by pump, and radiators of good area are fitted. The ignition is, of course, electric, and the coil with its vibrator is nested near the ignition plug, while the accumulators are carried under the front seat. There is storage room for luggage under the front seat, and in the hood shown in the illustration there is a detachable glass front with leather extension to meet the hood, so that the car is equipped for driving in the worst of weather. We believe it is only a question of time before all cars except those intended for "butterfly" work will be fitted with some such form of protection. We understand that since the run to Exeter the car has been driven nearly three hundred miles over the hilly Devonshire roads with the greatest satisfaction.

A South London firm which is devoting much attention to the repair of motor cars of all kinds is the Robin Cycle and Motor Works, of The Chase, Wandsworth Road, S.W. The premises have lately been considerably extended, so that there is now ample room, in addition to repairing, for the storage and cleaning of a number of cars.

EDITORIAL JOTTINGS.

Our Programme. THE CAR this week makes its curtsey to the public. In this age of progress, when the world is continually being startled by new inventions, there is nothing so striking as the advances made by mechanical locomotion in every form. When we consider M. Serpollet's "Easter Egg," with its recorded speed of over seventy-six miles an hour, and the speeds, hardly less great, attained by many petrol cars, as evidence of what can be done by road vehicles, or reflect that a train on the Northern Railway of France habitually averages over sixty miles an hour, surely we have here a subject of interest not only to the enthusiast but to the general public. The aim of THE CAR will be to give the latest and most accurate information on subjects connected with locomotion whether by land, sea, or air, and present it in a form easily understood by the non-mechanical mind.

Is there Room? Of course the inevitable question arises— Is there room for it? I think that the answer should be "Yes." From the very beginning there has been no idea that THE CAR should run in competition with any existing paper. Many of the present automobile papers are excellent, and have had a well-deserved success, but the time has come when there seems to be room for a sixpenny paper in which photographic skill and excellence in reproduction, coupled with interesting matter, can be presented to the reader. Naturally there must always be different classes in the automobilist public, just as there are in any other section of the community. I have never heard that *Country Life* has interfered with the *Field* or the *Sportsman*. Neither is there any reason why anything but the most friendly rivalry should exist between ourselves and the rest of the automobile press. We all press on towards the same goal.

NECK AND NECK—AN EXCITING RACE AT BEXHILL
(*A full account of this important meet will be found on pages 34, 35 and 36.*)

Cars and Country Houses. One of the features of England which strikes the foreigner most forcibly is the number and beauty of our country houses and the home life surrounding them. Just as these have been admirably illustrated as regards their gardens, so we shall endeavour to put before our readers, in text and pictorial form, descriptions of our great roads and the many beautiful houses which lie either close to or a short distance from the King's highway. To be worthy of our subjects we intend that all the resources of the papermaker, the printer, and the photographer shall be freely used. So far as THE CAR is concerned, no expense or trouble will be spared to give the reader the best that can be procured.

Advice as to Cars. Nothing puzzles the would-be buyer of a motor-car so much as the contradictory advice given to him as to which car is most suitable for his purpose. So far as lies in our power the staff of THE CAR will assist readers in their selection of automobiles and we can assure everyone

concerned that the advice will be wholly disinterested. THE CAR also aims at becoming a weekly *édition de luxe* for the motorist, and hopes to find a place on the table not only of every automobilist, but in every country home.

A Novel Form of Insurance. Fatal motor accidents are happily very rare, but from time to time lesser disasters may occur, even to the most experienced motorist, from some fault possibly not his own. It will be seen on reference to page 2 that THE CAR, by special arrangement with the Law Accident Corporation, provides a much-wanted form of insurance for the automobilist. Not only will £2 5s. secure for the subscriber a copy of this paper for a year, post free, but this sum insures the subscriber for the sum of £1,000 in the case of death arising from accident, and, what is personally more valuable, £6 a week will be paid for ten weeks during total disablement. No more need be said, for I am sure that this is a scheme which will recommend itself.

A Great Chance for our Seaside Towns. The suitability of Bexhill, coupled with the enterprise of Lord De la Warr, ought to be an example and a warning to other seaside resorts. There are many towns round our coasts where horse-racing is objected to by the locality for various reasons, but not even the Nonconformist conscience can object to motor-car competitions. I would suggest to the mayors and corporations who wish to keep the attractions of their towns well to the fore not to forget that automobilists are now greatly on the increase, and that large crowds, and consequent gain to hotels and tradesmen, will result from motor racing. In France it is estimated that the race over the Paris-Bordeaux course is viewed by at least 250,000 people—about five times as many as could obtain a glimpse of the Derby. But where Bexhill has led the way others may follow. All that is necessary is to obtain a straight or nearly straight course, the longer the better, or if possible a circular course. If the local municipal acts allow of it the municipal authorities should exercise their power and close the road during a portion of the day. Some of our corporations possess the authority to do this. I am quite positive that this would prove a great source of benefit and bring much local prosperity, besides being a new attraction to the people who visit these seaside resorts, the life at which is sometimes the very essence of boredom. I think that I may claim to have been the originator of the idea at Bexhill with Lord De la Warr, for I spoke to him about it at Monte Carlo in February this year, and, as I expected, he at once grasped the importance of the scheme to the automobile world and the resultant benefit to Bexhill. The work was only taken in hand at Easter, and here we are in May with Bexhill firmly established as the only racing course in England to-day on which motors can legally show what speed they are capable of. THE CAR congratulates Lord

THE BEXHILL RACES.

AS a vivid presentment of the power of the modern motor vehicle, the Whit Monday meeting at Bexhill may fairly be accounted historic. To ardent automobilists it fell far short of expectations, because of a variety of mostly unavoidable conditions, but to the crowds, numbering tens of thousands, who lined the track

winner, Mr. H. L. Belcher's 2 h.p. Humber, viz., 63 4-5 sec., was in the circumstances very creditable. The 2 h.p. Werner (E. H. Arnott) was second. The race for motor tricycles did not come off owing to the disqualification of the only entrant for overweight.

In the class for "light voiturettes" the weight limit was

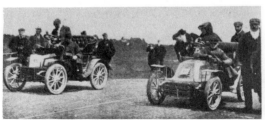

8 h.p. New Orleans   12 h.p. Gladiator

TOURIST VOITURETTES

Sir James Pender's 20 h.p. Darracq   Captain Lloyd's 20 h.p. Darracq

LIGHT RACING CARS

from end to end, the performances of the fastest vehicles must have been a veritable revelation. Nine-tenths of them had probably never seen a motor-car travelling more than twenty-5 miles an hour, yet double this pace was attained by ³ than one of the competitors, to the obvious delight of the spectators. It was unfortunate, indeed, that matters were not even livelier throughout, but as a matter of fact a strong wind swept along the course in the very teeth of the competitors, the ground was soddened with the rain of several days, while, as events showed, the take-off from Galley Hill to the entrance of the course was far too short to enable the cars to attain a really flying start, and several of the big racers never got on to their fourth speed at all.

The competitors were divided into two main sections, under the heads of "Tourist" and "Speed" respectively, with numerous subdivisions of class and weight. Races in the "Tourist" section were first completed, the way being led by motor-bicycles weighing not more than 1 cwt. The little vehicles were materially handicapped by the atmospheric conditions, but the time of the

A RACE IN A SQUALL—ONE OF MANY!

10 cwt. for cars with four seats, 9 cwt. for cars with three, and 8 cwt. with two. An easy victory was scored by Mr. F. Lewin's 5 h.p. (Baby) Peugeot, driven by Mr. C. Friswell, which won in 1 min. 30 3-5 sec., the second car home being the 6 h.p. M.M.C. of Mr. G. D. Barnes.

Weight limits of 15 cwt., 13½ cwt., and 12 cwt., according to seats, were imposed in the "voiturette" class, some curious juxtapositions being the result, as the figures permitted a four-cylinder New Orleans to compete against a two-cylinder car of the same make, a four-cylinder Panhard against a two-cylinder Panhard, a 16 h.p. Darracq against an 8 h.p. Renault, and so on. It may be said at once, however, that in this and in other races the French classification was taken as a model, and though the wisdom of this course has been questioned, the hard-working races committee could at least quote precedent in its own justification. The race was won in 1 min. 14 sec. by Mr. Herbert Smith's 8 h.p. Clement, driven by Mr. D. M. Weigel, Mr. Ernest de Wilton's 8 h.p. De Dion being second.

The "light car" class had a maximum limit of 18 cwt.,

9 h.p. Novelty   10 h.p. Georges Richard

RACING VOITURETTES

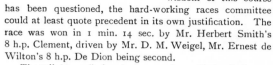

Gardner-Serpollet   Locomobile

STEAM V. STEAM

and provided no less than twenty-one entries, as well as some of the most interesting races of the day, several of the competitors being fairly equally matched, whereas in most of the competitions there was an absence of the " neck to neck " finish so dear to the heart of the spectator. Mr. Clarence Gregson's 12 h.p. Gladiator proved the ultimate winner in 1 min. 8 3-5 sec., Mr. A. C. Harmsworth's 15 h.p. New Orleans, driven by Mr. W. H. Astell, gaining second place.

Next came Class B, for cars of more than 18 cwt. and less than 25 cwt., the winner of which proved to be Mr.

Mr. A. C. Harmsworth's 15 h.p. New Orleans   Mr. C. Gregson's 12 h.p. Gladiator
LIGHT TOURIST CARS

Mark Mayhew on his 20 h.p. Panhard in 1 min. 2 4-5 sec., Mr. A. G. Schiff's 12 h.p. Panhard being second. The winner's time afforded evidence of the unfavourable nature of the course, for a 20 h.p. Panhard, as most people know, is capable of a much higher speed. The same remark will apply to the performance of Mr. W. G. H. Bramson's 50 h.p. Napier, driven by Mr. Cecil Edge, which could only do 56 2-5 sec. in the race for cars of over 25 cwt.; Mr. Edwin Midgley's 16 h.p. Napier was second. The winner took the Cordingley Cup, and also the Pape Cup for the fastest car in the tourist section without reference to class.

Hon. C. S. Rolls's 40 h.p. Mors   Mr. C. Jarrott's 40 h.p. Panhard
TWO NEW TYPE RACERS

The race for tourist steam vehicles was won by Mr. J. P. Petty's 6 h.p. Gardner-Serpollet in 48 1-5 sec., Mr. J. W. H. Dew's 10 h.p. Gardner-Serpollet being second. The tourist section was concluded with a race for electric vehicles, which was won by Mr. J. F. Ochs on a City and Suburban car in 1 min. 54 3-5 sec., Mr. T. G. Chambers on a British Electromobile car being second.

The tourist races had been enlivened, it may be added, by interludes on the part of M. Serpollet and Baron Henri de Rothschild, who were allowed to make trial trips with their respective racing cars before actually competing. The

whizzing flight of M. Serpollet's car startled the crowd considerably and was the first intimation of the livelier performances that were to be expected from the races in the speed section. M. Serpollet, by the way, was heartily cheered as he drove back to the Sackville Hotel after completing his first trial course.

A race for electric vehicles opened the speed section, and was won by Mr. E. W. Hart's 15 h.p. British Electromobile car in 1 min. 40 1-5 sec., Mr. R. W. Wallace, K.C., on a Krieger car being second. The winner received the Edmunds Cup. Then we reverted to motor bicycles, the race for the *Motor Cycling* Cup being won by the 2¾ h.p. Excelsior in 1 min. 1 3-5 sec., the 2¾ h.p. Shaw being second. The best time, however, was made by a 4½ h.p. Soncin, ridden by A. A. Chase, but the machine was disqualified owing to its not being fitted with a proper silencer; its progress along the course suggested the rapid firing of a Gatling gun. The race for motor tricycles and "quads" was won by Mr. Ralph Jackson on an 8 h.p. Eagle tandem. Then came the race for the De la Warr Cup, for racing voiturettes, the winner proving to be Mr. J. S. Overton's 10 h.p. Richard, the 9 h.p. Novelty car, driven by Mr. T. B. Browne, being second. The way in which latter car had been "skeletonised" to come within the weight limit of 7 cwt. 3½ qr. created no small degree of amusement.

The race for the *County Gentleman* Cup for light racing cars under 650 kilogrammes (12 cwt. 3 qr. 5 lb.) provided the

14 h.p. Déchamps   15 h.p. Mors
TWO CARS IN CLASS C (TOURIST)

fastest running of the day so far as petrol-driven cars were concerned. The entries included three cars of the new 20 h.p. Darracq type, and they proved to be veritable fliers, the winning car, driven by Baras for Captain Lloyd, covering the course in 43 sec., which is equivalent

BARON H. DE ROTHSCHILD'S 40 H.P. MERCÉDÈS

M. SERPOLLET'S NEW CAR ON FIRE

M. SERPOLLET AND MR. MONTAGU

to a speed of fifty-two miles an hour. Another well-known French racing man, Gabriel, drove Sir James Pender's Darracq to second place. In the race for vehicles weighing less than 800 kilogrammes for the Holder prize, Mr. S. F. Edge's 30 h.p. Gladiator had a walk-over, but the prize was not awarded owing to the absence of other competitors.

The next race was the *pièce de résistance* of the meeting, viz., the one for racers under 1,000 kilogrammes (19 cwt. 2 qr. 20 lb.) for THE CAR Cup, subject to the kilomètre being covered in not more than 40 sec. As 1,000 kilogrammes is now the maximum limit for racing vehicles under continental rules it followed that the entries for this race included the latest types of big racers.

THE NEW 30 H.P. WOLSELEY RACER

They comprised Mr. Harmsworth's 40 h.p. Mercédès, Baron de Rothschild's 40 h.p. Mercédès, Mr. C. Jarrott's 40 h.p. Panhard, Mr. H. Austin's 30 h.p. Wolseley, and Mr. Rolls's 40 h.p. Mors, all of which ran; but two of the most famous French drivers, MM. Réné de Knyff and

Girardot, who had also entered, did not put in an appearance. The winner proved to be Mr. Jarrott on a 40 h.p. Panhard, with Mr. Rolls second; Mr. Harmsworth's Mercédès, driven by Mr. Muir, was third, the new Wolseley was fourth, and the other Mercédès fifth. The winner's time was 44 3-5 sec., and therefore outside the limit, but the proprietors of THE CAR decided to award the cup to Mr. Jarrott notwithstanding. Only two competitors appeared in the class for vehicles over 1,000 kilogrammes for the *Daily Express* Cup, viz., Mr. Rolls's Paris-Berlin Mors and Mr. Edge's 50 h.p. Napier. Mr. Rolls won in 45 4-5 sec. The race for the Paris-Singer Cup for racing steam cars was won by M. Serpollet in 41 1-5 sec. on the "Easter Egg," his new car having been temporarily disabled through a flare-up. Mr. Edge gained the House of Commons Cup for appearance with a 16 h.p. Napier, Mr. W. J. Peall receiving the Bexhill Cup with his 12 h.p. Daimler, and the third prize fell to Mr. Harmsworth's New Orleans.

THE WIND-CUTTER ON MR. CLAY'S LOCOMOBILE

MR. MUIR ON MR. HARMSWORTH'S MERCÉDÈS

PARLIAMENT AND THE MOTOR.

TWO interesting motor-car debates took place in the House last week. The first arose on the vote for the Local Government Board. Mr. Chaplin made a bold yet very tactful speech pleading for more liberty for the motor-car, and pointing out the absurdity of the present system and the fact that the vast majority of motorists are willing to be registered if only they can be freed from the present ridiculous speed limit and the police persecution involved.

After Mr. Chaplin's speech the debate would have become interesting on the legal side of automobilism had it not been for Mr. Bayley, member for the Chesterfield Division of Derbyshire, at one time director of the Daimler Motor Company. We all thought that he was going to give us some interesting statements of his views on " motor-phobia," but not so. Mr. Bayley commenced a somewhat violent attack on the President of the Local Government Board by a question as to why lymph had been taken from a monkey instead of a calf on some particular occasion, and discoursed for some time on the relative merits of these two interesting animals, only to be floored by Mr. Muntz from the Government benches, who asked " why a monkey should be inferior to a calf," and the honourable member's concluding remarks were naturally somewhat drowned in laughter.

Mr. Long, when replying to the observations of Mr. Chaplin on motor-cars, took a fair and sensible line. He pointed out that he would be glad to find some way by which the present absurd regulations might be altered, and that if the House would support him and motorists consent to some further means of identification there might be an alteration made in the law. To this the House at once obviously assented. On some previous occasions when motor-car questions have been raised some members have seemed to a casual observer to be rather anti-motorist in feeling, but this time the sentiment was all the other way, and from all parts of the House there came signs of approval of anything which would make the present law more reasonable.

On behalf of automobilists generally I was able to say a few words before the close of the debate, pointing out that as a class they wish for nothing unreasonable, but only to be put on the same basis as other users of the road ; that is, not to be fined for dangerous driving when there is nothing dangerous about it, and not made victims of police per-secution by traps purposely made, and convicted by the evidence of policemen who are intentionally sent out to secure a " bag." I also stated that numbering or naming would be consented to if we were put on a fair legislative basis. Altogether the outlook from a House of Commons point of view has certainly improved, and I hope to be able to chronicle in next week's issue the definite steps which some of us have taken to meet Mr. Long's views and fall in with what seems to be the general feeling of the House.

Another interesting debate on the motor-car question arose on Friday on the Home Office vote. Mr. Norman opened the debate by referring to the case of Mr. Ashton-Jonson and Mr. Arthur Blomfield, who were fined £5 at Guildford police-court for driving at excessive speed. The constable had measured the distance with an ordinary bicycle wheel, and taken the time with the second hand of an ordinary watch. The hon. gentleman contended that it was a case of gross injustice, and the House generally seemed to agree with him. Mr. Norman then went on to state that the chairman of the bench had openly charac-terised motors as " noisy, evil-smelling, dangerous abomina-tions, which went madly about the country at a break-neck speed," and added that it was " the duty of magistrates to deal with offenders in an exemplary manner." At the worst, Mr. Norman contended, it was merely a technical breach of the law which had not been fully proved, and the Home Secretary was asked to reduce the fine and give some expression of opinion.

Mr. " Tommy " Bowles then endeavoured to turn the complaint into ridicule, and the House roared heartily when he declared that the ordinary watch used by a policeman was capable of timing a car to the twentieth part of a second. When several hon. gentlemen demurred to this Mr. Bowles said, " Well, a tenth of a second, I will give way a tenth."

The Home Secretary then rose to answer and, of course, carefully avoided dealing with the matter on its merits, as is the custom of a Government official. He admitted that the case was one in which there was serious conflict of evidence, but he could not interfere with the freedom of the local bench and intimated that he had practically no power in the matter.

Mr. Scott Montagu then complained of the gross prejudice which existed against automobilists in many parts of England and the excessive fines which were imposed for merely technical breaches of the law. Mr. Ashton-Jonson's case was only one of many, and because one or two motors were driven furiously the magistrates were apt to consider the whole class guilty. He was a magistrate as well as a motorist. There was so much prejudice that it was almost impossible to obtain justice.

Mr. Tomkinson, essentially a stern, unbending Tory and also a magistrate himself, thought it was a serious thing that magistrates preferred the flimsy evidence of a single police-man to the testimony of two unimpeachable gentlemen ; the conduct also of the chairman of the bench was distinctly that of a prejudiced party.

Had a division been taken on the motor-car question there would have been a very small majority for the Govern-ment, but as it was Captain Norton then drew attention to the pay of the Metropolitan Police, and the issue thus became an involved one, the voting being on ordinary party lines. Steps, however, are being taken to bring the matter up as a separate question, and all motorists will do well to bring the hardships under which they suffer before their local M.P.'s.   J. S. M.

THE AERO CLUB AT RANELAGH.

THE most important of the Aero Club functions up to the present was brought off on Saturday afternoon in the beautiful grounds of the Ranelagh Club. Though an important counter-attraction at Hurlingham caused the attendance to be smaller than usual, it was none the less considerable, and the aeronauts had a much more brilliant send-off than on any previous occasion. Three balloons had been announced to ascend, viz., Sir Vincent Kennett Barrington's " Shropshire," with a cubic capacity of 25,000 ft. ; Mr. F. H. Butler's " Graphic " (45,000 ft.) ; and Mr. Leslie Bucknall's " Vivienne " (35,000 ft.). The passengers in the first-named were Sir V. K. Barrington himself, with Mr. S. F. Edge and Mr. Percival Spencer. Mr. Butler took with him Mr. J. A. Holder, Mr. C. F. Pollock, and, of course, the indomitable Miss Vera Butler, who never misses an ascent. The " Vivienne " carried Mr. Leslie Bucknall, Mr. Edward Bucknall, and Mr. Stanley Spencer.

The balloons ascended with painful punctuality at half-past three, and many persons who had not noticed the alteration in the time from the originally announced hour of four, arrived too late to witness the actual departure. The weather was perfect, and as the balloons soared gracefully into the upper empyrean there were not a few among the spectators who envied the aeronauts their pleasurable excursion. All the balloons descended safely—the " Shrop-shire " at Bicester shortly after seven o'clock, the " Vivienne " near Warwick at eight o'clock, and the " Graphic " near Evesham at nine o'clock the same evening.

IT is with sincere regret that we note the death of Captain the Hon. Cecil Duncombe, who was one of the pioneers of the auto-mobile movement. He was a member of the committee of the Automobile Club, owned a Peugeot motor-car from quite the early days, and drove very often from his house in Pont Street to various points round London. Courteous and kindly, he was a type of the gentlemanly automobilist who acts as a moderating and conciliatory force, especially in his native county of Yorkshire, where, of course, his task was not always an easy one. His eldest son, Mr. William Duncombe, is also a keen automobilist, though not, however, as yet possessing a car of his own, and Mrs. W. Duncombe, who acts under the stage name of Mdlle. Lilian Eldee in A Country Girl at Daly's Theatre, is both beautiful and charming.

Motor Cycling & Motoring

Vol. 1, No. 1, February 12th, 1902.

SOME MOTOR CYCLE HISTORY, AND SOME PERSONAL EXPERIENCES.

By ANTHONY WESTLAKE.

In the following first instalment of a most interesting article Mr. Anthony Westlake relates some motor bicycle history which goes to show that motor cycles were engaging the attention of inventors so far back as 1781. Mr. Westlake commenced his experiments with motor bicycles in 1892, and he has since made a very close study of every development of the subject. The completion of this article, in which the gradual growth of the motor bicycle will be traced, will appear next week.

IN giving some experiences and descriptions of many motor cycles, my mind is inadvertently led back to reflect upon numerous men who essayed, even in bygone centuries, to make mechanical locomotion a practical thing ; and now that this is with us in all its present force, the somewhat crude and cumbersome efforts of those anachronic geniuses have a strange pathos about them.

To me they appeal strongly as my own early mechanical dreams were all in this direction, and I made many early efforts to realise them, which circumstance brings me to my first experience in motor matters, due to a fractured back hub on my safety in 1891. A friendly engineer on a traction engine entered into consultation, and finally volunteered a lift to within a quarter of a mile of my destination. The acquaintance afterwards ripened, and my progression in the art of driving increased until one day I managed with some adroitness to place the machine partly on its side in a ditch. I will draw a veil over the sequel, for with a maximum speed of nearly five miles an hour, and the now nearly-universal wheel steering, it was a wild and thrilling time ; and so now, with middle age coming upon me, and my 1902 racer (with a steady plod of fifty miles or so) in view, I settle down to a quiet and respectable view of life.

But *allons a nos moutons,* or perhaps more correctly *a nos velos.* My personal interest in motor power applied to bicycles was of even earlier birth At the French Exhibition of 1878 there was exhibited a steam motor bicycle, the invention of a Swiss mechanic, whose name I quite forget and which I have been unable, for the present, to obtain. I give a rough drawing (No. 2) from memory of this machine. The wheels were of hickory, with iron tyres, which had been superseded by the suspension wire-wheel in England some years before the date of which I speak. I have no knowledge of any records made on this machine, the boiler, according to my impression, being too small for any ride longer than 100 yards. In appearance it suggested a wild caricature of the Holden motor bicycle, which most of us I think know by sight.

The engine drove direct on to a pair of cranks attached to a small back wheel above which the boiler was placed, the rider sitting in the ordinary position common to the bicycles of those days. But a century previous to this masterpiece (1781), Murdock, Watts' foreman, had designed and constructed a small road carriage, or rather tricycle. See footnote. Small as the model was (I append sketch and dimensions), it proved however, from the mechanical point of view highly successful, for on one of its trials, made in the evening, on the road in front of Murdock's cottage, it literally ran away from its inventor, and charged down the street at twelve miles an hour, scattering fire cinders, steam, and the villagers in all directions ; the last-named fled shrieking that "Satan was unchained again. It ended its comet-like flight in the horsepond, and its inventor nearly followed it. Murdock under Watts' persuasion, very reluctantly abandoned his motoring ideas.

Apropos of Watt, a warning to inventors. When first designed, his engine and its piston and mechanism for transforming rectilinear into circular motion by means of the crank (before then never used in conjunction with steam and so constituted a valuable patent) being much elated with his success he

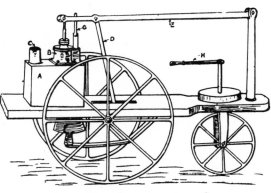

FIG. I. MURDOCK'S MOTOR CYCLE 1781.

A *Boiler.* B *Cylinder.* C *Chimney.* D *Connecting Rod.*
E *Beam.* F *Furnace.* G *Valve Stem.* H *Steering.*

The larger model had wheels of 20 inch and 9 inch respectively, and was some three or four feet over all.

WALKED DOWN TO THE VILLAGE INN,

and there, in the presence of the *élite* of the place, proceeded to explain with accuracy his most recent idea, by the simple expedient of dipping his finger in his mug of beer, and tracing with this medium on the counter an outline of the invention before all beholders or beer-holders.

Amongst the company was a smart gentleman from London, named James Pickard, who, recognising the importance and value of the invention, immediately returned thereto, and filed the patent before poor Watt had a chance to do so.

This same person actually sued Watt for infringement and Royalty on what was really Watt's invention. However

FIG. II. STEAM MOTOR BICYCLE, EXHIBITED AT THE PARIS EXHIBITION OF 1878.

A *Boiler and Furnace.* B *Cylinder.* C *Safety Valve.* D *Fuel and Water Tank.*

Watt immediately designed the sun and planet motion (geared facile movement) and thus evaded this imposition.

The foregoing, however apparently irrelevant to my sub-subject, is in reality most pertinent, as the crank and piston are the common foundation of nearly all motors.

However, to continue to relate these almost forgotten incidents in connection with the subject would be to risk running into many volumes, so I will proceed at once to deal with the petrol motor, the advent of which heralded the first tangible progress in our movement.

In 1885, Herr Otto Daimler made his

NOW FAMOUS MOTOR-BICYCLE,

with which most of us are familiar. The object of this construction was not to supply a practical vehicle so much as to

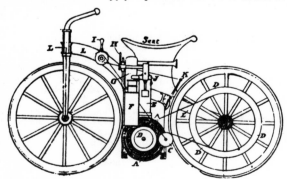

FIG. IV. DAIMLER MOTOR BICYCLE 1885.

A A *Crank Case.* B *Engine Pulley, Driving Strap, and* D D *Driving Wheel Pulley.* C *Jockey Pulley for tightening Belt D.* E *Cylinder.* F *Petrol Tank.* G *Carburetter.* H *Mixture Valve and Lever for altering same.* I *Lever and Ratchet for tightening Jockey Pulley C.* J *Valves and Lamp.* K *Brake.* L L *P Frame.*

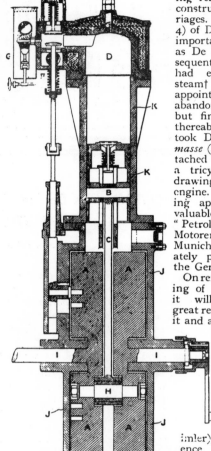

FIG. III. A SECTION OF ONE OF DAIMLER'S ENGINES 1880-5.

A A A A *Flywheels.* B *Piston and Wrist Pin.* C *Piston Connecting Rod.* D *Combustion Chamber.* E *Inlet Valve.* F *Exhaust Valve and Stem.* G *Ignition Tube and Lamps.* H *Crank Pin.* II *Axle Bearings.* J J J *Crank and Fly Wheel Case.* K K *Cylinder.*

provide a means of obtaining reliable data for the construction of other carriages. This machine (Fig. 4) of Daimler had a most important effect, however, as De Dion, a little subsequent to this period, had experimented with steam† with such disappointing results that he abandoned hopes of success, but finally in 1895, or thereabouts, he practically took Daimler's engine *en masse* (see Fig. 3), and attached it to the back of a tricycle. I append a drawing of Daimler's early engine. The original drawing appears in a most valuable work on motors, "Petroleum and Benzine Motoren," by G. Lieckfield, Munich, 1894, unfortunately published only in the German language.

On reference to the drawing of Daimler's engine, it will be seen that great resemblance between it and a sectional drawing of De Dion's motor, even down to the valve arrangements and the enclosed flywheels (afterwards abandoned by Daimler), the only difference being that De Dion's engine was entirely air-cooled. However, this was a huge step in advance, for in the Paris Toulouse races in 1897, and many others, the tricycles easily beat the cars of that period. De Dion also constructed a motor bicycle about this time. He placed his tricycle engine

JUST BEHIND THE BOTTOM BRACKET,

and drove from engine to back wheel by a train of pinions. One of these machines I know for certain came to England, and I believe that Mr. F. W. Baily, Hon. Secretary of the English Motor Car Club, had some amusement with it—principally in railway trains.

Contemporary with De Dion's invention was the Hildebrand-Wolffmuller bicycle (Fig. 5). This came into being in 1895. One in the hands of Mr. New was brought to England in 1896, and did some time tests and raced against a well-known cyclist on the C. P. track. This machine achieved a speed of some 27 miles an hour on level ground, but its great faults were its slipping propensities and its lack of ability to climb hills. It came to grief on the track, owing, I believe to the locking of the steering head, which caused it to charge the railings through which it passed in great style. It afterwards appeared at the great opening motor car run.

† In '95 he showed a steam tricycle at Paris. This is still to be seen in his works.

to Brighton in November, 1896, but it did not cover much of the distance. I made its direct acquaintance in 1897, while on a visit to the continent. Our intimacy was not of long duration. Being placed carefully in the saddle, and having got the control by means of the throttle and mixture, I went off in grand form at about 20 miles an hour. I felt very imposing indeed but suddenly became aware that there was a crossing some ten yards in front, and a large railway van just turning the corner. There was little time for reflection In a second I realised that I

COULD NOT GET THROUGH,

and in less time than it takes to relate pictured myself under the wheels of that van. My impulse was to swing the front wheel at right angles to the frame with the result that the machine and I came down at once—about four feet from the van—with a crash that resembled the discharge of a cartload of fire-irons. As I lay prostrate I saw my friend rushing up the road, swinging his arms about wildly and shouting "Put out the lamps! Put out the lamps!" As the machine was fitted with the tube ignition, the danger of the petrol firing can be understood. However, nothing happened in the way of an illumination, and I considered that I had got off cheaply with a cut knee and damaged

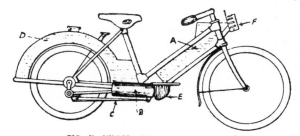

FIG. V. HILDEBRAND—WOLFFMULLER 1895.
A *Carburetter and Petrol Tank.* B *Cylinder.* C *Rubber Straps* D *Water Tank.* E *Case of the Ignition Lamps and Tubes.* F *Air Inlet and Mixture.*

hand. These I immediately dressed with petrol—a useful tip in such cases. The machine was absolutely uninjured.

Apropos of the Wolffmuller bicycle, it is well to mention that this was perhaps the first practical motor-bicycle.

THE ENGINE WAS WATER-COOLED.

The water reservoir took the form of a mudguard for the back wheel, the tank and carburetter (surface type) being placed on the fore part of the frame, and the foot-plates in the place usually occupied by the crank bracket. Pedal-gear there was none. The gear for valves was actuated by a small ball-bearing eccentric placed on the back axle. Large India rubber straps were attached to the big end of the connecting rod and cylinder to assist in overcoming the compression. As the outward stroke of the piston extended these, they, in returning, on the inward stroke exerted considerable force. A marked peculiarity of this machine was a funny tapping sound made by the carburetter. This was due to the two little non-return valves which served as air inlets. I have often wondered that this small feature has not been copied, for anybody who has placed his hand to the air intake of a carburetter when the engine is running will have felt the force of the "blow back," and will be able to appreciate the economy which such an arrangement, if efficient, will bring about.

Wolffmuller also constructed

A TANDEM WITH FOUR CYLINDERS,

arranged almost exactly as in the Holden engine, but it was not a success, chiefly owing to ignition troubles. In fact, for the first two years of its existence, the Wolffmuller bade fair to be a failure owing to this defect. I have a relic of the tandem in the shape of two of its cylinder covers fitted with two

separate insulated plugs in each head, their points converging to sparking distance. This machine was first fitted with the electrical ignition, but their system being faulty, lamps and tubes were substituted. These gave endless trouble, blowing out, going out, flaring, irregularly firing, etc., until, in 1895, I believe, Dr. Ganz, of Frankfurt, brought out his improved pressure-fed burner.

In 1897, Dr. Ganz employed an engineer named Baur to ride his Wolffmuller, so fitted in the Paris-Dieppe race (the first Gordon-Bennett). He duly competed, and would, in my opinion, have undoubtedly won this race for the road suited the now vastly improved machine admirably, but unfortunately by an oversight Baur had forgotten to close the drain tap of the water tank before starting, and only became aware that something was radically wrong when his engine was nearly red hot. Not being able to speak a word of French, he had much trouble in explaining his wants to the peasants at the *auberge* at which he stopped in the anticipation of procuring the necessary water. At length he obtained what he required and resumed his journey. Presently ominous sounds from the engine betokened more trouble. Dismounting he

FOUND IT ONCE MORE ALMOST RED HOT,

and the water tank again empty. At this juncture he thought of looking at the drain cock, which, of course, he found wide open. A horse pond being handy, he filled up and started again, and all seemed right. But not for long. His engine began to lose power in a remarkable manner, and upon examining his lubricators he found them empty. He had used the lubricant too lavishly on the cylinders before finding out the true cause of their over-heated condition. Managing to obtain some salad oil, he filled up with it and essayed

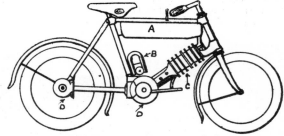

FIG. VI. HEIGEL—WEGUELIN 1896.
A *Carburetter and Tank.* B *Magneto Dynamo.* C *Cylinder* 4" x 4" D D *Crank case and bevel gear.* N.B —*No flywheel was fitted to this machine as first made, though one was added afterwards.*

to continue. As one may imagine, salad oil did not prove to be a very good lubricating medium, and owing to continual back firing Baur eventually abandoned the contest at Amiens.

Another machine (see Fig. 6), I might say an attempt to rival the Wolffmuller, appeared during 1896, made by Heigel-Weguelin, also a Munich firm. This machine was fitted with

ONE LARGE AIR-COOLED CYLINDER,

which occupied the position of the down tube from the head to the bracket, and drove a bevel gear therein which was continued to the back hub. The cylinder was 4 in. bore and with a 4 in. stroke, and was furnished with magneto-dynamic ignition. This cylinder, which I have still, is another interesting relic. This last-mentioned machine never achieved great notoriety, although one was to be seen about the streets of London, a year or two ago. In common with the Wolffmuller machine it was a bad hill climber.

In the next instalment of this article Mr. Westlake will deal with the advent of the practical motor bicycle, and the contribution, a really interesting chapter, will be fully illustrated by further striking diagrams.

THE 35 H.P. MERCEDES CAR.

Although this handsome and powerful vehicle has been running on the Continent and in this country for some time past, it has not as yet been so well illustrated as by the views we are now able to give. The mechanism and body alike are both the output of the Daimler Motor Co., of Cannstatt. In the design of the car great attention has been paid to stability, and with this desirable factor in view the centre of gravity is kept very low. Although the height of the frame is 23¾in., the lowest point of the engine crank chamber and gear case is not more than 8¾in. above the ground; in fact, it is too low for use on very uneven roads, but 25 h.p. cars are not designed for touring about in narrow and out-of-the-way lanes, or up little mountain by-paths. The engine is a four-cylinder motor of the now well-known Cannstatt type, water-cooled in the usual way, a centrifugal pump driven off the flywheel of the engine serving to circulate the water from the tubular cooler (seen filling the front panel of the motor bonnet) through the water jacketings of the cylinders and valve chambers, and return-

The 35 h.p. Mercedes engine- bonnet, removed. The separate floats for each pair of cylinders will be noted.

ing it to tank. The cooling tank, by its special construction, offers an enormous area of cooling surface to the heated water, the external air being drawn through the square tubes by a six-vaned rotary fan set immediately in rear of it, and rotated by suitable toothed wheel gearing from the engine-shaft. The makers claim that by this method of refrigeration, the water passing heated from the cylinder jackets into the cooler is reduced to, or very nearly to, the temperature of the outside air before it again leaves the cooler. With this system of cooling a comparatively small quantity of water is used, two and a half gallons being given as the total, while only a pint or two disappear during the course of a long day's run.

The drive from the engine, which is fired by the Simms-Bosch magneto ignition with the advance and retard improvements, passes through a friction clutch of large dimensions actuated by foot plate and side brake lever at will, and furnished with clutch brake to reduce the shock of gear changing to a minimum, to a Panhard type of change speed gear enclosed in an aluminium oil and dust-tight gear case most securely attached to the transverse and longitudinal members of the frame. This gear affords four speeds forward and reverse, and the drive continues therefrom through the countershaft, upon which is mounted the differential gear, to the sprockets at end thereof, and thence by chains to the chain wheels bolted to the spokes of the road driving wheels. The changes of speed and reverse are all obtained by the movement of one lever. Wheel steering of the worm and sector irreversible type is fitted. It should be noted that the gear wheels are ample in breadth of teeth. The lubrication of the engine, engine bearings, and change speed gear, is provided for by the fitting of an oil pump worked by a chain off the half-time shaft, and set on the dashboard in front of the driver. The petrol tank will hold sufficient petrol for a ten or twelve hours' non-stop run. The speeds vary from six to sixty miles per hour, and on the first speed the vehicle will climb gradients of one in four. The ability to climb rapidly is the great charm of a high-powered car. Notwithstanding the power of the engine, and the solid appearance of the vehicle as it takes the road, the car, with water, petrol, and all accessories aboard, weighs about 23 cwt. Messrs. Milnes and Co., of Motoria, Balderton Street, Oxford Street, handle these cars in this country.

THE EIGHT HORSE-POWER DURKOPP CAR.

The engine driving this machine is of the two-cylinder vertical type. The cylinders are in one casting, so that there are no water joints on the motor head. The engine is governed on the exhaust valves in the same manner as the Panhard (Phœnix) engines, and runs at about 700 revolutions a minute. The inlet valves are get-at-able by merely removing one nut, and another handy feature is found in an overflow cock in the crank case, so that when excessive lubrication takes place the superfluous oil is drained off, so that there is no fear of getting the plugs fouled with oil, or of smell from over-lubrication. The oil is fed by a sight feed lubricator on the dash, the oil before reaching the engine passing over the exhaust valve cams, and so lubricating them. Both accumulator and magneto ignition are fitted. The water circulating pump is of a new type, which, we are informed, has been found very efficient, and to which we hope to refer again before long. The clutch has a less abrupt incline than usual, but a very large area, by which it is claimed that great freedom from slipping and jumping is obtained. The transmission is of the usual modified Panhard type, and gives three speeds forward and a reverse, the bottom speed being seven miles an hour, and the top twenty-five, though, of course, considerably more can be done by the accelerator. Four brakes are fitted, two on the countershaft, and one on each sprocket. These are carefully balanced, so that there shall be no fear of unequal retardation of the rear wheels. Ball thrusts are fitted to the clutch and to the road wheels. The Durkopp light car is made in four sizes—8 h.p., 10 h.p., 15 h.p., and 24 h.p.—while the large cars are

made in the 10 h.p., 16 h.p., 24 h.p., and 40 h.p. sizes. The 24 h.p. light car is specially made and designed to compete in this year's French races,

The 8 h.p. Durkopp. Improved Britannia Motor Co.

being turned out to weigh inside the stipulated maximum of 1,000 kilogs. (19 cwt. 2 qrs. 10 lbs.), and it is guaranteed to maintain a speed of at least fifty-six miles an hour. It may be of interest to say that Messrs. Durkopp claim that they were the first to introduce the now so widely used single lever for speed changes and reverse. The entire car (including the artillery wheels and chains) is made at the Durkopp factory, at which over 8,000 men are employed. The cars, which are worthy of careful examination, are sold in this country by the Improved Briannia Motors, Ltd., of Long Acre, W.C.

AN EXPRESS PARCELS DELIVERY VAN.

Messrs. Whiteley, Ltd., the world-famed universal providers, who have been giving attention to the question of motor transport for some time, are now acquiring a number of Benz vans, one of which is shown above.   One of these vans is found to easily perform the work of three horses, and, as Messrs. Whiteleys have some 350 horses in their stables, they hope, when they have all been replaced by motor vans, to effect an enormous saving annually. During the present year Messrs. Benz are arranging to deliver one hundred of these vans.   The engine is at the back, and has a single cylinder 5⅛ in. bore by 5½ in. stroke, and the horse-power is given as seven. The speed change gear, which is of the toothed type, gives four forward speeds and one reverse. The car has a large carrying capacity, and is found particularly handy in all cases of urgent delivery, as it is easily capable of twenty miles per hour, carrying 5 cwt. of goods and the driver.   It is also a good hill-climber, and, we are told, will tackle a hill of one in four.   So there is nothing even in North London that can stop it.   The vans have been supplied by Messrs. Hewetsons, Ltd., the British representatives of Messrs. Benz.

—

A company has just been formed, with a capital of £1,000, to be known as Motormobile, Ltd., to acquire patents relating to motors, motor cycles and motor cars, etc.   The registered office of the company is at 27, Laystall Street, Rosebery Avenue, W.C.

The Automobile Club of Capetown recently held their inaugural run—a dozen cars and a couple of motor bicycles having triumphantly covered the distance between Capetown and Kalk Bay.   It was undoubtedly, as report hath it, a red-letter day for automobilism in Capetown.

A WALK THROUGH THE WOLSELEY WORKS.

Some months since we announced the removal of the Wolseley Tool and Motor Car Co., Ltd., to a much larger factory at Adderley Park, Birmingham. As we mentioned at the time, this factory is quite modern, it being less than four years since it was completed. With the exception of the offices and certain minor departments, the whole of the factory is on one floor, and lighted throughout by north lights. It stands on some three and a half acres of ground, and already the odd half acre available is to be built on and completely covered with extensions to the factory. It is not our intention to describe the works themselves, or any of the fine modern labour-saving tools with which they are installed—as these technical particulars would only be comprehensible to a comparative few, and would ne-

The "nearly completed" end of erecting department.
The "bare frames" or commencing end of erecting department.

A few of the automatic machine tools.

A view in the main machine tool shop.
Some heavy machine tools engaged on special work—a planer in foreground.
The wood working department.

cessitate a series of special articles—though we may say that many of the machine tools are made by the company themselves, and if it were not for the fact that time does not permit them, they would manufacture nearly all their own plant. With a vehicle of so many parts as the autocar, it is impossible to follow it right round the factory, however systematically it may be arranged, as so many of the processes are proceeding simultaneously, and are equally important, but it will undoubtedly be of interest to those of our readers who are unacquainted with the best modern factory practice if we give a brief account of a walk through the works, which was made, as far as possible, progressively, beginning with the designs and drawings, and finishing up with the completed car. The administrative side of the undertaking we do not touch on, though we may say a very interesting feature of the entrance hall and comfortable waiting room is a number of photographs of different Wolseley cars which have been supplied to automobilists all over the country. However, we turn from the offices to the factory itself, and commence our inspection with the drawing office. The drawing office, which is above the floor of the great main shop, and looks across it like a signal box over

A Busy Railway Junction,

is even more important to a motor works than the architect's plans are to a builder. In the drawing office the draughtsmen work out the new ideas and designs of the works manager and under his inspection. That is to say, if a new type of car is contemplated, here the drawings are made to scale for every part, so that there is no possibility of the workmen making a mistake, and here have to be worked out a great many other details, besides those of minute accuracy in the drawings themselves. The strength of all the parts must be considered in relation to the materials used, and the tools which will be used for making each part must be borne in mind, and often specially designed, and the number of operations on each article carefully considered, as there is a great difference between inventing or evolving a good idea and putting it into practical shape for manufacture on the interchangeable system. The drawings of the various parts are reproduced as blue prints for the use of the workmen all over the factory, and, as an instance of the up-to-dateness of the instalment, we may mention that a clockwork electrical printing machine is used to get the blue prints, as the daylight is too short and too weak this time of the year to be of much service, and a powerful arc lamp does duty as a sun. Having made the drawings, much has to be done in connection with most parts before they can be issued in the rough to the workmen, and the pattern shop, near the drawing office, is, in its way, almost as important. Here, in wood, are made patterns of all parts which are to be cast. Pattern making is, perhaps, the highest development of the carpentering art, and only skilled men are employed for the work. At the time we were in the shop we saw the wooden pattern for the gear box and several other parts of the new four-cylinder racing car, and we also noted incidentally that the firm were making their own steering wheels. The wooden patterns, to the eye of the untechnical, present distinctly curious shapes, and are almost as different from the cast-

ings which are to be made from them as a negative is from a photograph. In the foundry the reasons for these differences are at once seen, as the flow of molten metal has to be considered, and this or

That Unaccountable Projection

from a gear case or a crank chamber is found to form a channel in the fine sand in which the moulds are made for the metal to be cast. Aluminium and gunmetal are very largely used in autocar foundries, as well as iron, and this, of course, is easily accounted for when we remember the numerous parts which are made from one or other of the metals in a car. From the foundry we turn into the coachsmith's shop, where the metal frames of the wings or mudguards are made, and steps and similar ironwork of the sort carried out. All these are fitted on a dummy frame and body which are kept in the shop, so that there is no fear of the wings fouling any moving part of the car when they are assembled later. All the Wolseley wings are built with metal frame with patent leather stretched and stitched upon them, though, of course, the leather work is done in another department. The next shop is the general smithy, where heavier work is done. In this are four hearths and a steam hammer, and all such forgings as the exhaust levers, brake and change speed levers, and front and back axles are made. These axles are made from Vickers special axle steel, the same as is used in the best railway practice, and they are forged without a weld. That is to say, the front axle with a jaw at each end for taking the steering pins is made from one piece of steel forged out to shape. Here we noticed lamp irons, which are carefully turned from the bar, and merely sent into the forge to be bent at right angles. In the coppersmiths' shop, radiators, tanks, hoods, and exhaust pipes were being made. The hood of the engine bonnet, by the way, has been made of a somewhat more rakish type, as the front part is chamfered off at a sharper angle than hitherto. It will be remembered that in the Wolseley the hood is simply a hinged lid, as the sides of the motor bonnet are composed of radiating tubes, which are connected to two aluminium water columns, one on each side of the dashboard.

(To be continued.)

————◆————

The *Medical Press and Circular* is not a humorous publication, but it is quite capable of provoking a healthy laugh. After speaking of the slight distinction discoverable in the relative consequences of being thrown out of an applecart or an autocar, it notes a hidden danger in the case of the autocar "from the driving arm being suddenly thrown into forced extension by a sudden jerk of the mechanism. Not infrequently this determines indirect fracture of the lower extremity of the radius, following rupture or detachment of the anterior ligament of the wrist." Then on other occasions we have " a direct fracture at the junction of the middle and lower thirds of the radius, caused by the handle coming into violent contact with the limb. In one case the styloid process of the ulna was also torn away." This seems to be the apotheosis of Bosh.

A WALK THROUGH THE WOLSELEY WORKS.

(Concluded from page 127).

The radiators consist of copper tubes with brass gills, which are stamped out in three operations, and soldered by immersion to the copper tubes. The shape in which the gills are cut is such that they get plenty of hold upon the tube, and they are also correctly spaced from each other. This is a small point, and, of course, not a new one, but it is one of hundreds which one notices in passing through a good motor factory. Now all these departments through which we have passed are separated from the great main apartment of the factory, which is a shop of 220 feet by 300 feet, and the parts not taken up with actual erection are filled with machine tools of all kinds, the first one we came across being an 18ft. planer by Messrs. Gray and Co., of Cincinnati. Hard by was a boring machine which, we may say for the benefit of the uninitiated, may be very roughly described as

A Lathe at Right Angles

to its usual position. This boring machine is one of the Wolseley's own make, and was operating on another similar tool which was in course of manufacture. Then we came across two vertical turning machines engaged on turning pistons; four other planers at work on various tools; a slotting machine, which, by an upward movement and a downward cut, was making keyways in a gear sleeve; and a shaping machine busily shaping the choke slide

for the throttle—in other words, the sliding panel arrangement which cuts off the gas from the engine. A boring machine told off for boring crank cases was engaged in boring out the cradle or jig by which it holds fast the case when it is operating on one, as a slight improvement in the cases had necessitated the change. A big lathe was turning the fly-wheel and clutch of one of the 20 h.p. cars, while five new lathes with 8in. centres and 10ft. beds, by Messrs. Richards and Co., of Manchester, were hard at work on various parts, such as liners for the cylinders. Numerous machine tools of all kinds and of the best and most modern description were to be seen on every side working on almost every part one could think of connected with the motor or gear. Space forbids us to detail these, and the reader can easily imagine them for himself, for, as we have said, he has only to think of any and every part of a car and he would be almost sure to find it somewhere in the machine tool shop of the Wolseley factory in process of manufacture. As an instance of the number of operations which have to be performed on one part before it is finished we have only to mention the connecting rod, on which eighteen operations of turning, drilling, and milling have to be performed before the article has been completely machined, and then there is the bush or liner to the big or crank-end of the rod, which has been separately made, besides the necessary fitting of the other end to the piston. Hard by was an array of new capstan lathes, just delivered from Messrs. Alfred Herbert, Ltd., of Coventry, engaged on a variety of jobs, such as brakework, pumps, and gearshafts. We noted that each toothed wheel was separately mounted on the shaft, so that any one speed could be renewed when worn. We may perhaps explain to those unacquainted with machine tools that a capstan lathe is one which, in place of the ordinary slide-rest and tool-holder for a single tool, has, say, six different cutting tools mounted on a revolving turret or capstan. When the lathe is started the first tool completes its cut, and then the capstan automatically turns to bring the next tool into operation. This goes right through the series till the last of the tools has done its duty, and, if the nature of the work permits it, the material for the next article is automatically fed into position. Of course, there are many varieties of capstan lathes, but we may mention this as an example, for the principle is the same whether half a dozen or only three or four operations are necessitated. All working parts which require it, such as gears, are case hardened in the hardening shop. The process

The foundry.

The general smithy.

may be roughly described as baking for a long period in gas ovens. The articles to be hardened are packed in pots filled with a special mixture of bone dust and charcoal, and after a long period of steady baking at an even temperature they are dropped into oil or oil and water, according to the character of the metal and depth of hardening required. This heating and sudden cooling, which has the hardening effect, also tends to distort the article, and each part is passed on to the grinding shop, where, with various shaped emery wheels, it is ground to a perfectly true form. The hardening provides long resistance to wear, and the grinding to an absolutely true form gives very smooth running. As an instance, we may say that we revolved several change speed gears by hand, and found them perfectly smooth in action; that is to say, there was not the least difference in the resistance offered at any point in the revolution. We might dwell for a long while on the various processes we inspected, but we have said enough to show the care which has to be taken in the manufacture of

The Parts of a First-class Autocar,

and we pass on to the erecting portion of the establishment. First we come to the engines, which, after being assembled and adjusted, are tested for power on the brake, and we were informed that each engine has to give off its full power at 750 revolutions a minute for at least an hour before being unbolted from the testing bench and put into a carriage. The bare frames are found at one end of the department, and at the other the complete chassis is seen, each car, as one passes down the row, being found more nearly complete. With regard to the pistons, it may be interesting to note that it is now usual with all the best firms to pin the three rings, so that there is no fear of the cuts in each ring ever getting in line. Years ago this used to be a mysterious cause of occasional loss of compression, and we remember once having great trouble with a motor before we discovered what had happened, and others suffered similarly. The cranks on the two-cylinder engines are now parallel with heavy balance weights on the opposite side, and the crank case has been altered so that the lower half can be unbolted, and all the motion comes away with it except the crankshaft and connecting rods, as it is so made that the bottom half can be taken off without disturbing the crankshaft bearings. After examining the twenty odd cars in various stages of completion, we turned into the wood-working shop, where some particularly fine wood working tools of Canadian design and make were to be seen in operation, and various kinds of bodies in various stages of completion, all the work of forming, moulding, tenoning, and sand-papering being performed by machinery. After the cars have been run through their tests on the road of a hundred miles or more, the rough test body and wheels are removed, those belonging to the car fitted on, and then the otherwise finished vehicle is taken to the paint shop, which is an isolated department, completely closed from the dust of the factory, and lined throughout with white enamel bricks, so that it is easy to keep it free from dirt. Space does not permit us to refer to the several other departments, but we may mention that all

the upholstering is done on the premises. In fact, practically every part of the cars—except the chains, tyres, and one or two odd parts, such as the induction coils—is made in the factory. As we were passing out of the works—which, by the way, gives over four hundred men constant employment—we stopped to examine with interest the celebrated Wolseley which performed so successfully in the thousand miles. With its lever steering, quaintly-shaped bonnet, and somewhat cumbersome speed-changing device, it looked a very different machine from those of to-day; but its designer, Mr. Austin, is still very fond of it and its running, and has had it in almost daily use ever since it finished the memorable run. We reflected as we looked at this now historic vehicle what advances had been made in two years, as it was almost two years to a day since we first saw it exhibited in the Bingley Hall, Birmingham. Our short inspection of the works was a most pleasurable one, not only in itself, but because the enterprise is throughout a thoroughly British one. The design of the car was gradually

The engine room.

evolved by Mr. H. Austin, who commenced his motor experiments and continued them for some four years before he entered upon manufacture, so that he was able to turn out a thoroughly satisfactory machine directly he commenced to cater for the public. There is no doubt that with his ingenuity and enterprise, backed, as he is, by a practical board, who understand the necessities of the business and its requirements in the way of adequate capital, the Wolseley business will grow with its reputation. The works, if not the largest, are, so far as we know, the largest on one floor in this country devoted to automobile manufacture, and for general arrangement, system, up-to-date installation of machinery, and manufacturing methods are unsurpassed. In conclusion, we should like to express our indebtedness to Mr. Austin and his lieutenant Mr. Willson for the pains which they took in showing us everything, so that we could give our readers some idea of a few of the processes which go towards the building of a modern motor car.

A company has just been formed in Brussels with a capital of £20,000, to be known as La Société de Carrosserie et d'Automobiles.

THE RICHMOND HILL CLIMBING COMPETITION.

Argent Archer, Photo, Kensington.   Captain Locock on his 10 h.p. Wolseley.   Messrs. Astell and Swindley on the 12 h.p. New Orleans.
Setting out for the test hill.

Argent Archer,   At the top of the test hill.   *Photo, Kensington.*

The 8 h.p. De Dion double phaeton (Messrs. Stocks and Munn).   The 12 h.p. M.M.C. car, driven by Mr. Instone.

SOME SNAP SHOTS AT RICHMOND.

Captain Locock's 10 h.p. Wolseley.

Outside the Star and Garter. Mr. Hutton's Panhard between two New Orleans.

The four cylinder New Orleans.　　　　　　　　　　Lord Kingsburgh examining the cars.

In the Star and Garter stables. The new 16 h.p. Napier on the right and the 16 h.p. Panhard on the left.

Argent Archer,   The Lanchester at the top of Petersham Hill   *Photo, Kensington*

Argent Archer,   *Photo, Kensington.*
The Locomobile topping the crest of the "test" hill. Exhausting visibly from the temporary cause of shutting off condenser while sprinting

Automobilists, whether they are connected with the industry or not, are warned to be careful when dealing with any firms whose names are not known to them, but who may conduct their correspondence on very businesslike looking letter paper. One of our readers sends us particulars of a case of this sort, in which he received a letter from an address in North-west London. He sent a representative to see the firm, and found it to be a small private house with a woman in charge, who knew nothing whatever about the business. In fact, as far as he could gather, it was simply an address to which letters could be sent.

Under the auspices of the Bourguignon Automobile Club, an automobile congress is being organised to take place at Dijon in May next. Already most of the automobile clubs in France have decided to be represented at the meeting.

* * *

"With a view to checking the furious driving of motor carriages, the Dover Corporation have resolved to station police officers at various points with stop-watches to time the speed of drivers." If the sapient D.C. have the same kind of notions in properly performing with ordinary municipal business, the ratepayers are to be sympathised with.

THE RICHMOND HILL-CLIMBING COMPETITION.

On last Saturday, the 8th February, an unofficial hill-climbing competition was held on Petersham Hill, Richmond, under the auspices of the Automobile Club.

The competing vehicles met at the Star and Garter Hotel, Richmond, at twelve o'clock noon, and each vehicle climbed Petersham Hill with its full complement of passengers. Time was taken at the Dysart Arms, with flying start, and again at the entrance of the Star and Garter Hotel, Richmond, a distance of 600 yards, having an average gradient of 1 in 15.1, and at its steepest part a gradient of 1 in 9.5.

Mr. Harry J. Swindley and Mr. F. T. Bidlake acted as honorary timekeepers. The meeting was unofficial and informal, and was not held under the Competitions Rules of the club. Therefore, the results cannot be taken as official records. The results, which are not officially vouched by the club, but are only recorded in the Automobile Club *Notes and Notices* as a matter of interest, were as follows:

Petersham Hill—1,800 feet = 600 yards.

Car.	Driven by	No. of Passengers, including Driver.	Catalogue Price.	1st Ascent.		2nd Ascent.	
				Time.	m.p.h.	Time.	m p.h.
			£	min. sec.		min. sec.	
16 h.p. Panhard	Harvey du Cros, jun.. ..	4	1,250	1 $22\frac{3}{5}$	14 7	—	—
16 h.p. Napier	S. F. Edge	4	1,150	1 13	16·8	—	—
16 h.p. Panhard	C. Jarrott	4	1,150	1 $24\frac{3}{5}$	14 4	1 $18\frac{4}{5}$	15·5
20 h.p. Milnes	H. G. Burford	4	1,150	1 10	17·5	1 $5\frac{4}{5}$	18·5
12 h.p. Motor Manufacturing Co.	E. M. C. Instone	4 5	850	2 $6\frac{1}{5}$	9·7	2 $38\frac{1}{5}$	7·7
10 h.p. Napier	Charles Cordingley	4	600	2 $20\frac{2}{5}$	8·7	2 $21\frac{4}{5}$	8·6
10 h.p. Lanchester	Rowland Browne	4	525	2 $11\frac{4}{5}$	9·2	—	—
12 h.p. New Orleans	W. D. Astell	2	450	1 $17\frac{3}{5}$	15·7	1 $21\frac{4}{5}$	14 4
10 h.p. Wolseley	Capt. E. A. Locock	4	380	1 $53\frac{3}{5}$	10·8	1 55	10.6
7 h.p. Durkopp	P. Dodson	—	375	—	—	—	—
8 h p. De Dion	J. W. Stocks	4	328	2 $5\frac{2}{5}$	9·8	2 $6\frac{1}{5}$	9·7
4½ h.p. De Dion	J. M. Gorham..	3	320	3 $8\frac{2}{5}$	6·5	2 $16\frac{2}{5}$	9·0
7 h p. New Orleans	Jenner	4	290	3 $43\frac{1}{5}$	5·5	2 $36\frac{3}{5}$	7 8
4½ h.p. De Dion	Roger H. Fuller	2	240	2 $18\frac{1}{5}$	8·8	—	—
4½ h p. Locomobile	Ginder	2	190	1 $25\frac{1}{5}$	14·4	1 $14\frac{2}{5}$	16·5

The condition of the road on Petersham Hill was very bad, being covered with thick mud.

Luncheon was taken at the Star and Garter Hotel, and afterwards the cars were driven to the hill, which lies between Robin Hood Gate and Kingston Gate, in Richmond Park. The hill includes a bend. Times were taken over the steepest portion of the hill; that is to say, at the bottom at the oak tree on the right, the branches of which overhang the road, and at the top at the last (a small stunted oak) tree on the right.

The distance between these two points is 850ft. The average gradient is 1 in 11.3. The steepest gradient is 72ft., averaging 1 in 7.8. The number of passengers to be carried was in this case optional. The road was very loose and heavy. The results were as follow:

Test Hill.—850 feet = $283\frac{1}{3}$ yards.

Car.	Driven by	Price.	1st Ascent.			2nd Ascent.		
			No. of Passengers	Time.	m.p.h.	No. of Passengers.	Time.	m.p.h.
		£		min. sec.			min. sec.	
16 h.p. Panhard ..	Harvey du Cros, jun...	1,250	3	0 44	13·1	—	—	—
16 h.p. Napier ..	S. F. Edge	1,150	4	0 $37\frac{3}{5}$	15·2	—	—	—
16 h.p. Panhard ..	C. Jarrott	1,150	1	0 40	14·4	1	0 42	13·7
20 h.p. Milnes ..	H. G. Burford ..	1,150	4	0 $38\frac{3}{5}$	14·8	1	0 $30\frac{4}{5}$	18·6
12 h.p. M. Mfg. Co...	E. M. C. Instone	850	—	—	—	2	1 17	7·5
10 h.p. Napier ..	(Mr. Cordingley's car)	600	4	1 $20\frac{4}{5}$	7·1	—	—	—
12 h.p. New Orleans..	W. D. Astell	450	2	0 40	14·4	2	0 $40\frac{2}{5}$	14·4
10 h.p. Wolseley ..	Capt. E. A. Locock ..	380	1	0 57	10·1	1	0 $53\frac{1}{5}$	10·9
5 h.p. Panhard ..	J. Ernest Hutton, J.P.	—	—	—	—	1	1 $13\frac{4}{5}$	7·8
7 h.p. Durkopp ..	P. Dodson	375	1	1 $9\frac{3}{5}$	8·2	—	—	—
8 h.p. De Dion ..	J. W. Stocks	328	2	1 $9\frac{1}{5}$	8·3	2	1 5	8·9
4½ h.p. De Dion ..	J. M. Gorham ..	320	1	1 $5\frac{1}{5}$	8·9	2	1 $14\frac{2}{5}$	7·8
7 h.p. New Orleans..	Jenner	290	2	1 $8\frac{2}{5}$	8·5	—	—	—
4½ h.p. Locomobile ..	Ginder	190	1	0 $41\frac{3}{5}$	13·7	2	0 $43\frac{2}{5}$	13·4

A DOCTOR'S CAR.

The illustration shows one of the new two-cylinder 9½ h.p. light cars now being built by Humbers. The cylinders are 4in. bore by 4in. stroke, and the 9½ b.h.p. is obtained at a thousand revolutions per minute. The governing is on the exhaust, and the valve gear is particularly silent, and, as we have already said in regard to a trial run that we made on the vehicle, the governor is very sensitive. The transmission is geared throughout with universal and telescopic joints between engine and change speed gear, and also between the speed gear and live rear axle. The change speed gear gives three forward speeds and a reverse. Artillery wheels are pro-vided, mounted with New York tyres, and, except for the body, tyres, and chains, the car was made entirely at the Coventry works. The hood is of very ample proportion, and unites with the glazed exten-sion of the dash, so that protection can be obtained from the worst of weather, and this is very necessary, as the car has been built for Dr. Row, of Warbleton. The back seat accommodates two persons, and is entered from the rear by swinging the seat back-ward. The car is a substantially built vehicle, and looks thoroughly well suited for the work it is de-signed to undertake. Its running, too, is very com-fortable and smooth.

As we mentioned last week, an arrangement has been made between the Clipper Pneumatic Tyre Co., of Coventry, and the Continental Caoutchouc and Guttapercha Co., with the result that the Clipper-Continental tyres can now be obtained in this country. The Continental tyre is not so well known here as abroad, though it may be interesting if we say that it is widely used on the Continent, and has been fitted on many cars which have won important races, but up to the time the arrange-ment was come to between the Clipper and Con-tinental Companies the latter firm's tyres could not be used in Great Britain, owing to the patents they infringed, so that the makers had to content them-selves by selling their air-tubes (which are very well spoken of) for pneumatic tyres.

The first really fine Sunday this year, March 9th, brought a very considerable crowd of cyclists to Ditton, and the fact was made very evident to all observers that the motor bicycle is already a popular mount, a large number of these machines being seen on the road. J. H. Adams, clad in calf-skins, like a very Austria, was speeding quite up to the legal limit on an F.N. motor bicycle, H. J. Swindley was noted on the Fair Mile on a Chapelle, whilst A. J. Wilson alone on an Ariel quad also passed Cobham-wards. Harry Parsons, on a Holden, with Mrs. Parsons in a trailer, was also reported, whilst cars large and small were very numerous. That the motor bicycle will be a very popular mount this year there can be little doubt, and for a first show that of March 9th was decidedly indicative of the fact.

LE CHAT NOIR.

Mr. Oliver Stanton's "Le Chat Noir," which was first seen by most automobilists on the anniversary run to Southsea last November, is generally regarded as the finest English Daimler which has been made. Many of its special features are embodiments of Mr. Stanton's own ideas, and their intent is to simplify control as far as possible, and to place all items requiring attention in get-at-able positions. It is driven by a 24 h.p. four-cylinder Daimler motor fitted with tube and electric ignition and throttle valve, this last being specially finely graduated in order to obtain the best results, and it is found in practice that for town work it is invaluable, making the engine practically silent. The radiators and tank are all in front of the engine, which allows of a very much simpler arrangement of piping, circulation being effected by means of a double rotary pump, friction driven off the flywheel. These, together with the large cooling surface of the radiators, combine to keep the engine at a suitable temperature at all speeds, and as the petrol tank, which is fitted behind the front seat, has a range of over 200 miles, it will be seen that the car is well adapted for touring purposes. The body is arranged for four persons, the two front places being well seats, the back being really a mechanician's seat. The car is painted black, picked out with gold lines, and presents a very handsome appearance, the plating throughout being brass. The design of the patent leather wings keeps the car as clean as is possible in bad weather. The curved side extensions to the dash not only serve to turn

Front view of car.

Right-hand side of engine

Left side of engine showing separate exhaust pipes for each cylinder.

direct air currents completely away from the feet and legs of, the occupants of the front seats, but the space inside is utilised, as will be seen from the references, as a cupboard.   The illustrations we give, with the exception of two, are taken with the body and bonnet removed, and in the view which shows dashboard, gear box, countershaft, etc., it will be noticed that the gear box is very much shorter than usual, this being due to the fact that the sleeve is in two sections, thereby obviating the usual wear and tear on the third speed in Panhard type gear through changing on either side.   Attention should be drawn to the contact breaker B on the dash.   This is contained in a small mahogany case with glass front, which prevents any dust or dirt getting on to the commutator, which is driven by a chain from the countershaft.   Dynamo type brushes are employed, and found to be most efficient.   In the event of the water circulation tell-tale gauge glass D breaking, it may be cut out and the test cock F used for the purpose, which also fills the double-acting water-cooled band brake P through the small funnel, which will be noticed at F.   The sight feed lubricators C on the Daimler pressure feed system lubricate all the principal bearings throughout the car, and are brought into action by one cock.   The extreme left of the dashboard S is used as a receptacle for the accumulators, of which two sets are used.   It will be seen from the side view separate exhaust pipes are provided to each cylinder.   These exhaust into an expansion chamber at the side of the engine, so that the ex-

haust is free, and back pressure obviated.   A single pipe of large diameter runs from the exhaust chamber to the large silencer at the rear of the car, the exhaust gases finally escaping through a dust preventer very similar to that recommended in our columns a few months ago by Mr. Ernest Estcourt.   In the first expansion chamber a release valve is fitted, so that there is no possibility of the expansion chamber being burst, should a charge be fired past the engine.   The tyres with which the car is fitted are 36in. × 5½in. Goodyears, which have been put to extremely severe tests quite recently, and they have, we understand, withstood them most successfully, although we are not at liberty to divulge the nature of the tests.   "Le Chat Noir" possesses a special interest, as its behaviour so favourably impressed the King that, when he honoured Mr. Stanton with the command to draw up the specification for his new vehicle, he specially requested that many of the special fittings of Mr. Stanton's car should be included in his 1902 machine, which, it will be remembered, the Daimler Company have guaranteed to deliver in good time for the Ascot week.   We need scarcely add that in the first illustration the manipulator of the steering wheel is Mr. Oliver Stanton.

Last week, in the article "The Depression of the Freezing Point," a slip was made with regard to lithium chloride.   This is not a compound of two metals, but of one metal lithium with the halogen chlorine.

MOTOR VEHICLE REGULATIONS.

Manifesto of the Automobile Club in View of Pending Legislation.

In view of pending legislation with regard to autocars, the General Council of the Automobile Club have issued the following manifesto, which, from the fair and masterly manner in which it presents the arguments in favour of the removal of hampering restrictions from the industry and pastime of automobilism, ought to have some good effect :

The undersigned members of the General Council of the Automobile Club (a body appointed to confer with the committee of the club on matters affecting automobilism generally) ask permission to draw the attention of your readers to certain important questions affecting motor vehicle traffic and transport, namely, (a) the restrictions as to speed in respect of light vehicles, and (b) the restrictions as to tare weight and width of heavy vehicles used for commercial purposes.

We agree with Rt. Hon. Lord Thring, K.C.B., in the opinion which he expressed that there is no worse law than a law which is not respected.

In view of the powerful brakes with which all motor vehicles are fitted, and the perfect control which drivers have over motor vehicles, it is evident that the existing law which provides that even on a clear, straight road devoid of traffic, a light motor vehicle must not be driven at a speed greater than twelve miles an hour, does not command, and cannot command, respect or observance.

Careful observations made in our big cities and their suburbs show that electric and steam tramcars are driven at speeds up to eighteen miles per hour.

Recent experiments have shown that motor vehicles can be stopped on the flat on a fairly dry road when travelling at the undermentioned speeds, as follow :

From 11 to 14 miles per hour in 1 4·5 times the car's length.

From 15 to 17 miles per hour in twice the car's length.

From 18 to 20 miles per hour in 2¾ times the car's length.

From 20 to 24 miles per hour in 3½ times the car's length.

The figures given above are averages. As a matter of fact, one car travelling at 13 miles per hour was stopped in 4 yards; another travelling at 18 1-3 miles an hour was stopped in 7 yards; and another when going at 20 miles an hour was stopped in 12 2-3 yards. The average weight of the vehicles, without passengers, was 1 ton 4 cwts. From these results, it will be seen that motor cars can, on an average, be stopped when travelling at twenty miles an hour in less distance than the ordinary horse vehicle could be stopped when travelling at ten miles per hour.

Of these facts the General Council possess incontestable evidence.

The law, therefore, which prohibits travel on light motor vehicles at a speed in excess of 12 m.p.h., under any circumstances, and the systematic prosecutions and heavy fines imposed for technical offences against this law, cannot but fail to damage in this country an industry which is encouraged on the Continent and in the United States of America, by the chiefs of states, by the Government, by the press, and by the people; and which is providing abroad, and, if unencumbered by unnecessary legislation, should provide in this kingdom, work at good wages for many thousands of men.

The industry, even abroad, is admittedly only in its infancy. Owing, however, to the fact that, prior to the Light Locomotives Act of 1896, British invention and enterprise (which in 1830 and thereabouts had placed this country in the van of mechanical road locomotion) had been stifled by repressive and unnecessary legislation, foreign countries obtained considerable advantage over this country. Whilst in this kingdom six years ago inventors were being prosecuted for driving mechanical carriages at more than four miles an hour, and for failure to arrange that a man should walk in front bearing a red flag, invention on the Continent was being stimulated by competitions organised by leading journals with the concurrence of the authorities, and held on the public highway.

As a consequence, this kingdom, which seventy years ago, was in the van, is, owing to pitiably short-sighted legislation, now in the rear of this great industry, and we are face to face with the lamentable fact that money is being sent out of this kingdom to purchase motor vehicles made in other countries.

We are, in fact, repeating the same error of over-restrictive legislation which, in respect of electrical enterprise, stifled development in the United Kingdom so completely that the trade here has never been able to overtake the solid organisation which freer conditions enabled manufacturers to rapidly build up in Germany and the United States, where legislation does not blindly precede a new industry, but intelligently follows it.

In October of last year, perhaps the most inactive month in the year in the motor trade, money for the purchase of motor vehicles left this country for France, Germany, and the United States of America, to the value of £45,441, or at the rate of £545,292 per annum.

Being now face to face with the disastrous results of unnecessary legislation, it is imperative that without delay every obstacle to our progress in this industry should be removed, provided that the public safety is properly safeguarded.

First, we claim that the specific speed limit imposed under the Act of 1896 should be removed, and in support of this claim we can quote no stronger words than those of the Rt. Hon. Henry Chaplin, M.P., who, as President of the Local Government Board, introduced the Act of 1896 to the House of Commons, and thus secured some measure of liberty for this great industry. On November 14th last, Mr. Henry Chaplin, while urging that the Government should deal with this question during the present session, and deprecating the use on the roads of this country of motor vehicles capable of running at very high speeds, said:

"I see no reason whatever where there is a clear and open road, and where the other conditions of traffic are carefully observed, why an average speed, say, of twenty to twenty-five miles an hour should not very properly be permitted. Well, if that were so, the present limit of fourteen miles an hour must go. In my humble opinion there is very little object in maintaining it."

The Executive Council of the County Councils' Association have recently passed the following resolution :

"That the general law of the land for all vehicles, as extended by the special regulations issued, requiring the drivers of motor cars to stop on the request of any police constable, or of any person having charge of a restive horse, if scrupulously observed and rigorously enforced, is at present sufficient to secure the public safety, provided" (The Executive Council recommended numbering. We deal with this question later.)

The Executive Council of the County Councils' Association further resolved :

"That it is desirable that the statutory limit of speed be abolished."

It will be seen, therefore, that Mr. Chaplin on the one hand, and the County Councils' Association on the other hand, concur that the existing speed limit should be abolished.

We claim, secondly, that, provided the existing speed limit be abolished, and that only such restrictions are placed on motor vehicles as may be reasonable and proper for the safety of other users of the road, the proviso of the County Councils' Association, viz., "that there should be an easy and complete means of identification," is one to recommend itself to all drivers of motor vehicles, with perhaps the possible exception of cars which are not capable of being driven at any except slow speeds.

Mr. Chaplin, in the speech to which we have referred, also recommended that a system of identification should be enforced.

The Act contains oppressive restrictions for which no rational justification exists in regard to the tare weight and width of another class of vehicles—the motor waggon for carrying heavy goods—the development of which manufacturing industry is not less important than the manufacture of passenger vehicles, in view of the great benefits which heavy motor haulage is able to confer on the inhabitants of districts still unprovided with railways, whose industries are hampered and often destroyed by the prohibitive cost of cartage. The restriction to a tare weight not exceeding three tons is now preventing the manufacture and employment in this country of motor waggons, which would be capable of carrying loads up to ten and twelve tons, and use of which would reduce the cost of motor haulage to about one-third of the cost of horse haulage, thus practically extending the benefits of railway communication to every part of the country. The present Act also comprises useless restrictions on the speed of motor waggons, which prevent the development of the use by farmers and landowners of motor waggons, which would otherwise enable them to send vegetables, fruit, and other perishable goods direct to market without the risk and damage of the double transfer from road to rail and again from rail to road.

For reasons which have become only too apparent to make it necessary to specify them, we are of opinion that automobilists should have a ready form of appeal against decisions arrived at by benches of country magistrates. Such a provision would not be a new departure, as a similar appeal is provided under the Summary Jurisdiction (Married Women) Act, 1895.

We do not propose to enter into details as to what should be the other provision of a new Act dealing with motor vehicles.

We urge, however, upon your readers to secure that their representatives on the county councils and their representatives in the House of Commons should lose no time and spare no effort to induce His Majesty's Government to pass a Bill which would remove without delay the unnecessary and damaging restrictions which at present hamper mechanical traffic in this country, and, by providing for the identification of motor vehicles, prevent the dangerous or inconsiderate driving which is indulged in by a minority of motor drivers, and which has undoubtedly tended, in some instances, to bring the motor movement into disrepute. The Bill might also provide an increase in the penalties for infringement of the law, if at the same time it provided for the ready form of appeal before alluded to.

We are confident that the automobile movement which, in the eyes of many at present is only looked upon as the amusement of a minority, will most assuredly and very shortly become a beneficial factor in the general life of the community. It will afford speedy and cheap transport of agricultural produce from farms to the great centres of population and consumption, it will provide cheap and speedy communication between outlying districts and our great railway systems, and, as was pointed out by the Rt. Hon. Arthur Balfour, M.P., it is likely in the same way to prove an important factor towards the solution of the problem of the housing of the poor.

The letter is signed by the following amongst other members of the General Council of the Automobile Club: The Duke of Sutherland; the Earl of Shrewsbury and Talbot; the Earl of Onslow, G.C.M.G. (Under-Secretary of State for the Colonies); Earl Grey; the Earl of Verulam; the Earl of Wharncliffe; Lord Montagu of Beaulieu; Lord Robert Cecil, K.C.; Lord Brassey, K.C.B.; Lord Llangattock; Lord Saltoun; the Hon. Arthur Stanley, M.P.; Sir Francis Jeune; Sir Bernhard Samuelson, Bart.; G. Shaw-Lefevre (formerly president of the Local Government Board); General Sir Redvers Buller, V.C., G.C.B., K.C.M.G.; the Hon. Humphrey N. Sturt, M.P.; Sir Lewis M'Iver, M.P.; Sir James Pender, Bart., M.P.; Sir Edgar Vincent, M.P.; the presidents of the Automobile Clubs of France, Belgium, Germany, Austria, and Switzerland; Messrs. J. Williams Benn (chairman of the Highways Committee of the London County Council); Mr. A. G. Griffith Boscawen, M.P.; Mr. Charles E. Shaw, M.P.; Earl of Derby (president Liverpool Centre of the Automobile Club); the Rt. Hon. Sir John H. A. Macdonald, K.C.B., LL.D., F.R.S.S. (L. and E.), Lord Justice Clerk of Scotland, president of the Scottish Automobile Club; representatives of the Eastern and Western Sections of the Scottish Automobile Club, the Irish Automobile Club, the Manchester Automobile Club, the Yorkshire Automobile Club, the Lincolnshire Automobile Club, the Midland Automobile Club, and the Nottingham District Automobile Club.

ELECTRICAL VEHICLES.

Mr. James Swinburne took the chair at the house dinner of the Automobile Club held on Wednesday, the 26th February, and at the reading of the paper and discussion which followed.

The paper, which was the chapter on "Electrical Vehicles," intended for the Badminton Library Book on "Motors," was read by Mr. R. Lucas.

After the reading of the paper, a discussion ensued. Mr. Oppermann was doubtful as to the desirability of two motors. Dr. Playfair stated that he was the first man in London who had the electric light in his house, and he had wished to be the first man in London to have an electric carriage, but from enquiries made by him up to the present he had not found an electric carriage which could be purchased and run as cheaply as his landau and a pair of horses. Mr. Joel pointed out the great improvements which had been made in the way of accumulators. During six years the weight had been reduced by two-thirds. Six years ago an accumulator which weighed 66 lbs. now weighed 22 lbs.; six years ago accumulators which would only last one month now last for two years. Accumulators could be procured which could give 6,000 ton-miles, or, say, fifteen miles a day for 300 days. He could obtain estimates from independent sources which showed the actual cost of fuel energy per ton-mile was as follows:

Per petrol car, 1d. to 1½d. per ton-mile.
A steam car, burning petrol, 3d. per ton-mile.
A heavy steam vehicle with coke or other fuel, 3d. per ton-mile.
An electric car, taking the unit as costing 1½d., is 9d. per ton-mile.

Mr. Percy Northey spoke in favour of variable speed gears for electric cars which are required for touring in the country, or which are used in very hilly country. He also spoke in favour of the principle of the drive on the front wheels.

Mr. Leitner spoke in favour of the two-motor system.

Mr Chambers gave an example of his being able to get home by using one motor when the other had failed, and stated that he did not find that the wheels of cars fitted with front drive were apt to skid, except in going up a steep, greasy hill. The weight being then thrown off the front wheels, they were sometimes apt to skid.

Mr. Swinburne called upon Mr. Lucas to reply to the discussion, and Mr. Lucas pointed out that Dr. Playfair had evidently not heard of the arrangement made by the City and Suburban Co., by which they undertake the upkeep, storage, renewal of batteries, and renewal of solid tyres at £186 per annum. He thought that this would be a saving of £100 on the keep of carriage and horses. As regards Mr. Joel's figures, he thought that they were rather unfair on the steam car, inasmuch as he had not taken the steam car using paraffin instead of petrol.

Mr. Swinburne proposed a vote of thanks to Mr. Lucas, which was heartily accorded, and Mr. Phillips proposed a vote of thanks to Mr. Swinburne.

There was a large attendance of members during the reading of the paper and the discussion.

———◆———

Miss Eva Moore, the charming actress, was at one time an ardent cyclist, but recently she has taken to the autocar, and drives her own victoria very expertly.

* * *

An enterprising plan has been arranged by Mr. Wimshurst, of Coventry, who is interested in the sale of Progress cars. He is undertaking a series of tours, of which he announces the route in advance, and makes as many appointments as possible with automobilists and intending automobilists on or near the line of route. A project of this kind was suggested some years ago in connection with the first motor company established in this country, but, so far as we know, it was not taken up, and has never been systematically worked by anyone since.

THE CHICAGO MOTOR SHOW.

This highly-meritorious exhibition of American advance in automobile construction opened on Saturday night, March 1st, and will close to-morrow night, Saturday, March 8th, 1902. Up to Wednesday night the management played in very hard luck so far as gate money goes, owing to two wholly unforeseen contingencies: first the unexpectedly rigorous weather, and second the whirlwind rush of Prince Henry in our midst, which has been such an amazing example of metoric speed of travel, and such a stunning example of how to spend a thousand dollars a minute and never turn an eyelash, that it has been about all the average American could manage to keep track of the doings of this highly acceptable scion of the ruling house of the wooden shoe wearers. Americans like rapid action, and are always vastly delighted when some event of sport or State leads to celerity of movement accompanied by flinging money about in scoop shovelfuls. We did not know whether Prince Henry was a solemn ceremonial prig, or the courteous gentleman of quick sensibilities, ready wit, and wholly republican demeanour he has shown himself to be, but we made up our mind from the first to give him the whirl of his life, and we have done it: we took him as far south as Chatanooga, west to St. Louis, north to Milwaukee, and then east to Boston, where he was yesterday made a LL.D. by Harvard, and we filled about twenty hours out of every twenty-four of Prince Henry's dalliance with star-eyed Columbia, with such a very hurricane of lunches, banquets, and assemblages of all sorts from his ten-thousand-dollar two-hour luncheon at Sherry's with the "captains of industry," to the surging iron-gate crushing crowds of mere common folk which everywhere swarmed in countless hosts to see him, and presentations of city freedoms in gold cases, and elaborate memorial volumes in jewelled covers, and palace trains and operas and so on beyond all possibilities of enumeration, and wound up every day with such a divinely irrigated late supper that had

not Prince Henry been in the prime of life and the pink of condition, as well as wholly immune in respect of Katsenjanner, he would have been laid up for a month of repairs at about the end of the second day; and, as I said before, no real true-blue American has had time for the past week to do much of anything else than keep tab on Prince Henry's comings and goings and doings and sayings,

The Foster steamer. 6 h.p. Engine, boiler, and burner centrally placed, as usual. Centre of gravity lowered about 12in. Wheelbase, 72in.

which last have been in every instance highly creditable to him, prince of royal blood though he be.

Then the weather: the past winter has been the merest pretence to Snow King's rigours, but on the 21st of February he waved his icicle sceptre, and we had two days of snow and blow enough to satisfy a polar bear. This was followed by warm weather again, and on Saturday, March 1st, the New York thermometers climbed to 70°, and the floods came, and the trains all stopped right where they were. We had a sleet storm on February 22nd, which cased all the trees and wires in a glittering crystal armour, and the branches broke off the trees and the wires came tumbling to the ground, poles and all, and the trolley wires killed the horses, twenty-six horses being killed in Flatbush Avenue, Brooklyn, alone. We lost Philadelphia by wire for two days, and on the day the Chicago Show opened the postal telegraph had only fifty Chicago messages in place of the usual five hundred or so. No eastern road, except the Pennsylvania, sent through trains west, on Friday or Saturday. A great lot of folks who had purchased other Chicago transportation, either waited in vain for their trains to go out or, worse still, pulled out into snow drifts or were caught between flood breaks in the railways. The Great New York Central Western through line is not yet in any kind of schedule form. All of this kept everybody away from the Chicago Show, the first grand function of which was to be a convention of all the American Automobile Club magnates, with a view to a governing consolidation. The club delegates

The Stearns petrol car. 10 h.p. Horizontal single cylinder engine. Cylinder 5¾in. by 6¼in. Modified Panhard speed gear. Final drive by central chain to live axle.

were not in Chicago on Saturday or Monday, and it was only on Tuesday that the eight club managers' and delegates' conclave took place, with the result of forming a paramount body, "The American Automobile Association," having for its objects the advancement of automobile interests, and the betterment of common roads in the United States—and Heaven knows our roads need all the improvement they are likely to get. Winthrop E. Scarritt, of the (New York) Automobile Club of America, was elected president of the new organisation, and Jefferson Seligman, S. M. Butler, and A. R. Shattuck, of the same club, were elected treasurer, secretary and director respectively. The other organisations which figure as charter members of the American Automobile Association are the automobile clubs of Chicago, Long Island, Philadelphia, New Jersey, Rhode Island, and Utica.

Wednesday's advices show a fair gate at the Jackson Park Exhibition, with a prospect of sufficient

The Foster 15 h.p. steamer. The engine is placed in front, driving by chain through balance geared countershaft, and then by two outside chains to rear road wheels. The boiler is fixed below the seat and the water and petrol tanks behind it.

New Toledo steam car. 6 h.p. two-cylinder engine. 3½in. pneumatic tyres. 30in wheels. 84in wheelbase. Water tube boiler, 9in. diameter by 18in. high, and fitted with a super-heater. Large water and fuel tanks. Weight, 1,040 lbs.

increase of attendance to bring the promoters out even, or, maybe, with a little to spare. Jackson Park, Chicago, is the old World's Fair ground, many miles from the centre of that windy and highly-perfumed city. Hence, though the show building —known as the "Coliseum"—is very large, and also bare of decoration, except in the way of endless festoons of electric lights, it is not at all easy of access; it is reached, however, by steam surface lines and electric elevated cars, and this service has been, of course, vastly less uncertain than the electric surface trams in the recent cataclysmic tumble of wires and poles. The exhibition building is plenty large enough on the main floor, without touching the vast gallery space, to accommodate all exhibits, and the show has rather a bare appearance. There is none of the usual bunting display, and even the signs of the exhibitors take on a subdued effect. One of the enormous and very objectionable "Locomobile" signs, which so abominably disfigured the last Madison Square Garden Show, fell in process of placing, and killed an unfortunate workman standing beneath it. Such huge affairs

in the way of signs do not aid the makers who put them up, and should not be allowed by any show managers.

The characteristic of this Chicago exhibit is the appearance of a number of new waggons of American type, which are well powered and well finished, but of comparatively low price. Of these, T. B. Jeffery and Co., of Kenosha, Wis., show a very attractive example in a new Rambler, with a long wheelbase, at $750, and report the booking of no less than ninety-six orders in the two days this smart vehicle has been on view. I fully and certainly expected the appearance of really serviceable waggons at about this price, as I wrote of the distinctly French types of high-powered machines shown at the last garden show—these high-priced waggons do not meet American requirements—but I confess surprise at the considerable number of waggons by different makers, all looking to the same general end of producing a light-weight, low-priced, well-proportioned, and amply-powered vehicle really suitable for general road work. These waggons are not racers, though they have all the speed that is permissible on common roads, and they must be regarded as the skirmish line of what are to become the grand masses of the automobile

Buffalo petrol car. 6 h.p. single-cylinder engine under seat. Transmission by central chain to live axle. Change speed gear—Crypto on engine shaft. Inlet as well as exhaust valves mechanically operated. Weight, 740 lbs.

army which is soon to really invade the territory now held by the horse, and wage a warfare of extermination against the noble road-destroying and filth-compelling equine.

The Chicago list of exhibits is quite large, and some of the vehicles show decided novelty of outline, the International Motor Car Co. leading in this direction with no less than three distinctly original creations of different classes. Taken at large, the show very clearly marks a decided tendency to abandon French models and take up the production of thoroughly useful and satisfactory light-weight and low-priced waggons in earnest. The use of two long side springs, "Oldsmobile" fashion, reaching from axle to axle, seems to be meeting with favour, as several thus sprung waggons are shown. Another novelty is a waggon fitted with a "sprag," the first American example, I think.

There are no track exhibits in the Jackson Park Show. Waggons in motion have to be shown outside, and on roads which are not of the best.

The curio and antique loan exhibit feature does not appear, only one "relic," a steam tricycle, 1888, built by Edwin F. Brown, now V.P. of the Chicago Automobile Club, being shown.

I give no list of exhibitors, but shall specify one or two of the more notable exhibits, which are not mere

single constructions, but articles in manufacture, ready for immediate delivery. Two of these vehicles have friction drives. There will probably be builders of perpetual motions, rotary steam engines, and friction and ratchet motor waggon drives down to the

The Rambler. Single cylinder engine, centrally placed. Crypto gear, central drive to live back axle. The petrol is pumped to the carburetter.

end of time. That all of these moon-struck fabrics are fore-doomed to failure, and have all been tried out and thrown away, not by one, but by many, wild-eyed inventors who rose superior to the inexorable laws of applied mechanics, will have no deterrent effect on the waggon maker who becomes fascinated with the easy simplicity of the friction disc drive, and it is quite useless to call the attention of the friction-bug bitten one to the fact that all friction drives have an indeterminate pitch line, and hence must soon be destroyed in work. Nothing but bitter-ending experience will teach inventors of this class that machine part performance is always a certainty, and always ruinous if it transgresses well-known laws.

Perhaps the greatest innovation in the show is the Caloric motor carriage, of the Chicago Moto-cycle Co., Chicago. It is driven by what is described as a Caloric oil engine or hot air gas engine. It burns either kerosene or gasolene, and has neither carburetting nor electric or other ignition systems. No water is used for cooling purposes, the heat being all utilised and converted into power, an asbestos jacket to retain the

heat being used instead of a water jacket for getting rid of it. Its makers state that a new principle has been evolved in this engine. Working as a hot air engine, heat is applied to the bottom of cylinders, air is taken in and compressed in the cool upper end of cylinder, then transferred to the heated end, where it expands and forces the piston outward. The hot air is then expelled from the heated end; at the same time another cold charge is taken in at the upper cold end of the cylinder, and the operation is repeated, giving an impulse every revolution (or making a two-cycle engine). This makes the engine positive starting, as it does not depend on a proper mixture of air and gas as do all other engines. To increase the power gas is admitted with the air, according to the amount of power desired. If more gas is admitted than will unite with the oxygen it is wasted, but will not choke the engine. The engine will run without any gas internally, and so much gas cannot be used that it will not run. The vehicle in which this engine is incorporated does not differ materially from many types of runabouts. It is low, has a long wheel-base, wood wheels, solid rear axle, three speeds forward and one reverse, and three brakes. The engine is started from the seat. I hope to be able soon to present the readers of *The Autocar* with a more extended and more fully illustrated description of this motor. Full information is not now at hand.

I desire to present acknowledgments and thanks

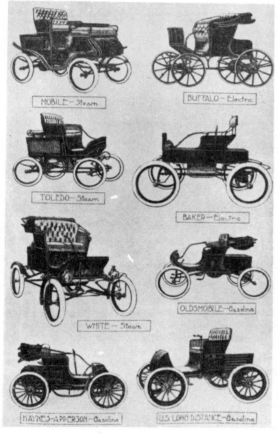

to the editors of the *Motor World* and the *Motor Review*, of New York, to whom I am indebted for generous assistance in the preparation of this notice of the Chicago Show, which is, taken all in all, the most satisfactory evidence of real advance in motor-waggon construction yet given in the United States.

New York, March 7th.   HUGH DOLNAR.

A new 8 h.p. Hozier light car, with double phaeton body.

THE CLUB QUARTERLY 100 MILES TRIAL.

The Automobile Club's quarterly 100 miles trial took place on Tuesday, the 25th inst., over the usual course on the Oxford Road. Six cars were entered, and five started, the results being as follow:

The 5 h.p. Peugeot, carrying two passengers, driven by Mr. A. Farrell, with Doctor Wyeth acting as official observer, made a non-stop run, consuming 3⅝ gallons of petrol and 2 pints of water. The passengers both alighted for last thirty yards of Dashwood Hill, which was climbed in 5m 14s., Aston Hill taking 9m 44s. The car was entered by Messrs. Friswell.

The 4 h.p. Rochet, entered by the British and Foreign Motor Co., of Liverpool, carrying three passengers (driver, Mr. T. Tridsch; observer, Mr. O. Gorman), accomplished the trip successfully with four stops, aggregating 10½m., due to leaky lubricator and brake detachment. It consumed 2¾ gallons of petrol and 5½ pints of water. Half-way up Dashwood, which was climbed in 5m. 22s., one passenger alighted, but the car climbed Aston well in 11m. 35s.

The 14 h.p. Deschamps stopped for 10m. on the outward journey to adjust clutch. It climbed Dashwood in 3m. 51s., and Aston in 5m. 58s. The driver accidentally stopped his engine in turning at the fifty-second milestone. It consumed 5 gallons and 1 pint of petrol. Driver, Mr. R. S. Elliott; observer, Mr. E. D. Wilton, four passengers being carried.

The 12 h.p. Gladiator made a non-stop absolute run. Driver, Mr. A. E. Perman; observer, Mr. Phil Paddon. It carried four passengers, and climbed Dashwood in 3m. 15s., and Aston in 6m. It consumed 4 gallons and 4 4-5 pints of petrol and ½ gallon of water.

The White steam car (driver, Mr. W. C. White; observer, Captain Lloyd, R.E.) started, and was reported met on outward journey by returning cars, but it had not turned up when our report left. The roads were heavy and bad as far as Beaconsfield, particularly between Gerrard's Cross and Beaconsfield, but were good afterwards. Dashwood Hill was in fair condition, and Aston very good. A gale of wind blew against the cars on the outward journey.

A company is likely to be formed in Burton for the sale of motor cars. We understand that some of the heads of the firm of Messrs. Bass and Co. are interesting themselves in the project.

* * *

"Provided the public safety is sufficiently guarded, automobilists may fairly claim to be delivered from all vexatious hindrances." This is a fair sample of general press views on the recent Automobile Club awakening.

* * *

The automobile postal mails have given such satisfaction in Paris that the horse-drawn mail carts are to be entirely superseded, while motor mails are to be introduced into the more important provincial towns, such as Marseilles, Lyons, Lille, Bordeaux, etc.

THE SIMMS MOTOR WAR CAR.

Russell and Sons, Photos.   *Crystal Palace, S.E.*

A full load for a trial trip.

This war automobile, of which whispers have been heard for some time past, was on Friday last revealed to a gathering of experts and press representatives on the terrace at the Crystal Palace. As will be seen from the illustrations, this armour-clad of the highway somewhat resembles in appearance a huge smooth-sided armadillo endowed with strange shaped horns in the guise of three pom-poms and a Maxim. This car has been designed and built to the order of Messrs. Vickers, Son, and Maxim, Ltd., for coast and road defence, after a number of separate designs had been made for the purpose by Mr. Fred. R. Simms. It is rightly considered that such war cars as these would prove particularly useful for defence against landings in this country, as there are few points on our coast which are far removed from good, or sufficiently good, roads, upon which the car could move with celerity to beat back the foe. It would also prove of great use in keeping open lines of communication, for hauling guns into position, or for searchlight operations. In the case of street riots, the appearance of this moving fort, furnished with arms capable of mowing down men by the hundred, would undoubtedly

exert a tranquillising effect. Moving along the roads which run coastwise of this country, the war car would offer a very small mark to the enemy's covering ships of war, and ample cover for it could be easily and cheaply provided at all points along its appointed patrol where landings might be attempted. It possesses at once great mobility and great range of action, as it has storage capacity for petrol or heavy oil to carry it no less than five hundred miles.

The rectangular frame is constructed of heavy U-section steel channel, and special attention has been given to the combination of the greatest strength with the minimum of weight. The frame is constructed to support a maximum load of twelve tons, while the tare will never exceed six tons. The frame runs 17ft. × 6ft. 2in. over all.

The motor—a 16 h.p. four-cylindered Daimler type of engine—fitted with Simms-Bosch magneto ignition and timing gear, and the speed gear, are carried on a special frame, mounted longitudinally on the car frame. This special frame is formed of Mannesman steel tubes, and strongly attached to the main frame by brackets and stays. The cylinders are each of 90 mm. bore, and the engine has a stroke of 130 mm., is governed by a centrifugal governor taking effect on the exhaust valves, and has compression of 60 lbs. per square inch. As in the Milnes oil war lorry, which ran in the War Office trials at Aldershot, the engine will run with either petrol or heavy oil. The cooling of the engine is obtained by means of what is now well known as the Cannstatt cooler, with inducing fan rotated by

Mr. F. R. Simms at the prow of his war car.

gear off the engineshaft. The engine and gear are set low down in the centre of the car, which is decked nearly all over some 2ft. 6in. below the top edge of the armour skirt.

The change speed gear, which is of the usual Cannstatt type, affords four definite speeds, viz., one and a half, three, five, and nine miles per hour with the engine running at 750 revolutions per minute. With the exception that there is one lever to each pair of speeds, and a reversing lever, the war

car is driven and steered by wheel and worm steering just as an ordinary road car, and with similar ease. The transmission of the drive from the gear is by countershaft and Brampton chains to road wheels in the ordinary way.

Ample brake power is supplied. A pedal actuated brake clutch takes effect on the first gear wheel shaft. A hand wheel just operates two powerful band brakes on the hubs of the driving wheels, and when these are applied the further rotation of the wheel applies two most effective tyre brakes on

The flexible ladder thrown over the side for mounting.

the driving wheels. It is claimed that when travelling on the top notch the car can be brought to rest within eight yards.

The main frame is carried on semi-elliptical springs at the rear, the frame and springs being outside the driving wheels, and by spiral springs on the steering axle, which are contained in horn plates. The wheels have wooden spokes and felloes built up on cast steel naves and steel tyres. The tyres of the driving wheels are provided with cross plates, and those of the steering wheels with annular rims of less width than the tread to afford easy starting on hard ground. The driving wheels are 4ft diameter and 6in. in width, and the steering wheels

The Simms machine in motion, and with guns in action.

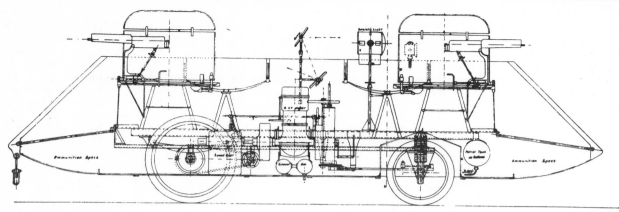

Elevation.

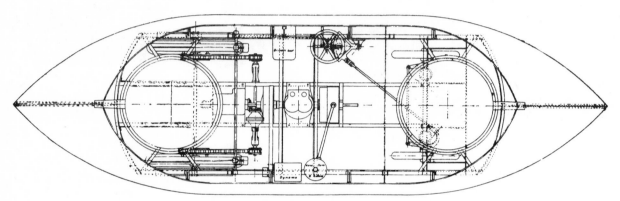

Plan.

3ft. diameter and 3½in. in width. Although not demonstrated on the afternoon of the 4th inst. owing to the soft nature of the Palace road surfaces, it is claimed that this war car will climb a gradient of one in seven and a half with a full load.

As can be seen from the illustrations we give, the armour skirt, which is of 6 mm. Vickers steel, and quite impervious to small arms (0.303) and projectiles, completely encircles the car frame. It is of crinoline shape and flattened longitudinally, but is provided with a ram fore and aft set at an angle of about 45°. The length over all is 28ft., beam 8ft., and height of top side of skirt 10ft. from the ground. The bottom edge of the armoured skirt is 18in. above the road level. Originally the skirt was fixed rigidly to the tubular frame, but it having been found that the road vibration shook the rivets loose, the skirt, as seen, is hung on semi-elliptical springs, which themselves are mounted on steel trestles braced and stayed to the main frame. The swinging action thus afforded the skirt has been found to increase its impenetrability. Distance links are provided to prevent excessive lateral movement. In the ends of the skirt provision is made for the storage of ammunition, and, if necessary, the road wheels can be protected by curtains of chain mail.

On the 4th inst. the war car was equipped with two pom-poms and one quick-firing Maxim on proper gun mountings, and these guns can either be placed in turrets or provided with the usual shields. If desired, however, a six-pounder could be mounted on this car. Over 10,000 rounds of ammunition can be carried, and the car can be adequately manned by four men, although it has deck space for over three times that number. Mr. Simms caused the car to be driven up and down the terrace with a full complement on board each trip, whereby its handiness was demonstrated to a keenly interested crowd. To give the whole thing an aspect of verisimilitude, Mr. Simms from time to time fired a few rounds from the Maxim. The press—both lay and technical—was largely represented, but, although ample notice had been given, no one was present from

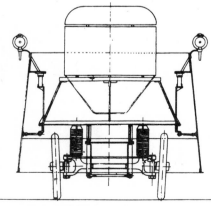

Front elevation.

the War Office. We were informed before the trial by Mr. Simms that a W.O. committee meeting precluded the attendance of the usual military officials. Doubtless they were most intensely employed in the alteration of a button die or in the design of some fresh form of dustman's cap, wherewith to further disfigure the Guards and alienate the nursemaid's heart. Such important matters must not be put aside for the consideration of such an airy and insignificant trifle as Simms's motor war car. We only hope the War Department will give proper attention to this important matter, and not leave it for foreign nations to take it up first, as was the case with the bicycle, and still is more or less with the motor car.

A NIGHT DRIVING CLOCK.

Among the many handy and clever accessories which Mr. Waterson has introduced for the benefit of automobilists, there is nothing which strikes us as more likely to meet with general approval than his new combined motor car clock and electric lamp. The outward appearance of the combination is plainly shown in the illustration, but it is impossible by this means to give a fair idea of the illuminating of the clock face. This is effected by a small electric lamp in the case above the clock, and the light is thrown right on its face in much

the same way as the lights are projected on to large public clocks. The clock face is lit up instantly by a button push, which, of course, can be actuated from any part of the car by means of a thin flexible cable. The battery, lamp, and clock are all contained in the one case, which is 10½in. by 4½in. by 2¾in., and the total weight of case, lamp, battery, clock, duplex wires, and switch is under 5 lbs. The capacity of the battery is ten thousand two-second flashes—more than sufficient for one year's use in night driving. The case is absolutely waterproof, and the four-cell battery can be moved from the case without disturbing the clock, while the clock can be wound or taken out of the case without disconnection of or interference with any other parts. No electrical knowledge is required to replace either battery or lamp. Apart from its great usefulness, there is quite a cheery fascination when one sees the clock face illuminated on a dark night, and it is one of those things which can be appreciated by all who have gone through violent contortions in endeavouring to get their watch into a ray of light from the side lamps, or who have vainly struck matches to see the time by the dashboard clock, and we have no doubt it will come into very wide use.

A service of autocars recently started running from the Obelisk at Lewisham to the village of Southend, on the Bromley Road, at a fare of threepence.

A COMBINED BALL AND ROLLER BEARING.

The section we are able to give shows a combination bearing which has been brought out by Mr. J. R. Churchill, 115a, Queen Victoria Street, E.C. At one end of the hub—the inner end—a set of rollers in a cage is placed, and these receive nearly all the dead weight on the wheel. The balls at the outer end bear very little of the dead load, their function being to take the side stresses or thrusts coming on the wheel when in actual use. It is claimed that by their joint action the two bearings

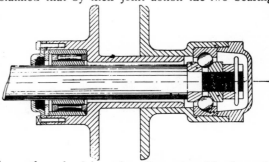

keep the wheel in strict alignment with the axle. In the case of rear wheels for side chain drives the roller bearing is placed so as to take direct the full pull of the chain on the sprocket, as well as the dead weight on the wheel itself. The section shows a rear hub. Front hubs are very similar, but the rollers, instead of being placed inside the spoke line, are placed directly under it. It will be observed that any side play in the bearing can be taken up in the usual manner by adjusting the ball bearing cone on the axle. We understand that several leading firms have decided to use these hubs. We may add that a patent for the device is pending.

The Vicar of Barlaston, near Stone, Staffs, had an interesting experience last week in running down two poachers on his motor car.

* * *

To-day the Motor Cycling Club, recently formed, will hold its opening run, the objective of which will be Brighton, and to join in with which all motor cyclists are cordially invited. The gathering points are Hyde Park Corner at 2.30 p.m., and Station Hotel, Purley Corner, 3.30 p.m. Start punctually half an hour later. Tea at Crawley at 5 p.m., and dinner at Gloucester Hotel, Brighton, 8.15. Tickets 4s. Ladies are invited.

* * *

What appears to be a good design of sparking plug has been sent us by Messrs. J. C. Meredith, Ltd. The porcelain is in two parts, which, it is stated, allows for expansion and prevents breakage from over-heating. Moreover, the top half of the porcelain is held to its seat by a spiral spring, so that there is an appreciable give in the fitting, and as the spring encircles the central wire running through the insulators, a certain amount of lateral flexibility is given. Consequently, there is very little fear of the porcelains being broken by the mere strain of the high-tension wire. This, particularly if it should be a little short, puts a very hard pull on the plug at times.

THE AUTOMOBILE MEETING AT NICE.

Baron Zuylen's big nine-seated touring Panhard decorated for the "Battle of Flowers."

The automobile meeting at Nice promised to be of an exceptionally interesting character, with the engrafting upon the usual programme of the Nice-Abbazia-Nice race and the trial of heavy industrial vehicles from Paris to Monte Carlo, and though the great race was, unfortunately, prohibited at the last moment, the meeting was nevertheless entirely successful, and visitors had plenty to interest them in the many new cars that foregathered in view of the speed events.   To begin with, the trial of industrial vehicles may be regarded as by no means the least important part of the programme, if we consider the influence which this type of car may have on automobilism generally.   It is clear that as soon as the public become impressed with the value of the autocar as a commercial vehicle, and see that its utility extends far beyond the pleasure carriage, the automobile will occupy a much higher plane even than it does at present, in the sense that it will become universal.   So far, it must be confessed that the commercial autocar has received far less attention in France than it deserves, probably because there have been wanting definite data as to the economy and durability of the vehicles.   The trials held from time to time have certainly been valuable, but the results on the whole have not been sufficiently conclusive, and they have not always been carried out over a long enough period.   There could, of course, be no longer any question as to the economy of mechanical traction over horse haulage, both in time and working cost, but it was doubted whether the vehicles would be able to run regularly for any length of time without giving rise to trouble and probably serious breakdowns.   In organising his trials from Paris to Monte Carlo, M. Paul Meyan, director of the *France Automobile*, aimed at proving the reliability of heavy cars by running them with full loads under the most arduous conditions an average of sixty miles for twelve consecutive days.   At first, it was supposed that the test was much too severe, and that the failure of the vehicles to get through such a long run would do more harm to the industry than good, but as events showed the industrial cars did even more than was expected of them, and at the end, indeed, seemed capable of continuing the journeys indefinitely.   The trials were not only a great success, as proving the economy and trustworthiness of the vehicles, but the long run through France must have done a vast amount of good in awakening interest in mechanical locomotion, and it is to be hoped that it will have the effect of giving a renewed stimulus to this branch of the automobile industry.

We accompanied the industrial cars from Paris right down to Nice, and propose in another issue to give a full account of them and their performances.   It will suffice to say now that all but four accomplished the trying journey of over seven hundred miles most successfully.

The Nice-Abbazia Race.

On reaching Nice we found the world of automobilism that centres around the Automobile Club was in a turmoil of excitement over the prohibition of the race to Abbazia and back.   This was to have been the big event of the week, and promised indeed to be the most interesting of the year.   The makers had been preparing for it by building special cars, and Panhard, Serpollet, Mercedes, Darracq, Decauville, and others had all sent down a large number of vehicles, while they had gone to enormous additional expense in making preparations along the route through Italy—storing petrol and tyres, and carrying out arrangements for repairing cars on the road. The blow was the more serious in that it was so sudden and unexpected. The Automobile Club de Nice had received official sanction from the Italian Minister of Public Works, and there did not seem to be the slightest doubt that the race would be run off. Then, a few days before the event, it was announced that the race had been suppressed between Coni and Turin on account of the roads being encumbered with cattle on the occasion of the market in the former town, and finally the interdiction extended to the entire course. Other explanations were that the road was too dangerous, and that the Minister of Public Works had no authority to sanction the race. But at Nice it was stated that the real reason of the prohibition was the conduct of drivers of certain competing cars —not English or French—who raced over the course and caused several accidents, one of them ending fatally. The populations were so alarmed that the Government was obliged to interfere. We merely repeat this rumour for what it may be worth. This, however, can be no excuse for withdrawing a sanction for a race which was to have been run off with every possible guarantee for the safety of the public. As the Italian authorities had promised to keep the course clear, and the populous centres were to be neutralised, the incidents referred to could not have changed the nature of the race, and it was obviously an extremely arbitrary proceeding to suppress it at the last moment, and thus involve the autocar industry in a loss that can scarcely be estimated.

Feeling was very bitter against the Italian Government, not because it compromised the success of the Nice meeting—for that was a comparatively small matter—but because it threatened to strike a blow at racing generally, and consequently at the industry, for the influence of the one on the other is considerable, as was evident from the progress observable in the cars specially built for the Nice meeting. It is feared that the action of the Italian Government may have disastrous consequences for the Paris-Vienna race, and the Cannstatt people consider prospects so doubtful that they have decided not to proceed with the new cars being constructed for that event, though it is true that after the fine performances of the Mercedes at Nice it scarcely seems as if a new type of racing vehicle were necessary.

The New Cars.

It is to the Cannstatt works that we have to look at the moment for the most remarkable advance in autocar engineering. During the past three years the Mercedes car has been improved to such an extent that nothing but admiration can be felt for the splendid new vehicles which made their first appearance in view of the Abbazia race. The first thing that strikes one is their wonderfully quiet running. When the vehicle is standing, a rapid rhythmical beat is only just audible, scarcely more than a low hum, and there is absolutely no vibration. It is generally supposed that the motor is then turning at not more than 150 revolutions a minute, but Herr Daimler assured us that it was still running at 500 revolutions, and one explanation of this quietness is the method of synchronising, as it were, the exhaust with the admission, both of which are operated mechanically, and in this way, at whatever rate the motor may be running, the exhaust

Degrais upon one of the new 40 h.p. Mercedes-Simplex racers, which did fastest (petrol) time for the flying kilo.

is always rapidly cleared at the precise moment the charge is being drawn in. The motor is regulated by the well-known Mercedes tubular regulator, with ports, forming part of the carburetter, and the running of the engine can be varied instantly from 500 to 1,200 revolutions by means of a small lever on the dashboard moving on a toothed sector. The four cylinders are in a line, and the motor develops 40 nominal h.p. On some of the cars magneto ignition is employed, and on others a small dynamo is fitted, similar to the well-known form of American "self-sparker," and with both systems great facility has been obtained in retarding and advancing ignition. The petrol is carried in a cylindrical tank under the back of the car, and being at a lower level than the motor, it seems as if the spirit is brought to the carburetter under a certain pressure, but we were unable to understand from the German mechanics precisely in what way this is done. In some of the cars the ventilator behind the tubular water tank forming the front of the bonnet has been done away with, as it is found that the fly-wheel is quite sufficient to create a draught through the

Lemaitre, and H. Degrais; and we were surprised to see the large number of Mercedes cars at Nice belonging to private owners, many of them having apparently come from Marseilles. All the racing cars naturally had to come within the 1,000 kilogs. limit, and two of the Mercedes-Simplex weighed exactly 999 kilogs., which implies an extremely close calculation. The cars were weighed stripped of absolutely everything, and we believe that an allowance was made even for the magnetos, as the accumulators were also taken out of the cars when weighing.

M. Serpollet was terribly disappointed over the prohibition of the Nice-Abbazia race. He had specially prepared eight vehicles for this event—three of 12 h.p. and five of 6 h.p.—and he says that he had counted very much on the race to show the regularity of his cars. He apparently did not expect to beat the big petrol cars in point of speed, but he certainly hoped to run more regularly, and was confident of being able to show up well at the finish. His cars were fitted with a tubular condenser in front with thin metallic gills of the usual

Mr. Louis Barrow's Mercedes-Lohner on the left, and M. Porsche's on the right.

tubes, especially in cars which are propelled at a high rate of speed. The weight of the motor is said to be only 407 lbs. Owing to the great elasticity of the engine, it is rarely necessary to use the change speed gear, and the vehicle can be slowed down to a crawl with the highest gear in mesh, while speeds can be changed with perfect ease and silence without throwing out the motor. The underframe is built of channel section steel, tapering away in front with a long extension, so that the front axle is brought forward underneath the end of the frame. The wheelbase is exactly eight feet. All the moving parts run on ball bearings in oil, and the vehicle can be pushed forward with only a slight effort. Every part is made of the best material, the steel for the underframe being supplied by Krupp, of Essen, and the wheels and springs are made by leading French firms. It is difficult to imagine how elasticity of engine power and economy of effort can be brought to a higher stage of development in an autocar, but it is nevertheless certain that finality has not yet been reached, and we may now confidently look to the time when the petrol car will become as quiet and docile as the electric vehicle. There were four Mercedes-Simplex racing cars, driven by Messrs. E. Stead, W. Werner, A.

type, and M. Serpollet stated that he could run 370 miles without taking in water, which would have allowed of his covering each stage in the race without stopping. For the short events, such as the La Turbie climb and the mile competition, the condenser was suppressed, and the exhaust was allowed to escape freely. The cars were fitted with the new self-starter, and were in every way identical with the cars we recently described. M. Serpollet, however, had a novel form of racing body in the shape of a shoe which, while serving as an admirable windcutter, afforded plenty of protection to the driver.

One of the novelties at Nice was the light carriage of Turcat-Méry, of Marseilles. The firm have for years been engaged in the construction of autocars, but they have recently struck out in a new line, and are building vehicles in which they have sought to combine the advantages of the Mercedes and Panhard mechanisms at the same time that they strive after the greatest possible simplicity. The three cars they sent to Nice for the Abbazia race are really splendid vehicles. They have a very close resemblance to the Mercedes, with the same form of body and the same tubular tank. The four cylinders are in line, and the carburetter, with regulator, is of the Mercedes type. The wheelbase is

7½ft., and the car weighs a little more than 12 cwts. We were informed that the car has been timed to run at the rate of fifty-two to fifty-five miles an hour on good level roads. It is certainly very fast, and we were given an opportunity of trying the vehicle by a run through Nice and down the sea front, when the motor showed a great elasticity, and the speeds were changed promptly with perfect ease. It was only during a few seconds that the way was sufficiently clear to allow of the car being sent along at top speed, but we could easily believe that the vehicle was quite as fast as the makers made claim for it. Had the race been held, the Turcat-Méry cars would undoubtedly have shown up well, barring accidents, in the light carriage class. We learn that one of these cars has been disposed of to Mr. Guinness, the famous brewer, of Dublin, and that other British automobilists have purchased vehicles of this make.

Prepared for the Corso fleurie.

A great deal of curiosity had been manifested in the new mixed type of vehicle which was being constructed for the Nice meeting by Messrs. Lohner and Porsche, of Vienna. Prince Lubecki was looking after the interests of these cars, one of which was owned by Mr. Lorraine Barrow, of Biarritz, and the other was driven by Herr Porsche. Its proper designation is a Mercedes-Lohner, and it is, in fact, merely a 28 h.p. Mercedes car with electrical transmission. On the clutchshaft is a dynamo, which only runs when the petrol motor is put in gear, and the electrical energy thus developed is conveyed directly to the motors on the front wheels. Resistances are interposed between the dynamo and the motors to get fifteen different speeds. There was no battery in the cars at Nice, but we believe that in some of the vehicles a small battery is used to start the petrol motor, though apparently this was suppressed in the racing cars for the sake of weight. The theory of this system is, of course, that electrical transmission is much more economical than mechanical transmissions, and that nearly the whole of the power developed by the petrol motor is utilised on the front driving wheels. At the same time, it is clear that in practice there

must be a certain loss, not only in the dynamo, but also in the two electric motors, and it remains to be seen whether it is appreciably less than in the mechanical transmissions, which have been so considerably improved as to be far less wasteful of power than formerly. At the same time, there remains the old objection, that the owner must not only be thoroughly acquainted with his petrol motor, but must also be an electrician as well. However, the value of the system can only be proved by its

The Concours d Elegance at Monte Carlo.

performances, and, unfortunately, the suppression of the race prevented us from seeing what it was capable of doing. There is no doubt that the car is extremely quiet, and runs with every possible variation of speed without gearing of any kind.

M. Jenatzy went to Nice with a new racing car fitted with the huge engine which he had on his petrol-electric vehicle. The motor is rated at 40 h.p., but it is believed to develop fifty per cent. more. The four cylinders are very high and big, and

A graceful quartette in the Concours d'Elegance.

look powerful enough to propel the car at fantastical speeds. The transmission is by shaft to the differential on the rear axle. Charron, Girardot, et Voigt sent down the first car they had turned out of their new works, and it was driven in the Nice events by M. Etienne Giraud. As is well known, this vehicle is propelled by a four-cylinder motor, and the propelling mechanism has many new practical devices which assist in increasing the efficiency and reliability of the car. For this firm also the suppression of the race is a serious matter, as they were very anxious to take advantage of this opportunity to show the speed and reliability of their vehicles. Three Italian makers had entered cars for the race —Messrs. Fiat, Rondine, and Lanza—but, owing probably to the race being prohibited, they did not turn up at Nice.

The Tourists' Caravan.

While M. Paul Meyan was carrying out his very interesting and successful trial of heavy cars, another event was being run off under the direction of M. Georges Prade, of the *Auto-Vélo*—that is to say, a caravan of tourists from Paris to Nice. There were about forty vehicles starting from Paris, and for the first half of the journey they seemed to be no better favoured than the industrial cars, and it was partly on account of the inundations that so many tourists failed to get through the journey. There were several accidents, chiefly caused by cars running off the water-logged roads, and Madame Gobron was one of the victims, though, fortunately, none of them had serious consequences. Some of the daily runs of about 125 miles also encouraged the tourists to indulge in fast driving, which had

Floral decorations. The two ladies on the front seat are not visible from the point of view from which the photograph was taken, as they are completely enshrined in their floral bower

the effect of still further diminishing the number of vehicles. The dropping of so many tourists out of the caravan does not seem to have been due so much to mechanical failures to the unsatisfactory conditions of the run, chiefly meteorological, and only fourteen succeeded in reaching Nice. During the journey the cars were tested over a kilom. course, and some of the performances were rather astonishing, though the satisfaction of competitors at beating record times was somewhat minimised when it was found that one of the timekeepers had lost his head and got the results mixed up in curious confusion. With the arrival of the tourists' caravan, and the immigration of autocars from all the automobile centres of the south, Nice was alive with mechanical vehicles, and on approaching the town there was quite a stream of automobile traffic, with only a rare horse-drawn vehicle, looking entirely out of place in its new surroundings. Outside the carage

of the A.C. of Nice autocars were coming and going, small touring cars fraternising with powerful racers, whose potentialities were still to remain a mystery. Along the sea front cars were being driven at high speed, and, rounding the avenue, were brought up suddenly in front of the carage. A modest-looking gentleman on board then inscribed something on a card and inspected the certificate of the driver. This was the official engineer, who was trying the brakes, and seeing that the drivers were in possession of their necessary permits. Automobilists were there from all the countries of Europe, as well as from America. For the moment Nice was the hub of the automobile universe.

The Corso Automobile.

On Sunday took place the Corso Automobile *fleuri*, or battle of flowers, on the Place de Masséna, where no car could gain admittance unless it was decorated. The severe outlines of the cars were softened down by floral adornments, and some of the vehicles were extremely pretty, while the decorations of others were of a distinctly humorous character. Here was a rear-driven Peugeot made up as a road roller symbolical of the A.C.N., whose "speciality was to smooth away little difficulties and inconveniences," but, unfortunately, it was powerless to overcome the very big difficulty of the Nice-Abbazia prohibition. Then followed a De Dion voiturette, with harp in front, and adorned with white and blue flowers, and a war car in white marguerites with guns pointing fore and aft. M. Paul Chauchard's orange-coloured Panhard was much liked for its unpretentious decoration of orange trees, and Baron de Zuylen's big Panhard brake was also a prominent feature. The No. 3 De Dietrich omnibus was decked out in roses and marguerites with palm trees on the top, while, as a contrast, was a smart Kriéger electric carriage with a fan of pale roses at the back. Several of the cars were sufficiently adorned with feminine grace, which was perhaps unnecessarily hidden by the flowers. After the distribution of banners the battle waged furiously with the gaiety for which Nice is famous, and the promenade in front of the stands was soon lying a foot deep in flowers.

The La Turbie Hill Climb.

At an early hour on Monday morning the industrial cars left the carage for Monte Carlo by way of La Turbie gradient, where we were to halt to see the hill-climbing competition. The famous mountain begins on the outskirts of Nice, and rises to the village of La Turbie for a distance of 9.6 miles. It had been arranged that the cars should go up in procession, but the line was soon broken, as the Daimler lorry pushed steadily forward, and seemed to make light work of the gradient. The Panhard omnibus was also going ahead, followed by the Peugeot berline, and then came the De Dietrich omnibus and the De Dietrich lorry, with an enormous case carefully covered up with a tarpaulin.

It is true that the case was empty, but it looked well on the lorry climbing up the mountain road. As the trial had terminated, all the cars now ran without load, except the omnibuses with passengers. On the whole, the La Turbie climb is not so hard as the Esterel gradient, owing to the road being better graded, but the turnings are, nevertheless, extremely sharp, and very dangerous for cars going at full speed. For only about half the distance does the road rise about eleven per cent., though here and there the incline is very severe, and then for the rest of the way the road grades up slightly to La Turbie. After such gloriously fine weather it was with some little misgiving that we saw the top of the mountain wrapped in clouds, and very soon the cars were running in a fog, which increased in density until we arrived at La Turbie, when we could scarcely see twenty yards ahead. Like all the other vehicles, the Gillet-Forest van got to the top without any difficulty, and reached La Turbie in about two hours from the start, including a couple of halts by the way to bring all the cars together. La

five seconds better than that of Werner. After this it was with considerable uneasiness that we watched for the arrival of the succeeding cars. H. Degrais, on another Mercedes-Simplex, took more than nineteen minutes, but Mr. E. Stead, on the same type of vehicle, accomplished the best time of the day by covering the course in 16m. 37s., though he declared that he would never risk his life under such conditions again. At one moment a wheel actually left the road, and hung over the precipice, and it was only by a sudden turn of the steering wheel that a catastrophe was avoided. The Serpollets flew past the control with the flames roaring out of the top of the boiler, the best time for the steamers being 19m. 16s. Then the Jenatzy, driven by Baron de Caters, came up powerfully in 22m. 23s., but the motor was evidently not running well, for Jenatzy spent a long time overhauling it. Osmont, on an 8 h.p. De Dion tricycle, got to the top in 18m., with his hand cut where it had grazed the rocks at a turning. Five Darracqs finished well, doing from 16m. 50s. to 18m. 36s. The Decauvilles took from

Werner climbing La Turbie on his Mercedes-Simplex.

Turbie appears to be a favourite summer resort for the inhabitants of Nice and Monaco, but for the moment it was depressing in the extreme with the fog rapidly gaining in thickness. Seeing that it was highly dangerous to run off the competition the officials had telephoned to the club at Nice to postpone the start, but for some reason or another the warning was not heeded, for about seven minutes past nine the bugles began sounding down the hill, and a vehicle loomed out of the fog, and, after rapidly passing, disappeared again with the rasping of brakes. It was Werner on a Mercedes-Simplex, who had taken 18m. 30s., or about two minutes more than the time in which he won the race last year. After a short interval, another Mercedes-Simplex car came out of the fog, driven by M. Lemaitre, and accompanied by his young wife, who shares all the dangers through which her husband may be running, and there is no doubt that the race up La Turbie in the fog was extremely dangerous. M. Lemaitre declared that he had to finish on the second speed. Nevertheless, his time was 20m. to 29m. The times of other cars were as

follows: Cottereau, 25m. 41s.; Gladiator, 27m. 59s.; Renault, 40m. 52s.; Lorraine Barrow on a Mercedes-Lohner, 19m. 20s.; Howard Johnson on a Mors, 32m. 22s.; Charron Girardot et Voigt, 27m. 20s.; Count Zborowski on a Daimler, 25m. 21s.; and a Clément motor bicycle, 22m. 24s. It can easily be imagined that none of the competitors were satisfied with the conditions which prevented them from beating records with more powerful cars, and many protests were lodged with the committee, but it was clear that the event could not be run off again. It was, indeed, matter for great satisfaction that the competition did not give rise to serious accidents. On the following day, in clear weather, a 20 h.p. Decauville car, driven by Gabriel, beat the La Turbie record in 15m. 4s., which is at the rate of more than thirty-seven miles an hour.

Concours d'Elegance at Monte Carlo.

In the descent from La Turbie to Monte Carlo the winding road proved a very severe test for the brakes, which were set a hard test in holding vehicles weighing two tons and more on a gradient

Lefevre at the finish of the kilometre.

nine miles in length. The danger, of course, lay in the possibility of the brakes burning, in which event they would have become utterly useless, but, fortunately, all the cars got to the bottom without trouble of any sort, and most of the drivers had so much confidence in their brakes that they gave no attention to them at all. They usually descended with the band brakes, and left the differential brake as a reserve, while in the event of these not acting powerfully enough the compression of the motor itself would have helped to slow the vehicle. The brakes were thoroughly efficient, and in this respect it does not seem as if any notable improvement is

needed. The run down the mountain was also a test of skill and coolness, for now and then the cars had to turn in almost their own length, and at one moment we saw the Peugeot van stopped against the low wall bordering the precipice when it had to reverse to turn. If the industrial cars got down safely, a couple of racing vehicles were not so fortunate, for while a Turcat-Méry car was coming up the hill, a Darracq driven by Marcellin dashed into it with considerable force, completely smashing both vehicles. The drivers escaped unhurt by a miracle. The descent opened up a magnificent view of Monaco and Monte Carlo, and on arriving at the

Stead on the Mercedes-Simplex, which did second fastest time amongst the petrol cars for the flying kilo.

outskirts the vehicles were drawn up in a line for procession into the town. The nine cars certainly made a remarkably fine display, looking none the worse for the journey of seven hundred miles through France. It was only to be regretted that the Turgan tractor was not present to make the sight still more impressive, but though absent on this occasion, the vehicle with its artillery waggons arrived at Nice three or four days afterwards. The weather was brilliant, and even the heights of La Turbie were bathed in sunshine. On starting the procession into the town the vehicles were carefully watched by the police, who warned the drivers against running at more than ten kilometres an hour, and sufficient space had to be left between the cars. The law concerning traffic is evidently not to be trifled with in Monaco. The Concours d'Elégance took place in the afternoon, when the industrial and touring cars ran in procession around the fine gardens in front of the Casino, when awards were given for the most attractive vehicles. This was a fitting termination to the great trials, which had brought a larger number of heavy vehicles on a longer journey than had ever been accomplished before. The procession then broke up, the cars returning to Nice by the shorter road along the coast, and on the way we passed the Panhard omnibus with a punctured tyre, and Herr Daimler busily engaged in assisting the mechanics to put on a new cover. This was the only puncture to pneumatic tyres that took place during the whole run.

The Mile Competition.

The next two days were devoted to a public exhibition of vehicles in the carage of the A.C.N., and on Thursday was to have been held the mile competition and the flying kilometre for the Rothschild Cup on the Promenade des Anglais. This promenade is along the sea front, forming a broad cement track quite straight for about two-thirds of the distance, and then bending slightly to the finish. It is admirably adapted for a competition of this kind. Thursday opened very threateningly with heavy rains and squalls, which developed into a violent storm. Nevertheless, an attempt was made to run off the mile, but when Mr. Stead's Mercedes-Simplex skidded on the wet cement it was clearly too dangerous to continue, and the event was postponed. The next two days the storm continued unabated, but on Sunday the morning opened with brilliant weather, and the success of the mile and kilometre races fully compensated for the failure of La Turbie climb. It has, indeed, become historical for the wonderful performance of M. Serpollet with his 20 h.p. racing car of the shoe pattern, of which we publish a photograph. He pulverised all previous records by covering the flying kilometre at the phenomenal rate of seventy-five miles an hour. It is difficult to imagine how this performance can be beaten, for it seems to represent the maximum at which a driver is capable of steering a vehicle, and M. Serpollet was quite pale when he got down from his car, and his companion appeared utterly exhausted. He complained that he could not breathe, and had to turn his head to avoid suffocation. Osmont, on his 8 h.p. De Dion tricycle, also did remarkably well by covering the mile in less than a minute, and a good performance was that of. Williams on a Clément motor bicycle, with a 3 h.p. motor, the two cylinders being inclined V wise. As was to be expected, the Mercedes-Simplex did the fastest time among the big cars, but they can hardly do justice to themselves on a mile from a standing start owing to the loss of time in getting momentum on heavy vehicles. The only light cars to compete were the 20 h.p. four-cylinder Darracqs, which have certainly proved themselves very fast and reliable vehicles, and they are likely to show up very well in their category in this year's events. The following are the times for the standing mile: Osmont, De Dion tricycle,

M. Serpollet on his record steam car. Photographed on the Promenade des Anglais, Nice

57 4-5s.; Degrais, 40 h.p. Mercedes-Simplex, 1m. 9 3-5s.; Werner, Mercedes-Simplex, 1m. 9 4-5s.; Bardeau, 6 h.p. De Dion tricycle, 1m. 10 2-5s.; Baras, 20 h.p. Darracq, 1m. 10 4-5s.; Renaux, Darracq, 1m. 11 2-5s.; Williams, 3 h.p. Clément bicycle, 1m. 12 1-5s.; Lemaitre, Mercedes-Simplex, 1m. 17 2-5s.; Rutishauser, 12 h.p. Gardner-Serpollet, 1m. 21 2-5s.; Edmond, 20 h.p. Darracq, 1m. 21 4-5s.; Stead, Mercedes-Simplex, 1m. 27 1-5s.; Guillaume, Darracq, 1m. 27 4-5s.; Jenatzy, 40 h.p. Jenatzy, 1m. 40 3-5s.; Gasté, 20 h.p. Automotrice, 1m. 44 2-5s. The results of the flying kilom. competition for the Henri de Rothschild Cup, confined to big vehicles carrying two persons, were as follow: Léon Serpollet, 20 h.p. Gardner-Serpollet, 29 4-5s.; Degrais, 40 h.p. Mercedes-Simplex, 36 1-5s.; De Caters, 40 h.p. Jenatzy, 37 1-5s.; Chauliaud, 12 h.p. Gardner-Serpollet, 38s.; Stead, 40 h.p. Mercedes-Simplex, 38 1-5s.; Werner, Mercedes-Simplex, 38 3-5s.; Chauchard, 40 h.p. Panhard, 38 4-5s.; Pinson, 40 h.p. Panhard, 39s.; Cottard, 12 h.p. Gardner-Serpollet, 39 1-5s.; Lemaitre, 40 h.p. Mercedes-Simplex, 40 4-5s. During the mile and Rothschild Cup competitions five vehicles covered the flying kilometre at the rate of more than sixty-two miles an hour. As an outcome of the Nice meeting a sporting match has been arranged between Mr. W. K. Vanderbilt and Baron Henri de Rothschild over a distance of 124 miles. They will both drive Mercedes-Simplex cars. The race is to take place between Paris and a seaside town which it is perhaps inadvisable to specify.

THE CARLTON COMBINED CARBURETTER AND INLET VALVE.

The accompanying lettered section shows the construction of the above-named carburetter, made and used by the Carlton Motor Co., of 19, Elm Grove, Cricklewood, London. The section is from the size of carburetter adopted for use with engines from 4½ to 6 h.p. To those who have a general knowledge of the interior and working of carburetters very little description in addition to that afforded by the lettered section and reference thereto is needed for a full comprehension of its construction and working. The carburetting device is set immediately above the induction valve L, of which it is a part, as the hollow column I¹ set within it forms the inlet valve stem guide. The valve spring Q surrounds the partially-hollow valve stem K, and takes a bearing on the upper surface of the upper diaphragm J J, from which it exerts its returning effect on the valve by its pressure upon the underside of the valve stem nut K¹, secured in any desired position by lock nut K¹¹. The carburetter is secured to the valve chamber of the engine cylinder by set screws passing through holes in the flange X X, or is made to be screwed into the wall of combustion chamber. The needle valve F is set to move perpendicularly in the hollow stem K of the induction valve L, its upward position being retained by the spiral spring I. The needle valve is made with a slot, as shown, to permit the introduction of the pin G fixed in the valve stem K at any desired point. The socket, in the lower part of which is formed the seating for the needle valve F, is adjustable to

that valve, and by this means, together with the control afforded by the pin G, the petrol feed can be adjusted. Thus it will be seen that when the valve L is drawn downwards by the suction of the piston in the engine cylinder, the needle valve F, held in the upper part of the stem K, is likewise

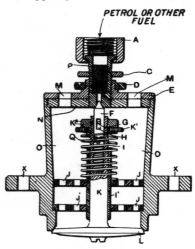

A, union for petrol pipe. Screwing socket affording adjustable needle valve seating. C, lock nut for ditto. D, lock nut for an adjustment. E, rotating air valve. F, needle valve. G, pin controlling movement of needle valve F. H, slot in stem of induction valve. I, spiral spring to needle valve. I¹, inlet valve spindle guide. J J J J, perforated diaphragms acting as atomisers. K, inlet valve stem. K¹, valve spring nut. K¹¹, lock nut to ditto. L, inlet valve. M, air passage. N, perforated cap for carburetter. O O, mixing chamber. P, filtering plug to wire gauze. Q, inlet valve spring. X X, holes for set screws securing carburetter to valve chamber.

withdrawn from its seating, and petrol flows into the mixing chamber O O, air penetrating thereto in any desired quantity through the orifices M M in the rotary valve E and carburetter cap N. The passage of the air and petrol at speed through the perforations in the upper and lower diaphragms, J J J J, effectually atomises the spirit and brings about a thorough and effectual mingling before it passes on to the cylinder through the annular space left by the opening of the valve L. The makers claim that this carburetter will serve for either ether, petrol, alcohol, paraffin, or common gas. A dust-cap is fitted when required over the perforated cap N. The carburetter being also the inlet valve is, of course, so close to the combustion chamber that freezing never occurs.

The Reading Automobile Club will tour to Dulverton, via Hungerford, Frome, Wells, Glastonbury, Taunton, and Wiveliscombe on Whit-Saturday. The next day they will go on to Porlock. The next day will be spent there, and the return to Reading at the rate of 140 miles per day will be made on Tuesday and Wednesday.

* * *

Mr. C. Jarrott has certainly put his new 16 h.p. light Panhard, of which we published a small photograph last week, to a pretty severe test. The following is his fortnight's record: Paris to Dijon, Dijon to Avignon, Avignon to Nice, Nice to Turin, Turin to Nice, Nice to Grenoble, Grenoble to Dijon, Dijon to Paris, and he wound up with Paris to Dieppe, and Newhaven to London.

AN AMERICAN PETROL CAR.

This machine is interesting, as it shows the tendency among the builders of petrol cars in the United States to copy the European outline of car. In fact, they go further than copying the outline, as the positions of the motor and chief parts of the mechanism are the same. The particular vehicle we illustrate, which is rather a smart-looking machine in many respects, is driven by a three-cylinder vertical motor, which is stated to be of 16 h.p. The bore is 4½in. and the stroke 5½in. This engine is placed in the hood in the front, and fuel is served by a float feed and single carburetter, in which an old idea is revived, as there is a fan revolved by the suction current, to assist the thorough mixing of the petrol vapour and air. The speed-changing gear is either of the Panhard sliding type, and the transmission from the change speed to the rear wheels is by outside chains, or, instead of this, an epicyclic train is used for speed variation, and the central transmission shaft and live back axle take the place of chains. In fact, this second system is applied to the particular machine which we illustrate. The motor speed is regulated by a governor of the ordinary ball type. This does not work on the exhaust valve or throttle, but advances or retards the time of the spark, the explosion occurring early or late, as the engine may be running rapidly or the reverse, while a lever on the steering column controls a throttle for adjusting the supply of gas to the engine. Two band brakes on the rear wheel drum are hand-applied, and the countershaft brake is pedal-applied as usual. The pedal-controlled clutch is placed between the engine and gearshaft, while the frame, which provides a 7ft. wheelbase, is of the accepted channel steel section. The weight of the vehicle is just under a ton.

* * *

At Easter, Messrs. Mann, Egerton, and Co., of 5, Prince of Wales Road, Norwich, advise us that they will have their depot open day and night. This is for the convenience of Easter tourists in general and the Automobile Club men who will be at Cromer in particular.

* * *

The English Motor Club will be making Worthing their headquarters at Easter, taking tours from that centre into the surrounding country. On the 12th of April they have a run to the " Swan " at Bedford, and on May 3rd to the " Mitre " at Oxford, where it is hoped the Reading Club will be able to join them. On the 31st May the popular contest in the grounds of the Crystal Palace, open to everybody, will be repeated, but with several new and interesting features added, of which more anon, and on July 12th another popular fixture will be repeated—the hill-climbing contest up Tilburstowe. Other fixtures during the coming season will be announced later.

One of the leading physicians of Norwich, Dr. Burton-Fanning, owns a four-seated Locomobile. He uses it professionally as well as recreationally, and thinks nothing of covering fifty miles a day when on his " rounds " into the outlying districts. Mrs. Burton-Fanning is also an enthusiastic automobilist, and drives the car entirely alone, often in the wet, and she braves a solitary drive in the darkness without the least hesitation.

* * *

We hear that Mr. Joseph Pennell is getting on very well with his Phœnix motor bicycle. The other day he ran it from London to Nottingham, and climbed everything with scarcely any pedalling. He found the roads very loose in places, and the only semblance of loss of power was caused by a little belt slipping and some slight slackening after leaving Kettering, due presumably to over-heating or want of lubrication. We also hear that he climbed High Street, Guildford, without pedalling on the same machine.

COSTUMES AND CHATTER.

MY Dear Diana,—I am so glad you have been amusing yourself so well. London also is very bright and gay just now. The Coronation seems to be coming very close, and people are smartening up their clothes, houses, and carriages for it. *À propos* of these last, more electric broughams than ever are being used, and several people I know have actually given up the delights of a box at the opera to indulge in one of these charming horse-less carriages. And how right' they are! The sweetest notes, even of a Melba or a De Reszke, die away on the ear and are forgotten, becoming as completely a thing of the past as a supper at the Carlton, but the utility of a motor brougham is always with us.

I hear that the firm of **Mr. Paris Singer** are taking in orders for these electric carriages at the rate of one per day, which, you will agree, is enormous considering the work involved and the money that it represents. But there is no doubt but that they will be quite equal to the demand. Lady Charles Beresford has ordered one, which will be particularly useful to her, as she is always flitting between her house at Ham and her rooms in Claridge's Hotel.

A COAT OF GREY CLOTH WITH ASTRAKHAN COLLAR

no protection whatever, and nothing but cloth, serge, or fur seems really comfortable.

Coat of Silver Baboon.—I was first shown a coat of silver baboon, a very rare skin from the West Coast of Africa. So rare indeed is it that although this one is obtainable for the modest sum of £11, it would be a matter of some difficulty for the firm to obtain another to order. The collar and revers are made of lynx, a fur which is more becoming near the face. This is a coat which could be worn for ordinary carriage driving as well as motoring, and there are very few days in chilly England when a light wrap of this kind is not enjoyable.

Another Charming Coat.—A fetching long coat of wild catskin was being made for Lady Algernon Gordon Lennox. It was adorned with a large collar of racoon cloth. Yet another useful coat of grey cloth had a roll collar of astrakhan to match.

Costume of Russian Colt.—But this is not all, and as I know you like an infinite variety of choice, let me tell you of a costume of Russian coltskin which I saw, made in the evergreen blouse bodice and skirt style, the latter being completed round the feet with leather to match the shade of the costume. This trimming was also repeated on the bolero and on the small cape which formed a part of the collar. The sleeves were slightly fulled into bands round the wrist, and the whole effect was indescribably smart and unique.

Motor Toques.—As for headgear, here are two pretty toques of Jay's, both eminently suitable for summer motoring, being both practical and becoming—a combination only too seldom found in motor headgear. One, which is most serviceable for country wear, is entirely composed of straw

Costumes and Coats from Jay's.—And now listen to the description of some absolutely irresistible creations from Jay's in the line of coats and muffs suitable for motoring, and do not look at the bright sunshine of June and wonder when I break to you gently that they are mostly of fur. Remember, as I said before, that when rushing through the air at—well, we won't say what pace, out of deference to the law—nearly all thin wraps afford

A MOTOR TOQUE AT JAY'S

ANOTHER TOQUE

—soft, crumpled, black straw below and burnt straw above— and has two smart quills of the same ornamented with steel buttons. The other, which is perhaps more suitable for town wear, is a coarse straw, sailor shape, bound with black velvet, and made very becoming by the decoration on one side of a closely arranged bird and twists of blue soft silk ribbon.

Modes at Ernest's.—Ernest's, that very excellent firm in Regent Street, are turning out some charming dresses for mid-season and summer wear, and though not very severe they are just the thing for smart motor excursions when well covered by long dust cloaks. His great specialities are the beautiful hand-made embroideries with which the dainty little boleros are trimmed. I quite fell in love with a brown corduroy bolero and skirt, which would be the very thing for the dull days which come to us even in June. This gown had the simplicity of all really smart creations. The little bolero was most daintily shaped, and ornamented down the fronts with passementerie and cord of the same delicate shade of mouse colour.

Another delightful gown was of palest blue cloth with large revers which were completed in the gold embroidery, done by hand. This embroidery was repeated down the sides of the bolero, forming a kind of zouave, across which again tiny straps of the blue cloth were drawn upwards, while a necktie of spotted foulard coming from beneath the revers and loosely knotted in front completed the charming effect.

The skirt was finished at the bottom by the introduction of this same gold embroidery, which traversed it at the back, ending in two points in front, this embroidery being again crossed, as in the bolero, by straps of the cloth.

I can put these dresses into words for you, my dear Diana, but you must pay a visit to this establishment yourself, as nothing else can so well make you understand their daintiness and the indescribable air of smartness which clings to all of Ernest's emanations. In fact, I was so delighted with them that I must describe one more to you, although it is more suited to a garden party than a motor.

Picture to yourself a black garment made of some gauzy summer fabric and finished off round the feet with innumerable little frills. Both skirt and bodice of this were made up over an underdress of a creamy flowered silk, which showed softly through its veils of black, an exquisite touch of colour being given by a sky-blue sash, the long ends of which hung behind towards the left side. There was an air of daring simplicity about this dress which made it specially attractive, and, my dear Diana, believe me I have never seen anything which would so exactly suit your style.

A COSTUME OF RUSSIAN COLTSKIN

A New Veil.—Of course you are wearing the new motor veil lined with white or pink chiffon! I think those are most becoming which have the largest black spots, and those not too close together, although I am told that they are very bad for the eyesight. But I am sure you will not mind that, so long as they are pretty! THE GODDESS IN THE CAR.

ON COLOURS FOR CARS.

A BROUGHAM painted bright red would remind one of a fire engine; and in fact any horse-drawn vehicle of a bright colour seems to be an eyesore. But it is curious that a bright-coloured automobile is a charming and cheery spot of colour and often enlivens the otherwise dismal street. After all, the coaches of old days were painted brightly enough, and in our own time no one can say that the bright green of the Great Western, the chocolate of the Midland, or the buff of the London, Brighton and South Coast Railways are not becoming to engines of speed. But always remember that the brighter the colour, the cleaner your car must be kept.

IN connection with the grand charity bazaar to be held at the French Embassy on the 12th, 13th, and 14th instant, a "grand automobile battle of flowers" is to take place on the 13th at the "Paris in London" Exhibition at Earl's Court, when prizes will be given for the best decorated cars. For the purpose of the procession a continuous route has been planned out in the Exhibit on gardens, along which the motor-cars will proceed decked with flowers or ribbons. After the presentation of banners to successful competitors the procession will again cover the course. For the convenience of intending competitors it may be stated that an ample supply of flowers will be procurable at the Exhibition beforehand. The first section will be given up to two-seated cars driven by ladies, the second section being for larger cars, also driven by fair automobilists. Sections three and four will be for men under similar conditions, section five being for a pair of cars, and section six for a team of four. Princess Henry of Battenberg has promised to distribute the prizes, and all the prettiest actresses in London are to act as flower and programme sellers. The prices for seats on the various grand stands will be £1 1s., 15s., 10s. 6d., 7s. 6d., and 5s. respectively.

HAPPENING to be close to the entrance gates of Bushey Park on a recent Sunday afternoon one of our staff noticed ten automobiles pass through in as many minutes, amongst the number being Sir Francis Jeune on his smart 12 h.p. Daimler "Lonsdale" waggonette. Although, as usual on a Sunday afternoon, all the approaches to the park were crowded with horse-drawn vehicles, the advent of the various motor-cars did not appear to cause the slightest perturbation to equine nerves. How different was the case three years ago! Contrary to the practice of the Surrey constabulary, which posts its men in ambush along the most unfrequented parts of the country roads, it was noticed that at Bushey Park the police were stationed only at points where a slow speed was absolutely necessary for safety, and that each driver of an automobile was individually warned to use special caution.

THE PARIS-VIENNA ROUTE

— JUNE 26 - 29, 1902. —

PARIS

START

CHAMPAGNY

GRETZ
TURNAN
ROZOY

NANGIS PROVINS

NOGENT

MAISON
ROUGE

ST. HILAIRE

R. SEINE

TROYES

VENDEUVRE

EVAR ST. AUBE

CHAUMONT

LANGRES

FAYSBILLOT

COMBEAUFONTAINE

LURE

BELFORT

PORT sur SAONE

PLAIN OF LANGRES

R. SAÔNE

VOSGES MTS.

JURA MTS.

DELLE

BÂLE

FRANCE

R. RHINE

BRUGG

RHEINFELDEN

WINTERTHUR

ZURICH

ARBON

RORSCHACH

FRAUENFELD

WEINFELDEN

OTTENBURG

LAKE CONSTANCE

SWITZERLAND

RHEINECK

BREGENZ

FELDKIRCH

BLUDENZ

RAINECK

IMST

LANDECK

ST. ANTON

STUBEN

TELFS

INNSBRUCK

HALL

SCHWAZ

RATTENBERG

WÖRGL

ST. JOHANNI

REICHENHALL

ST. JOHANN

KOCKLABRUCK

SALZBURG

R. DANUBE

WELS

STRASSWALCHEN

ENNS

LINZ

MOLK

TULN

AMSTETTEN

STRENGBERG

KEMMELBACH

ST. PÖLTEN

STOCKERAU

VIENNA

AUSTRIA

LENGTH OF 4TH DAY'S RUNNING

LENGTH OF 3RD DAY'S RUN

LENGTH OF 2ND DAY'S NEUTRAL RUN

NEUTRALIZED

LENGTH OF 1ST DAY'S RUNNING

N

THE PARIS-VIENNA RACE.

LATEST DETAILS.

THIS great race, which starts to-morrow from Paris and finishes on Sunday evening next at Vienna, has attracted, up to the time of closing the official list, no fewer than 208 entries. The four days' journeys are clearly shown on the accompanying plan, that portion of the course which is shown by a dotted line being the neutralised section, set down for the second day's trip, which will be of a processional character, until racing recommences at Bregenz, after emerging from Swiss territory. This point of recommencement of high speed coincides with the change of the rule of the road, for in Austria the same regulation holds good as in England, that one keeps to the left of approaching traffic, whereas in all other European countries this practice is reversed. Special shortened formalities have been arranged for the racing vehicles at the customs offices in order that the frontiers may be passed with but a moment's delay for the purposes of identification. Among the excitements of a race which will provide a thrill at every corner, not the least startling experiences will be the jumping of the hundreds of *caniveaux*, or cross channels, which, like miniature fords, cross the road and scar its surface almost as badly as railway crossings, and with even greater risk when they are swollen with heavy rains. Numerous leapings may be expected also at the many small bridges, colloquially known as donkey-backs, which, with a steep run up, endue a fast car with powers of aerial flight for a brief moment, and the descent may or may not be on the road. It was on one of these hump-backed bridges that the only English representative came to grief in the Paris-Berlin race last year. May the Englishmen's luck be better on this occasion!

A FINE RUN.

A REMARKABLE feat was performed on Thursday last by a 10 h.p. Décauville car, which accomplished a non-stop run from the General Post Office, Edinburgh, to the Motor Car Company's depôt in Shaftesbury Avenue. Such a run of 400 miles of consecutive travelling is quite without precedent either on the road or on the rail, for the best expresses between London and Edinburgh change engines at York and at Newcastle. The Décauville made the trip without the least symptom of trouble. No adjustments were necessary, nor any replenishments of the petrol supply, for the car carried sufficient for the whole trip. The level railway crossings were all opened in the nick of time, and, by careful driving through the towns and villages, no stops were necessitated by the exigencies of traffic, nor was the run marred by any difficulties with the tyres. Mr. F. T. Bidlake acted as observer, and the driving was done in relays by two of the Motor Car Company's experts, who alternately drove and slept in the tonneau.

THE third meeting of the members of the Aero Club took place at Ranelagh on Saturday afternoon, when three balloons made an ascent in the presence of a large number of spectators, the majority of whom were ladies. The balloons had to be dragged from the 8 in. main half-way up the ground, as owing to the recent heavy rains it was extremely wet under foot. The first balloon to go off was Mr. Frank H. Butler's "Graphic" (45,000 ft.), the passengers being Miss Vera Butler (who has already made eight ascents), the Hon. C. S. Rolls, Mr. C. F. Pollock, and Mr. Butler. Mr. Leslie Bucknall's balloon, "Vivienne" (35,000 ft.), contained also Mr. Ernest Bucknall and Mr. Arthur Spencer, whilst the "City of York" balloon (53,000 ft.) had Mr. E. Pitman, Mr. J. Talbot Clifton, and Mr. Percival Spencer. The "Graphic" and "Vivienne" both descended at Rainham, Essex, at about twenty minutes to seven, each touching ground in the same field. An unusual proportion of the visitors on this occasion journeyed to and from the club by motor-car.

THE Motor Power Company, Ld., have just supplied the Duke of Connaught with a 9 h.p. Napier car. This car will be particularly used during the coronation time for inspecting the various bodies of troops spread over a large area. The company desire us to notify that their address is now 14, New Burlington Street, and not 14, Regent Street.

THE PARIS-VIENNA RACE:

AN ENGLISHMAN WINS THE GORDON-BENNETT CUP.

THE great automobile race from Paris to Vienna has been fought and won, and there is every justification for supposing it to have been one of the most exciting struggles on record. At the time of going to press, however, full details are necessarily wanting, and uncertainty even prevails as to who may be declared the actual

BEING TOWED TO THE STARTING POST

winner, as the officials at Vienna were unable to make a positive declaration on the subject until the figures were to hand of the previous days' performances of all the competitors.

It appears highly probable, however, that Englishmen will have good cause to congratulate themselves on the double event of the Paris-Vienna race and that for the Gordon-Bennett or International Cup, which was run over a portion of the route of the former. The cup has been won by Mr. S. F. Edge on his Napier car, while if, as is reported, the winner of the Paris-Vienna event should prove to be Count Zborowsky, it is only necessary to point out that he is a naturalised Englishman, and a well-known member of the Automobile Club of Great Britain. Englishmen may therefore take pride in his achievement, although his car, a Mercédès, was, unlike the Napier, not of native construction. The prominent position occupied by other drivers of English nationality, such as Mr. Jarrott and the Farman brothers, is also a matter of gratification.

MAKING READY IN THE COURT OF THE FRENCH
AUTOMOBILE CLUB

As regards the Paris-Vienna contest, the first arrival at Belfort on the opening day was Chevalier de Knyff, who covered the distance of 253 miles in 7 h. 11 min. 56 sec. He was closely followed by Messrs. Henry Farman, Maurice Farman, and C. Jarrott, and the fact that this quartette finished the long journey within a few minutes of each other shows how keenly the race was contested.

The second stage of the race was neutralised for the whole distance, 120 miles, from Belfort to Bregenz, and the Swiss police are stated to have been very strict in their enforcement of the prescribed limit of fifteen miles an hour. It became known during the day that M. Fournier and the Hon. C. S. Rolls had been obliged to abandon the race. The third stage, from Bregenz to Salzburg, a distance of 370 kilometres, was the most trying of all, for the road lay over the Arlberg Pass, which rises to a height of 5,000 ft., and was found to be somewhat liberally strewn with stones. M. de Knyff seemed to be strongly in the running for both events, but unfortunately broke down before Innsbruck was reached, and, as the other Gordon-Bennett competitors had already retired, Mr. Edge was left the winner of the cup. It is rumoured that the unsuccessful competitors for this trophy have lodged a protest on the ground that Mr. Edge was assisted by peasants in extricat-

MR. C. JARROTT, ONE OF THE ENGLISH DRIVERS

ing his car from a river bed, whereas one of the rules of the contest is that no one but the occupants of a competing car are to move it at any time during the race. Mr. Edge, however, denies that he has incurred any disqualification, or even that any such accident had occurred to him at all. Innsbruck marked the termination of the Gordon-Bennett race, but the third stage of the major event was completed at Salzburg, where the first car home was Henry Farman's, with Count Zborowsky and Baron Forest, each on a Mercédès, second and third respectively, and Maurice Farman's Panhard fourth.

The concluding stage from Salzburg to Vienna was run on Sunday. The first man in was M. Marcel Renault on a light car of his own construction, while Count Zborowsky was second on his Mercédès, Baron de Forest third, and Maurice Farman fourth ; then came M. Edmond on a Darracq, followed by M. Pinson on his Panhard. Mr. Edge arrived twenty-first.

A private note from Mr. Montague Grahame-White informs us that the crank-shaft of his 45 h.p. Wolseley broke within 200 yds. of the start, and he had to wait until another was sent on from Paris.

In describing the scene during the weighing operations at the French Automobile Club our special correspondent writes: "The cars present a spectacle well calculated to gladden the heart of the *chauffeur*. Never before were vehicles so full of interesting points. The *chassis* of these racing cars is now a mere skeleton, but the engine a raging lion, immense in size and power although exceedingly light. In fact, the ingenuity displayed in reducing the weight of this year's racing models, while at the same time greatly increasing their power, is such as to reflect the greatest credit on the designers and constructors who voluntarily took upon themselves this difficult task.

"It is to be feared, however, that the proportion of the starters who succeed in reaching Vienna will be comparatively very small. The course is the longest and most difficult that has ever yet been undertaken and most of the cars will start utterly untried. The constructors have been at work, day and night, for weeks past, but owing to the fact that almost every item in the vehicles is new it has been impossible to complete them in time for even a short trial. It has been necessary in many cases to tow the racing cars to the club for weighing owing to details of the mechanism being incomplete.

"Several of the *chauffeurs* have already been over the whole course, and the most complete reports are to hand regarding the nature of the road. That portion lying in France and

MR. HENRY FARMAN ON HIS 70 H.P. PANHARD

Switzerland is reported to be sufficiently good, but the road from Bregenz to Vienna is said to be terrible, full of *caniveaux* and *dos d'âne*, well calculated to destroy any but the most substantially constructed cars."

There were 147 actual competitors in the Paris-Vienna race, of which twenty-five were on motors driven by alcohol. In the Paris-Berlin race of 1901 there were 120 starters. It has been calculated that the machines driven by steam and petrol that started for the east from the gay capital last Thursday represent a money value of about 3,000,000 francs (£120,000).

The following is a *resumé* of the past contests :—

1895 (Paris—Bordeaux—Paris).—Won by M. Lévassor on a 4 h.p. Panhard. The distance was 1,152 kilometres, covered in 48 h. 48 min. Average per hour, 24 kilometres.

1896 (Paris—Marseilles—Paris).—Won by M. Mayade upon a 6 h.p. Panhard and Levassor. The distance was 1,720 kilometres, covered in 67 h. 42 min. Average per hour, 27 kilometres.

1898 (Paris—Amsterdam—Paris).—Won by M. Charron upon an 8 h.p. Panhard and Levassor. The distance was 1,502 kilometres, covered in 33 h. 4 min. 34 sec. Average per hour, 45 kilometres.

1899 (Tour of France).—Won by M. René de Kynff upon a 16 h.p. Panhard and Levassor. The distance was 2,300 kilometres, covered in 42 h. 33 min. Average per hour, 54 kilometres.

1900 (Paris—Toulouse and return).—Won by M. Levegh upon a 24 h.p. Mors. The distance was 1,348 kilometres, covered in 20 h. 50 min. Average per hour, 66. kilometres 200 m.

1901 (Paris—Berlin).—Won by M. Henri Fournier upon a 40 h.p. Mors. The distance was 1,198 kilometres 600

VIEW OF ENGINE OF MR. H. FARMAN'S PANHARD

m., covered in 15 h. 33 min. Average per hour, 71 kilometres 100 m.

From the point of view of speed, according to *L'Auto-Vélo*, the famous average of 86 kilometres in the Paris-Bordeaux has been beaten by M. René de Knyff, who covered 380 kilometres of the course, with the neutralised portion deducted, in 4 h. 16 min. This represents an average of 90 kilometres per hour. It was upon one of the new Panhard-Levassor machines with a Centaure motor that this splendid feat has been achieved, and it was with alcohol that M. René de Knyff scored this triumph and carried off the Arenberg cup.

Between Fontenay, Trésigny, and Rozoy the line of route was marvellously straight, with a very slight declivity of about one per cent.; the ground was firm and good. There was a space of 200 metres measured off exactly, and at the start M. Lamberjack stood with a flag, and at the other end M. Alphonse Baugé, a journalist, with a chronometer. When the vehicle passed him, M. Lamberjack lowered the flag, and M. Baugé at once started the seconds hand of his chronometer. A motor-car swept on, bounding like lightning in a cloud of dust. It was Fournier, who had covered 200 metres in six seconds, or at the rate of 120 kilometres per hour, and he swept swiftly out of sight a few moments later.

Fuller details of the Gordon-Bennett and the Paris-Vienna race will be given in the next issue of THE CAR, together with photographs taken on the spot by our special correspondent. The official classification, if the Paris-Berlin event be any criterion, will not be ready in its entirety, but there is no doubt but that the world will know the results so far as the men in the first flight are concerned.

BARON DE CATERS' MORS

THE PARIS-VIENNA RACE:

FROM OUR SPECIAL CORRESPONDENT.

WRITING from Vienna, our special correspondent, who went over the whole course, says: "The Paris-Vienna race has now been brought to a successful conclusion, and it must unhesitatingly be recorded as the greatest achievement yet accomplished by motor vehicles.

"A journey of 1,420 kilometres, spanning three countries and traversing the most mountainous quarter of Europe, successfully accomplished in four days by eighty-five cars out of 137 starters, and these practically all of types new and totally untried, reflects the greatest credit alike on the engineers who have designed and constructed them, and on the *chauffeurs* who have guided them over this arduous journey.

"It is a matter for regret that so few Englishmen know what one of these great automobile races means to Paris. The sight of the preparations on the night before a race is one which no other country can show, and is certainly one of the things to have lived to see. This midnight throng of humanity, 50,000 strong or more, streaming up the hill of Champigny and out along the route, these thousands of cyclists with their fairy lamps and cars with flashing acetylenes illuminating the animated scene, and finally, as the hours draw on towards dawn, the racers flitting past darkly—for they carry no lamps, to save weight—but known by their thunder-

ing engines and speedy gait, make up a scene not easily to be forgotten, and once seen not easily to be resisted again.

"The night before the Paris-Vienna race was as that

MR. HENRY FARMAN ON HIS 70 H.P. PANHARD

before the 'Paris-Berlin' contest, but with interest and enthusiasm even more intense. From 8 p.m. on Wednesday, June 25th, to 2 a.m. on Thursday, the hill of Champigny was traversed by a mighty army, motorists, cyclists, and pedestrians proceeding together, so that one would suppose that a long list of dead and wounded could be the only result; but this is

MR. S. F. EDGE AND MR. NAPIER ON THE 40 H.P. NAPIER

not so; somehow they manage these things better in France. Soon after midnight came the racers, swiftly and darkly, along the narrow lane left clear for them, and taking up their places one by one, according to the numbers

VIEW OF THE FINISHING POST AT VIENNA

on the now classic trees which line the hill. At 3 a.m. the dawn, rising in pink and gold of exquisite purity, revealed more distinctly the monster racers stationed at the summit of the hill, cleared for action and manned each by some well-known *chauffeur*, waiting once more to risk his hardly-earned reputation in arduous combat. There was the redoubtable Henry Fournier, who last year carried off the honours of both Paris-Bordeaux and Paris-Berlin, with René de Knyff, Girardot, Farman, Edge, Rolls, and a host of others whose names are bywords for skill and daring in the automobile world at home and abroad.

"At 3.30 a.m. Girardot, on a Charron-Girardot and Voight car of about 60 h.p., was sent on his way to head the race so long as fortune should favour him. The Wolseley car failing to appear, at 3.32 Fournier on a 60 h.p. Mors was sent off amidst the greatest enthusiasm and overwhelmed with good wishes for success, and two minutes later Edge on the new 30 h.p. Napier sped on his way, followed by René de Knyff on a 70 h.p. Panhard. These four cars were the competitors for the Gordon-Bennett Cup, the race for which was run off simultaneously with the Paris-Vienna race, but ended at Innsbruck, 618 kilometres of racing distance and 930 kilometres actual distance from Paris.

"After the Gordon-Bennett cars came a stream of competitors, 133 in number, for Paris-Vienna, the last car being sent off at 7.45 a.m. The chief controls on the first day were at Troyers, Bar-sur-Aube, Chaumont, and Langres,

THE FIRST OF THE MORS CARS TO ARRIVE

and the final destination was Belfort, near the Swiss border. At Troyers Fournier was leading, followed closely by de Knyff, and twenty minutes later by Edge. Girardot had disappeared since Langres, 74·5 kilometres from the

start. At Bar-sur-Aube and Chaumont Fournier was still the leader, closely followed by de Knyff. At Langres de Knyff took the first place, and he arrived first at Belfort, having covered the 408 kilometres from Paris in 4 h. 6 min. 30 sec. of running time, or at an average of nearly 62 miles per hour. Fournier had smashed his car on a dangerous winding hill between Chaumont and Langres, and Edge was thus left as the only competitor with de Knyff for the Gordon-Bennett Cup.

"By midnight 106 of the cars had arrived at Belfort, amongst the chief defaulters being Rolls and Foxhall Keene, both driving 60 h.p. Mors cars, and both came to grief at a sharp curve 11·5 kilometres from the start. The greatest care was taken to give warning of these dangerous curves, otherwise there would no doubt have been many more accidents. It is to be regretted that the three Wolseley cars did not start as expected; all were delayed from minor defects which showed themselves on the road between Birmingham and Paris. One of the Wolseleys, however, a 30 h.p., ran unofficially over the first and second stages, but was not seen after Bregenz; it passed Chaumont on the first day at 8 p.m., having suffered from a broken crank-shaft amongst other troubles.

"The whole route from Belfort to Bregenz, for the second day, June 27th, was neutralised, the cars simply travelling in procession and falling out of place as any trouble arose from

MR. C. JARROTT ON HIS 70 H.P. PANHARD

accidental causes. From Bregenz the start was made at 3 a.m., René de Knyff being first, followed closely by Forest on a Mercédès, No. 26, the Farmans on 70 h.p. Panhards, and Edge on the Napier. During the night the cars were all retained *en parc* in a large plot of ground near the town As the time arrived for departure the driver and *mécanicien* of each car in order were allowed to enter the *parc* and take their car from the ranks, the haste to get off being productive of many amusing scenes. Difficulties in starting the engines were usually overcome by having the car pushed along, with clutch in, until the engine started.

"The third day's run was over a most difficult and, in places, dangerous route, passing by Landeck and Innsbruck to Salzburg, and was productive of some unexpected changes in the order of the competitors. The most notable event was the breakage of the differential on René de Knyff's Panhard, which put him completely *hors de combat* about 50 kilometres from Innsbruck, and left a certain victory for Edge in the Gordon-Bennett race, provided all went well with his Napier. As the event proved, the English car ran consistently well throughout, and for the first time an Englishman on an English-built car has won an important continental race. De Knyff being *en panne*, the first place amongst the arrivals at Salzburg fell to Baron Forest, who was followed three-quarters of an hour later by Henry Farman, Panhard No. 7, and Marcel Renault, No. 147. In all, seventy-one cars had entered the Salzburg control before 9 p.m., and eighty-seven cars before midnight on June 28th.

"The fourth and final stage of the race, viz., Salzburg to Vienna, was run off on Sunday, June 29th, the start being

COUNT ZBOROWSKI FINISHING

made at 6 a.m. Throughout the day there was a keen contest for the first place between Forest and Zborowski on Mercédès cars, Nos. 27 and 26 ; Maurice Farman, Panhard No. 6, and M. Renault. The result, witnessed by a great gathering on the racecourse at Vienna, was of a quite sensational nature. The first arrival, 2.18 p.m., was Marcel Renault, whose little car, weighing 630 kilogrammes, and with an engine of about 20 h.p., has actually made the fastest time over the whole course. Half an hour after the Renault came Count Zborowski, followed by Maurice Farman, and almost simultaneously by three Darracqs, Nos. 35, 38 and 39.

VIEW OF THE CARS IN THE ROTUNDA AT VIENNA

Baron Forest had broken down a short distance from the Prater, and was towed in by another Mercédès car. The first of the big Mors cars, Baron de Caters's No. 3, arrived fourteenth at 3.54 p.m. S. F. Edge, on the Napier No. 45, arrived twenty-first at 4.11 p.m., thus gaining a highly creditable position in the Paris-Vienna race, besides having won the Gordon-Bennett Cup.

"It will be impossible to give the actual times for the race until all the control times are worked out, but it is interesting to note that the total time, including that in control, for the first six cars arrived at Vienna is about twenty-six hours, and that all repairs were carried out during this time. It requires nearly double this time to traverse the same route—Paris, Belfort, Bregenz, Vienna, by train.

The fact, then, that by Monday morning at 9 a.m. 85 cars had arrived shows very strikingly how perfect is the mechanism of the modern motor vehicle.

"These 85 cars included 12 Panhard-Levassors, 4 Renaults, 3 Mors, 2 Mercédès, 6 Darracqs, 5 Georges-Richards, 2 Déchamps, 1 Napier, 5 Clement and Clement-Gladiators, 2 De Dietrich, 5 Gobron-Brilliés and Gobron-Nagants, 5 Serpollets, 7 Decauvilles, 1 Crouan, 2 Werner and 2 Mulders Pipe motor cycles, 1 De Dion tricycle, &c.

"On the whole the race has been a triumph for lightness, confirming in every respect the desire of the Automobile

THE NAPIER AFTER THE RACE

Club de France and of French constructors to reduce the maximum weight of the largest types below 1,000 kilogrammes."

The following is an official communication from the Automobile Club de France : "The International Commission of the Gordon-Bennett Cup, composed of Mr. C. Johnson, representing the Automobile Club of Great Britain and Ireland, and the Comte de Chasseloup-Loubat, representing the Automobile Club of France, who have Mr. Thorn associated with them as president, assembled on July 4th and 5th at the Automobile Club de France, and

M. MARCEL RENAULT'S CAR

after examination of the course declared that Mr. Edge had won this trial, and that in consequence the Automobile Club of Great Britain becomes the holder of the cup.—The Secretary of the Sportive Commission, R. Hochmelle."

It need hardly be said that this decision will be received with much satisfaction by British automobilists.

THE PARIS-VIENNA RACE.

MR. MONTAGUE GRAHAME-WHITE sends us his impressions of the Paris-Vienna race as follows:—

"Perhaps no international automobile contest which has taken place up to the present has evoked more interest and given rise to greater criticism than the great race which started from Champigny on June 26th last. The graphic accounts of the route from one capital to the other, which were so fully detailed in the continental newspapers, must certainly have intensified the public interest in the final outcome of the race. *L'Auto Velo*, the leading French automobile journal, and practically the official organ of the French Automobile Club, devoted pages to the description of the cars and of the roads to be traversed by the racers. Indeed, when one had read these narratives, it was difficult to think how these monster cars, fitted with engines of increased horse-power and diminished weight, were going to bring their drivers safely through to the eastern capital.

"The arrangements

THE 45 H.P. WOLSELEY CAR

over, it is surely to their advantage to get their neighbours accustomed to the use of automobiles, and dispel the uninterested feeling that at present exists.

"Perhaps none of the great French races that have taken place hitherto have given the smaller cars a better o portunity of showing their capabilities. It is over a straight and moderately level course that the powerful 75 h.p. Panhards and 60 h.p. Mors cars can show their enormous speed powers, but over a route such as the Paris-Vienna, full of *caniveaux*, *dos d'ânes*, and corners, the rate of travelling of these 'fliers' cannot exceed the margin of safety which is equal for the small as well as the high-powered car.

"To refer to the performances of the principal high-powered cars, it is curious to note that few of these even reached Vienna in anything approaching decent time. I refer more especially to the Panhard and Mors racers, out of which Messrs. René de Knyff, Henri Fournier, and Girardot all remained *en panne* before arriving at Innsbrück, whilst 'Charlie' Rolls was put *hors de combat* but a few kilometres from Champigny, and Max came to grief on the Arlberg on a 40 h.p. Darracq.

for the information of the competitors were by no means what they might have been, and I am sure that this opinion will be endorsed by the majority of those who took part in the contest. As regards the flagging of the route, in some districts nothing was left to be desired, whereas in others dangerous crossings and corners were left unnoticed. Then, again, at some of the controls the arrangements were anything but satisfactory, and some of the protests already lodged are amply justified.

"In conversation with many of the *chauffeurs* who took part in the race, the question has invariably arisen as to why the contest should ever have been carried outside the country. They argue that, in the first place, the French roads are infinitely superior, and the country folk far more accustomed to seeing automobiles on the roads; whilst another point in favour of this suggestion is the fact that in Switzerland and Austria cars are not looked on altogether with a favourable eye, and the roads are about the last a *chauffeur* would care to drive on. On the other hand, it would seem that from a commercial point of view it would be advantageous to the French manufacturers to show the capabilities of their machines by running them in foreign countries on roads that few cars have yet traversed. More-

"As regards the Gordon-Bennett Cup, Edge alone arrived at Vienna. Fournier was *en panne* near Chaumont, and left his car with his *mécanicien*, whilst he himself proceeded by train to Belfort. Girardot was *en panne* also before reaching Belfort. De Knyff was stranded near Innsbrück, and what happened to the Wolseley cars comes next. For myself, I was down to drive car No. 171 ; this was the 45 h.p. car on which the Wolseley Company pinned their faith and I my hopes. To me the contest seemed to have started many days before it actually did, as all was bustle and hurry at the company's works three weeks beforehand to enable the cars to be turned out in time for a sufficient brake and road trial. At one time there was a great uncertainty of the race ever taking place at all, owing to the inability of the French club to obtain the sanction of the Swiss and Austrian authorities to race through the country from Belfort to Vienna. It was due to this uncertainty that the Wolseley Company, already far behindhand in coping with the numerous cars on order, decided to put aside the work on the racing cars until some decision was arrived at. Finally, when the announcement was made by the French club that the permission of the Austrian authorities had been obtained, little or no time was allowed to finish the cars and submit them to severe brake tests and road trials ; in fact the 45 h.p. three-cylinder car, on which the Wolseley Company mainly relied for the Gordon-Bennett Cup, only arrived in Paris about ten hours before the cup racers were timed to leave Champigny.

"In conversation with M. René de Knyff at the Automobile Club de France, I learned that he had driven his 75 h.p. Panhard over 4,000 kilometres, a very good road trial. I believe Mr. Jarrott had likewise driven his car a few hundred miles before the start for the race took place. The three-cylindered 45 h.p. Wolseley not being ready when I left for Paris, it was decided to take over the two 30 h.p. cars, Nos. 169 and 170, and give them a good road test. Mr. Claude Johnson accompanied me on No. 169, and Callan drove the other from Boulogne to Paris. Owing to heated bearings, No. 170 kept us from a fast run to Paris, but, on leaving Callan some 70 kilometres from Paris, Mr. Johnson and myself set off for the French capital to try the running of the car on the many straight strips of road on the journey. The only trouble experienced was from misfiring through the faulty English sparking coil, a trouble from which, I afterwards learned, Mr. Edge had likewise suffered on the Napier.

"After awaiting the arrival of the 45 h.p. for some days I learned by wire from Mr. Austin that it was decided not to enter No. 171 for the race, as no time had been given for a road test, and, much to my regret, I had to turn my attentions to No. 169, one of the thirties. Punctually at 2.30 a.m. on the morning of the race a start was made, from our *garage* in Paris, with car No. 169, myself driving and Mr. Austin accompanying me, to be ready for the *départ* at Champigny. Neither Mr. Johnson, Mr. Austin, nor myself had had above four hours' sleep during the preceding forty-eight hours, owing to the work necessitated in fitting only English parts to the car which was *now* to run in the Gordon-Bennett instead of the Paris-Vienna race, so that at the start none of us were as fresh as we might have been. The car had given a very satisfactory account of itself within the four preceding days, and we had hopes of getting through by making a good steady average all the way, instead of pressing the car unduly. We had gone steadily within about 500 yards of the *départ de la course*, when the motor stopped with a thud. Quickly dismounting we found on examination that a serious mishap had occurred—the crank-shaft had snapped in two.

"No words could express our thoughts, but without wasting a moment I suggested flying off to Paris for the new crank-shaft with Callan, on car 170, whilst Mr. Austin and the other mechanic took down the whole motor. On my return the motor was out, and being taken down, and I at once helped on the work whilst Mr. Johnson and Callan drove off to the start ready to be signalled away. In 5½ hours we had the motor back and the car running. The work of taking down a four-cylinder motor on the road can be realised only when replacing it starts ! By taking down I mean *the whole engine casting.*

"When all was ready, we left Champigny exactly 10¾ hours after our scheduled time, and after travelling well for 30 kilometres we came across three Mors cars at a railway station which had come to grief at the level crossing, the first met with from Champigny. One of these we were sorry to find was painted with "Charlie" Rolls's number. Hard luck—and so near the start ! The car kept running well, and we soon passed two or three cars *en panne.* When we reached Chaumont we heard that Fournier was also *en panne.* Here we lit up, and kept going with scarcely a change of speed until daybreak came, and we reached Belfort about 3.20 in the morning. The road was not flagged, and hence the apparently long time taken over the journey. With scarcely any time for eating we soon had to set to, to oil up and adjust the car outside the first control ready for the next day's spin, both of us practically done up for want of sleep ; in fact we had to keep changing places to give one another's eyes a rest, owing to the strain in keeping a clear look-out through the clouds of dust thrown up by preceding cars. At Belfort I noticed practically a complete Panhard car in pieces, ready to replace any part that might have given out on one of the firm's cars, one car, I believe, being refitted with a complete new gear-box.

"After leaving the Belfort control, the car still running well except for the continuous missing fire caused by the faulty English induction coil, we passed many cars on the stiff gradients before reaching the Bâle control, where sufficient time was allowed for a hasty lunch. After leaving Bâle we experienced two punctures on the near side front tyre, which caused some delay, as the last to occur necessitated fitting a new cover in the broiling sun by two men who had had no sleep for three days. After the tyre was fitted we had a good run to Bregenz. From Bregenz the car ran excellently, and it was not until we reached the commencement of the stiff rise over the Arlberg that we passed some dozen or more cars by the roadside *en panne.* M. Deutsch was walking up whilst his mechanic adjusted a slipping clutch. A 75 h.p. Panhard, a 30 h.p. Decauville, and a Gladiator were amongst the disabled ones. At the top of the pass were walls of snow banked up some five or six feet, which had already been brushed on one side to allow the cars to pass.

"On the descent we passed Max's engineer on the side of the road where the car had fallen, and another Darracq some few hundred yards further on with a broken spring. (The corner where Max fell was extremely dangerous, sloping the wrong way, with a huge rock on the inside of the curve.) On arrival at the Landeck control we heard that De Knyff was *en panne* near Innsbrück ; this being so, and our car running well, we knew that only Edge and ourselves were left in the Gordon-Bennett. At the Landeck control we waited for petrol without stopping our motor, and just as we were leaving again for Innsbrück the motor stopped. 'Accumulators down,' I said. No such thing, however. Off came the lids of the motor crank-chamber and, lo ! another crank-shaft had gone, with only 63 kilometres to the finish.

"This was the end of the Wolseley car No. 169's luck, as no other crank-shaft was to be had. Had there been any possible way of repair we would have done it, but nothing was available, much to our disappointment. I craved for broken steering gear, no spare tyres, a broken chain, anything but so hopeless a fracture ; but such is luck in war or racing, and we can only console ourselves by the old saying, 'Try, try again.' "

MR. C. JOHNSON'S VIEWS.

A representative of THE CAR happened to run across Mr. Claude Johnson, the secretary of the Automobile Club, shortly after he had returned from the thick of the battle that raged from Paris to Vienna, and from the wordy warfare which followed the actual struggle. Mr. Johnson himself started as an amateur mechanic on the Wolseley car driven by Mr. Austin, but was obliged for the purpose of following the details of each day's racing to proceed to the close of the stage by rail, and it was at his urgent request that the judges' committee sat, after the race, in Paris to dispose of the rumours of infractions of the racing rules brought against the winner of the Gordon-Bennett Cup.

Without committing himself, Mr. Johnson let it plainly appear that he did not think very highly of the system of making the awards in the Paris-Vienna competition. Count Zborowski, for example, whose position as first in the class for 1,000 kilogramme racers was taken from him by the imposition of an additional time, has not to this day been informed what sin against the rules it was that he committed in neutralised Switzerland to justify this action. He left the country in the same position relative to the other competitors as he entered it, and apparently his real offence was arriving first in Vienna on a German car.

Essentially the race was conceived as a means of introducing business into fresh districts, and the professional drivers of French cars were out to push business, while the Count was out for pleasure only, and it so happened that his car was the type which its manufacturers had expressly withdrawn from the race. Not entering themselves, and not running a team, the makers of the Mercédès nevertheless scored an actual victory, and all the talk of would-be buyers in Vienna was of the German house of Daimler. There can hardly be any doubt but that trade jealousy was largely responsible for the displacement of Count Zborowski by the addition of a penalty just sufficient to degrade him to third place.

But the dodge was really too late, for the Viennese actually saw him arrive, and the talk was all of him and his car, amid the glum looks of the expectant Frenchmen who had to wait while the honours were showered on him, until their representatives came along playing second fiddle. All along the journey Count Zborowski, out for sport, only treated the trip as a picnic. He would arrive at a control, discard a dust coat, and reveal himself in faultless attire and spotless linen, take out his gold cigarette case, light up, enjoy a smoke, and casually remark, " I think I had better be going on now," and then start off in a casual canter. It was too much for an amateur to saunter through in this apparently lackadaisical way and win !

Mr. Johnson's impressions of Vienna were not greatly in its favour. It seemed to be an off season, and the town was as dull as a third-rate provincial city, with the opera house shut, the theatres closed, and life at a standstill. The official reception also fell flat owing to the banquet being fixed for the night of the arrival, when most men preferred to hide themselves and rest rather than attend a formal function.

MR. EDGE'S IMPRESSIONS.

Seeking Mr. S. F. Edge, our representative found him fully corroborative of the lack of sportsmanlike feeling in connection with the races. He stoutly condemned the system under which the records are summarised by a single official, and the details are not made known either to competitors or the public. There is no check on him even for clerical errors. No competitor knows his own official score from point to point, nor where he has points deducted or adjustments of his time made. In his own case he declared he was quite sure that in more than one control he would enter the neutralised section immediately on the axle of a preceding car, and would follow it exactly to the outward control, and yet have to wait a considerable time after the word to depart was given to such preceding car before he himself was allowed to go. Yet no details of times were vouchsafed, no copies of the records were permitted, and it rests solely in the hands of one official to make or mar any man's success.

In regard to the protests made against him, Mr. Edge explained that they were not formally lodged. A formal protest required the lodging of a deposit of £40, but Mr. Johnson and he both desired investigation into the rumours current against him, and an immediate clearing up of all false reports. The case alleged against him of receiving help when he ran off the road was entirely worked up by one of the timekeepers of the race, an official who, one would imagine, should of all men be strictly neutral, and the only written evidence that help was given was found to have been officially written for the witness, who not only denied the writing of the document but repudiated the

statement it contained ; while as to the absurdity set going about his using French tyres, the fact that his Dunlops were certified before the start, and officially viewed in accordance with the rules, disposed of that mare's nest.

In reply to a query, Mr. Edge explained that he did not drive into a river when the trouble came to him near the bottom of the long descent of the Arlberg. He had stopped to attend to the valve nuts of his driving tyres, and while replacing the air-tubes many cars passed him, raising dust that hung in clouds, and, owing to the road being sheltered, this dust fog did not disperse. Thus handicapped, he dropped down the pass, taking a big risk at each corner of the zig-zag. At most of them he swung out with a huge swerve rather than slow to a crawl. At all of them it was touch and go, and at one of them he mismatched the pace and the curve, and swung too far and slid down the bank into a field. " I thought the race had ended for me," remarked Edge, " at this point, and I got off after collecting my thoughts, and began to have a good look round. Peasants offered to push the car back up the slope we had slid down, but this was a physical impossibility, and to replace the car on the road at that point would have required a crane. I got under the car and found only a water-joint loosened. This I wired up at once, and my cousin wandered along to find a place where the car could regain the road, and in a very few minutes we drove her out of the field and were going again, unaided, unhurt, and with only the loss of a few drops of water." " Not enough water to account for the fiction of the river bed ? " " No, nor the least atom of help to account for the worse fairy tale about our being pushed out."

The corners, Mr. Edge explained, were not the only bad features of the Austrian hills. Frequent flat spaces occur, intended for resting-places for horses, like the landings of a staircase, and at the edge of each landing is a prominent ridge to scotch the wheels of the waiting carriage. Coming down the hills one would hit these ridges at the rate of three a minute, and the wonder is that all the cars that hurried on this part were not knocked to pieces.

Shortly after his lucky escape Edge passed de Knyff, but did not then know that he was in trouble, but assumed that he had won the Gordon-Bennett Cup and was resting content with his laurels, and it was not till an English confrère came along with a whoop of delight, and told Edge that the laurels were his, that he knew that he alone had survived the bad going and secured the Gordon-Bennett Cup for England. Ruts and 150 miles of newly-laid stones made speed a secondary consideration to strength and reliability on the last stage, and yet the winning car could not be set down as a sluggard when it was clocked to do seventy-four miles an hour on a down grade, and ran for many a mile on the French roads (when its faulty coil had a temporary good fit) at sixty-five miles an hour. Already Mr. Edge has in hand a defender car. The course is not settled, but the fact that he will fight is certain. He would like a neutral country if the race cannot be permitted here, and suggested America if a course could be found. One interesting fact concerning the car Mr. Edge explained. It is solely a racing type, and the live axle with direct drive will not be adopted on standard Napiers. His view is that the advantages only exist when racing is the sole object of construction, and that for general use, and for equal efficiency on all the gears, and for renewals in case of accident, a chain drive from the countershaft is altogether preferable.

THE Belgian manufacturers who had cars engaged in the Paris-Vienna race, says *La France Automobile*, are much gratified by the results. A Brussels firm had four vehicles which completed the distance, the first gaining an excellent position. A Liège house was equally fortunate. The severe conditions of the trial showed that Belgian constructors have manufactured a strong, durable type of car, equal to all the exigencies of the roads.

THE NORTHERN ALCOHOL RACE.

Jarrott entering Arras.

The speed test organised by the Minister of Agriculture as part of his alcohol programme fully disposes of the agitation which was worked up last year by a certain class of politicians who sought to make capital out of the benevolent attitude of the Government towards the sport of automobilism. Being close to the general election, the Government at that time prudently dissociated itself from anything which might help to give colour to their protest, and the refusal to sanction racing of any kind on the public highways seemed to show that the days of automobile racing were numbered. Then arose the question of alcohol, which gave a vast interest to automobilism. Instead of being regarded as the sport of a few, the autocar was looked upon as the regenerator of a national industry, and the Minister of Agriculture made it a patriotic question by organising his series of trials and tests, of which the principal events have been held during the past week. Since it was necessary to institute a comparison with petrol, the Minister decided to include a race in his programme, with a view of showing that the agricultural spirit could be used equally well for vehicles running at high speeds, and he has also, at the same time, done a useful work by proving that with proper precautions the racing cars can be driven without the slightest danger to public safety. It is, of course, certain that in automobile racing, as in most other sports, there is a big element of risk to the drivers themselves, who have to display exceptional qualities of coolness, judgment, and nerve, but during the race last week not one of them met with any personal injury.

A Great Success.

The event went off without a hitch, and must be regarded as an unqualified success. The interest of the race lay not only in the fact of its being promoted by the Government as a demonstration of what can be done with alcohol, but it was expected to bring together the new vehicles which had not been given an opportunity of being put to the test through the suppression of the Nice-Abbazia race, and, moreover, it was to see the first appearance of

the new cars that were being constructed for the Paris-Vienna event. Had all of these cars competed the Northern Circuit would have been of exceptional interest. Panhard, Mors, Charron, Girardot et Voigt, and other firms who were building cars specially for Paris-Vienna hastened forward with their construction in the hope of being ready for the alcohol race, but in matters of this kind there is nothing to be gained by hurrying, as some of the firms found out when they came to test their cars, and seeing that there was a good deal to be done to put them in thorough racing order, they wisely preferred not to run the risk of courting the inevitable *panne*. There was, consequently, a lot of disappointment, and no one felt it more keenly than Henri Fournier, who had to stand down at the last moment on account of his losing a pin or something in his new Mors, which he was unable to replace. The only big Mors to start was the one driven by Baron de Caters. The abstention of these cars was the more regrettable, as the firm expected to do great things with their new system of direct transmission on the fourth speed. The C.G.V. cars were also unable to start through not being ready in time, but Panhard et Levassor ran one of their Paris-Vienna vehicles, of a nominal force of 50 h.p., but developing something like 75 h.p., and driven by Chevalier René de Knyff. This is a fine-looking vehicle, with an unusually large engine, having a copper jacket, and M. de Knyff is convinced that it is the fastest petrol vehicle yet turned out. Gobron et Brillié are always to the fore in alcohol demonstrations, as they claim that their motor is particularly adapted for using this spirit, and for the first time they entered the lists with the racing cars. M. Serpollet hoped to follow up his success at Nice by showing that his cars are not only remarkably fast, but that they can stay, and in order to fulfil the conditions of the race he adapted his burners for alcohol. In this respect he seemed to have an advantage over the internal combustion engines, as alcohol is certainly not inferior to petroleum for steam raising, and M. Serpollet says that he is surprised at the excellent results obtained with this spirit. Darracq and Decauville ran the same vehicles that were down at Nice, and Renault Frères were represented by half-a-dozen cars.

The Course.

The total length of the course to be covered by the racing vehicles was 572½ miles. It was divided into two stages, starting the first day from Champigny, and then going through Châlons-sur-Marne, Rethel, and Saint-Quentin to Arras, and on the second day from Arras to Boulogne, Abbeville, Dieppe, Rouen, and Saint Germain. All the towns were neutralised, and every dangerous place was marked out with red, blue, or yellow flags when the competitor had to proceed slowly, cautiously, or stop, according to the nature of the signal. For two days previous to the race the vehicles had been weighed in the Tuileries Gardens for the purpose of seeing if they were within the weight limit for their respective categories. Chevalier René de Knyff's

Henri Farman, 16 h.p. Panhard; Baras, 20 h.p. Darracq; Marcellin, 20 h.p. Darracq; Renaux, 20 h.p. Darracq; Hemery, 20 h.p. Darracq; Edmond, 20 h.p. Darracq; Guillaume, 12 h.p. Darracq; Baron de Caters, 30 h.p. Mors; De la Touloubre, 20 h.p. Decauville; Comte de Failly, 20 h.p. Decauville; Achille Fournier, 18 h.p. Gobron-Brillié; Rigolly, 15 h.p. Gobron-Brillié; Osmont, De Dion tricycle; Bardeaux, De Dion tricycle; Gustave Lazon, De Dion tricycle; G. Richard, 10 h.p. Georges Richard; Canesse, Lamaudière bicycle; Théry, Decauville; Ulmann, 20 h.p. Decauville; Page, 20 h.p. Decauville; Marcel Renault, 9 h.p. Renault; G. Grus, 9 h.p. Renault; V. Oury, 9 h.p. Renault; C. Cormier, 9 h.p. Renault; Baret, Bruneau bicycle; W. K. Vanderbilt, jun., 45 h.p. Mercedes; M. Richer, Metropole bicycle; Albert Collins, 20 h.p. Darracq; Corre, 10 h.p. Corre; Buchillet, 8 h.p. Corre; Georges, Werner bicycle; Bucquet, Werner bicycle; Domptet, 20 h.p. Clé-

The new 75 h.p. racing Panhard, driven by the Chevalier René de Knyff.

new car looked heavy beside the other Panhards, but curiously enough it scaled 22 lbs. less, so that with a considerable increase of force there is actually a diminution of weight. All the vehicles got within the 2,200 lb. limit, but some of them were very close to the mark. Neither the C.G.V. cars nor the Gillet-Forest racing vehicles were weighed. The start took place on Thursday morning at Champigny on the outskirts of Paris. The little suburban village was alive with automobilists and cyclists, who kept up a stream of traffic through the night, and some hundreds of visitors went down by the last train and over-ran the *cafés*, waiting for the dawn when the vehicles were to be sent on their long race. The weather was far from promising, for the rain kept drizzling from time to time, though, fortunately, it was not heavy enough to do more than lay the dust.

The Competitors.

Exactly at four o'clock the start was given to Chevalier René de Knyff, and the others were sent off at intervals of two minutes as follows: Maurice Farman, 35 h.p. Panhard; C. Jarrott, 35 h.p. Panhard; Teste, 35 h.p. Panhard; Georges Berteaux, 16 h.p. Panhard; Gondoin, 16 h.p. Panhard;

ment; Tart, 12 h.p. Clément; Barbaroux, 10 h.p. Clément; Volatum, 10 h.p. Clément; Dacier, Clément bicycle; Derny, Clément bicycle; Rutishauser, 12 h.p. Gardner-Serpollet; Chanliaud, 12 h.p. Gardner-Serpollet; Barbereau, 6 h.p. Gardner-Serpollet; Le Blon, 6 h.p. Gardner-Serpollet; H. P. Déchamps, 20 h.p. Déchamps; René Cozic, 20 h.p. Déchamps; Louis Renault, 16 h.p. Renault; Vauthier, 16 h.p. Renault; Berrué, 18 h.p. Gobron-Brillié; Deckert, 20 h.p. Deckert; Marot, Decauville; Arthur Ducros, 16 h.p. Panhard. In giving the foregoing horse-powers it should be explained that they do not always represent the actual powers developed, and the term is employed by most firms to classify types. In some cases the powers developed are considerably above those given, while in others it may safely be said that they are appreciably below the nominal powers. In certain of the leading makes of engines the brake power is something like twenty per cent. more than the force stated.

The Race.

On a circular course like this it is impossible to follow the various phases of the race except through the medium of the telegraph and telephone, which were naturally at the service of the Government to indicate the arrival of the vehicles at the different controls. Nevertheless, the Minister of Agriculture organised a special train for the benefit of a number of privileged automobilists and journalists who were able to see as much as possible by going to Arras in time for the arrival, and returning to Saint-Germain for the finish. The special started from the Gare du Nord at 8.15. The Minister, M. Dupuy, was there, together with the Baron de Zuylen, Baron Arthur de Rothschild, MM. Michelin, P. Chauchard, Jeantaud, and many other prominent makers and automobilists. The special ran from Paris to Arras without a halt, the magnificent compound locomotive of the Nord flying through the country with its five cars at the rate of 78.8 miles an hour, despite a slowing down when passing through Amiens. On arriving at Arras, the streets were decorated with flags. There was a long walk out of the town to the control, which was situated at the top of a gradient that gave an excellent view of about two miles of straight road. The course was kept clear by soldiers and the police, and military cyclists were ready to pilot the cars through the town to the garage where they were to put up for the night. The weather was mild but damp, with gusty winds and occasional showers, but over some parts of the route the rain fell heavily and made the going here and there somewhat dangerous, especially at the turnings. On arriving at the control, telegrams were coming in with news of the cars, stating first that De Knyff was en panne, and then that Maurice Farman was leading. It was the first time the big Panhard had gone out, and De Knyff had trouble with the friction clutch, while he complained that the carburetter got clogged up with the alcohol. Maurice Farman covered the first fifty-six kiloms. in fifty-two minutes, being in advance of Jarrott by a minute and a half, after deducting the difference in time at starting. Montmirail—82 kiloms.—was reached by Maurice Farman in eighty-seven minutes,- when Teste had now taken the second position, and at Châlons-sur-Marne the leader had augmented his advance on Teste, while Jarrott was third, and Marcellin fourth. On leaving Châlons, Baron de Caters had to give up through one of the wheels of his Mors car breaking when taking a corner. Jarrott was now going remarkably well, for at Rethel he was only ten minutes behind Farman, while Marcellin was eleven minutes to the rear of the second, but on the way to Saint-Quentin the positions changed through Jarrott being obliged to stop to see to his carburetter. The want of a piece of wire made him narrowly miss losing the second place. At Saint-Quentin he was eighteen minutes behind the Darracq, but during the next fifty kiloms. he cut down this advance by seven minutes.

Speeds Compared.

By calculating the speed of the cars when running with petrol it was expected that the leader would reach Arras at about half-past ten, and up till now the race had shown that so far as concerns speed alcohol was giving results by no means inferior to the petroleum spirit. A few minutes after the schedule time a bomb was fired half a mile down the road to announce the arrival of a car, and a bugle was sounded at the control, when the police and soldiers cleared the road. This was done at all the towns through which the cars passed. A moving object rapidly approached along the road, and flew up the gradient at a terrific speed, and Maurice Farman stopped at the control without hat or glasses, while the state of his vehicle showed that there had been plenty of mud on the course. To the questions put to him as to what the others were doing he could say nothing, for after passing M. René de Knyff in trouble he saw no one else, and this was his experience during the whole race. He confessed that he started with little hope of finishing first, but with the big Panhard out of the way he raced to win. His time for the 254.6 miles was 4h. 54m. 5 4-5s., excluding, of course, the neutralisations in passing through the towns. The next arrival was Marcellin in 5h. 26m. 4 2-5s., and then in order of their times came the following: Louis Renault, 5h. 35m. 27 2-5s.; C. Jarrott, 5h. 43m.; H. Farman, 6h. 1m. 32 2-5s.; Osmont, 6h. 2m. 24s.; Bardeau, 6h. 13m. 28s.; Guillaume, 6h. 14m. 13 4-5s.; Collins, 6h. 17m. 1 4-5s.; Edmond, 6h. 23m. 7 2-5s.; Marcel Renault, 6h. 23m. 35s.; Chanliaud, 6h. 26m.; Rutishauser, 6h. 40m. 19s.; Grus, 6h. 54m. 34s.; Cormier, 6h. 56m. 4s.; Rigolly, 7h. 4m. 9s.; Barbaroux, 7h. 14m. 25s.; Oury, 7h. 15m. 11s.; Berteaux, 7h. 30m. 39s.; Gondoin, 8h. 5m. 55s.; Tart, 8h. 6m. 23s.; De la Touloubre, 8h. 11m. 7s.; R. de Knyff, 8h. 17m. 50s.; Cozic, 8h. 28m. 7s.; Ducros, 8h. 31m. 44s.; Le Blon, 8h. 32m. 7s.; Barbereau, 8h. 40m. 51s.; Derny, 8h. 51m. 27s.; Buchillet, 9h. 3m. 27s.; A. Fournier, 9h. 22m. 15s.; Bucquet, 10h. 7m.; Georges, 10h. 9m.; Corre, 10h. 49m. All the Renaults and Darracqs finished the course, but nothing was heard of the Mercedes of Mr. Vanderbilt, which does not seem to have reached the first control. Several vehicles came to grief on the winding and dangerous turnings and gradients between Coulommiers and Montmirail. Altogether thirty-three cars arrived at Arras out of fifty-six starters.

The End of the First Stage.

As the vehicles reached the end of the first stage they were put up at the garage, where no one was allowed to enter except the officials, and thus for the first time came into operation the system of "closed parcs," by which the cars are not allowed to be touched between the time of arrival and of starting the following morning. All repairs had to be carried out on the road and included in the racing time. This undoubtedly gave additional interest to the race, but on the first day it did not affect the positions of the competitors, as all the vehicles arrived in good condition. Drivers of vehicles which got damaged in accidents did not find it worth their while to continue to Arras. M. de Knyff was extremely disappointed at the trouble he was put to with the clutch, and possibly had he been able to repair overnight he might have had a good chance on the second stage, but as it was he doubted whether he would continue the race. On the following day the heavy rains had made the roads so muddy that he decided not to start, as he felt that it would be extremely dangerous to drive such a vehicle at top speed. It appears that when on its good behaviour the car is marvellously fast. After the first cars had arrived, the Minister of Agriculture offered a lunch to those who had come down by special train, and he delivered a speech, in which he spoke hopefully of the future of alcohol, which he believed would in time entirely replace petrol and bring back prosperity to the agricultural industry.

The Second Stage.

If the weather on the first day was hardly what would have been expected in the month of May, it was absolutely disastrous on the second stage. The heavy rains along the coast had left the roads very muddy, and it was raining more or less the whole day, and cars which had been driven safely at forty miles an hour skidded dangerously on the granite setts when passing through the neutralised towns at walking pace. Under these circumstances it is not surprising that the average rate of speed was not so high as on the previous day, or that several competitors gave up in despair. At Arras it was raining heavily when Maurice Farman was sent off at four o'clock, and then followed Marcellin at 4h. 15m., Louis Renault at 4h. 24m., C. Jarrott at 4h. 32m., H. Farman at 4h. 27m., and the others at intervals of two minutes. Maurice Farman reached St. Pol (sixty kiloms.) in sixty-four minutes, absolutely smothered with mud, and Marcellin followed seventeen minutes afterwards, with Jarrott fourteen minutes behind the second. Collins gave up on account of a derangement to his vehicle. Still they raced through the mud and rain to St. Omer (135 kiloms.), which was reached by Maurice Farman at 6h. 33m. The interest of the race was now centred in the struggle between Marcellin and Jarrott, who was rapidly cutting down the Darracq advance, and had gained five minutes up to St. Omer. Rain and mud all the way to Boulogne (188 kiloms.), where Farman arrived at 7h. 14m. Nearly half an hour afterwards Marcellin passed, followed after an interval of three minutes by Jarrott, who, however, lost a quarter of an hour in changing his plugs. Marcel Renault broke a wheel through slipping on the paved roads; Louis Renault broke a pinion, and the motor cyclist Osmont also gave up. Edmond lost the bolt of the transmission shaft of his Darracq, when he had a lead of a quarter of an hour on the other light cars. The weather was responsible for many of these failures, and bad luck for still more, or rather it may have been the "closed parc" arrangement, which prevented the cars being overhauled at the end of the first day's journey. While Jarrott was replacing his plugs he had been passed by Edmond, and at Abbeville he was fourth, only six minutes behind Marcelin, but up to Eu he again lost five minutes on account of his plugs and his carburetter. At Dieppe (330 kiloms.) the weather improved slightly, though it was still very bad. Farman arrived at 10h. 9m., followed by Marcellin at 10h. 44m. and Jarrott at 10h. 55m.

The Finish.

At St. Germain there was a large crowd of spectators to see the finish, despite the stormy weather, which made patience a distinctly precious virtue, and the refreshment tent, the officials' cabin, and other temporary structures had hard work in resisting the violent gusts of wind. A special telephone installation had even been fixed up for receiving news direct from the different controls. And thus we learnt how the cars were racing down along the coast from Boulogne to Dieppe, and then came news from Eu, Vernon, and Mantes, punctuated with occasional reports of accidents, but always qualified with the statement that they were slight, and that no one had sustained any personal injury. In fact, so far as we have been able to learn, not a single driver was hurt, and this, too, under conditions that were certainly not conducive to the safe driving of racing machines. At five minutes past one the approach of Farman was announced, and a few seconds afterwards he was at the control plastered up with mud. His time for the 318 miles was 7h. 7m. 56s., and he had covered the total distance of 572½ miles in 11h. 56m., or at the rate of 47.69 miles per hour. There was a wait of fifty minutes for the second arrival, and there was a good deal of speculation as to whether this would be Jarrott or Marcellin, for the latter was still leading at Mantes, but when not troubled with his plugs Jarrott was going much the faster. At five minutes to two Jarrott came flying to the control, which he passed at full speed. An inspector of police who was running across in front of the car was caught by the off-side wheel and thrown a distance of several yards. He was picked up in a fainting condition, but happily it was found that he had not sustained the slightest injury beyond a few bruises. The reason why Mr. Jarrott raced past the control was that he was closely followed by Marcellin, and he feared that by stopping too suddenly there would be a collision. He just succeeded in securing the second place by ten seconds, his time for the full distance being 13h. 3m. 12s. Mr. Jarrott stated that he had a great deal of trouble with his sparking plugs, and also had to stop frequently to clean his carburetter, while the motor ran somewhat sluggishly. He got to the end of the journey, and wrested the second place from Marcellin, by sheer persistency. Henry Farman finished more than an hour after Marcellin, and after another hour arrived Gondoin, followed at short intervals by Grus, Oury, Rutishauser, Rigolly, and Bardeaux, the latest arrivals reaching St. Germain during the night, when a violent storm was sweeping the country and bringing down the refreshment tent. Nineteen vehicles finished before the control was closed, and the full times were as follow: Maurice Farman (Panhard et Levassor) 11h. 56m. 1s., C. Jarrott (Panhard et Levassor) 13h. 3m. 12s., Marcellin (light Darracq) 13h. 3m. 22s., Henry Farman (light Panhard et Levassor) 14h. 9m. 36s., Rutishauser (Gardner-Serpollet) 16h. 0m. 54s., Grus (Renault) 16h. 4m., Bardeaux (De Dion tricycle) 16h. 2m., Oury (Renault) 16h. 17m., Rigolly (light Gobron-Brillié) 16h. 31m., Gondoin (light Panhard) 17h., Barbaroux (Clément voiturette) 17h. 49m., Cozic (light Déchamps) 18h. 29m., Le Blon (Gardner-Serpollet) 18h. 46m., Tart (light Clément) 18h. 47m., Chanliaud (Gardner-Serpollet) 18m. 57m., A. Ducros (light Panhard) 19h., Barbereau (Gardner-Serpollet) 19h. 16m., Guillaume (Darracq) 20h. 27m., and Cormier (Renault voiturette) 21h. 3m.

A Triumph for the Panhards.

The race is a great triumph for the Panhard cars, of the type that ran last year in the Paris-Berlin event, but lightened considerably to bring them within the weight limit. The axles are hollow, and, while being lighter, are capable of resisting much heavier strains. Weight has also been cut out of the springs, of which there are now only three, the front one being placed transversely under the end of the frame, but in Maurice Farman's car one of the springs broke after leaving Arras, and the vehicle ran for more than three hundred miles with the body banging down on the frame—a sufficiently severe test of strength and solidity. The motor develops about 50 h.p. The new vehicles being built for Paris-Vienna are said to give 70 b.h.p. It is a pity that the car of this type was not able to do itself justice in last week's race. The event was also a success for the light Darracq, in which the maker has accomplished a remarkable feat in putting a 25 b.h.p. motor into a vehicle weighing less than 12 cwts., and running it at high speed over such a course without trouble of any kind. The Renaults confirmed their previous performances by winning in the voiturette class, but the most interesting thing was the behaviour of the steam cars. Down at Nice M. Serpollet regretted the prohibition of the Abbazia race, because he wanted to show that with his new system of condenser the cars would run with great regularity over long distances, and he has proved it in the Northern Circuit by entering four vehicles and seeing them all finish in times ranging from sixteen to nineteen hours. Except for the Panhard cars of Messrs. Maurice Farman and Jarrott, the Gardner-Serpollets were the only vehicles to finish in the class of big cars. The race was also a particularly trying test for the pneumatic tyres, as they could not be replaced except on the road, and the competitors therefore had every advantage in using them until they punctured. We cannot say what was the experience of the number of automobilists who were unable to complete the course, and whether their

Maurice Farman in full flight.

made no complaint on this score. The value of alcohol can only be judged from careful observations in the industrial and touring cars, and its interest in the racing machines lies principally in the fact that it has resulted in a very successful race, and may do still more in bringing about a revival of the sport of automobilism.

A 20 h.p. Decauville, photographed at Nice by Mr. W. H. Sydney Smith.

failure was to be attributed more or less to the tyres, but the winners in the different categories had much less trouble than might have been expected, and the tyres appear to have come out of the ordeal very satisfactorily. As for the alcohol, the results prove sufficiently that the spirit is perfectly suitable for racing vehicles, but whether it can be compared with petrol for reliability is another matter. Some of the competitors complained of the carburetters getting clogged up, and the motors did not always develop their full power, but it is difficult to say whether this can be due to the alcohol, since the winners have

MRS. LEWIS WALLER AND HER MOTOR CAR.

The hearing of this case was resumed on Wednesday of last week, when the defendant, Mrs. Waller, was put into the box, and explained the unsatisfactory way in which the Peugeot car worked.

In cross-examination by Mr. Young, witness admitted that she made no attempt to procure a steam car, inasmuch as she was then coming to the end of her tour. Moreover, a steam car would have been less suitable, as being more noisy than the Panhard she had ordered, as she required it for use in the last act.

Witness, further cross-examined, denied that there was any discussion about the size of the wheels between her and Mr. Farman at any time. The contract she signed was wholly conditional upon the satisfactory working of the Peugeot lent her while the new car was being got ready. She described an interview with Mr. Clingo, Mr. Farman's agent, who called and saw her at the Imperial Hotel. Mr. Clingo asked her to sign a document. He heard her complaints about the Peugeot, and endeavoured to make the best bargain he could on behalf of Mr. Farman. She signed one document—in fact, she believed she signed two documents—and in the result, Mr. Clingo cancelled the original bargain for the building of the new car.

Mr. Young pointed out that the plaintiff never treated the loan of the Peugeot as an essential part of the contract for the new Panhard.

His Lordship: But you said so, Mr. Young, two days ago. And it is the common sense view of the whole transaction that it was an essential part of the bargain that she was to be lent the Peugeot while the Panhard was being got ready. The Peugeot being faulty, Clingo did the best he could for his master, and cancelled the contract.

Judgment was entered for the defendant (Mrs. Waller) on the claim and on her counter claim for the return of the £100 deposit, with costs.

CONTINENTAL NOTES AND NEWS.

The Alcohol Motor Show.

The series of alcohol tests carried out by the Minister of Agriculture have been terminated by the holding of a show in the Galerie des Machines, where the utility of the spirit is being demonstrated in many different ways, but by far the greatest prominence is given to motors and autocars which occupy more than half of the entire space. All the

The Northern alcohol race. Henry Farman on the 16 h.p. Panhard-Levassor light car.

vehicles competing in the recent trials and race are exhibited, and the public are thus able to make a closer acquaintance with the Panhards of Messrs. Maurice Farman and Charles Jarrott, the singular-looking racing Darracq, utterly devoid of anything behind the dashboard except the cylindrical tank surmounted by a seat, and the many other vehicles which show a very strong line of demarcation between the racing vehicle and the touring carriage.

The Northern alcohol race. The winner's car, Maurice Farman's 40 h.p. Panhard. It will be noted that the transverse front spring has given way.

One of the most interesting of the vehicles is the Krieger electric car, which, it will be remembered, got to Arras on the first day, and then retired from the tourists' competition. It has one battery of forty-four cells in the front of the car, and behind is a De Dion motor, with a dynamo on the crank-

shaft for recharging. While, of course, there is a great advantage in having a self-contained electric carriage so as to be able to recharge on the road if necessary, the motor and dynamo, nevertheless, represent so much dead weight, though probably not more than if a second battery were carried, but, on the other hand, the vehicle can only run half the distance it could if two batteries were used, and the process of recharging is somewhat tedious. Again, with a motor of a little extra power the battery could be dispensed with altogether. This car is an interesting experiment, but it remains to be seen whether it will open up new possibilities of improvement in electric carriages. Among the motors the most interesting exhibit from an automobile point of view were the two Centaure engines on the stand of Panhard et Levassor, the larger one of

Northern alcohol race. Jarrott and Geo. DuCros on 4) h.p. Panhard. This shows the new front springing very plainly. The two nuts in the axle just below the spring shackles secure the ends of the light hinged compression rods which run back to the main frame of the car.

70 b.h.p., and weighing only a shade more than 6 cwt. or 9.68 lbs. per h.p. We have already published an account of this engine, which looks remarkably novel with the copper jacket coming half-way down over the steel cylinder. The installation of Peugeot and De Dion-Bouton et Cie., with motors driving all sorts of mechanism from dynamos to threshing machines, show that there are many side lines in the motor trade that may be turned to profitable account.

The Alcohol Awards.

The general classification in the Northern Circuit has been somewhat modified by the final results, for after an examination of the control sheets it is found that Marcellin, on his light Darracq car, was second, while Mr. Jarrott, who was believed to have beaten him by ten seconds, takes the third place, though, of course, he is still second in the big vehicle class. Over the entire course the average speed of Maurice Farman was 44.8 miles an hour, of Marcellin 41.2 miles, and of Jarrott 41.15 miles. This average would have been much higher if it were not for the abominably bad weather on the second day, which made a difference in most cases of nearly four miles an hour. In the trials of touring vehicles a Chenard-Walcker car is first with the remarkably low consumption of 65.31 litres per kilom. ton, and then follow two Bardon cars (the lowest with 78.66 litres), a Delahaye, a De Dion-Bouton, and a Société Nancéienne. Prizes were awarded to

The Northern alcohol race   A conversation at the control.   Rigolly on the 15 h.p. Gobron-Brille.

Chenard-Walcker in the big carriage class, to Delahaye for a light car, and to Peugeot for a quadricycle. Among the industrial cars prizes have been awarded to the Société Georges Richard for a light vehicle, and to the Société d'Automobiles Bardon for a lorry carrying more than a ton.

The Paris-Vienna Race.

Arrangements are making satisfactory progress for the Paris-Vienna race, and all the mayors along the route through France have given their consent, though one of them has suggested that something should be done for alcohol, and it is probable that

The Northern alcohol race.   The 9 h.p Renault with Aster engine.   The inevitable dog insists on being photographed.

a special class will be set apart for vehicles using this spirit. It is expected that the alcohol cup of the Prince d'Arenberg will be offered as a prize. It has also been practically decided that the race for the Gordon-Bennett cup will be run off at the same time. A course will be marked off, over which the vehicles will be timed, but it is not yet known whether they will be required to go on to Vienna. The race will start from Champigny, and will go by Fontenay, Nangis, Provins, Troyes, Bar-sur-Aube, Pont-sur-Saône, Amblans, Ronchamps, and Belfort. From thence the course will go either through Switzerland or Bavaria. This will be settled in a day or two.

A Philanthropical Automobilist.

The automobile industry is often regarded as a very profitable enterprise, and people usually engage in it for the sake of making money, but the example of a French millionaire may very well be followed by others whose financial situation places them above

Northern alcohol race.   Rutishauser on a Serpollet.

[We have to thank the Hon. Leopold Canning, J.P., for kindly placing at our disposal the photographs, from which the Circuit du Nord illustrations published this week are made]

the necessity of securing profits out of the manufacture of autocars. Baron Henri de Rothschild is a very enthusiastic automobilist. For years he has been taking a practical interest in the sport and pastime, and has closely identified himself with the Mercedes cars, which he was the first to introduce into France, and the creation of the Henri de Rothschild Cup at Nice is evidence of the active part he is taking in furthering the interests of automobilism. Besides this, Baron Henri de Rothschild is a doctor, and under the name of Doctor Pascal gives his services to the hospitals, and he is the founder of an infirmary in Paris, and also, we believe, of a hospital near Chantilly. The Baron is now associating automobilism with hospital work by taking up the manufacture of autocars. He has designed a new car something upon the lines of the Mercedes, and propelled by a 30 h.p. motor, which is being built at the Bardon works at Puteaux. For the moment, only this one type is being constructed, but doubtless smaller cars will be turned out as soon as the factory is properly equipped for the work. Dr. Pascal will not take a penny profit from this enterprise, but the whole of it will be devoted to the maintenance of his infirmary and hospital.

THE ANNIVERSARY RUN:

CLAIMS FOR NON-STOP CERTIFICATES.

SINCE our last issue the Automobile Club has issued a list of applicants for non-stop certificates, in connection with the anniversary run on the 8th instant. It is intimated that other applications have also been received, but in some cases the applicants have failed to have the times filled in on their time cards by the official timekeepers. The records consequently are incomplete, and the certificates cannot be granted. In other cases the time records attached to the applications show clearly that the drivers have failed to adhere to the speed rules; and as the committee recognise that rules are useless which can be disregarded, the applications in such cases could not be entertained. In other cases complaints have been received that drivers have broken the rules which prohibit passing on

Photo. by]   MR. C. JARROTT ON A 10 H.P. NAPIER   *[The Car*

going down hill, and in controls. These complaints have been forwarded to the drivers concerned, and if they can satisfy the committee that the complaints are unjustified, the names of the cars will be published later.

It will be noticed that the number of applicants whose claims the Automobile Club has recognised as *primâ facie* valid is not particularly large; in fact, it only attains a total of thirty-four. No doubt this may seem small enough in proportion to the total number of vehicles which took part in the run, but it must be borne in mind that not by any means all of the latter were entered for non-stop certificates. So many of the occupants of the cars, moreover, were wet through long before arriving at Reading, that it was quite excusable for them to retire on that ground

Photographed specially for THE CAR *by]*   THE START FROM GROSVENOR PLACE   *[the Biograph Studio*

alone. No one expected such drenching rain, coupled with half a gale of wind and occasional hail. Then, again, it is not known how many were the "other applications" that have been received. There may have been a fair number of cars, which, under the trying conditions prevalent, made

THE PIPE CAR WHICH WAS DAMAGED BY A BUTCHER'S CART

non-stop runs, but not in conformity with the limits of time imposed by the club.

The following is the official list of applicants :—

Official Name.	Name of Owner.	Name of Makers, etc.	H.P.
Aboras -	*Mr. W. Stocks -	De Dion-Bouton, Ld.	8
Albany -	Locomobile Co. - -	Locomobile Co. of America.	$5\frac{1}{2}$
Albatross -	Dennis Bros., Ld. -	Dennis Bros., Ld. -	12
Anglo-Saxon	*Mr. G. A. Barnes -	Mitchell Motor Co. -	2
Attractive -	*Mr. William Glass -	Firefly Motor and Engineering Co.	12
Blind Man -	W. Payne and Co. -	Motor Manufacturing Co., Ld.	10
Bull Dog -	Dennis Bros., Ld. -	Dennis Bros., Ld. -	9
Certiorari -	*Mr. Ernest de Wilton	De Dion-Bouton, Ld.	8
Chelmsford -	Clarkson and Capel -	Clarkson and Capel Steam Car Syndicate, Ld.	12
Creeper -	Mr. Alf. C. Wright -	Ormonde Motor Co. -	$1\frac{3}{4}$
Diana -	*Mr. H. H. L. Lewis -	Daimler Motor Co., Ld.	6
Doubter -	Mr. Arthur F. Smith -	Darracq et Cie. -	12
Fireworks -	*Mr. W. J. Crampton -	Decauville - -	10
Flying Fox -	Mr. Stuart B. Yoakes -	Germain - - -	$7\frac{1}{2}$
Irene - -	*Mr. H. Melvill Simons	Durkopp - - -	10
Lenthall -	Rawlings Bros., Ld. -	Marshall and Co. -	12
L'Orvet -	*Mr. Arthur F. Mulliner	Gladiator - - -	12
Mars - -	Mr. F. P. Marshall -	Benz - - -	10
Noiseless -	*The Hon. A. Verney Cave.	Wilson and Pilcher, Ld.	8
Patti - -	Mr. E. B. Palmer -	Singer Cycle Co., Ld.	$2\frac{1}{4}$
Petrolls -	*The Hon. C. S. Rolls -	Panhard et Levassor	10
‡Rambler -	*Mr. Walter C. Allen -	Jeffrey Co., U.S.A. -	$4\frac{1}{2}$
Reliable -	John Marston, Ld. -	John Marston, Ld. -	10 to 12
Rosalind -	*Mr. John H. Gretton -	Motor Manufacturing Co., Ld.	7
Sluggard -	Mr. William Exe -	New Orleans Motor Co., Ld.	14
Soupac -	*Mr. S. F. Beevor -	Daimler Motor Co., Ld.	6
Steadfast -	Speedwell Motor Co. -	Gardner-Serpollet -	6
Tempter -	Mr. Harry Martin -	Bayliss Thomas and Co.	$2\frac{3}{4}$
Toronto -	Locomobile Co. - -	Locomobile Co. of America.	$5\frac{1}{2}$
Tourist -	*Mr. Geo. Iden - -	Motor Manufacturing Co., Ld.	20 bhp
Violet - -	*Mr. C. F. Wahl - -	De Dion-Bouton, Ld.	$4\frac{1}{2}$
Wanderer -	*Mr. Syd. D. Begbie -	Century Engineering and Motor Co., Ld.	12
Watsonia -	Mr. Herbert Watkins -	Durkopp - - -	10
Weary Will	*Mr. Philip Simpson -	Panhard et Levassor	6

* Gentlemen whose names are marked with a * are members of the A.C.G.B.I. and Motor Union.

‡ Protest lodged on the ground of a stop.

The list of cars other than the foregoing which arrived at Oxford and which adhered to the rules will be published when the time records have been checked.

The annexed illustration reveals the damage that was done to Mr. Frank Atherley's 15 h.p. Pipe car by the carelessness and bad management of the driver of a butcher's cart. The accident took place at the dip between two hills not far from Goring, on the road to Wallingford. Mr. Atherley was descending on his proper side of the road as the butcher's cart was descending the opposing rise. At the dip there is a by-lane, and the butcher, without any warning, suddenly crossed over to his wrong side and attempted to get in between the car and the end of the lane. Not carrying any brakes he was of course unable to slacken speed when he found that he had miscalculated his distance, and he has to be grateful to the fact that motor-cars carry powerful brakes that he was not seriously injured. As it was, the pony between the shafts had a leg broken and had to be shot accordingly, while, as will be seen from our photograph, the lamps and other details of the car were damaged.

Another interesting picture which we publish herewith is a snapshot of two police spies at Nuneham, near Dorchester. A car in which three members of The Car staff were travelling was duly warned by Mr. Carter, the obliging cyclist who displayed to each vehicle as it approached a board with the legend "Police Trap" in large letters. A few hundred

POLICE SPIES AT NUNEHAM

yards further on the man seen at the left of the photograph was discovered standing at a hedge corner, and, suspecting that this was the trap, one of the occupants of the car jumped out and discovered a second spy behind the hedge. Seeing that the game was up he came from his hiding place, and the pair of worthies were promptly photographed.

Another and more important aerostat *v.* automobile contest is being promoted by Mr. Leslie Bucknall, who will fly his new balloon, "Vivienne II.," the largest in Britain. The ascent will be made at Reading during December, and prizes to the value of £30 will be offered. The previous evening the aeronauts and automobilists will meet at a dinner.

ARRIVING AT A CONTROL STATION

MR. AND MRS. S. F. EDGE ON A
16 H.P. NAPIER

SOME OF THE
CARS DRAWN UP AT READING

A GROUP IN THE STATION YARD,
READING

DESERTED CARS AT LUNCH TIME

ROYAL DESPATCHES BY MOTOR-CAR:

A SIGN OF THE TIMES.

"IN the King's name!" has been the cry of the royal *legati* for centuries as they hurried by chariot or coach, on foot or horseback. Many as have been the methods of the messengers in carrying despatches of the State, it was not until last week that the Foreign Office mail was ever carried by motor-car. The distinction of being the first King's messenger to carry such despatches *en automobile* has been gained by Lieutenant W. G. Windham, late Royal Indian Marine, who utilised his 9 h.p. Darracq "in the King's name" between Charing Cross Station and Whitehall.

Lieutenant Windham, the King's foreign messenger, carried the Foreign Office despatches for Brussels, Berlin, Darmstadt, Copenhagen, and intermediate stations. These

duties. One can imagine the shade of a king's messenger of Chaucer's days, booted, spurred, armed, and armoured, gazing, with ghostly eyes, round with wonder upon Lieutenant Windham driving his Darracq within the confines of historic Whitehall. Truly a change has come o'er the spirit of our dream !

ENGLISH AS SHE IS WROTE.

THE following is a literal copy, save for the suppression of names, of a letter received by a London firm of engineers from a French correspondent :—

Masters —— and ——, Engineers, London.

I invite you to come at home, as soon as possible, to finish of regulating the movers you have furnished at me,

THE KING'S MESSENGER ARRIVING AT THE FOREIGN OFFICE WITH DESPATCHES

included letters from His Majesty to the Queen, who was at Copenhagen. The same route was taken for the return journey, and this time the lieutenant carried letters from Her Majesty to the King. He arrived at Charing Cross Station a few minutes before six o'clock, and there his motor-car was waiting in readiness. The porter at the Foreign Office was probably astounded at the sight of the King's messenger driving a motor-car—an outrage to the custom of centuries !

As His Majesty himself is such a keen automobilist, this seems a fitting innovation and one which he will undoubtedly look upon with favour. The time will come when many others of the officials of the royal household will adopt the ubiquitous motor for the more rapid execution of their

there are two or three months. By the same occasion I shall have any littles goods bespoken to bespeak. I shall pay your travel's expenses. Besides, you shall be entertained at home if that thing agree you. I beg Master —— to indicate his arrival's day.

Receive, dear Sir, my better salutations, ——.

I beg Master —— to come here before the 10 November, because I shall depart in voyage at this epoch.

"Movers" is intended for "motors." The rest of the quaint epistle is self-explanatory, but it is long since we have seen a letter couched in such palpably "French-English."

AN international exhibition of all the industries connected with the automobile and the cycle is to be opened in May next at Idrott's Park, Stockholm.

THE UNCONTROLLABLE HORSE.

A Record of Five Days' Accidents with Horses. Five Persons Killed and Sixty-five Injured.

As so much has been written within the last week or two about motor accidents and so-called motor accidents which are not such at all, we think it advisable, in the interest of automobilism, to give a record of five days' accidents to horse-drawn vehicles. We have, therefore, kept all the reports which we have been able to come across, though there are undoubtedly many in local papers all over the country which have of necessity escaped our attention, and many more accidents that are not recorded at all. At any rate, it is obvious that those who clamour for new legislation in connection with the regulation of motor traffic should also, to be consistent, do the same with regard to horse traffic. As any interference with horse traffic would be looked upon as little short of ridiculous, we need hardly point out that it is most unwise at the present time to disturb the motor regulations. At any rate, those who talk of the dangers of the motor have only to read the incomplete summary below to form an idea of the unreliability of the horse and its driver, for although we hear so much about incompetent motor drivers no one ever says a word about incompetent horse drivers, which, as a matter of fact, are far more numerous in proportion. As we have so often pointed out the more logical lines for the Legislature to move upon in this matter would be to improve the facilities for travel on our highway, so as to accommodate the new form of traffic which has been legalised, and to frame regulations applicable to all forms of traffic alike. It will be noticed that the list includes some accidents caused by horses taking fright at motor cars, but our justification for noting these is to be found in the fact that horses ought to be properly broken in to these vehicles. It should be understood that we give this record impartially, and not because we are in any way prejudiced against the use of horses. All we ask is that the horse and the motor shall be treated in the same way, because it is obviously not equitable that the often uncontrollable horse should be allowed to be used free of restrictions imposed upon motors which are so certainly controlled, and the action of which does not depend upon the whims of a dumb creature.

AUGUST 26TH.

Collapse of a cab at Rotherham; cabman's leg broken.

Waggonette accident near Chester-le-Street; one man killed, nine or ten injured.

Fatal trap accident at Kirkby-in-Ashfield; pony shying at lights.

Two carts in collision at Salford; child injured.

Brake overturned at Stanford Rivers; twelve persons thrown out, six seriously injured.

Collision between two traps at Unthank, near Brechin; man seriously injured.

Carriage horses bolting on Tomnamoon Brae, Perthshire, precipitating driver and a lady and child into the road.

Trap accident at Heywood; two men injured.

Trap accident at Colchester, throwing out driver and a boy.

AUGUST 27TH.

Trap accident at Newbury, pony taking fright, and injuring a young lady.

Landau accident at Blackpool; horse took fright, injuring itself and driver and knocking down some palings.

Carriage accident at Dufftown; young lady injured.

Trap accident at Burgess Hill, Sussex; horse startled, collided with another trap, two ladies and gentleman injured and horses cut.

Carriage accident in Oxford Street, London; gentleman and lady seriously wounded.

Accident at Bedale, Yorks; horse killed.

Man killed at Sheffield; knocked down by a *char-à-banc*.

Miller's waggon at Coventry collided with a stationary motor car.

AUGUST 28TH.

Runaway horse with trap collides with dray at Burton; occupants thrown out.

Little girl knocked down by horse and waggon at Bradford.

Pony and cart overturned by tramcar at Bradford.

Pony (with trap) shied at motor car at Market Weighton.

Horse frightened at passing object at Lisnaskea, Ireland.

Cart upset at Arbroath; four young men injured.

Horse frightened at motor car at Truro; three injured.

Car horse frightened at Ballymena; lady injured.

Vehicle overturned by a horse at Cromer; two injured.

Boy killed by van at Bristol.

"Runaway" at Newport damaged a wall and hoarding.

AUGUST 29TH.

Horse took fright at motor bicycle at Annan.

Man thrown from waggonette at Northampton; arm broken.

Four-in-hand collided with tramcar at Edinburgh.

Horse frightened at gipsy's tent and fire at Sandy, Beds.; coachman lamed.

Pony shied at Romsey; man thrown out of trap, and plate glass window smashed.

Horse startled by steam roller at Whitby; heavy cart overturned.

Cab and butcher's cart collide at Birmingham, and bring down two cyclists; machines wrecked.

Farmer's horse frightened at motor car near Caithness and injured.

Van horse frightened by motor car at Lowestoft, and woman injured.

Pony took fright at Lewisham, and threw doctor and coachman out of trap.

Horse-drawn van furiously driven at Deptford; knocked down a boy.

One trap run into by another at Redditch, and driver of one seriously injured.

AUGUST 30TH.

Two boys injured by runaway horse at Irthlingborough.

Pony (with trap) startled, and collided with stationary cart; lady rendered unconscious.

Mayor of Evesham injured by pony being frightened at a dog.

Collision between two traps at Cropthorne, and boy thrown out.

Trap collided with motor car at Pickering.

Horse frightened at "something" at Retford, and bolted, colliding with other vehicles and causing much damage.

At Hope Horse Show one of the animals, while being judged, kicked a judge, and rendered him unconscious.

Waggonette collapsed at Tickhill; driver's leg broken and other people injured.

Child killed near Beccles by cart being overturned.

Horse attached to a hay-making machine took fright at steam-roller, and man injured.

Cabs collided in Sloane Street, W.; one overturned and driver and a lady injured.

Cab horse fell down on tramlines at Yarmouth.

We might go on indefinitely, but we think we have given a sufficiently long list to convince the ordinary reader that there is quite as much danger with horses as with motors.

THE AUTOCAR

A Journal published in the interests of the mechanically propelled road carriage.

EDITED BY H. WALTER STANER.

No. 372. Vol. IX.]   SATURDAY, DECEMBER 13TH, 1902.   [Price 3d.

THE AUTOCAR.

EDITORIAL OFFICES:

COVENTRY.

PUBLISHING OFFICES:

3, ST. BRIDE STREET, LUDGATE CIRCUS, LONDON, E.C.

CONTENTS.

COLONIAL AND FOREIGN EDITION.

IN ADDITION TO THE USUAL EDITION OF "THE AUTOCAR," A SPECIAL THIN EDITION IS PUBLISHED EACH WEEK FOR CIRCULATION ABROAD. THE ENGLISH AND FOREIGN RATES WILL BE FOUND ON THE LAST PAGE. ORDERS WITH REMITTANCE SHOULD BE ADDRESSED "THE AUTOCAR," COVENTRY.

The Autocar can be obtained abroad from the following:

AUSTRALIA: Phillips, Ormonde, and Co., 533, Collins Street, Melbourne.
FRANCE: Nice, Levant, and Chevalier, 50, Quai St. Jean Baptiste.
UNITED STATES: The International News Agency, New York.

Notes.

The Numbering Proposals.

On the 3rd inst. a conference was held at the Automobile Club between the legislative committee and the club committee with reference to the Bill placed before Parliament by the Hon. Scott Montagu, and drafted in conformity with the recommendations of the legislative committee of the club. The club has issued the following report of the conference: " After discussion it was unanimously resolved, ' That this meeting hereby confirms the action of the legislative committee in accepting the principle of the identification of motor cars coupled with the abolition of the speed limit, but considers that, before the formal assent or approval of the club is expressed, some assurance should be obtained that such regulations will be made as will, as far as possible, minimise the risks to automobilists which might arise from abuses of identification.' A resolution was passed asking the Hon. Scott Montagu to insert, if possible, in his Bill a provision that the speed of the motor car, irrespective of the circumstances of the case, need not necessarily constitute ' furious driving.' The arguments used in connection with these decisions were that if every motor car be identified, a driver who might be driving, for instance, from London to Liverpool, with moderation and conformity to the law, might, a fortnight after the completion of his journey, receive a summons for alleged furious driving said to have taken place in a village quite unknown to him by name. The summons might arise from a complaint lodged by some cantankerous person having a strong antipathy to any means of road locomotion except horse-drawn vehicles. The driver of the vehicle would probably have no knowledge as to the precise portion of the road alluded to in the charge, inasmuch as the name of a certain district only might be mentioned, which might extend for some six miles of the road. He would, naturally, have a very poor recollection of the traffic and other circumstances existing on that portion of the road at the time he passed over it, and he would have no opportunity of finding the names and addresses of persons who witnessed his passage. He would therefore not be in a position to defend himself against any accusation, however preposterous or vexatious it might be. It was suggested in the course of the discussion that the Act, or regulations made under the Act, might provide that the method of identification should not be made use of unless the driver could be charged with having driven to the danger of other passengers then on the highway, or with having failed to stop when called upon to do so by a police constable or the driver of a restive horse. If every driver of a motor car is to be at the mercy of every other passenger on the highway who may see fit to charge him with furious driving the life of a careful driver of a motor car may be unendurable, as it is at present under the twelve-mile-an-hour limit. It is therefore suggested that the new Act should incorporate a provision which will make it impossible for a motorist to be prosecuted for furious driving in circumstances under which a speed considerably in excess of the

145

speed of horse drawn traffic might be legitimate; for instance, on a portion of open straight highroad with no cross roads, no houses, and which is unoccupied by horse-drawn vehicles. It was agreed that there is no reason why, under such circumstances, the speed of a motor car should be confined to the speed of a horse-drawn vehicle; on the other hand, it is recognised by automobilists that it is only right and proper that the drivers who propel motor vehicles at high speeds through villages, past cross roads, and round corners, might be, and should very properly be, prosecuted for furious driving." This is the official summary of the club's new attitude towards the Bill as disclosed at the conference.

An Attempt to Improve the Bill.

It will be seen from the above that the additions which are now suggested by the club put a very different complexion on the Bill as compared with the one which has been placed before Parliament with the unqualified approval of the legislative committee. As the Bill stands, and without the additions now suggested, it merely provides for abolition of the speed limit and the numbering of cars, reference also being made to a method of facilitating an appeal from magisterial decisions to a superior court. The points brought up in the discussion, and mentioned above, show that the opposition with which the Bill has been received by

the bulk of automobilists has had partial recognition, and that many of the arguments used by its opponents have been taken to heart, particularly in the attempt to limit the abuse which would arise from improper use of the identification facilities offered by numbering. These additions to the Bill, if they are practical and possible—and this is a point we are not prepared to discuss at the moment, though, as we have frequently shown, there is a great risk of some clauses being accepted, and others (and perhaps more vital ones) thrown out when it comes before the House—undoubtedly greatly improve it; but it is necessary to bear in mind that but for the fortunate fact Parliament could not consider the Bill in the present session it would have been passed in its original and very imperfect state. We think the changes which are now suggested are another argument in favour of our suggestion—that for the time being it is far better to leave the law alone, and not to bring forward this or any measure till such time as it is practically forced upon automobilists. The discussion at the club showed that the club committee were very much more fully aware of the objections to the Bill in its original state than were the legislative committee, and it is more than probable that when the opportunity promised later for general discussion of the subject by the club is given the membership at large will be found even more opposed to it than the club committee. The statement made

Mr. J. B. Dunlop, the inventor of the pneumatic tyre, driven by Miss Dunlop on their new 12 h.p. Argyll.

on behalf of the club, that the majority of sober-minded men believe in the Bill as originally drafted, is an entirely mistaken one, and it is necessary to remember that less than two years ago the club was absolutely opposed to numbering propositions of any kind, and in its then attitude was backed up practically by the whole of the British automobile world. However, now the matter has been brought forward, the best course is to discuss it fully, but the presentation of any bill should be postponed as long as possible; if it can be two or three years hence, so much the better. As the matter stands, automobilists throughout the country have to thank the congested state of Parliamentary business for their escape from a measure which has been shown by the position now taken by the club to have been imperfect. Had it passed into law as drafted, the last state of the automobilist would have been very much worse than the first, and this has been patent all along to almost everybody except the members of the legislative committee. We recognise very fully the good which the Automobile Club has done and is endeavouring to do on behalf of the movement, but we feel in this matter a very grave mistake has only been most narrowly averted. Automobilism has escaped a great damage merely by a piece of good luck, as only circumstances altogether outside the control of the legislative committee have prevented the incomplete and dangerous Bill they have fathered from becoming law.

Mails by Motor.

Although the Post Office authorities have been experimenting at different times with motor vehicles, they do not, so far as London is concerned, appear to have taken up the matter with anything like thoroughness. In fact, it would appear that they are not by any means favourably impressed with the motor, as it was stated in the *Daily Mail* last week—in reference to the accident to the Brighton horse mail coach which had part of its load taken to its destination by the motor mail van which runs between London and Redhill—that the Post Office authorities explained that only a few mail hampers were taken up by the motor van, and, further, that no motor vehicle had been found which could carry heavy weights; and, consequently, the authorities were not departing to any extent from the older method of horse draught. Whether this is an official statement from the Post Office chiefs or merely the opinion of subordinate officials does not really matter very much, as the policy of the Post Office with regard to motor vans is ample proof that no really serious attempt has been made up to the present time to supersede the horse-drawn mails, except, of course, in instances like the Liverpool and Manchester motor service; but, then, as we stated a moment since, we are dealing with the London policy. All our older readers know that from time to time we have recorded experimental runs by the Post Office authorities from London to Redhill, and, further, that they have referred to at least three different makes of motor vans, but, despite this, the authorities have, with the exception of a few trifling loads, stuck to the horse. The reason for this is not difficult to find. The Post Office requirements are altogether of a special character—quite different from those of any other user of heavy traction—but the authorities expect to get the exact type of vans they want practically without paying for them. The manufacturers may design and make as many different types as they like, and the Post Office, in certain cases, will consent to try these vehicles and even to pay for their hire, but they take an isolated machine, and if it should fail once, that is practically the end of the matter, and the unfortunate maker, who may have spent anything between £2,000 and £5,000 in endeavouring to secure their contract, is left with some unwieldy machine on his hands, which is neither a heavy tractor nor a light delivery van, and which can hardly be transformed into a *char-à-banc*, and is, consequently, more or less useless. If the Post Office had any real desire to take up motor traction it would decide to spend a little money on the matter. As it does not do this, it may have to wait some years, and then, as all sorts of commercial motor vehicles will have been made, it is quite likely that with the multiplication of models and types, there will be one or two which, by comparatively small modification, can be made to meet the requirements of the Post Office. It is a strange thing, however, that, despite the accidents which happen too frequently to the Brighton horse-hauled mail, nothing is said about relinquishing that archaic method of conveying His Majesty's mails.

Prevention of Side-slip.

Probably no competition organised by the Automobile Club will be of wider service to automobilists generally than the trials which are being organised of devices to prevent side-slipping. Already one very promising method has been tried, and has met with the most satisfactory results. We cannot at present give a description of the arrangement, but it is one which can be attached and detached in a few minutes to or from any existing tyre, whether pneumatic or solid. It has been tested upon two cars of absolutely different build and weight distribution belonging to members of the Automobile Club, and has proved completely reliable. The first trial was made on a very wet night from Queen Victoria Street, along the Embankment, over Westminster Bridge, down the Kennington Road, and up Brixton Hill to Streatham, the roads being in an exceedingly treacherous condition. The car was driven with great freedom, and intentional swoops and curves were made, and, in fact, a serpentine was steered in and out of the greasy tram-lines without any side-slip whatever. Trials were also made over asphalt and, in fact, every description of road surface. When the brakes were jammed on suddenly the car could be pulled up without deviation, and in taking bends or corners it seemed to follow its true course without any slip. The arrangement has also been tried on an ordinary pedal bicycle, and with conspicuous success. So far as we can gather, there is no doubtful element about the arrangement, except, possibly, the effect it may have on the tyre. We do not think it will damage it, though we can scarcely regard this as proved at the moment. It is not likely that it will have any appreciable slowing effect on a car, at any rate. This may possibly be apparent on a bicycle, though even if it is it will be due to outside causes rather than to any inherent defect of the device itself.

The Gordon-Bennett Cup.

Last week we referred to the nomination of two Napier cars by the Automobile Club to defend the Gordon-Bennett cup for England, and also mentioned that an eliminating race would be run to decide which make should be the third car to represent this country, three being the maximum number of machines allowed to each competing nation. In addition to the Wolseley and Star vehicles which are being built to take part in the eliminating race, we hear that cars of nominally 40 h.p. are being constructed by the Dennis Co. of Guildford and by the Rex Co. of Coventry. (The latter will be completed in seven or eight weeks.) Further than this, a Napier will take part in the eliminating contest, and in the event of it beating the other vehicles, there will be three Napiers in the race proper, as, of course, the one intent of the eliminating test is that the best vehicle shall be selected. The participation of a Napier in the test will undoubtedly add interest to it, as it will enable some sort of idea to be formed of the capabilities of the two other cup defenders of the same make. In any case, if no further competitors are found for the eliminating trial in April, it will be exceedingly interesting, as there will be at least four specially-built racing cars taking part in the trial. The Napier cars are being built suitable either for racing in Ireland or for the picked roads of France, as, of course, it is still doubtful where the race will be run next year, though the probabilities point to France. Since the above was written we have been informed that the Wolseley Co.'s proposition to put in a car for the race has been withdrawn so far as the Gordon-Bennett contest is concerned, though the company will enter Wolseley vehicles for races on the Continent during the year.

The 1903 Reliability Trials.

It will be seen from the conference reported elsewhere that the regulations for next year's reliability trials embody many of the practical improvements which we and others have suggested from time to time. These trials will unquestionably be the most interesting which have ever been held by the club, as nothing whatever will be permitted to be done to the cars except during their running time and while actually on the road. Even the operation of filling up the tanks with petrol and water will have to be performed after the cars have been officially started on their day's run. At the same time, it will be necessary to take some special precautions to prevent abuse of the replenishment rules. If this is not done, some competitors may obtain a misleading advance on others, and stops for refilling should be recorded entirely separately from those for repair or adjustment of the machine.

Lord Pirbright's 12 h p. Dennis car. This is one of Messrs. Dennis Brothers' new models, and is known as the Pirbright pattern. It has been built to the order of Lord Pirbright, and is driven by a 12-14 h.p two cylinder engine. The gear-box is large, and big wearing surfaces are provided, and the drive is direct when running in the top gear. The power is transmitted from the change speed gear to the rear live axle through universally jointed arborshaft and bevel gear. The bevel gearing is also specially large to provide against wear. The car has five brakes, three of which are operated by two pedals, while the two back wheel brakes are worked from the side lever as usual The tyres are Goodyears. The body is built throughout of aluminium, and is painted and upholstered in Lord Pirbright's colours. The car is very quiet and smooth in running, this feature being largely due to the new Dennis governor In appearance, as will be seen from the illustration, it is a decidedly handsome vehicle. It was driven in the Oxford run of the Automobile Club recently, and was one of the three cars of the same make which earned non-stop diplomas

STUDIES IN EXPRESSION.

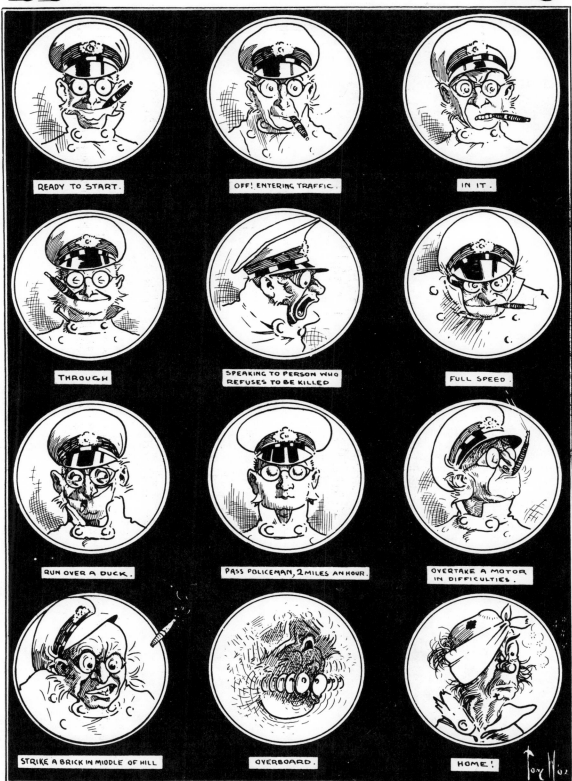

THE MEDICAL MOTORISTS OF BOURNEMOUTH.

Mr. George Frost, M.D., Mayor of Bournemouth, on his 7 h.p. Daimler car, with his 5 h.p. Wolseley hard by.

Automobilism has taken a strong hold upon the medical men of Bournemouth. Conspicuous amongst those who have adopted the autocar is the retiring Mayor, Dr. George Frost, who keenly appreciates the increased facilities given by an autocar in visiting his patients. This genial and popular gentleman is an enthusiastic motorist, and keeps two first-rate cars. His motoring experiences have been of a most exciting description, and include, amongst other things, a hairbreadth escape. On first taking to driving a car, and on coming down one of the many steep hills in Bournemouth, he failed to make proper use of his brake, and on taking a corner his car turned a complete somersault, throwing out his chauffeur into the road, but imprisoning the doctor underneath it. He escaped with a slight scratch, whilst his passenger came off scot free. The doctor spent his holiday this year motoring in the New Forest.

Dr. F. W. Cory is one of the oldest motorists amongst the Bournemouth medical men. He possesses a wonderful capacity for improvements in detail connected with his Bollée tandem, and has designed and remade several parts of it. A noticeable feature is the fitting of convex air fans that direct a continual stream of air to parts liable to become overheated when the machine is in motion. Another clever contrivance of his, which he terms a hurricane shield, is fixed as a protective measure to the lamp, making it impossible for it to blow out.

Dr. F. W. Cory and Mrs. Cory on their 2 h.p. Bollee tandem.

Dr. F. W. Ramsey, on his 7½ h.p. Benz; his 3½ h.p. De Dion standing on the left.

This improvement only refers to the tube ignition with which his tandem is fitted. Moreover, he has made a specially-designed funnel, which has the addition of a small tube that allows the air to

Dr. H. Nankivell on his 6 h.p. White steam car.

escape from the petrol tank when filling it, and also acts as an overflow, directing any petrol in excess of the amount required to fill the tank to a receptacle placed for the purpose. The use of this will allow the operation to be carried out in the dark. This method would be appreciated by many who are in the habit of using a naked light in close proximity to the petrol tank. His method of fixing a large carriage umbrella to the tandem is very ingenious, and in use efficiently protects both himself and passenger from rain, wind, and sun.

Dr. W. T. Gardner and Mrs. Gardner on their 3½ h.p. De Dion.

Dr. Harold Simmons was the first to efficiently demonstrate to his *confrères* in Bournemouth the possibility of continuously running a De Dion voiturette in medical practice for two years. He also enjoys the distinction of being the police surgeon, and of being on the most cordial terms with all grades

of the force. He is responsible for many converts to automobilism amongst the Bournemouth medicals. Amongst the latest converts is Dr. Roberts Thomson, who is awaiting the delivery of the car he has on order. This gentleman is colonel of the 1st Hampshire Volunteers, and, doubtless, will use the car extensively for military purposes.

Dr. Rolt Davidson, who has a car turned out by a Coventry firm, is also experienced in the use of a motor bicycle. Dr. Davidson is a firm believer in the necessity of owners having the knowledge of

Dr. A. McCall at the helm of his 6 h.p. Serpollet.

enabling them to deal with any hitch that may occur under any circumstances.

All the medical men whose portraits are here given are unanimous in declaring that the horseless carriage has firmly established itself in the medical world as a distinct advance on the older method of progression.

The Mayor of Bournemouth.

FRENCH ROAD SIGNS.

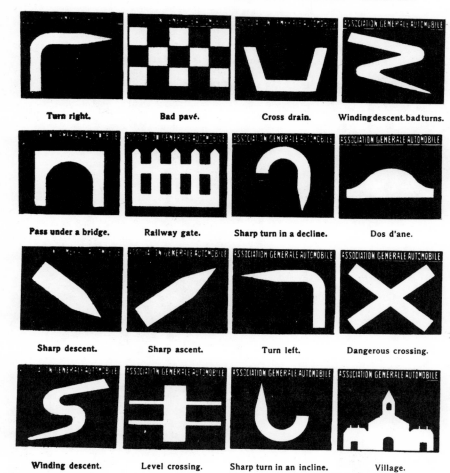

Turn right.   Bad pavé.   Cross drain.   Winding descent. bad turns.

Pass under a bridge.   Railway gate.   Sharp turn in a decline.   Dos d'ane.

Sharp descent.   Sharp ascent.   Turn left.   Dangerous crossing.

Winding descent.   Level crossing.   Sharp turn in an incline.   Village.

The French Association General Automobile are, as we mentioned in *The Autocar* of November 29th, 1902, suggesting the erection of direction boards on the principal highways for the guidance of automobilists. A very numerous assortment of these boards is contemplated, and a few of them are shown in the annexed illustrations. Some of these signs appear to us to be particularly useful, such, for instance, as those showing a steep ascent or descent when they occur unexpectedly. The level crossing sign is good where the crossing is approached by a bend, and the winding descent sign is a useful warning to a driver. Some of the other suggested designs are rather wide of the mark, and would be apt to destroy the value of the really useful signs, which to the tourist would be of the greatest benefit. The signs are to be painted in white upon a black or green background, and should show up well.

The Pershore magistrates are certainly not to be congratulated upon their sense of justice. Only a few days since they fined Mrs. Biddulph Martin's driver £10 and 25s. costs for an alleged excess of the legal limit along a stretch of road by the village of Eckington, Worcestershire. Now, the constable who brought the charge stated that the measured distance over which he timed the car with an ordinary watch was a quarter of a mile and four yards, and he measured this distance out by pacing. A local butcher and a relative of his—a baker— also stated that in their opinion the speed was about eighteen miles an hour, and on the strength of such evidence the magistrates actually inflicted the maximum penalty. It appears to us that a great injustice has been done, as no owner is more careful than Mrs. Martin, and her men are good and considerate drivers. Since she has taken up automobilism she has covered many thousands of miles without any complaint whatever. So far as we can gather, it would appear that the witnesses were planted ready at the time the trap was set, but how a bench of magistrates could accept paced measurement and times with an ordinary watch taken by one man from one end of the paced stretch we really do not know. Still less can we understand why General Davies and the bench over which he presided should accept evidence prepared in so slipshod a manner. What would be thought of weights and measures prosecutions in which the inspector guessed at the inaccuracies or measured them by the span of his hand, and yet the one is no more ridiculous than the other.

* * *

The Worcestershire County Council have been considering the preparing of regulations to govern motor cars, but have not shown any excessive degree of enlightenment in the matter. In addition to the usual identification and certification proposals, they go so far as to recommend that motors should be chargeable with higher rates of duties than at present. That "indication boards" should be placed on main roads at the termini of towns and villages, and also at any places where it is advisable that motor cars should slow down. The outlay for these boards would be recouped to the council out of the fees to be charged for registration of the cars. That Section 7 of the Act of 1896 should be amended so as to provide that £100 shall be the maximum penalty for an offence instead of £10 as therein provided.

COUNTY COUNCILS AND HIGHWAYS.

From a County Councillor's Point of View.

The article on this subject in your issue of December 27th attracted my attention, inasmuch as I have seen the practical working of the Highways and Local Government Acts so far as county councils are concerned, and the Highways and Locomotives Acts so far as traction engine traffic is concerned.

A few words, therefore, from the point of view of the county councils may enlighten your readers who take an interest in this topic. In the earlier portion of the article contributed by Mr. Morrison he speaks as if he were interested in traction engine traffic, complaining that county councils, by closing certain bridges against such traffic, have, *ipso facto*, debarred traction engines from using certain roads. In speaking against the iniquity of such a procedure, he makes certain statements which, to my mind, are not capable of proof, such as the following: "These highways, which are unfit for a traction engine, are, as a rule, unfit either for a bicycle or a motor car." Although I have cycled over most of the principal main roads in England and Scotland, I prefer to base my deductions from roads I know very intimately. To take Northumberland as an example, the main roads in that county are excellent, well kept and maintained, and are eminently fitted for cycle and motor car traffic, yet they are unable to stand the constant heavy traffic of eight and ten-ton traction engines, drawing one, two, and sometimes three waggons behind them. As a matter of fact, I know of no macadam roads in any county having a good surface and fitted for light fast traffic, that will stand rough work of this class for any length of time.

Again, Mr. Morrison asserts "that it is absolutely essential that the character and the condition of our highways shall minister to the new *régime*—pounds, shillings, and pence being a secondary consideration." This may be all very well from the point of view of the traction engine proprietor, but there is the other side to be looked at. I happen to be a member of the Northumberland County Council, and I can speak of the great damage done to the main roads in that county by the increasing number of heavy traction engines using the roads—once purely agricultural roads, as Mr. Morrison terms them, and which I am prone to admit were never made or intended to bear the weight of such heavy traffic; and in speaking of Northumberland I know from what I have seen that I am simply re-echoing the sentiments of other county councils as to the great damage done to their roads. During the last eight or nine months the damage done to the Northumberland County Council main roads by heavy traction and steam locomotive traffic has amounted to something like £8,000. This has chiefly been caused by the constant and heavy traction engine traffic from and to quarries. A great portion of the damage would doubtless be recoverable under the head of "extraordinary traffic," but, as a matter of practice, very little of it is recovered, the legal proceedings for the recovery thereof being complicated and slow, and quarry companies and contractors not always being keen to pay, often going bankrupt instead.

To repair the damage thus done has caused the county rate to go up at least 1d. in the £ during the last six months.

Amongst some of the proprietors of traction engines there has been displayed—possibly unintentionally—a great lack of consideration for at least nine-tenths of the traffic that use our main roads. Cyclists and owners of motor cars would, I think, feel rather ashamed if they thought that, through their use of the roads, they were putting the authorities who have to pay for the whole maintenance of the roads to a great deal of extra expense; with some traction engine proprietors it seems to be different. They pay something like £10 a year for a county license for their engine, and they seem to think that this payment is equal to an insurance premium for any damage their engines and vehicles cause to the roads. Travelling as they do through a county—in times of frost as well as during wet seasons—hauling furniture vans or brewers' rolleys, they do an incalculable amount of damage, which cannot be recovered under the head of "extraordinary traffic," as it is not confined to any one particular road, but is spread over a number of roads.

My personal experience of the best surface on main roads for cycles, motor cars, and ordinary carriage and vehicular traffic is good macadam, well rolled in by a steam roller, and systematically looked after and maintained. A smooth macadam road will not stand for any length of time the heavy weight of the traction engine. If the macadam be laid upon a proper foundation, the surface, if much used by traction engines, always gets broken, and becomes soft, and is never the best for cycle, motor car, and other vehicular traffic, and the road, so far as surface is concerned, must always be classed as a second-grade one. If traction engine traffic goes on increasing, as it has done of late, then all our first-grade county main roads will in a few years become second-grade roads, something similar to what they were some ten or fifteen years ago before the benefits of the steam roller were felt on our roads.

Foundationless Roads.

These roads—so termed by Mr. Morrison—undoubtedly predominate in the different counties in the United Kingdom. They do so in Northumberland, where the whole of the main roads are managed by the county council and by one official—the county surveyor—and his deputies. The main roads in that county are excellently kept, and their surface is of the best, and I can honestly say that I have cycled over none better in England or Scotland. Yet they are "foundationless roads"!

Now comes the crucial point! We have something like 450 miles of county council main roads in Northumberland—wholly maintained by the county—and the county surveyor estimates that to remake the roads with a foundation to withstand heavy traction engine traffic will cost something like £800 per mile; so that £800 multiplied by 450 gives us £360,000.

May I ask Mr. Morrison where the money is to come from if this expenditure has to be incurred?

The nation which he speaks of " that can afford millions for war and that can well afford to defend its internal welfare by the possession of efficient highways at home " is, in my humble opinion, not likely to provide the money required. Neither can the existing highway rating authorities, who will undoubtedly resist any further large expenditure upon their roads, willingly accede and provide this large sum of money. If it has to be done, who then must bear it?

In England and Wales we have something like fifty-two counties, and, taking an average expenditure for re-forming the county council main roads of, say, £250,000 for each county, something like £13,000,000 would be required to place our county main roads in anything like a condition fitted to bear the heavy weight of constant traction engine traffic. I am afraid that a sum like this would make a hole in the profits of even traction engine owners! It cannot be reasonable for them to expect others to provide this money, which would only be for their benefit.

When I speak of £13,000,000, I am only estimating for county main roads. In each county the district councils maintain a larger mileage than the county councils, so that I feel sure that I am within the mark when I say it would cost £26,000,000 to remake the roads of England and Wales to stand traction engine traffic. I would rather see a portion of this money spent on light railways adjoining our main roads and tramways upon the highway waste lands. Instead of having traction engines on our roads we should see light railways and tram roads conveying the goods and traffic of the district at much less cost, and at much greater speed, and at the same time interfering very little with our present roads.

A Question of National Importance

The last portion of Mr. Morrison's paper is occupied with a dissertation under the above heading. He seems to dread the electric tramway and its extension, and longs for an independent and active agency, which, while equally efficient, need not be imprisoned within the limits of special tracks. My answer to this is to be found in the motor car or light locomotive, which will go beyond the radius covered by the electric tramway, and which will in a few years cause many country places to become, as it were, the suburbs of large towns.

When he longs for a corps of inspectors—paid red-tape mercenaries, I prefer to call them - operating under the control of the Local Government Board, and who, thoroughly conversant with the circumstances and exigencies of modern road user, shall gradually manœuvre British highways into line by friendly counsels with the existing road surveyors, I am led to sigh. I am afraid my friend has had little experience of the Local Government Board and its red-tape officials. I would have no hesitation in choosing as the lesser evil the local highway authority—even if it be an independent little oligarchy of itself, having its own special ideas and antipathies, and practically recognising no superior authority—to a paid band of Government mercenaries who know as little about a macadam road as they do about a traction engine.

A Larger Question.

I am inclined to think that Mr. Morrison in his article raises a larger question than he imagines. To my mind, instead of getting any appreciable number of light locomotive owners to help the traction engine proprietors in their agitation against the county councils, he will find in course of time that the county councils will get the assistance of all cyclists and owners of all motor cars and vehicular traffic to resist the increasing traffic of heavy traction engines breaking up their roads. From what I see ahead, I feel sure that the whole of the county and district councils will be taking joint action on this head themselves, and that at no distant date the cry will not be that of the traction engine proprietor against "foundationless roads," but that of the county and district councils clamouring to keep heavy traction engines off their roads altogether. I have often been pained to see the way some roads have been cut up and spoilt by traction engines, and if the traffic continues the surface of all our principal roads will deteriorate, and we shall find that, instead of good surfaced roads fitted for fast light traffic, we shall have nothing but bumpy roads, such as those who use the main roads of the kingdom find when they approach to within some four or five miles of large towns.

JOHN A. WILLIAMSON.

THREE TYPES OF FINISHED HONEYCOMB COOLERS (see page 11).

Lozenge cooler with side tanks.   Hexagon cooler with round air tubes and fan complete.   The Mors type of lozenge cooler.

HONEYCOMB COOLERS.

We find that a good many who have not been able to see the new types of radiators and coolers are somewhat mystified as to the actual construction of what has hitherto been known as the Mercedes type of radiator, but which the French prefer to call the honeycomb. The three illustrations we give of different forms of complete coolers on page 10 will make their construction clear. The fan shown behind one of them is driven by the engine, and its mission is to induce a current of air through the air tubes of the radiator, so as to ensure cooling. It is not always necessary at high speeds or driving against strong winds, but when the car is hill-climbing or running very slowly artificial circulation is imperative. These coolers take the form of a flat box some three or more inches thick, which is pierced by a number of tubes. The genuine Mercedes has square tubes packed very closely together, but there are numerous other sections, several of which are shown (round, square, diamond, and lozenge), but the principle in all is the same—that is to say, the tubes which pierce the tank are surrounded by the hot water as it comes from the engine, and this runs around these tubes, and is cooled by the circulation of air through them. Of course, the principle of all radiators, coolers, or condensers is the same. That is to say, the heated stream or water which it is desired to condense or cool, as the case may be, is passed either through or around tubes exposed to the cooling influences of the atmosphere. In the case of the flanged coils of radiators

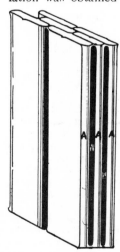

Fig. 1.—The original shape of the tube

which have hitherto been mainly used, the water is pumped through the cooling pipes; but with the honeycomb type the air passes through the pipes, and the water surrounds them; but in each case the object is the same. As the lozenge type of air tubes was one of the puzzles of the French show—people being unable to understand how the circulation was obtained—we give a couple of illustrations which will explain the apparent mystery. The tubes are oblong in section, as shown in fig. 1. Both ends are slightly expanded, and at the centre on either side a slight lip is formed, as shown in figs. 2 and 3. The tubes are then nested together, as shown in both the figures, and are soldered together at the ends. Now the expanded lips of the tubes coming close together leave a space around each separate tube, as is depicted by the heavy shading in fig. 2. The air spaces—the interior of the tubes—are lettered A, while the water spaces are lettered W. The object of the central lip in the side of each tube is to form an abutment for the tube lying next to it and its

Fig. 2.—A vertical perspective view of a nest of tubes. The out-turned lip is shown more clearly. A A A are the air tubes, W W being the water spaces.

The New Type of Radiator.

opposite one; in this manner a very neat joint is secured, and the lip on each tube being very slight it is very difficult to detect any deformation, as is shown by fig. 3. In the illustration, fig. 2, the water spaces are slightly exaggerated in order to show them more clearly; in reality they would be little more than half the size shown. Though this is a very small space indeed, it is claimed to be sufficient for the purpose, and it certainly results in a very large area of thin films of water being exposed to the cooling surfaces of the tubes. The tubes are all soldered in position, and so far as appearance is concerned the lozenge form of radiator is very neat, though we should question whether it would prove so durable as the types with the

Fig. 3.—A perspective view of five complete tubes and a finishing one nested. Note the central lip which forms the abutment for the neighbouring tube.

round or square tubes, in which greater clearances are given. We have to thank Mr. H. Waterson, of Aston, Birmingham, for his courtesy in lending us the photographs from which our illustrations are produced and the sections from which our drawings are made, Mr. Waterson having taken up the agency for this type of radiator and tubes, and is, in fact, supplying large quantities in France as well as in England to manufacturers, either to

Fig. 4.—Alternative sections of tubes which may be used in constructing this form of radiator.

Fig 5.—Another type of cooler. This is simply a tank with a large number of round section tubes passed through it.

make up or in the form of radiators, or, when preferred, they can buy the coolers complete. We understand that many cars in the forthcoming shows will be fitted with honeycomb coolers.

THE LIGHT DELIVERY VAN TRIALS.

Under the chairmanship of Mr. G. H. Burford, a fairly representative meeting of the Society of Motor Manufacturers and Traders was held on the 31st ult. to discuss the above. The meeting approved of the trials lasting for three months, no maker to be allowed to enter more than two vehicles in each class, and the judges to be independent technical experts, and not connected with the industry. A commercial committee was formed to draft rules and conditions for the competition under which the members of the Society of Motor Manufacturers and Traders will consent to enter vehicles.

Mr. A. E. Pearson, of 13, Stonegate, York, informs us that he is making arrangements by which he will shortly open a motor garage and repairing depot, which will be known as the York City and County Garage and Motor Agency. It will be situated near the Market Place in the centre of the city within two minutes' walk of all the main roads passing through York.

A SHIP OF THE ROADS.

The 16 h.p. Napier car, shown by the two accompanying illustrations, has been supplied by Messrs. S. F. Edge and Co., of 14, New Burlington Street, W., and fitted by the Coupe Co., of 14, Regent Street, W., with a body of somewhat novel design supplied by the owner. Mr. Stuart Ogilvie, who is the well-known dramatic author, is an ardent convert to automobilism. He depends entirely upon the reliability of his Napier car not only for tours, country calls, and shoots, but for station work and business appointments, and has disposed altogether of his horses and carriages.

The Napier with the hood up

So far as the engine and change-speed gear are concerned, these are those of a standard 16 h.p. Napier, but in order to take the owner's special body, the channel steel frame has been particularly constructed. The artillery-built road wheels are (fore and aft) 36in. in diameter, and are shod as to the drivers with the well-known and most durable Sirdar Buffer tyres (solids); and as to the steering wheels, with Midgley's armoured pneumatic tyres. In the conception of the body, Mr. Stuart Ogilvie has endeavoured to embody therein numerous conveniences which, up to the present, are not commonly found on automobiles. It will accommodate six passengers, including the mechanic. The central seat within the brougham body is raised nine inches above the driving seat in front for the purpose of giving those occupying it a good view of the road forward, which, of course, cannot be obtained in the seats of the ordinary double phaeton-bodied cars, where the occupants of the vehicle all sit on the same level. These seats, as can be seen, are most adequately protected by a hood, which when down forms an efficient dust screen for the passengers. This hood is so designed that by the addition of two detachable side columns and a roof section, all of which are carried on the car, the vehicle can be converted from its open form into a single brougham or landaulette in less than three minutes. This covered portion of the vehicle is intended for refuge in bad weather and for night driving.

The hood down.

The rear spider seat is level with the central or hooded seat, and accommodates, too, the mechanic and a passenger when the former is not driving.

This overcomes the difficulty of finding a seat for the driver without having to depose a passenger.

The question of baggage, carriage, and stowage has had the particular attention of the gifted writer. Beneath the central seat is a boot, on the lines of that of the old-fashioned mail coach, access to which is obtained from the rear. This boot accommodates two canvas dress cases, each 29in. by 19in. by 13¼in. Under the spider seat a large dustproof tin box, made like an uniform case, is accommodated. This case measures 30½in. by 18½in. by 10in.; and Mr. Ogilvie trusts that these dimensions will satisfy the requirements even of a lady passenger. On the underside of the boot or box provided for this case are slotted carriers, which carry the brougham top and side columns when these are unshipped. Upon the footboards of the spider seat being raised, two trays are discovered, divided into several suitable compartments, to take all necessary spare parts and tools.

Nor do the above particulars exhaust all the conveniences of this remarkable body. The box seen below the frame gives shelter to the Castle and Bleriot lamps during the day, and when this landcraft is commissioned for a long trip, picnic, or shooting parties, the box will accommodate extra baggage or a luncheon hamper, guns, ammunition, etc., the lamps meanwhile remaining on their brackets. When not in use, the brougham seats are protected by a waterproof covering, which can be stowed beneath the box cushion of the spider seat when not required.

The body is finished in "Napier" green, with black mouldings picked out red. The wheels are in red to match the lines, and picked out with broad green lines of the body shade. The upholstery is in green morocco, with rich broad laces throughout.

The car has been christened, and will answer to the name of "Stai," the warning cry of the Venetian boatman as he swings his gondola round a corner on the wrong side.

We believe we are correct in saying that Mr. Stuart Ogilvie was for many years a Surrey magistrate, and graced the benches of both Kingston and Guildford, but a fate cruel to automobilists of the South has spirited him away to the eastern counties, where, nevertheless, we feel assured he will spare no effort to temper magisterial prejudice wherever it shows itself.

THE NEW NON-SKIDDING DEVICE.

Mr. Crampton's 10 h.p. Decauville, to which the antiskidder is fitted. By Mr. Crampton's side the inventor of the device is seated.

Recently we referred to a device which had been tried on different cars with great success for the prevention of side-slip. We are now able to give some more definite details. The arrangement is known as the Parsons non-skidder. As will be seen from the reproduced photographs, the device consists in its approved form—there are a number of alternative ways of obtaining somewhat similar ends—of two flexible wire hoops, one on each side of the wheel and of slightly larger diameter than the rim. The hoops are connected together by steel chains passing diagonally from one hoop to the other round the tyre. The hoop or ring on the inside of the wheel is endless, but the outer hoop is supplied with a right and left-hand screw coupling, which affords a ready means for adjusting the non-skidder to the tyre. The diameter of the hoops is such that they cannot pass over the periphery of the tyre, and we are assured they cannot come off even when it is

A rear view of Mr. Crampton's car.

deflated. The non-skidder is not fitted tightly enough to impress the tyre visibly, and in running "creeps" slightly, so that the chains never bear on the same point of the cover at any two consecutive revolutions. Any very slight loss in efficiency from this cause is probably more than made up by the superior adhesion of the wheel and non-skidder as one. That is to say, the loss is probably far less than it would be with a plain tyre on a greasy road; but not only so, there is the immunity from danger at good speeds, and the entire freedom from nervous stress, which can only be obtained with plain tyres by driving at a very low speed indeed, and even then, in certain conditions of road surfaces, a little slipping may take place. We are informed that some dozens of wheels have been running on different cars over long distances, and that none of the covers have shown any signs of wear from the non-skidder having been used. It will be seen that the arrangement can be easily fitted to any wheel without taking the car to pieces in any way, and the chains can be renewed, if desired, in sections, as each zigzag is a separate member. Side-slip is caused by the tyre failing to bite the road proper, the mud, when being in what is known as a greasy state, acting as a sort of lubricant, and presenting a film between the tyre and the road surface, so that the car has little lateral stability; and any deviation from the line of progress, whether caused by steering or by the disturbing effect of brake application, results in a side-slip more or less serious, according to the speed and general circumstances of the moment. The action of the non-skidders appears to be that they cut through the grease and get a bite upon the road itself. The arrangement was first tried upon a bicycle, and as soon as Mr. Parsons had satisfied himself that it was right he fitted it to a car, and a number of practical motorists were so thoroughly impressed with its value that a strong syndicate is being formed, in which Mr. Henry Edmunds, Mr. Paris Singer, Mr. W. J. Crampton, and other well-known members of the automobile world are interested. They have all given the non-skidders a good test, and Mr. Parsons has already had the honour of supplying a set to His Majesty the King. We have not yet had the opportunity of testing the non-skidders ourselves, but, as we have shown, they have been given a thorough trial, and there appears no doubt that side-slip has been, to all intents and purposes, overcome. It is hardly necessary to say that the arrangement is equally applicable to motor cycles, though in this case we presume that both wires are

One of the King's wheels. Goodyear tyres with non-skidders fitted.

One of the Collier-tyred wheels of Mr. Edmunds's Daimler car Antrona.

fitted with pipe nuts, so that the hoops can be put on and taken off without pulling the machine to pieces. We should perhaps add that it has not been found necessary to fit the chains to the front wheels. All the tests have been made with them fitted to the back only, and even when braking violently the car could be always pulled up in its straight course without slewing. At the same time, if absolute security is desired, it would probably be better to have all four wheels chained. Mr. Harry Parsons's address is the City and Suburban Electric Carriage Co., Ltd., 157a, Manor Street, Clapham Road. S.W.

Sir Thomas Lipton at the helm of his latest car, a 10 h.p Panhard. The Hon C. S. Rolls, from whom he bought it, occupies the tonneau seat

AMERICA'S SWIFTEST CAR. THE BAKER ELECTRIC RACER.

By Hugh Dolnar.

It is said that there are in the United States three hundred factories all told building mechanically-driven road vehicles, which factories turned out nearly 19,000 vehicles in 1902, and that the total automobile output for 1902 reached twenty millions of dollars in value. This vast industry has grown up within the last ten years, and no one, it may be said, yet realises the plainly evident truth that next to bringing out the grass and putting the leaves on the trees in spring, the job of building the horses and the waggons is the very biggest on earth; and now that it is here, it is sure to stay and to grow larger every day until this little world freezes up and puts the human race in peaceful cold storage for all eternity, or else drops into the sun and is vaporised in a jiffy, and so end all our proud achievements, automobile building included.

So lately as 1895 there were really no automobile factories and no automobiles. A few men—Duryea, Haynes and Apperson, Pennington, Morris, Salom, and Whitney — were working on autocars here in America, and Benz in Germany was building machines that would run. The French had only just borrowed the Daimler motor from the little German town of Cannstatt, and were trying to drive vehicles with it. England—having most effectually turned down the first really successful motor car makers in the 1830's, and driven the commercially successful steam passenger coaches of Dr. Gurney and Sir Charles Dance off the road by absurd horse-favouring laws and taxes—was building no automobiles in 1895, and almost none in 1900.

But now things are changed. The Stanleys—Newton neighbours of East Boston Whitney—brought out their elegant little steam cars, which were to the slow and ponderous early English steam carriages what a greyhound is to an elephant; and so from the work of Whitney and Stanley came the Locomobile with its superb factory at Bridgeport, the Mobile with an elegant plant at Tarrytown, the White Steam waggons at Cleveland, the Toledos at Toledo, Ohio, and others; and we have even imported some of the heavy English truck manufactures of England, so that now Gurney and Dance are well pulled out from under the hoofs of the horses that, with the aid of fine conservative British legislation, trampled on Dr. Gurney's sound engineering and smashed Sir Charles Dance's bank balance in 1831.

Not all of the automobile makers have made money, and many of them up to now are heavy losers; but those wonderfully successful twins, the Stanley Bros., of Newton, who began all over again with little steam vehicles, after selling out to the Locomobile in 1899, told me the other day that they were running one hundred hands on steamers at their Newton shop, and had so far turned out a large number of vehicles at a good profit, all sold at the shop door without advertising or agents, for $650 each, clearly demonstrating that money can be made building mechanically-driven vehicles if the maker goes the right way about it.

Baker, of Cleveland, is another builder of light vehicles of the "runabout" type who knew his letters and could read his little book. But while the Stanley Bros. were first country school teachers and then photographers, and next and now large makers of photographic dry plates, and became road carriage makers by accident, and succeeded by force of natural ingenuity and sound business sense, with no previous engineering knowledge or training at all, Baker came in through the other door, being thoroughly trained in factory practice, and becoming a ball-bearing expert before he touched motor making. As the Stanleys leaned towards steam, so Baker was won by electricity as a motive power for waggon driving. The Stanleys were "natural mechanics," and while all of their remarkable work was strong and original, much of it was raw and needed reshaping; but both Stanley and Baker were full believers in ball bearings from the first, both fully recognised the imperative need for light weight in construction, both made vehicles which the automobile heavy construction school derided as flimsy toys—the Stanley steam and the Baker electric vehicles being about the same weight, something over 600 lbs. ready for work on the road—and both used ball bearings in all possible places, so that little power was needed to drive their work.

The Baker electric runabout starts from rest with 6½ lbs. drawbar pull, and both Stanley and Baker have made money, and will so long as they stick to their present light-weight autocars and grease them with steel balls and sell them at fair prices.

The Stanleys paid for a good solid thorough engineering education in small steam-engine construction right in their own shop and under their own tutorship, and went from their first little sopping wet steam motors using 140 lbs. pressure of saturated steam to their present practice of superheated steam at 300 lbs.; and Baker, having combed all the snarls out of his elegant little electric "top buggies," was bitten by the speed bug; and the virus, thus transferred to his young blood, of which he has plenty, drove his brain to the task of devising the fastest possible car — electrically driven, of course—to carry its two operators only: one to manage the motive power and one to steer and brake the waggon, but to carry these two in safety and at ease over a common road as swiftly as the swiftest bird can fly; and having thought out his scheme, Baker built this "Baker racer," which cost about $10,000, and can run on a good common road at an eighty-five miles per hour rate, and which is here illustrated and described for the first time.

In designing this uttermost machine, Baker had many questions to answer and many riddles to read. Because of storage battery driving, the weight must be great; it is about 3,100 lbs. To give steadiness the wheelbase must be long and the wheels must be large, ball bearings must be used everywhere to decrease the friction to its lowest possible point, the centre of gravity must be kept low, the mass must be carried as nearly as possible in the horizontal plane of the two axles, and the carriage must be many times stronger in every part than mere carrying of its load requires. Wind resistance must be carefully avoided, the two passengers must be enclosed and protected from the air through which they rush, and, above all, the steering mechanism must be absolutely ideal, with a prodigious strength and safety factor, and without the slightest lost motion, proof against wear, and responsive to slight muscular effort on the part of the driver. At high speeds life and death depend on small fractions of seconds in direction operations, and it would be no less than suicide to attempt to guide a machine hurling itself through space at the rate of a mile in less than forty-three seconds if the steering gear did not at all times rigidly control the positions of the steering wheels. There are locomotive engineers who

Fig. 1. Front view of Baker electric racer as it appears with driver and electrician out of sight, inside the shell.

have more than once perhaps ridden at the rate of seventy-five miles an hour on their rail-guided machines, and so know something of the sensations due to rapid transit on wheeled vehicles; and these swift road runners can tell how much "go and come" they would tolerate in their steering gear if called upon to drive eighty-five miles an hour on a trackless course. It is possibly not so very difficult a task for so very experienced and skilful a designer as Baker to get out a machine capable of holding together at great speeds; but it certainly calls for ingenuity of the highest order to produce such directing elements as shall guide a projectile weighing a ton and a half with ease and certainty when flying eighty-five miles an hour over a common road surface. Hence, while all engineers must admire the sound and bold designing shown in the choice of elements and their placing and securing in the Baker racing automobile, they will be most impressed with Baker's turning to marine practice for his wheel and axle and wire cable-steering device. This steering rig is powerful enough, so that I myself, old and not at all strong, was able to move the steering wheel without extreme effort, when two muscular men—one at each wheel—grasped the steering wheel tyres on each side, and did their best to resist the movement I imparted to the wheels. I thus enlarge upon the abundant leverage and holding power of this steering gear, because, after the most regrettable fatality which occurred at Staten Island

on the occasion of the only public exhibition of the speed of Baker's racer, it was asserted that the accident was due to a failure in the action of the steering gear. Mr. Baker and Mr. Denzer, who were the driver and electrician in the Staten Island event, both assure me that the cause of the accident was in no way due to any weakness of the machine or failure of the steering gear or any part to work perfectly, but wholly from the fact that hundreds of over-anxious and excited spectators had crowded into the road or track near the end of the course, not in the least realising at what speed this electric machine was moving; but Mr. Baker with his tachometers know just what he is doing. He knew his wonderful speed, and reckoned the havoc that would occur if he did not stop. Hence he applied the only available mitigation—he shut off the power, applied the brakes, and within 650 feet brought the machine to a standstill with its nose on the track, where the machine took the natural skid to a right-about position. It was the skid that proved fatal to the unfortunate onlookers; and, appalling as it was, Mr. Baker's cool head doubtless saved a score or more of lives that must have been lost had he pursued the course to the end.

The factors of strength and safety of the machine were proven under this great and instant strain. When the brakes were applied, they locked the rear wheels. One wheel rim gave way, and with one corner of the racing car frame touching the road bed, the steering was seemingly impossible; but Baker kept it on the road, with the steering gear, steering wheels, and axles uninjured; and to-day all the steering parts are still unchanged, in their places, and in perfect working condition.

Baker's conception of the body form of his racer also reverts to marine types. The underframe of the waggon takes the form of a shallow flat-bottomed barge, somewhat narrowed at each end, suspended beneath the axles. The upper body closely follows yacht-hull lines, and the whole vehicle is really a decked yacht-hull turned bottom side up, so that the deck forms the bottom of the carriage body, smooth and free from all projections, while a very small and low hatch coaming, provided with a curved

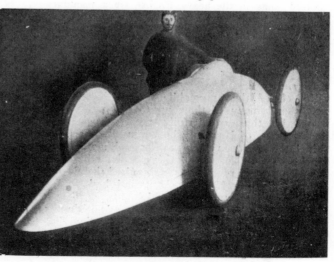

Fig. 2. Right rear view.

mica window, rises from the upturned keel to contain the driver's head, and permit him to have an unobstructed view of the sides and front of his road. It is, of course, absolutely necessary that the driver's face and eyes should be protected against wind and small missiles, and glass would have been a most unsuitable material for this purpose. The use of mica has been criticised as not being a perfectly lucid material; but the photograph of Mr. Denzer's face partly covered by the mica window light, gives the irrefutable testimony of the camera and photograph in favour of the suitableness of mica in this place. It will be observed that Mr. Denzer's upper face and eyes, covered by the mica, are but little darker than the lower face, fully exposed in a room freely lighted by midday sunshine.

The reproductions of photographs given herewith show all the details of the racer's construction so clearly as to render extended description needless, as the titles of the illustrations give sufficient information to the technical reader.

The placing, seating, and securing of the bodies of the driver and the electrician of this vehicle included difficult problems, which were met by hammock canvas seats and cross bands of heavy webbing, passing from the front rail of the seat over the shoulders and back to the rail again where the free ends are buckled. This confines the riders in a woven material support, and leaves their limbs free, while protecting their bodies from accidental displacement by rough road jolting or even by violent collision. At the fatal ending of the Staten Island run, someone said to Edison, who was a spectator, "Baker and Denzer are both killed." "No," replied Edison, who had seen the riders seated in the machine, "they are not hurt at all; they could not be hurt, supported and protected as they are." And Edison's judgment was correct. The only mark on Baker or Denzer, when removed from the crippled racer, was a lump on Denzer's head, due to the removal of the hatch by the club of a heroic policeman on rescue bent.

As seated in the pictures, the driver has the steering wheel close to his breast and his legs extended nearly horizontally forward, each foot resting in a slidable brake stirrup fastened to cables extending to the rear axle brakes. The left foot brake is a plain brake action, but the right foot brake cable is made to work the brake the same as the left foot

Fig. 3. Driver's head inside the coaming behind the mica window.

movement; and in addition the right cable is connected to the cut-out switch, so that when this right foot brake is applied the current will be shut off the motor before the brake is applied.

The electrician has the voltmeter and tachometer under his eyes, and so knows the rate of travel at the instant of observation, and communicates the same to the driver, who has switches at his right and left hands enabling him to apply any moiety of the battery current to motor propulsion; and the motor, nominally 7 h.p., can be driven up to 14 h.p. for a short time.

Fig. 4. Rear view, with cover removed.

The transmission from the motor is through coiled springs under compression to the motor sprockets and then through Whitney Company chains to the rear axle.

The metallic bottle seen standing upright at the left of the electrician's seat contains liquid carbonic acid gas, released to blow the "hooter."

The wheelbase is 9ft. 9in., the wheel gauge 56½in., and the wheels are all 40in. in diameter. The tyres are single tubes made by the B. F. Goodrich Co. They are 3in. cross section diameter, and are blown up to 125 lbs. for use. There are in each wheel fifty-six wire spokes, each .195in. in diameter, wood rims being used.

As shown by figs. 1, 2, and 3, the outer upper surface of this racer has very easy entering and leaving lines, the least air resistance form being similar to that of least water resistance, made familiar to the eye by yacht hulls. The material is light wood, either pine or basswood, ribbed inside with light wooden ribs, and enamelled white inside and out. This cover is very light in weight, as it is only about ¼in. thick, and is slotted, as shown in figs. 1 and 2, to permit rise and fall on the axles. The springs are long, but, of course, are heavy, as they have to support about 1,500 lbs. on each axle. The general arrangement is front steering, the stub-axle arms leading forward, the steering action being had from the hand wheel and axle shown in figs. 4, 6, 7, 8, and 9. The grooved cable drum and the cable yoke secured to the steering arms link are quite clearly shown in fig. 7. There are three wire cables, each taking a full turn about the spirally-grooved drum on the steering wheel axle. These

Fig. 5. Motor, rear axle, brakes, driving chains, rear spring, and rear batteries.

wire cables are stretched by heavy coiled springs at each end, the springs being mounted on threaded rods having adjusting nuts, so that the spring tension can be regulated to suit. This arrangement allows some elasticity to mitigate shocks caused by road bed roughness, in case of an unusual obstruction, but is rigid under ordinary conditions. As there is no lost motion whatever in this steering rig, the Baker racer "minds the helm" promptly, and the spring-stretched wire steering cables reduce the chances of breakage of the steering gear to their lowest limits.

The small raised hatch on top of the shell body

Fig. 6. General front view, cover removed.

covers a hatchway barely large enough to house the heads of the electrician and the driver, and is secured by leather straps inside the cover. The inside of this tortoiseshell-like hatch cover is thickly padded, so as to avoid bumping the heads of the crew. As shown in fig. 3, the driver has a wholly-

unobstructed view in front and sidewise, as the mica window is curved.

To avoid air resistance and the catching up and throwing of pebbles and road drift, the wheel spokes are covered with white enamelled cloth, which is whole on the outsides of the wheels, except for a

Fig. 7. Front axle, front spring, and steering cable drum, with three-wire cables, spring adjuster, and the enamelled cloth spoke covers.

hole for the hub end, and is carried over the wheel rim, under the pneumatic tyres, and then turns down the inside of the wheel for a couple of inches or so, leaving the insides of the wheels to be covered by other pieces of the same white enamelled cloth, which are laced at their outer edges to the outer cover, as shown in figs. 1, 4, 5, and 7. Figs. 1, 4, and 5 show this inside spoke cover partly unlaced for a little way on one wheel. The motor sprockets are rigidly secured to the motorshaft; the rear axle driving sprockets are loose on the rear axle, and drive through heavy coiled springs, which keep both chains always equally at work.

Fig. 8.—Electrician and driver seated in the racer. The cover is removed, showing the webbing crossbands which hold the men securely to their seats.

Figs. 8 and 9 show clearly the hammock seats for the crew, and the method of securing the bodies of the men in their seats, so that they cannot be jolted out of place. The dials of the recording instruments are seen by the electrician between his legs, as he sits with bowed head, as shown in fig. 8.

Nothing of the position of the riders is left to chance or accident; their bodies cannot move into injurious contact with any part of the vehicle.

All of the electrical work is most carefully designed, and placed so as to reduce chances of failure as much as is possible. The switches (see fig. 11) have a quick action mechanism, to avoid the large spark caused by dragging.

Fig. 9. Driver's and electrician's seats, carbonic acid bottle, recording instruments, steering wheel, electric switches, side and front batteries.

The axles are hollow, and have a very large factor of safety. The wheel rims are of wood, as are those of all Baker electric waggons, Baker being firmly convinced that a wooden wheel rim is in every way far better than a steel rim.

While a road car which can run eighty-five miles an hour is not in any sense a practicable vehicle, the durable construction and safe operation of such vehicles involve problems requiring the highest engineering skill and the greatest ingenuity

Fig. 10. Motor, driving chains, rear axle, and brake bands.

on the part of the designer, and the lessons taught by the working of such wonderfully swift machines are of the highest value to the art of automobile building at large. It is from extremes and tests to destruction that the truths must be learned, and there will always be costly and hazardous fast waggons built in the endeavour to discover the very best possible constructions.

That the best automobile is a problem not beneath the consideration of the highest grade of engineering and constructive genius will soon be fully proven by the enormous rewards which will come to those who really meet the demands of the self-driven road vehicle.

The identical machine described here is, we understand, to be seen on the Anglo-American Motor Car Co.'s stand at the Palace Show.

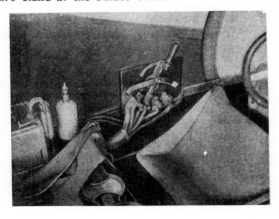

Fig. 11. Switch construction, carbonic acid bottles, gauges, and operators' seats.

To those who employ high tension current for firing their engines, Messrs. Peto and Radford's (of 55, Hatton Garden, E.C.) price list of accumulators for ignition, contact breakers, coils, and plugs, will prove both useful and interesting. Four-volt accumulators for motor cycles in both ebonite and celluloid cases are first treated; then follow sections dealing with accumulators for motor tricycles, light cars and voiturettes, and accumulators for big cars. The now well-known and much-appreciated "armoured accumulator" is, of course, specially treated. We might say here that we have had a pair of two-volt armoured accumulators in continuous use since the early part of June last, and they have given us the utmost satisfaction, never once having played us false, although we have once or twice run them considerably lower than was wise. In the catalogue will be found an interesting illustrated description of the "P.M." sparking plugs and a description of the manner in which they are made. In the "P.M." plugs mica and not porcelain is used as the insulating material, the central pin being first encased in several leaves of mica, like a cigarette wrapping, the mica-enwrapped pin then being surrounded by a series of mica discs of various suitable thicknesses, which are threaded on to the central pin, and there subjected to considerable pressure by a hydraulic press which renders the mica envelope of the pin into a homogeneous mass which can be chucked and polished on a lathe. So treated, the mica becomes a first-class insulating material, and though we have not personally tested these plugs, we have heard them extremely well spoken of by those who have. The method of testing these plugs is described; as also are the "P.M." contact breakers. Details are given of a moderately priced primary battery for recharging accumulators.

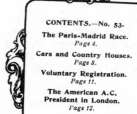

Editorial Jottings.

Our First Birthday. I feel I must this week indulge in a chortle. THE CAR has now completed its first year of existence, and this number, No. 53, begins our second year. Neither I nor any of my friends contemplated that THE CAR would be quite so successful as it has been, and the policy to which I have endeavoured to adhere of conducting the journal on absolutely independent lines has been fully justified by the result. The press as a whole was most friendly to us at our birth, and now that we have attained to the dignity of being a year old, I take the opportunity of thanking them, our advertisers, and the public and automobilists generally for the support which they have given us. I wish also to thank many kind readers who have recently written letters congratulating us on the completion of our fifty-second number.

Paris-Madrid : Nothing certain yet. The account of the casualties in the Paris-Madrid race is, at the moment of writing, hardly definite enough to enable one to form a sound judgment. From our special correspondent's telegrams, printed elsewhere, it appears that the cars will go on *en promenade*, but not as in racing form. The number and seriousness of the accidents also appear to have been exaggerated. The majority of the disasters seem to have been caused by cars trying to pass one another in blinding dust, which, of course, at the high speed they were travelling, is a most difficult and dangerous process.

The Rules must be altered. As my readers know, I have doubted for some time past whether these cars of gigantic horse-power are really serving any useful purpose. Motor racing until recently has assisted the evolution of the touring and commercial car, tending, as it has done, to produce a type of automobile which has great power and lightness combined. But now that 100 h.p. and over can be placed in the frame of a car weighing under a ton, we have reached the limit of what is useful. The suggestion which I made some weeks ago, that in future the rules for racing will have to be revised, and cubic capacity of cylinders substituted for weight as a limiting factor, seems to have received an additional argument in its favour when the occurrences of Sunday are taken into consideration. These contests, too, are not in the ordinary sense of the term sporting affairs, but titanic commercial struggles between various makers, immense sums of money depending on the result of whether a particular firm can win the race as against another firm.

The Gordon Bennett Race quite different. Let us keep our heads ! Disastrous as have been the accidents in the Paris-Madrid race, and greatly perturbed as is sure to be the public mind owing to the wide publicity which has been given to these unfortunate occurrences, the thoughtful public generally will not absolutely condemn motor racing. For instance, as regards the Gordon Bennett race in Ireland, the most strenuous precautions have been taken to protect spectators and the competitors themselves. The rules governing the speed of competitors through crowded places will be most rigidly enforced, and flags will be placed at all dangerous corners and points on the road at which it is thought that an accident might occur. There will also probably be at the most only twelve cars in the race as against 216 which started for the Paris-Madrid race.

If it had been a Motor-car ! Apropos of the sad events in the Paris-Madrid race the following accident, which has just happened in Ireland, is worthy of notice. A horse while running in the Bay Plate at Dundalk (Mr. W. T. Brabazon's " Culloden Delight ") bolted with its rider, Mr. Christopher Hope, and dashed into the spectators, many of whom were knocked down and severely injured. The horse then came down and rolled over its rider, who, when picked up, was found to be suffering from internal injuries. The injured spectators and Mr. Hope were taken to the hospital. Just fancy if a motor-car had run off the road during an automobile race what an anti-motorist howl there would have been, and yet an accident like the above was relegated to an obscure back page in a paragragh of half-a-dozen lines. According to the public's theory death is sweet and acceptable if caused by a horse, but bitter and detestable if caused by a motor. Perhaps they think one kind of death leads to the happy land and the other to a kind of extra hot inferno. The injuries to one or two spectators in a race in New York last year was made the excuse for all kinds of anti-motor legislation, but our old friend, the horse, which has gone on gaily killing people for the last 6,000 years, is yet called the friend of man ! It is wonderful how little human beings reflect ! It is not death, but a novel kind of death they apparently dislike !

Legislative action approved. The tabulation of the voting papers returned in answer to the questions of the Automobile Club Committee, shows that the Legislative Committee were quite right in assuming that the majority of the members of the Club are willing to concede conspicuous identification in return for an increase in the speed limit and the other concessions which were named in the circular. Now that this result, showing a majority of two to one, is known, Lord Russell and his friends are, I know, only too anxious to help the Club to produce a workable measure which is likely to pass the Houses of Parliament. As Mr. Long is to introduce his Bill into the House of Lords, the ground is free for our Bill in the House of Commons. As I pointed out last week, it is important we should have a measure to show our *bona fides* in the matter, and I have always fought for numbering, because I have considered that the speed limit has no chance of being increased without it.

In the Lords. Elsewhere in our pages will be found an account of the debate which took place last week on the so-called motor problem in the House of Lords. Both Lord Wemyss and Lord Granby made reasonable speeches on the subject. I was standing at the bar of the House of Lords when the latter was speaking, and for all the world might have been listening to speeches at the Automobile Club or to a repetition of the arguments I have so often put forward in these pages. The Government's Motor-car Bill will be introduced first of all into the House of Lords, a method which, I think, has many advantages, as the discussion and ventilation of the subject will be more easy there than in the House of Commons, where we are, at the present moment, struggling in the throes of the London Education Bill. Should the noble lords pass the Bill without serious amendment there might be time towards the end of the session for its discussion in the House of Commons. I begin to see daylight, and a chance that 1904 will be a year of deliverance.

In the Commons. The debate in the House of Commons on Thursday last was in sharp contrast to that in the House of Lords. During question time Mr. Wason wanted to know why the police were ridiculed while trying to enforce the speed limit. He does not seem to see that the reason is that they are trying to enforce a ridiculous law which is unenforceable. Mr. Weir also complained that he had been nearly knocked down by a motor at the entrance of the House of Commons. Later on, on the vote for the salaries and expenses of the Metropolitan police, the same hon. member again raised the subject of motor-cars, and suggested that the police might use lassoes. To use his own words, he "hoped that means would be adopted for catching, upsetting, and smashing up these destructive wretches, who had no more regard for human life than if they were flies." The hon. gentleman also included apparently in his denunciation motor cycles, bicycles, in fact everything that was not horse-drawn. One is almost tempted to suspect that Mr. Weir must have been in the tramway-horse trade or have been walking about with his eyes shut. Does he know the number of people knocked down and run over by horse-drawn carriages, or does he think that motors are the only "murderous" vehicles? The Home Secretary, Mr. Akers-Douglas, agreed that legislation was necessary, and said—as the House already knew—that a Bill was about to be introduced by the President of the Local Government Board dealing with the whole subject. The attitude of the House generally to the motorphobes was shown by the committee's laughing and jeering attitude. It is only fair that the anti-motorists should have representatives of their case in Parliament, and from our point of view Mr. Wason and Mr. Weir are ideal spokesmen.

An Excellent County. Next Thursday the Mayor of Hertford is inviting automobilists to come down for an automobile demonstration in his town. It is hoped that as many motorists as possible will attend, especially as the Chief Constable of Hertfordshire, the Mayor of Hertford, and other county authorities have always been most reasonable in the matter of enforcing the twelve miles an hour limit. The local police are only put at dangerous corners and at the entrance to narrow village streets, and warn drivers rather than spy upon them. This eminently sensible attitude is one which ought fully to be recognised by automobilists, and I hope the Mayor's kindly intentions will meet with the good reward they deserve.

Owing to the Whitsuntide holidays the next issue of The Car will not be published until Wednesday, June 3rd.

Our frontispiece this week is a charming photograph of Mrs. C. Arthur Pearson. Like her husband, Mrs. Pearson is an enthusiastic motorist, and has experience of several cars, including the new type of Mors

THE PARIS-MADRID RACE.

UNFORTUNATE ENDING OF A GREAT CONTEST.

MOTOR-RACING with all its terrific excitements has received a grievous, but we hope only a temporary, blow; and, of all things the worst, two brave men at least will race no more. Danger we knew there was, but those who drove in the Paris-Madrid contest no doubt counted the possible results well worthy the risk.

Late on Sunday night the news came through. Those who are as yet outside the movement cannot realise how painful a shock was created in the minds of those who had not crossed the Channel and yet whose interest was focussed upon the great race. Everything had promised so fairly. The Paris-Madrid race—the greatest motor contest in history—with beautiful weather, a record entry, and the favour of the thousands of inhabitants along the route, was a prospect of the brightest. Saturday's mails brought glowing accounts of the gathering of the cars from our friends in Paris, Bordeaux, and Madrid and then this black news! The newspaper reports so far are contradictory, confusing, exaggerated; but at the best it is bad. And over all there is mourning for those who have been killed—to some of us they were personal friends.

Briefly, one gathers from the garbled accounts that the story of the race is this:—At daybreak on Sunday morn-

LOUIS RENAULT AND HIS CAR

ing the cars started from Paris. The scene, witnessed by 300,000 people, was a memorable one—eager racers, alert *mécaniciens*, bustling officials, enthusiastic multitudes—and then the excitement as one by one the 216 racing cars shot from Versailles *en route* for Bordeaux, 324 miles distant. Ill-luck from the start marked the contest. M. Louis Renault was the first to arrive in Bordeaux, with Jarrott next. Gabriel on his Mors was third, having covered the 343 miles distance in 313½ minutes, averaging over sixty miles per hour, and actually passing 118 competitors. These were the first in, and over fifty of the 216 starters had reached the end of the first stage within twelve hours. Marcel Renault, winner of the Paris-Vienna race, made a mistake at a corner of a hill at Poitiers, and has since succumbed to his injuries. Mr. Loraine Barrow ran over a dog, he and his *chauffeur* being thrown out. The latter was reported killed and the former terribly injured. Mr. Stead—Stead, the Leeds man, a genial, cool-headed Englishman—had his car wrecked at Montguyon, and was seriously injured. Fournier, W. K. Vanderbilt, and Baron de Forest came to grief and had to abandon the race, as did Mr. Mark Mayhew and the Hon. C. S. Rolls. Mme. Du Gast (the only lady competitor) arrived safely. Mr. L. Porter's Wolseley was overturned and smashed up. He was caught underneath, and was reported to have been severely crushed. A private telegram now informs us he is still alive, but Mr. Nixon, a

THE CAR.

M. RENÉ DE KNYFF AND HIS PANHARD
M. HENRI FARMAN AND HIS PANHARD
M. AUGIERS AND HIS MORS
MR. W. K. VANDERBILT, JR.'S MORS

MME. DU GAST

MR. C. JARROTT ON HIS DE DIÉTRICH
WERNER ON HIS MERCÉDÈS
BARON DE FOREST'S MORS
BARON DE CATERS AND HIS MERCÉDÈS

Belfast gentleman who was with him, was killed. M. Georges Richard was upset and broke several ribs. M. Tourand, and his mechanician were killed or most terribly injured. Several other drivers had mishaps, it is said, but, though wounded, pluckily continued the race. In view of these calamities, the race was stopped by the Government.

The following telegrams have been received from our special correspondent at Bordeaux :—

"Bordeaux, Monday afternoon.
"Great confusion prevails here about the race, and

J. B. WARDEN'S MERCÉDÈS

even yet information is wanting concerning many factors of importance. Only 114 competitors have arrived out of 216 starters and include no English cars, and only Jarrott and Holder as English drivers of French cars. Mayhew and four Wolseleys started but nothing heard of first named. Lieutenant Cumming broke down when going well, but stopped through bent crank shaft. Porter, who drove Mr. Allan's Wolseley, reported on one hand burned to death but on other to have escaped unhurt though car overturned. Rolls was picked up by another car and came in on step. None of the English motor cycles have arrived.

"Best car performances are as follows :—Gabriel (Mors), 8 hr. 7 min. 31 sec.; Renault, 8 hr. 27 min. 45 sec.; Salleron (Mors), 8 hr. 40 min. 1 sec.; Jarrott, 8 hr. 45 min. 55 sec.; Warden (Mercédès), 8 hr. 50 min. 27 sec.; Gastaud (Mercédès), 8 hr. 56 min. 16 sec. Of course uniform deduction

P. BARAS AND HIS DARRACQ

from each must be made for neutralisation, i.e.,about 2½ hours. Best motor cycle time is 11 hr. 51 min. 1 sec., by Bucquet on Werner. Several fatal accidents reported to have occurred but nothing confirmed. I learn, however, that Minister of Interior has annulled the race to frontier, therefore report of Marcel Renault's death may be assumed correct. It will probably be decided this afternoon whether cars will proceed *en promenade* to frontier and resume race in Spain.—C. L. FREESTON."

Anxiety anent the safety of Mr. Mark Mayhew was set at

rest by the following telegram received from our representative at Bordeaux :—

"Bordeaux, May 25th.—Mayhew. Steering went wrong. He struck tree, and hurt ribs, but not seriously. Mechanic turned several somersaults but unhurt.—

C. L. FREESTON."

The general impression among automobile circles in London seems to be that, although this calamitous race will do much to prejudice the public against motor racing, it will have no effect upon the motor movement generally. That the chain of disasters will not enhance the popularity of the Gordon Bennett contest and connective events is certain, but there is no reason why it should interfere with the arrangements of the Automobile Club.

Many questions are naturally being asked as to the condition of the roads on the Irish route and those between Paris and Bordeaux. The former compare rather unfavourably with the French itinerary, but this argument is no proof that equal dangers will exist in the International Race. The excessive number of competitors, the blinding dust, and a certain amount of recklessness inherent in some racing motorists, are responsible for what has occurred. In the case of the Gordon Bennett race none of these risks will be present in anything but a very slight degree. Each driver will be of necessity much more cautious than when, as on Sunday, he feels that the road is level.

The road between Versailles and Bordeaux, says the

GIRARDOT ON HIS 50 H.P. "C.G.V."

special correspondent of the *Daily Mail*, in the days when motor races were run at an average speed of thirty miles an hour, was considered to be an ideal racing road. With very few exceptions a car could be run round any of the bends without slowing. Now, with cars which can travel at eighty miles an hour, these bends amount to veritable obstacles, to negotiate which speed has to be reduced some fifty per cent., and they occur every twenty or twenty-five minutes. For this reason the driver of the racing car of to-day has greater risks to face, and is required to exercise more frequently the judgment as to the maximum speed at which a corner can be taken. An error of judgment means a catastrophe—perhaps death.

Saturday's issue of the *Allgemeine Automobil Zeitung* contained a leading article strongly condemning the construction of cars with exceptionally powerful motors. After referring to one or two recent fatal accidents the writer said, with almost prophetic instinct, "When I think that perhaps 250 cars will start in the Paris-Madrid race, and that at least fifty of these will be provided with such terribly powerful motors, and finally that, of all the drivers probably only twenty are capable of mastering these 'speed monsters,' I feel inclined to pray to Heaven that the race may not be the occasion of some frightful accident. Forsooth, I am no prophet of evil, but if accident on accident should take place in the Paris-Madrid race, what a clamour there would be in that section of the press which persistently opposes automobilism,"

PARIS-MADRID—A RETROSPECT:
CARS, COMPETITORS, AND SOME CRITICISMS.

ALL that can be said for and against the great and ill-starred Paris-Madrid contest has surely been said, and our criticisms, though in no essential altered since last week, can only be a recapitulation of facts and opinions already set forth in the public press. Ignoring the screamings of the less sober of the journals, who seem to fail to see that automobilists deplore more deeply the misfortunes of the competitors in the race than the non-motorists themselves, we may frankly admit that the seeds of prejudice have been sown in the minds of thousands whose powers of discrimination may not be very great. But we are thankful that things are not so black as they first appeared.

Poor Marcel Renault succumbed last week, but others whom we feared were dead are now on the highway to recovery. The first wave of sensationalism having passed over it has been recognised that there is motor-racing *and* motor-racing, and Parliament, the leading dailies, and the local government boards of Ireland have not been carried away by the first alarm, and they only rightly insist that

JUST OFF! VAN DE HEYDEN ON HIS PANHARD.

be framed. We would suggest:—(1) That there be a *minimum* weight and not a *maximum* weight as at present; (2) that the cubic capacity of cylinders should be limited. It is quite possible now to get 40 h.p. in four cylinders having a *maximum* of 5 in. diameter and 6 in. stroke.

Were such regulations made, the tendency would be—(1) to get more perfect vaporisation of the petrol, technically called carburation; (2) improvements in the methods and ease of transmission between the power developed and its result on the road wheel; (3) to obtain greater safety, from more strength in the frame and engine. Such results would form valuable *data* for the further improvement of touring and commercial cars, which undoubtedly form the backbone of the motor trade of this country or any other. Just as the formula which governs " rating " in yacht racing has had to be altered several times in order to avoid the development of dangerous and unseaworthy boats, so the rules of

THE SCENE AT DAYBREAK: AWAITING THE START.

the Gordon Bennett Cup contest shall be run with the strictest regard for the safety of the public. The Paris-Madrid misfortune may thus prove a blessing in disguise; for it is truly a lesson, a salutary lesson, and all are agreed that the regulations appertaining to such contests must be revised.

" Motor Massacre," " Jehu on the Juggernaut," " The Petrol Death," and similar absurdities flaring from the contents bills of evening papers of Monday week were painful to those mourning the tragedy of brave men. It was unreasonable that these sad occurrences should have been made the excuse for so much " yellow " journalism. Every year people are killed and injured in many sports—at football, at cricket, steeplechasing, polo, hunting, shooting, yachting, mountaineering, and yet these pastimes go on with public approval, and if accidents happen there is no storm of sentiment aroused against them.

As we pointed out last week, we have long doubted the practical utility of these struggles between cars of enormous horse-power, and are convinced that similar demonstrations must not recur. Private tracks must be built—there will soon be one laid down at Purley—and new regulations must

MARK MAYHEW READY TO START.

motor racing ought now to be altered, not only in the interests of the public and the competitors, but for the

MAYHEW TAKING THE HILL AT PETIGNAC.

GABRIEL ON THE HILL AT PETIGNAC

eventual advantage of manufacturers as well. Cogent and cool-headed is the general criticism which the letter issued by the Automobile Club with reference to the comparison between the Paris-Madrid and Gordon Bennett races has elicited. The text is worth reprinting :—

Fears have been expressed that some of the accidents which have characterised the first day of the Paris-Madrid race may be repeated in the Gordon Bennett race. It is desirable to explain, therefore, that the latter contest will be held under totally different conditions to the one which has just taken place on the Continent. In the first place, it must be remembered that in the race on Sunday week over 200 cars competed. Moreover, in that race, cars of varying types and speeds were inexplicably mixed up, with the result that there was a continuous passing and repassing, at racing speed, of one vehicle by another. In the Gordon Bennett race all the twelve cars will be approximately of the same speed, and there will not be, in consequence, the constant overtaking of one car by another.

It is manifestly impossible properly to protect the total distance of 800 miles between Paris and Madrid by police and soldiers. In the Gordon Bennett course, however, the whole

AUSTEN ON HIS WOLSELEY.   PORTER AND NIXON WITH THEIR CAR ON RIGHT.

length of the road upon which the race will take place is only ninety-three miles, and it has already been arranged that the road shall be kept clear by 7,000 police officers, assisted by troops and club stewards. These will have strict instructions to keep spectators off the roads and on the other side of the walls, ditches and hedges bordering the course and away from corners altogether.

Another source of danger in the Paris and Madrid race was the character of the road surface. A constant cloud of dust hid the sharp corners, and prevented the drivers from seeing the gulleys, which are occasionally cut across the road. In Ireland, however, arrangements have been made to spend nearly £1,500 in removing gulleys and sharp bridges, and all corners will be treated to prevent the dust being raised. The whole road throughout the course will be put into proper condition for high speed racing cars. On the road between Paris and Madrid there are several dangerous railway level crossings. There are no level crossings on the Irish course.

Interest in the sporting and technical points of view has naturally been somewhat submerged by the unhappy importance of the ending of the race. Our photographs

BERTEAUX'S PANHARD TAKING A NASTY CORNER.

LORAINE BARROW AT PETIGNAC.

give an excellent idea of the appearance of the cars and of the excitement that prevailed when the start was made from Versailles. We feel proud, in spite of everything, that Jarrott did so well in the race, and the performances of

J. B. WARDEN AT PETIGNAC.

Gabriel and Louis Renault, to whom premier honours are due, are nothing short of marvellous; 343 miles in 313½ min., or an average of sixty-six miles an hour, is a world's record on any track, rail or road. Jarrott started first and reached Bordeaux second, accomplishing the journey in 5 hr. 51 min. 55 sec.

The following is a record of the principal times made between Paris and Bordeaux (343 miles) :—

CARS (up to 1,000 kilogs.)

		H.	M.	S.
1. Gabriel (Mors)		5	13	31
2. Salleron (Mors)		5	46	1
3. Jarrott (De Diétrich)		5	51	55
4. Warden (Mercédès)		5	56	30
5. De Crawhez (P.L.)		6	1	8
6. Voigt (C.G.V.)		6	1	9
7. Gasteaux (Mercédès)		6	8	0
8. Arch. Fournier (Mors)		6	11	39
9. Rougier (Turcat-Mery)		6	16	7
10. Montei (De Diétrich)		6	17	54

LIGHT CARS (up to 650 kilogs.)

		H.	M.	S.
1. L. Renault (Renault frères)		5	33	59
2. Baras (Darracq)		6	12	49
3. Page (Décauville)		6	19	8
4. Hemery (Darracq)		6	52	33
5. Pelisson (De Dion-Bouton)		7	12	43

VOITURETTES (up to 450 kilogs.)

		H.	M.	S.
1. Masson (Clément)		7	19	57
2. Barillier (G. Richard)		7	39	0
3. Wagner (Darracq)		7	47	12
4. Combier (G. Richard)		8	7	26
5. Holley (De Dion-Bouton)		8	22	19

MOTOR CYCLES (up to 50 kilogs.).

		H.	M.	S.
1. Bucquet (Werner)		8	57	1
2. Demester (Griffon)		9	3	44
3. Jollivet (Griffon)		9	25	54
4. Cissac (Peugeot)		9	39	36
5. Lanfranchi (Peugeot)		9	50	40

We have spared our readers the details of the accidents and the fatalities, but news of the progress of the injured

JARROTT'S ARRIVAL AT BORDEAUX.

will be found in another part of this issue as received from our Paris correspondent yesterday.

The financial loss to the French and German manufacturers must be something enormous. The average cost

THE ARRIVAL OF GABRIEL AND HIS WINNING MORS AT BORDEAUX.

of each of the heavy cars may be put down at £1,000, that of the light cars at £600, that of the voiturettes at £320, and that of the motor cycles at £100. Two hundred and sixty-seven vehicles of all classes were entered for

COOLING THE TYRES EN ROUTE.

the race, which gives a total expenditure for the construction of the cars of all classes of nearly £200,000. Such firms as the Mercédès, Mors, and Panhard, must have lost, at a moderate estimate, from £8,000 to £12,000. *La Presse* calculates that the French automobile constructors spent £2,000,000 over their preparation. Probably they realised that this was to be the last of the great road contests, and strained every nerve to gain fame and fortune.

It is pleasant to record that there was no accident of any kind in the tourist class, and about one hundred motor-cars from Bordeaux entered Spain on May 26th. This is a striking contrast to the chapter of accidents in the racing class, and is strong testimony in support of the fact that touring cars may travel at comparatively high speeds without danger to drivers or other users of the roads. The Spanish Automobile Club organised an expedition to meet the "tourist" motor-cars at the Escurial. Fifty-nine motors assembled there and continued to Madrid. Arrived in the capital, a procession headed by the Duke of Santo Mauro, president of the Spanish Club, and other notabilities was formed and proceeded through the streets of the city, which were kept clear by police with flags. Passing the royal palace, the automobilists saluted the Queen-Mother and the Infantas. The principal festivities were cancelled.

WRIGHT WITH HIS ORMONDE BICYCLE AT THE
CHATEAUDUN CONTROL.

The following has been received from our special correspondent in Bordeaux :—" It is still uncertain whether the Mercédès cars will compete in Gordon Bennett race. I have travelled to-day with a prominent official of Cannstatt-Daimler works, who tells me the matter is by no means settled. Mr. Foxhall Keene, though nominated by the

German Club, would be unacceptable to MM. Jellineck and Charley where driving abilities are concerned, and in this connection it may be mentioned that he was the only driver of Mercédès cars who did not start on Sunday week. Jellineck states that if his cars cannot start under conditions of which he approves he will not allow any under his control to take part. At the same time both Keene and Baron de Caters are amateurs owning their cars, and could not be prevented from participating if themselves willing, and the only car over which Jellineck could exercise veto would be that of Hieronymus. Another factor of uncertainty, however, is that De Caters may not care to drive. I have discussed the matter with the Baroness, who is very unwilling that he should form one of the team, and, if feminine persuasion can succeed, he will not start.

"Concerning the Panhard team the Bordeaux journey affords no evidence. In the first place De Knyff's car broke down with a cracked cylinder head, and Farman abandoned the race because of Marcel Renault's injuries. Moreover, I am told it is probable Panhards will build other cars for the Cup race. Henri Fournier also broke down, so that we know nothing of either Panhard or Mors capabilities. The

REMOVING INSECTS FROM THE RADIATOR OF
WARDEN'S CAR.

record of the Mercédès team in the Bordeaux course presents several interesting features. Of eleven starters nine finished. Werner went round a corner on two wheels. He struck the kerb and they collapsed with resultant broken back axle. Terry, a young amateur, driving his own 60 h.p. car, had the misfortune to have it set on fire by back flames from a Serpollet, and the Mercédès was destroyed.

"Jenatzy, on a 90 h.p. car, had an extraordinary experience. He was making faster time than anyone, when the car mysteriously stopped, and for three hours he endeavoured in vain to allocate the cause. On taking carburetter to pieces he found a fly in the jet was stopping the flow of petrol. Dergais, also on a 90 h.p. car, had made excellent progress when the car began to give trouble. He took three and a half hours to determine cause, which proved to be analagous to the incident in the Glasgow-London trial. It appears that on the weighing-in he had great difficulty in bringing his car down to the maximum weight, and as a last resort removed the water-cooling attachments for brakes. He filled his petrol can with water, however, to be ready if wanted, but his mechanic not knowing this subsequently emptied tin into petrol tank. The contents, of course, had to be thrown away when the error was discovered."

(For latest news see " Paris Gossip ")

171

"PARIS-MADRID."—SOME POSTSCRIPTS:

BY C. L. FREESTON.

WERE the issues less momentous it would be amusing to observe the extent to which alarmists have been airing their motorphobic frenzy during the past few days. Returning from Madrid as THE CAR is going to press I have been glancing through the diluvial invectives in the English journals resulting from unveracious narratives of the abortive race, and am moved to chronicle herewith a few facts and impressions which may shed a soberer light on its melancholy details.

Judged by the vitriolic comments to which such liberal vent has been given, it might reasonably be assumed that automobilists had proposed to hold races on the highways every day, and claimed the right to monopolise the road from Paris to Madrid in perpetuity. But a race is an exceptional event, liable to produce exceptional happenings both in number and in kind. It is with vigour, therefore, that one must protest against the unwarrantable—nay, unscrupulous—attempts that have been made to convert the public to the belief that the Paris-Madrid race and the use of ordinary automobiles under ordinary conditions are one and the same thing.

Ere I had left Madrid a copy of the *Times* had come to hand, in which was published a long telegram from its Paris correspondent containing all but hysterical references to the "dangers" of motor vehicles in Paris, references which were entirely untrue, and enough to make M. Blowitz turn in his grave. He at least could look facts in the face, but his successor must perforce be asked to choose between the accusation of wilful perversion of the facts or of being so lacking in objectivity as to betray gross journalistic incompetence. So far from automobiles being the terror of the Paris public, it was shown only a week or two ago that out of over 600 street catastrophes not a single one was due to motor vehicles. And as regards the race itself, what can be said of the *Times* description of the cars passing at headlong speed through populous districts when in every town and village they were compelled to crawl behind a cyclist pilot? The time devoted to these official checks on each competitor alike amounted to more than three hours out of a journey which the fastest car covered in little more than eight, but the impression sought to be conveyed by the *Times* allusion was that every competitor drove throughout as though the Furies were at his heels.

A general tendency has been displayed, moreover, to utilise the cumulative effect of the several accidents as though all had occurred to spectators and not, with a solitary exception, to the *coureurs* themselves. Terrible as was this one catastrophe, however, to all concerned, let the fact at least of its isolation not be forgotten. That the race was stopped because of the Angoulême tragedy is certain ; equally so is it that the Governments of France and Spain would not otherwise have interfered. Let us examine, moreover, the facts of this lamentable incident. All the world over the statement was telegraphed that the car had charged into the crowd and killed several people, including a woman. The mental vision thus suggested was that of an innocent crowd being victimised by an uncontrollable vehicle. In the first place the number of fatalities resultant from this one calamity has been greatly exaggerated ; they did not include a woman, and the driver, M. Tourand, was in no way to blame. The accident occurred outside the control, and any spectators who clustered by the roadside were well aware that they did so at their own peril. M. Tourand, having left the town, had therefore legitimately got up speed, when suddenly a child of nine years of age darted into the road right in front of the car. He made an heroic attempt to save the child by turning the car violently to one side.

The child's life indeed was saved, but at the cost of causing the car to swerve to the side of the road, with the distressing result that two spectators were killed, while M. Tourand himself narrowly escaped with his own life,

and his mechanician was even less fortunate and was killed outright. All the anti-automobile prejudice in the world cannot alter the fact that the only catastrophe in which any member of the public was injured along a route of nearly 350 miles was due entirely to the action of a feckless child, who ought to have been under the control of his parents at the time. I may add that the arrangements at Angoulême generally appear to have been far from satisfactory, and M. Serpollet complained bitterly to me of the way in which the competitors were harassed. It may be further stated that the soldier who was one of the spectators killed by M. Tourand's car was not on duty, but was merely present out of curiosity.

With regard to the accidents to the racers themselves, let us now consider how many of them were due to special and fortuitous circumstances, or how many tended to prove the racing vehicle of 1903 to be unmanageable and unfit for use on the road at all. Naturally the calamity which most appeals to the English automobilist is that which befell Mr. Porter's 50 h.p. Wolseley, which was overturned at a level crossing. Mr. Porter's own explanation is that this spot was one that was guarded by flag holders, but at the time of his arrival the two custodians concerned had gone to lunch ; consequently he approached the dangerous spot at a higher speed than was consistent with safety. His mechanician, it may here be stated, was killed by the shock of the car falling on his body, and though the vehicle took fire he was not incinerated as has been described. An official enquiry has been held by the local authorities, who have expressed the opinion that the custodians were justified in leaving their posts in that they regarded the race as over, and that, having been detained so long *en panne*, Mr. Porter should no longer have regarded himself as in the running, nor continued to travel at racing speed. Be that as it may, the accident was clearly due to the fact that Mr. Porter had no suspicion as to the presence of danger, and by no means implies that under the normal conditions of the race a certain number of vehicles were of necessity uncontrollable.

It is surely no stretch of argument, moreover, to describe as accidental the catastrophe in which Mr. Loraine Barrow was grievously injured and his mechanician killed. Mr. Barrow had to swerve to avoid a dog, and by a cruel mischance there was another dog on the road just beyond. It was the impact with the second animal, occurring while the car was still swerving aside from the first, which caused the upset. These facts demand the fullest emphasis, because the untutored public, including the sub-editors of daily journals *passim*, continue to labour under the misapprehension that racing or even ordinary motor-cars are inherently liable to "explode," or fall to pieces, or otherwise become uncontrollable when running in a straight line.

And now we come to the question of accidents due to the fact that this memorable journey was a race, with resultant risks from that fact alone, as in every other event into which the element of keen competition is imported. Poor Marcel Renault met his death when endeavouring to overhaul another competitor immediately in front. The latter, Théry, slowed down because he came in sight of a danger spot, but Renault, being behind, did not see the warning flags. It is said, moreover, that he did not know the details of the road at this stage. He had to swerve aside to avoid running into Théry, and the circumstances did not allow of any deviation of this kind with safety. This accident to Renault, and the one, which was not fatal, in which Stead endeavoured to pass Salleron, who swerved outwards, however, at the wrong moment, were the only two which could be set down as resulting from ordinary racing risks. It is, indeed, surprising that there were not more of this type of casualty. Certainly, it was in the matter of passing that automobilists themselves feared the possibility of catastrophes, from the presence of so many cars on the road with engines of such enormous power.

It must be remembered that no less than 215 competitors set forth from Versailles ; that they had 342 miles of road to cover on the fastest vehicles in the world ; and that much passing was inevitable from the fact that only one minute intervals could be allowed between the competitors at the start. Gabriel, for example, who was the eighty-first to leave Versailles, had necessarily to pass no less than seventy-eight fellow competitors before he reached Bordeaux. Is it not rather food for wonderment—not that any accidents occurred, but that they were not more numerous ?

A fact which is altogether ignored, moreover, in considering the race, is that it was not merely a competitive event, but the greatest ever held. In what other field of sport do 215 competitors come to the post ? In what other event do they cover such tremendous variety of ground ? Accidents occur, in far greater proportion to the number of persons engaged, in other forms of sport, and no outcry is made. At Auteuil on Sunday, so an eye-witness informed me yesterday, there were accidents in every race ; but steeplechases are common enough, and no one proposes to stop a meeting when a jockey is killed. A fatal case occurred only on Monday at Cartmel.

The most valid objection to be urged against an event such as the Paris-Madrid race is that it is altogether too colossal. In the case of entries by firms, not individuals. only one type of car should be admitted, and in any case a maximum number of competitors should be prescribed beforehand. Engine power, moreover, has undoubtedly grown too high, and a limit of cylinder capacity should be imposed henceforth ; nevertheless one cannot forbear from pointing out the fact that, despite the retention of the 1,000 kilos. limit, no car is known to have failed through weakness, even though so much weight was necessarily appropriated by the engine itself. Consequently when constructors have shown their ability to produce such substantial under-structures within the 1,000 kilos. limit, the ordinary tourist palpably benefits thereby, for if the materials of which the *chassis* is composed will stand the enormous strain of racing, it is obviously not difficult to make an ordinary car, of infinitely smaller speed capacity, which shall be trustworthy in every particular. If road races are to be held in France they must be on more manageable lines, so as to reduce the limit of probability of accidents from fortuitous causes ; but it is simply monstrous that such widespread attempts should have been made to class even the racing automobile as *per se* a dangerous vehicle, and to prejudice the use of ordinary cars by comparison with the circumstances of this gigantic and ill-starred race.

The greatest disappointment has been felt in Madrid at the abandonment of the race. No less than 700,000 pesetas had been expended in improving the roads and in other preparations for the arrival of the competitors. The Spanish prizes were magnificent ; a finer cup than that offered by the King has rarely been seen, while several others which were exhibited at the Automobile Club premises in Madrid were almost equally handsome. The stands which were erected at the finishing point would have accommodated some thirty or forty thousand spectators.

I was informed officially in Madrid that the Spanish Government agreed to follow suit to France in stopping the race, for fear that if any pedestrian were killed the peasantry would barricade the roads and fire upon approaching cars. Such a hypothesis was scouted at, however, by the numerous tourists who journeyed in such large numbers to Madrid. One and all declared that they had everywhere been acclaimed with enthusiasm and loaded with flowers. Several of the tourists were Americans, and one of these described to me the hospitable way in which—despite his nationality—he was entertained at the house of a Spanish officer.

While driving one day in Madrid I was suddenly attracted by the appearance of a car with an unmistakable Daimler bonnet. At first I thought that the vehicle must belong to an English tourist, but recollected that the Duke of Santo Mauro, president of the Automobile Club of Spain, was the owner of a 24 h.p. Daimler, and that this must be his car ; so, indeed, it proved. The car was painted yellow, and was the largest and most imposing of all that I encountered in the Spanish capital.

PARIS GOSSIP:

FROM OUR OWN CORRESPONDENT.

WE have learned with much pleasure that the Paris-Madrid disaster will have no effect on the Gordon Bennett Cup race. The two contests are totally dissimilar. All that can be said against the Paris-Madrid is that the course was absolutely overcrowded with competitors. In Ireland you will not have more than ten or twelve racers and comparatively no public, and the danger will only be for the competitors themselves, if it can be called a danger to ride at an express speed on such a clear track as the Irish course promises to be. As Gabriel told me after the race, "The speed is nothing on a clear road, but it is awful between two lines of people."

The Automobile Club of France have not yet decided how the prizes will be awarded in the Paris-Madrid race.

It is to be noted that René de Knyff, Henri Fournier, and Henri Farman—the three representatives of France for the Gordon Bennett Cup—were victims of early breakdowns. Their cars had hardly been tested, and, of course, their poor performance has been much commented upon here. Concerning Maurice Farman, it must be said that he only stopped when he learned of Renault's accident. Madame du Gast also lost a few hours on account of the help she gave to an unfortunate competitor. In spite of this, however, she proceeded to Bordeaux and covered the distance in 17 hr. 46 min.—a splendid feat for a lady. She was cheered from Versailles to Bordeaux, and was presented with bouquets in every town she passed through.

The affair was thrashed out in the House of Deputies and it was feared that there would have been a very hot discussion, but the Prime Minister, M. Emile Combes, though declaring that he would not allow any further road racing, added that it was necessary to abstain from taking excessive measures in a moment of panic, for such a course might tend to compromise an industry which ought to be encouraged. However, the Périgueux kilometre race, which was to take place this week, has been forbidden. What will be the luck of the many "weeks" prepared in all parts of France?

Except the victorious ones, the most powerful cars did not do well, and the new 90 h.p. Mercédès were beaten by the 60 h.p. cars. The new Panhards did not finish, and only the new 100 h.p. Gobron Brillié arrived just to "lift" the Prince d'Arenberg's Cup from the Panhard firm. It

BARRAS CHATTING WITH M. DARRACQ.

is the same story with the 4 and 5 h.p. motor cycles. The voiturette class was won by an old Clément voiturette, which was first in many hill-climbing contests last year.

M. Georges Prade, in the *Auto*, sums up the results of the race regarding the merits of the machines as shown on their arrival at Bordeaux. The performance of the Mors machine, he thinks, is nothing short of wonderful. The

Sud-Express is looked upon as one of the fastest trains running, and it covers the 552 kilometres between Paris and Bordeaux in seven hours. But Gabriel, on a Mors, took only 5 hr. 13 min. to do the same distance. This speed works out at 36 sec. a kilometre, or 30 metres a second.

The question of a motor track is now much discussed, and I hear that a company is to be formed for the acqui-

ARRIVAL OF SALLERON AT BORDEAUX.

sition of an immense arena to the north of Paris. Another motor track is being built at Etaples, but I fear this is too far to be a very great success. The proposed Chambord track is also too inaccessible.

The *Auto* is opening a subscription fund for the erection of a memorial monument at the spot where Marcel Renault's accident occurred.

The annual "Fêtes des Fleurs" in the Bois de Boulogne last Saturday and Sunday was the occasion of a new triumph for the automobile. For the first time electric carriages were admitted in company with the time-honoured landaus and victorias. No doubt petrol or steam vehicles will also be admitted eventually.

THE SCOTTISH A.C. (Western Section).

THE Committee of the Scottish Automobile Club have drafted tabulated results of the Glasgow to London Non-stop Trial from the Observers' reports. The following cars and motor cycles were awarded marks (maximum 1,000 for non-stop):—

Description.	Bhp.	Tyres	Drivers.	Marks.
14 h.p. Chenard and Walcker Tonneau	17	Dunlop	Walter G. Gutmann	999
Gladiator	12	Dunlop	Miss D. E. Levitt	994½
24 h.p. De Dietrich	30	Michelin	Charles Jarrott	990
10 h.p. Lanchester	10	Michelin	E. J. Hartenfeld	1,000
10 h.p. Wolseley Tonneau	10	Continental	Harry Prosser	9.6
4-Cylinder Sunbeam Car	10 12	Collier	Thos. C. Pulliner	1,000
4-Cylinder Sunbeam Car	10 12	Clipper Continental	Jas. Reid	1,000
Argyll	10	Clincher Michelin	Douglas H. White-head.	991
6-seated Double Phaeton (Gardner - Serpollet steam) English made.	12	Falconnet Compounds.	W. E. Townsend	994
Rochet and Schneider	22	Clipper Continental	Captain Deasy	999
12 h.p. Georges Richard Light Car.	13	Clipper Continental	M. Ross Browne	989
24 h.p. Georges Richard Light Car.	26	Clipper Continental	D. Edwards	808
Arrol-Johnston Dogcart	12	Solid—Shrewsbury. Chalinor.	Thos. Wardell	1,000
De Dion-Bouton	10	Dunlop	J. W. Stocks	997
6-seated Atrol-Johnston Carriage.	12	Solid—Shrewsbury Chalinor.	P. Mitchell	1,000
10 h.p. Wolseley Tonneau	11	Clipper Continental	Thos. Shaw	1,000
12 h.p. Argyll	16	Clincher Michelin	Alec Govan	1,000
2 seated Peugeot	6½	Clipper Continental	J. A. Peacock	985
Quadrant Motor Bicycle	2½	Clincher	Thos. Silver	995
Brown Motor Bicycle	2½	Palmer	F. E. Coles	951
Humber Motor Bicycle	2½	Dunlop	Bert Yates	988
Humber Motor Bicycle	2½	Dunlop	J. F. Crundall	980

IMPRESSIONS IN PARIS CAUSED BY THE CALAMITIES IN THE PARIS-MADRID RACE.

(By our Paris Correspondent.)

The most important event of the year in the automobile line, apart from the Coupe Internationale Gordon-Bennett, should undoubtedly have been the Paris-Madrid race in successive stages, but owing to several inevitable accidents this contest was suppressed by decrees of the French and Spanish authorities, and consequently ended up at Bordeaux, the first stage. The start was at Versailles, chief town of the Seine-et-Oise Department, about twelve miles south-west of Paris. Early in the evening crowds of cyclists, coming from all the surrounding parts, poured into this town to view the drivers and their powerful cars, and the soldiers along the path had great difficulty in keeping them off the competing monsters.

It is estimated that over two million onlookers were along the almost straight stretch of road which separates Versailles, starting point to Bordeaux, which shows how deeply interested people in France are now in the motorcar, but it must be said that many of them were most imprudent, standing in the middle of the road until the cars were almost on them, for the simple purpose of reading the number of the vehicle first, and reporting to others more sensible than themselves, who did not venture their lives. It is not to be wondered therefore that so many accidents occurred.

These various accidents prove once and for all that speed races should be entirely prohibited. Most of the automobile manufacturers are decidedly against races of this kind, contending that speed is useless to prove the capabilities of the motor for ordinary usage; and they now propose races, such as the reliability trials lately run in England, which would not only safeguard the public, but would also tend to greatly decrease the large amount of money spent in constructing special cars, which are of no commercial advantage.

As was expected, the matter of road racing was duly brought before the Chamber of Deputies. In automobile circles it was much feared that, through an almost natural feeling of sympathy towards the victims, many parties would have voted very extreme measures for the future, and thereby compromise this flourishing industry, which employs so many workmen in France; but happily such was not the case.

After the Paris-Berlin race, the former Minister of Interior, M. Waldeck Rousseau, declared that no further automobile races would be authorised in the country, but his successor, M. Combes, gave his signature allowing the race from Paris to Madrid among others. This is precisely where the people blame him, and consider that he is fully responsible for the accidents which occurred; but to this he states that, since the time the races, such as the "Epreuve de l'Alcool" and the Paris-Vienna, were allowed, and no objection had been raised, he had come to the conclusion that Parliamentary dispositions had been modified. He further states that the accidents which occurred were entirely caused on account of the unexpected speed attained by the vehicles; but he considers that these fatal occur-

rences should in no way affect the ordinary use of motors. Moreover, the deputies were unanimous with regard to this matter and seeing no reason for the law regulating automobiles being revised, order of the day " pure et simple " was passed.

The reasonable stand taken up by the Chamber is fully appreciated in France,

J. Lombard and the Bachot, which failed to get through to Bordeaux.

and it shows once more how motoring has extended in the country.

After all these accidents, if high speeds are to be attained to prove the advantages of machines, there is only one course open, viz., to have a motordrome of, say, about one to two miles long and forty yards wide, and to fully protect the spectators. A committee has now been formed in view of seriously considering the construction of such a track in France.

Of all the various incidents on the road, the death of Marcel Renault has caused the greatest impression, and the following is the declaration of his mechanic with reference to the occurrence. " I wished to grease the gears, but M. Marcel told me to wait until we had passed Thery; but all of a sudden we fell, and I do not remember anything further."

He was running at the rate of 100 kilometers an hour, when at a curve he could not see through the dense cloud of dust caused by the car in front, the left side wheel caught in a ditch, and collided with a tree, the car making a somersault twice over. He was carried to the first village, where he was attended to by several of the best known doctors in the district However, there were still hopes of his recovering, though he never regained consciousness, but on Wednesday night he succumbed.

It is sad to notice that many of the drivers were not expert hands at the wheel, and it is to be hoped that this lesson will be fruitful to organisers, who appear to desire to sacrifice quality for quantity, as was the case with this contest. These drivers not only put their own lives in danger, but were the means of others being killed as well, which should not be allowed.

It is a sure thing, and this is fully recognised by all French dailies, that many of the accidents were caused entirely on account of the fact that the sightseers were really too bold, and it is to be hoped that the Gordon-Bennett race will not end in such a manner.

Towing one of the racers through Bordeaux.

HOW ARE THE MIGHTY FALLEN!
*The high-powered racing cars were not permitted to leave Bordeaux under their own power, but were to
return drawn out of the town by horses—a contrast to the outward journey!*

Nearly every Sunday a fine show of motors may be seen in the courtyard of the "White Lion," at Cobham. All types will be found, from the lordly Mercedes to the humble motorcycle. Quite a crowd of motorists walk round, inspecting and criticising each other's cars.

Motor-Bicycles in the Austrian Army.

The Austrian military authorities are convinced that for campaigning in a civilised country the motor-bicycle will play an important part in the future, and orders have been placed for 20 machines to commence with. These will be used in trials connected with despatch carrying, scouting, inspection of posts, etc. If the experiments are successful, the number of machines will be largely extended.

Motor Volunteer Corps.

Mr. Ker-Seymer and Lieut. Trippel have been doing duty for the General Officer Commanding Home Districts for the last week. Mr. Noel Kenealy is doing duty in connection with the large signalling scheme by the Brigade Signalling Officer, Second London Volunteer Infantry Brigade, on 30th to the 1st. The General Officer Commanding Fourth Army Corps has requisitioned for the services of members on the 13th and 23rd of June. The Inspector-General of Fortifications is also employing the services of a member of the corps for his inspection of Hounslow and Wi   on June 2nd.

A J.P. Gets a Fine Discounted.

Sir Alfred Cooper, who sits on the Kingston bench, was recently fined 10s. at Chertsey for exceeding the legal limit. Inspector Marks had half a dozen cases, but the other five victims had to pay 20s. So it would appear from this that there are some advantages even in being a J.P.

Messrs. Flamand and Elskamp, the winners of the Circuit National, held in Belgium, and the Minerva Motor-Bicycles they rode.

Keep the Motor-Bicycle Belt Free from Grit.

It pays to thoroughly clean the belt from grit after every long ride, as much unnecessary wear on the pulley can be thus avoided. Use a rag soaked in petrol to wet the belt surface, and then get an old knife and scrape the belt with the back of it. When clean, redress th belt.

The Motor Cycling Club Prospectus.

We have before us a copy of the prospectus issued by the Motor Cycling Club. It is a nicely got up little pamphlet, setting forth lucidly the aims and special features of the club. It should prove a very useful production to intending members, who will be supplied with a copy on application to the secretary, Mr. G. E. Roberts, 7, Fieldhouse Road, Hyde Farm, Balham, S.W.

A New Detachable Tyre for Single Tube Rims.

The Swain Patents Syndicate, Ltd., Horwich, Lancs., inform us that they have been successful in producing a tyre 3½ inches diameter, suitable for fitting on American single tube rims. The price will be £23 per set of four tyres. This will be a distinct advantage to users of light American cars, as these tyres can be fitted without the wheels having to be rebuilt. The tyres are, of course, of the double tube detachable type.

A TOUR IN FRANCE.

By W. H. Goschen.

Ready to start after settling all preliminaries. The official number in position.

A complete independence of timetables is perhaps the great advantage of a touring car, and with this idea in our minds we left London a few weeks ago for Southampton and France. The day was fine, and the car—a 10 h.p. M.M.C., with a roomy tonneau—was running well, so that, lunching at Winchester, we ran on to Southampton in good time, and drove into the docks. Here the London and South-Western Railway took charge of the car, and after emptying the tank of petrol, a crane picked up the car by ropes attached to each axle, with spreaders to prevent the body being injured, and gently deposited it on the deck of the steamer, where it was carefully made fast under cover, without even a scratch on the paint. The boat sailed at 12 p.m., and the next morning soon after seven o'clock we arrived at Havre. As I happened to have friends in Havre who were used to dealing with the Customs authorities, I did not take advantage of the arrangements the Automobile Club have now made for their members, and an account of the necessary formalities may possibly be of use to others who may think of visiting France.

The Necessary Permits.

To drive in France, two permits are necessary—the *permis de circulation* or *carte grise* and the *permis de conduire* or *carte rouge*, as they are commonly called. The first affects the car, the latter the driver.

As regards the former, if the car is a French one, there is no trouble, as the French makers supply the purchaser of the car with the necessary papers required by the authorities, and as the recognised French makes of car are known and registered by the Prefecture, no delay is experienced.

With an English car, if one makes one's arrangements in time, there need be no delay either.

My friends in France informed me what details were necessary, and put the matter in the hands of an excellent motor car agent and dealer—Monsieur Burton, of Havre.

The Motor Mfg. Co. kindly furnished me with a complete specification of the car, and this I sent to France a month or so before I intended to start. It was then duly forwarded with the demand for the *permis de circulation* on properly stamped paper to the Prefecture at Rouen, with the result that on my arrival I found everything practically arranged. I understand that once the specification of a car made out of France has been registered by the authorities, other cars of the same maker, horse-power, and type, are granted the *carte grise* without any difficulty, especially if the applicant for the *permis de circulation* can refer to the number stamped by the Prefecture on the specification of the original car obtaining the licence.

At Havre.

On arriving at Havre the car was run off the steamer by hand, and there I found Monsieur Burton awaiting me with petrol, etc. After filling our tank and sending our luggage to the hotel, we left, accompanied by a Custom House officer and piloted by M. Burton on a little Georges-Richard car, for the weighbridge, where the weight of the car was duly recorded, and then back to the Custom House, where the wheels were measured, the papers completed, and the necessary deposit made, the whole formalities not occupying more than half an hour.

M. Burton had arranged for an official of the Department des Mines to be available at ten o'clock

A sticky valve, the only roadside repair.

to grant driving certificates to myself and my man, so after leaving the car with him to be washed, he drove me back to the hotel. At ten o'clock he reappeared, and I shortly found myself driving a polite French official through the streets of Havre. He was apparently soon convinced that we could both manage the car, so that before twelve o'clock I found myself in possession of a provisional *permis de conduire* and the information that our definite certificates and the *permis de circulation* would be ready in Rouen, the head prefecture of the district, the next day.

I would strongly advise anyone intending to take a motor to France to instruct some reliable motor car agent or dealer in good time to make the necessary arrangements for him and to meet him on arrival. The fee charged is not large, and the comfort and saving of time are great. The local man has all the necessary formalities at his finger's end, and will from his experience and acquaintance with the French officials probably save any intending tourist much trouble, time, and possible annoyance.

We had not expected to be able to complete all the formalities so soon, so had originally intended to stay that night at Havre; but finding ourselves free to leave, my wife and I decided to start that afternoon, as, beyond the docks, which, of course, are very fine, there is not much of interest in Havre.

En Route.

From Havre to Rouen we chose the route *viâ* St. Romain, Bolbec, and Yvetot. There is a little *pavé* as one leaves Havre, but one soon reaches the magnificent Route Nationale, and I then began to wish I had followed the makers' advice, and had larger sprockets than I used in England fitted to the car. I should imagine that any car that is of ample power for its size in England would on the fine French roads take sprockets with at least ten per cent. more teeth than one is accustomed to use here. We arrived at Rouen in good time that even-

ing, and the next day went at once to see about our certificates, etc. Here a Mons. Drance, a motor car agent, who had been recommended to me at Havre, rendered me great assistance, and although he could not get us the definite certificates that day, he was able to find out what number was allotted to us—a car in France must carry a number in front and behind—and have it painted for us by the afternoon, while we spent the morning in seeing part of the cathedral, etc. As we intended to pass through Rouen on our homeward journey, we left in the afternoon for Lisieux, M. Drance promising to forward us our *carte grise* and *carte rouge* as soon as they were signed. We had intended to take the route *viâ* Bourg, the Roulde, and Brionne, which is the shorter, but took a wrong turn; and, finding ourselves on a splendid road *viâ* Pont Audemer, decided not to go back, and after a lovely drive through a country sufficiently undulating to be picturesque, found ourselves at the Hotel de Normandie at Lisieux, which, in addition to being very comfortable, has, like most French hotels, every convenience, including a pit for motors.

After visiting the beautiful cathedral at Coutanees, and one or two churches, we left for Mont St. Michel *viâ* Granville, a pretty little town built on two sides of a valley with a hill down into the town and one up the other side. Thence to Avranches, which is built on a hill celebrated as being the highest steep in Normandy, and the road up to it is a stiff ascent with an almost acute angled turn halfway up. It looked formidable, especially as the surface was greasy, and we had to face it from a dead stop at the bottom for a level crossing, but the car ran up it without difficulty, and we were soon at lunch at the Hotel d'Angleterre, where we again found an excellent garage and pit. There is a lovely view from the gardens here across to Mont. St. Michel. Leaving Avranches there is a rather steep descent. At Pontorson the road turns to the right for Mont St. Michel. One can drive up to the rock itself along the causeway, but the car must be sent back to Madame Poulard's garage, which is situated at the beginning of the causeway about one kilometre from the hotel.

At Pontorson we made the mistake of taking a cross country road, which was curly, rather greasy,

Saumur from the bridge in the early morning.

and heavy from the rain, and we were glad to meet the main road again at St. Hilaire, from which place the going is all excellent to Domfront, Juvigny, Couptrain, Pré, and Alencon, and the country picturesque.

Beyond the church of Notre Dame we found little of interest in Alencon, and the next afternoon we were on a perfectly straight road *en route* for Le Mans. Here the cathedral is well worth seeing, especially the view it presents from the market-place. From Le Mans there is a good road to Angers *viâ* La Flèche and Durtal, which is a lovely little place.

Our First Panne.

Soon after leaving Durtal, and finding we could get no power out of the car, we examined the carburetter, and finding the jet was clear, we were lucky enough to locate the trouble in the inlet valves; these were very sticky, owing, I think, to some new kind of petrol a man had persuaded me to try, and which I never came across again. We discovered afterwards it had a tinge of yellow in it, possibly due to impurities, which may have accounted for the sticky deposit it left in the cylinders. After this I never used anything but the well-known brands of " essence," which can be obtained in every town from the firms mentioned in the excellent book published by either the Automobile Club or the Touring Club of France.

The next morning, after exploring Angers, we followed the road skirting the right bank of the Loire. The view as one drives across the river into Saumur is superb. From this place one should follow the road on the left bank of the Loire to the quaint little village of Candes. Here we left the main road to see the Abbey of Fontevrault, now a convict prison, where one can still see the cloisters and the chapel that contains the tombs and coloured effigies of Henry II. and Richard I. Returning to Candes by road, we ran through lovely scenery along the banks of the Vienne, and crossing this river, found ourselves in the pretty little town of Chinon. After staying here two days, we took the road on the right bank of the Vienne to Beaumont and Port Boulet, where we again met, and crossed the Loire. The road on the right bank of the Loire after passing the picturesque town and beautiful chateau of Langeais runs through lovely scenery along the river to Tours, where one crosses to the left bank.

The country round Tours is very interesting, and we spent two or three days in excursions to Chinon-ceaux, Loches, etc., and were always able to go and return by different roads. The drive from Tours to Blois *viâ* Amboise (where there is a lovely chateau overlooking the Loire, which is well worth seeing), and Chaumont is most attractive.

Ignition Troubles.

A few miles from Blois we experienced the advantages of a double system of ignition, for, finding there was something wrong, we lit our burners, and ran comfortably into Blois, where we found both the tremblers on the coil and the brushes on the commutator required adjustment. Two days were spent pleasantly at Blois and its surroundings, including a beautiful drive to the chateaux of Chambord and Chevorny, and back to Blois through the forest of Beauregard.

Should one visit Paris, it may be well to remember that the octroi on petrol is very heavy, and that, although a greater speed is allowed in the streets, twelve kilometres (= 7½ miles) an hour is the official limit in the Bois de Boulogne.

From Versailles to a little beyond St. Germain-en-Laye, there are long stretches of bad *pavé*, in-cluding a steepish hill, the condition of which defies description; but after leaving St. Germain, the road to Mantes (a pretty old town) is good. Here we crossed the Seine, and followed the road along the right bank through the forest of Vernon. There are several steep hills on this road, and after passing the ruins of the famous old chateau of Gaillard, put up for the night at the sixteenth century hotel of Le Grand Cerf in Grand Andely.

The Return Journey.

We varied our route from Rouen to Havre by taking the far more beautiful road along the Seine *viâ* Caudebec (a lovely spot), Lillebonne, and St. Romain, arriving in Havre in plenty of time to complete the formalities for the return of our deposit at the Custom House before it closed at six o'clock. The car was put on board, and the next morning we drove back to London from Southampton thoroughly satisfied with our tour. We had been extremely lucky, for not only had we no trouble with the car, but during the 1,500 miles we ran

The Courtyard of Le Grand Cafe.

while we were away, we did not have a puncture, although the tyres were not new when we started.

France is admirably adapted for a motor tour. The roads are good, and there are plenty of sign-posts. Further, at any cross roads of importance and in most villages there are boards erected by the Touring Club of France giving the direction and distance of the important towns. Warning boards are apparently erected at the top of every steep hill. All the hotels we came across had a garage of some kind, many of them a pit also; and essence, grease, and oil could generally be obtained from the man in charge. Indeed, one need never be afraid of running short of petrol in France, for there seems to be a stock in every village. Taradi's road maps are excellent, and the annuals of the Touring Club, or of the Automobile Club of France, afford one endless information about hotels and their prices, mechanics, depots of essence, oil, etc., together with many other useful details.

If the ubiquitous " Baedeker " and Hare's books dealing with the district one proposes to visit are also included, one has, I think, everything necessary, provided the weather is fine, for a complete change and a pleasant holiday.

POLICE AMBUSCADES.

AS announced in our issue of August 29th, we now give a new and revised map showing the whole of the police traps of which we have been advised. We shall be glad if our readers will communicate with us when any of these are withdrawn, together with particulars of any new traps which may be established, as we are desirous of keeping the map as up-to-date as possible. That it is of great service to automobilists is obvious, from the numerous appreciative letters which we have received since it was first issued.

1. Near Newmarket Inn, 2½ miles on Brighton to London road.
2. Between Newbury and Thatcham.
3. Between Newbury and Hungerford.
4. Between the top of Godstone hill and Caterham.
5. Between Sutton and Carshalton from railway bridge to convent walls.
6. Yarmouth, Acle, and Blofield routes.
7. In and around Garstang.
8. In and around King's Heath, near Birmingham.
9. Three miles from Wetherby on the road from Boroughbridge.
10. Near Horndean, 62 miles on Portsmouth-London road.
11. Measured quarter-mile at Twyford from Reading.
12. Between Heacham and Snettisham, near Hunstanton.
13. Top of Buck Ha Brow on the Clapham side of Settle, and passing under railway bridge through Settle.
14. Four Alls publichouse, 6 miles from York; between the seventh, eighth, and ninth milestones; at Barton Hill; 1½ miles from Malton across Old Malton Lane.
15. Entrances to Alton, Hants.
16. "The Avenue," Southampton.
17. Numerous traps on entering Winchester—all sides; also a quarter-mile from the middle of Alresford going towards Winchester.
18. Measured quarter-mile at Potterspury, 3 miles north of Stony Stratford.
19. Measured furlong from Benhilton Church into Sutton, Surrey, and a measured distance on Cheam Road.
20. Between Towcester and the first milestone towards Daventry; and on Stow Hill entering Weedon from Towcester.
21. Top of Acomb Hill to Acomb Schoolroom, Wetherby to York road.
22. Approaching Beckenham from all sides.
23. Ilford, Hinton, and Totton from Bournemouth to Southampton.
24. Half-mile, both entering and leaving Shifnal.
25. Entering Penkridge from Wolverhampton.
26. Near Wheat Sheaf, Sheldon, on the Coventry-Birmingham road.
27. All entrances to Oxford.
28. Near Crowborough, between Uckfield and Tunbridge Wells.
29. Two miles from Lymington on the road to Brockenhurst.
30. Measured quarter-mile outside Burley, just past Malt Shovel, near Bradford.
31. 220 yards between entrance to Ranelagh Club and the Common, Barnes.
32. About 1 mile from Ashford, Kent, on Hythe road.
33. About 1 mile beyond Utley on the Keighley-Skipton road.
34. Lowfield Heath, 2 miles London side of Crawley.
35. Entering Epsom from the south.
36. Near Hickstead, about 10 miles from Brighton on London road.
37. "The Bloody Oaks," 6 miles N. of Stamford.
38. A measured furlong leaving Slough towards London.
39. A series of traps on the Great North Road between Stamford and Grantham, the positions of which are being constantly changed by the police.
40. The Newark side of Gonerby Hill, 2 miles from Grantham.
41. At Bagshot, entering from Camberley side, and level crossing at Sunningdale Station.
42. At Weybridge, traps laid daily.
43. At the bottom of Jonn-o'-Gaunt's Hill entering Leeds.
44. Between Norbury and the fountain at Croydon, two measured quarter-miles.
45. Between the church at Horley and the Gatwick racecourse.
46. On the Sevenoaks Road between Bromley and Green Street Green.
47. On the Addiscombe Road, Croydon.
48. Hill at Stonebridge approaching from Coventry; also between Berkswell and "George in the Tree."
49. On the road between Lincoln and Newark, several traps.
50. Between Atherstone and Lichfield.
51. At the foot of a hill between Merstham and Redhill.
52. From York to the New Inn on the Tadcaster Road

(6 miles), a series of constantly changing traps; at Dringhouses, 2 miles from York, a measured piece at the corner of a by-road leading over the railway bridge.
53. In the straight which commences after leaving Old Windsor for Staines.
54. At Aston Clinton, midway between Tring and Aylesbury.
55. On the York to Knaresborough road, near Poppleton railway bridge, and along the wall at Allerton Park.
56. Numerous traps in the neighbourhood of Harrogate, Knaresborough, and Boroughbridge.
57. Between Billinghurst and Pulborough and south of Pulborough on the Portsmouth Road.
58. From Kew Bridge Station to Gunnersbury Station (As an alternative route, take Wellesley Road, which runs parallel.)
59. A measured furlong just past Rake on the Godalming Portsmouth road.
60. On the Andover-Devizes road, about 4 miles past Weyhill towards Devizes.
61. Half-way between Chichester and Arundel on the open road.

62. A complete trap at Phiddingley, 4 miles north of Hailsham, fitted with electrical apparatus.
63. At the bottom of the hill leading out of Warwick towards Stratford-on-Avon.
64. On Altrincham-Northwich road between third and fourth milestones out of Altrincham.
65. At Buckden between Huntingdon and St. Neots.
66 A measured distance of 250 yards at the entrance to Sandwich on the Ramsgate road.
67. On the Basingstoke-Salisbury road between Worthing, Oakley, and Deane Gate; also between Overton and Whitchurch.
68. Four miles beyond Selby towards Doncaster.
69. Between the second and third milestones out of Henley-in-Arden on the Birmingham side.
70. From the top of Liveridge to Hockley Heath.
71. Between Sawbridgeworth and Bishop Stortford.
72. On the high road from Warton to Lytham, near old Lytham Docks.

A WELL-TRAVELLED RENAULT.

A few weeks since we recorded the fact that Mr. H. R. Willding was starting on a commercial tour of England on a 10 h.p. two-cylinder Renault. Since then he has travelled from London down to Margate, right round the south coast and to Land's End. Here he turned north-east, and drove through Taunton, Bath, and Bristol to Gloucester and Hereford, thence to Birmingham. While there he visited our Coventry office, and we took a short run in the car, which had been driven just 2,300 miles in the month, which concluded on the day Mr. Willding called, it having been run over 1,000 miles before that in the Irish fortnight and preliminary drives. We were very much struck with the smooth running of the vehicle; in fact, it is one of the smoothest, if not the smoothest, two-cylinder cars we have ever tried. Not only is the engine free from vibration, but the gearing throughout is very quiet, and the car altogether is silent in its running. It will be remembered that the drive on the top speed is direct, and the way the two-cylinder engine pulled up a steep slope on the top gear was remarkable, although it

had been so slackened by the load that it was only just running. The same car will be entered in the 1,000 miles trials, and its record will be watched with great interest. It will probably have covered another 800 or 900 miles before then of its long run round England. Up to the present, we understood from Mr. Willding, no part had been renewed, with the exception of a sparking plug and a new blade on the commutator. We need say nothing about the smart appearance of the car, as that is well shown in the illustration.

AMERICAN ENDURANCE TRIALS.

When criticising the endurance or reliability trials organised by the American Automobile Club, we pointed out that the system of observation, particularly with regard to the repairs, adjustments, and renewals which were made upon the road, was not so good as it might be. Now, the National Association of Automobile Manufacturers are about to have an endurance test of their own, and the regulations they have got out are practically a copy of the English rules. The condition of each competing motor at the finish will be taken into account as well as the cost of repairs to each vehicle, and the time required to make them, the efficiency of the brakes and hill climbing capacity. One mark will be lost for every minute the car stops from any cause whatever except necessary traffic stops. An observer will be appointed to each car, and will be changed every day, and repairs will only be made in the presence of the observer. The classification

will no longer be by weight but by price, as in England. Altogether, a distinct advance has been made, and, provided the rules are impartially carried out, the test will be a very valuable one, but it is a pity that the makers and the American Automobile Club are not working together. It is as unsatisfactory for trials of this kind to be managed entirely by the manufacturers and interested parties as it is for them to be wholly in the hands of amateur users such as the Automobile Club. The best plan is the one we have, in which the makers and the club are equally represented on the managing committee of the trials. By this arrangement absolute impartiality is ensured, and the confidence of the public in the English trials is absolute. At the same time, as the makers are well represented our trials are so conducted that no impractical or unreasonable tests are included in the series of daily drives.

ONE YEAR'S HORSE ACCIDENTS.

3,991 Accidents: 411 Persons Killed, and 2,991 Injured.

IT IS NOW TWELVE MONTHS SINCE WE COMMENCED TO SEARCH THE NEWSPAPERS FOR REPORTS OF ACCIDENTS DUE TO HORSES. DURING THAT PERIOD THE NUMBER OF SUCH ACCIDENTS WE HAVE DISCOVERED IS 3,991, RESULTING IN INJURIES TO 2,991 PERSONS, AND IN THE DEATH OF 411 OTHERS.

The above are alarming totals, considering that the horse is generally believed to be such a safe animal to control and drive. The object we had in view was to show the necessity for some more stringent regulations in regard to horse traffic than those which obtain at the present time; or, in the alternative, that no greater necessity exists for special legislation in regard to motor cars than horses. Our contention all along has been for equality of legal restraint upon all kinds of traffic on the highways of this country. As a matter of fact, the question has been dealt with by Parliament since the commencement of the compilation of these statistics, but we need hardly say that it is not yet finally settled, and will not be till such time as motor cars are placed under the ordinary restrictions of the common law.

Horse accidents have become so common that they are disregarded, except in the particular locality where they happen, and all manner of obscure local newspapers have to be searched in order to find reports even of the most serious mishaps in which persons may be killed. It is quite a common occurrence for a fatal horse accident to be dismissed with less than half a dozen lines of newspaper space. The occurrences are so lacking in novelty that newspaper editors find they do not make good copy. This is one reason why the impression is abroad that horse accidents are rare. A motor car accident, on the other hand, is much more of a novelty. There is the glamour of the "snorting, vibrating, pulsating mechanism," which to the common mind is invested with a kind of superstitious horror, as though it were a unholy death-dealing creation imported from the infernal regions. These features give to motor car accidents a sensational interest in the public mind akin to that which attaches to ghastly crimes. The newspaper editor, therefore, must needs instruct his reporters to "write them up," so as to tickle this craving after sensationalism. This also accounts for the fact that whenever a horse takes fright and causes an accident on the road or in the street every effort is made by the penny-a-liner to import, though only in imagination, a motor car upon the scene. If only a suspicion of a motor car can be dragged in the accident is at once, and without further enquiry, attributed to that cause, and is blazoned abroad in large type as "A Terrible Motor Accident." A case in point occurred at Durham recently, when a lady was thrown out of a trap and killed. The first reports of the accident stated in the most positive manner that the lady "died from the effects of an accident sustained by her horse taking fright at a motor cycle." The motor in this case existed only in the imagination of the reporter, for at the inquest it was elicited that there was no motor nor motor cyclist about at the time, but that the sad affair came about by reason of the lady being unused to horses.

Again, drivers of horses are always too ready to assume that their animals are bound to take fright on the approach of a motor, and, by undue solicitude for their poor animals (who in most cases are not nearly so frightened as the persons in charge), bring about accidents which otherwise would not occur. There is, without a doubt, quite as much need in the interests of public safety for certificates of competency to be taken out by horse drivers as there is in the case of drivers of motor cars. Indeed, at all points it is not overstating the case to say motor cars are far more controllable, reliable, and free from vice than horses. In regard to the horse there is always an element of uncertainty. The peculiar characteristics of the animal's mental and moral development—if such a term may be permitted—have to be taken into account. A motor, on the other hand, is entirely devoid of these doubtful mental or moral characteristics, so that the driver's will, in regard to its management, is never disturbed by speculations as to how the machine will act. The competent driver knows to a certainty how his vehicle will behave under given conditions, but this cannot be said even of the most competent coachman in regard to the behaviour of his quadruped. As we have already pointed out, horse accidents are so common that they are unheeded; reports of them are not sought after by the public, and hence the general, though entirely erroneous, impression that they are few in number. That they are pretty plentiful is abundantly shown by those we have been able to discover during the past year. These are by no means exhaustive; probably the half has not been told. Our last return was made in *The Autocar* of June 13th. The following details are for the last three months—June, July, and August—during which period the accidents numbered 980, the persons injured 849, and the killed 82. For the whole year, the figures show an average of 76.75 accidents per week, with 57.52 persons injured, and 7.9 killed every week.

TABLE SHOWING NUMBER OF HORSE ACCIDENTS, AND PERSONS INJURED AND KILLED THEREBY, DURING THE YEAR ENDED AUGUST 29, 1903.

Number of accidents enumerated.		Persons injured.	Persons killed.
3,011	Brought forward from *The Autocar* of June 13th, 1903 ...	2,142	329
90	Week ending June 6th ...	68	5
79	,, ,, ,, 13th ...	57	8
86	,, ,, ,, 20th ...	77	7
91	,, ,, ,, 27th ...	62	7
88	,, ,, July 4th ...	67	7
58	,, ,, ,, 11th ...	47	5
66	,, ,, ,, 18th ...	41	3
66	,, ,, ,, 25th ...	42	8
68	,, ,, August 1st ...	56	7
58	,, ,, ,, 8th ...	61	6
93	,, ,, ,, 15th ...	79	13
83	,, ,, ,, 22nd ...	54	1
54	,, ,, ,, 29th ...	38	5
3,991		2,991	411

LEGISLATION AFFECTING AUTOMOBILISTS.
By John A. Williamson.

THE HEAVY MAXIMUM PENALTIES SPECIFIED IN THE MOTOR CAR ACT FOR 1903 FOR OFFENCES COMMITTED UNDER THE ACT HAVE NATURALLY EXCITED A GREAT DEAL OF DISCUSSION, AND SOME AUTOMOBILISTS HAVE BEEN INCLINED TO TAKE A DESPONDENT VIEW OF THE SITUATION. THE FOLLOWING SYNOPSIS OF ACTS OF PARLIAMENT OTHER THAN THE MOTOR CAR ACTS SHOW THAT THERE ARE MANY OTHER OFFENCES FOR WHICH SEVERE PENALTIES CAN BE INFLICTED, BUT WHICH ARE SELDOM OR NEVER EXACTED.

EXCEPT in very serious cases, it is improbable that the maximum penalties will ever be exacted under the 1903 Act, and the modified power of arrest which is given in Section 1 (clause 1) to any police constable to arrest without warrant the driver of a motor car driving recklessly or negligently, who refuses his name and address, or fails to produce his license on demand, or who has not the identifying mark on his car, is a very mild one compared with the powers of arrest contained in the Highway Acts, Towns' Police Clauses Act, and other statutes.

Although the maximum fines under the Motor Car Act 1903 are as a rule heavier, yet the powers to apprehend any person committing an offence under these Acts are much more severe than in the Motor Car Act, and upon perusal they would appear to be capable of being very harshly applied. In practice, however, these powers of arrest have not proved oppressive, and the same state of things may occur under the Motor Car Act of 1903. Yet all these powers and penalties are applicable to automobilists in addition to those imposed by the new Act.

It may interest automobilists to peruse a synopsis of a few Acts of Parliament which, since the Motor Car Act of 1896 was passed, have been applicable to motor car drivers.

Nearly all of these Acts contain powers of arrest, but seldom do we hear of these powers being exercised. For the last seven years drivers of cars have been liable to be arrested for furious driving, for not obeying the rule of the road on meeting vehicles, and other offences within the meaning of these Acts of Parliament.

List of Offences under the Highways Act, 1835.

72.—(1.) Wilfully driving upon any footpath or causeway by the side of any road made or set apart for the use or accommodation of foot passengers.

(2.) Causing injury or damage to the highway, or hedges, posts, rails, walls, or fences thereof.

(3.) Wilfully obstructing the passage of any footway.

(4.) Wilfully destroying or injuring the surface of any highway.

(6.) Breaking, damaging, or throwing down the stones, bricks, or wood fixed upon the parapets or battlements of bridges, or otherwise injuring or defacing the same.

(8.) Pitching any tent or encamping upon any part of any highway.

(9.) Making or assisting in making any fire within 50ft. of the centre of the carriageway or cartway.

(10.) Laying any timber, rubbish, or other matter upon the highway to the injury of such highway, or to the danger of any person travelling thereon.

(11.) Wilfully obstructing in any way the free passage of any such highway.

PENALTY.—A fine not exceeding 40s. over and above the damages occasioned thereby.

Under Section 79 of the Highways Act a power of arrest is given in cases where the offenders are unknown to the surveyor, assistant surveyor, or district surveyor, or such other person as he may call to his assistance, or to any other person witnessing the committal of an offence under the Act, to take the unknown offender before a justice of the peace; there to be dealt with according to law.

78.—(1.) By negligence or wilful misbehaviour causing any hurt or damage to any person, horse, cattle, etc., being upon the highway.

(2.) Leaving a carriage on the highway so as to obstruct the passage thereof.

(3.) *On meeting any other carriage and not keeping on the left or near side of the road.*

(4.) *Wilfully preventing any other person from passing or from passing any carriage under his care on the highway.*

(5.) By negligence or misbehaviour preventing, hindering, or interrupting the free passage of any person or carriage on the highway.

(6.) *Not keeping his carriage on the left or near side of the road for the purpose of allowing such passage.*

(7.) Driving any carriage furiously so as to endanger the life or limb of any passenger.

PENALTY.—In addition to any civil remedy, a fine not exceeding £5; £10 if the offender be the owner of the carriage. In default a term of imprisonment not exceeding six weeks hard labour. Any person witnessing an offence under this section can arrest the offending driver, with or without warrant, and take him before a justice of the peace to be dealt with according to law.

Any driver refusing to disclose his name may be committed to gaol by the justice of the peace for a term of hard labour not exceeding three months, or he may be proceeded against for the penalty aforesaid by a description of his person and the offence only without adding any name or description.

Towns Police Clauses Act, 1847.

21 and 22.—Disobeying the orders of the authorities as to the route to be observed by car-

riages during times of public rejoicings, or illuminations, or in cases when the streets are liable to be thronged or obstructed, or in the neighbourhood of theatres and other places of resort and churches during divine service.

28.—Every person who *in any street*, to the obstruction, annoyance, or danger of any resident, commits any of the following offences :

(1.) Repairs any part of a carriage (except in cases of accident where repair on the spot is necessary).

(2.) In meeting any other carriage *does not keep to the left* or near side of the road (except in cases of actual necessity or some sufficient reason for deviation).

(3.) In passing any other carriage does not keep his carriage *to the right or off side of the road* (except in cases of actual necessity or some sufficient reason for deviation).

(4.) By obstructing the street, wilfully preventing any person from passing him or any carriage under his care.

(5.) Drives furiously any carriage.

(6.) Causes any public carriage to stand longer than is necessary for loading or unloading goods or for taking up or setting down passengers (except hackney carriages standing for hire at appointed stands).

(7.) Wilfully interrupts any public crossing by means of any carriage.

PENALTIES.—A fine not exceeding 40s. for each offence, or in the discretion of the court imprisonment not exceeding fourteen days.

Any constable may arrest without warrant and take into custody and forthwith convey before a justice of the peace any person committing an offence under this Act.

The Metropolitan Police Act, 1839. The City of London Police Act, 1839.

These two Acts contain almost similar provisions to the Towns' Police Clauses Act 1847, which are applicable to the Metropolitan police district and the City of London.

A power of arrest is given to constables who witness the commission of offences under the Acts.

PENALTY.—A fine not exceeding 40s., or in default imprisonment not exceeding one month.

Offences Against the Person Act, 1861.

(1.) Whosoever having the charge of any carriage by wanton or furious driving or racing or other wilful misconduct or by wilful neglect causes any bodily harm to any person.

PENALTY.—This offence is a misdemeanour, and is punishable by imprisonment for a term not exceeding two years, with or without hard labour.

Power of arrest is given in the Act.

The Municipal Corporations Act, 1882.

23.—(1.) Grants municipal authorities power to make byelaws for the good rule and government of the borough, such as carrying of lamps, etc.

PENALTY.—A fine not exceeding £5 ; in default a term of imprisonment not exceeding one month. No power of arrest is granted.

The Local Government Act, 1888.

16.—(1.) Grants to county councils similar powers.

PENALTY.—A fine not exceeding £5 ; in default a term of imprisonment not exceeding one month. No power of arrest is granted.

Photo.   *Levick, New York.*

AUTOMOBILE RACING IN AMERICA. Our Transatlantic cousins are notorious for the immense scale upon which they conduct their affairs. Motor racing forms no exception to the rule, and since the Empire City track was opened to racing autocars some exciting events have been witnessed. The illustration above shows how by careful classification really interesting races can be secured, as it depicts a round in a fifteen miles race. The track is only a mile in circuit, so that the Purley track, when built, should provide far better sport.

THE MOTOR RACES AT EMPIRE CITY.

Rounding the bend after the start for the five miles open race. It was won by a 10 h.p. Franklin car in 6m. 54⅗s. The starting post is seen on the right opposite the grandstand and lawn.

One of the most exciting series of motor races ever seen in the United States took place on the Empire City track at Yonkers, New York, on July 25th. It will be remembered that a plan of the track was given in *The Autocar* of July 11th, page 90. Beautiful weather favoured the races, which were very largely attended, there being no less than 303 autocars parked in the enclosure. Eleven events were down on the programme, nine of which were run off, the remaining two being abandoned on account of there not being a sufficient number of entries.

The first event—a five miles race open to cars of any power, but not weighing more than 10 cwts. 2 qrs. 24 lbs.—brought five out of the nine cars entered to the starting line. The most powerful of these cars was a 16 h.p. Darracq, while the lowest-powered car was a 4 h.p. Orient Buckboard. The winner turned up in a 10 h.p. Franklin, which covered the distance in 6m. 54⅗s., the fastest mile being done in 1m. 22s. The Darracq ran second in 8m. 6⅘s., the little Orient Buckboard coming last in the remarkably good time of 8m. 30s., having maintained an average speed of over thirty-five miles per hour. It is interesting to note that the 10 h.p. Franklin has an air-cooled engine, and that it ran with remarkable regularity throughout the day, in spite of the atmospheric heat prevailing. Two firsts and a third places were obtained, the latter among a class of much higher-powered cars than itself.

The second event was the *pièce de résistance* of the day, as Barney Oldfield, driving a 70 h.p. Ford

racer, made an attack on the mile record flying start, which he was clocked to cover in 55⅘s. It was a wonderful performance, considering it was not on a straight track, and was duly gloated over in the American evening press in the following strain:

"Oldfield went for the record with a flying start. The big car got under full speed almost at once, and as Oldfield, bareheaded and alone, sat in it and crossed the tape, everyone caught a breath and realised that he was moving at hitherto unseen speed. There was no time to think of much, to marvel at the daring of the man, or to wonder why he kept to the outside of the track away from the pole, before there came an exhibition of hair-raising

Barney Oldfield going at full speed in his attack on the world's mile record. His time was 55⅘s.

The 35 h.p. Panhard leading in the fifth event, an open ten miles race. The three other competitors are seen coming up in the Panhard's dust   A 40 h.p. Darracq finished first.

daring and nerve and skill that explained. Keeping near the outer fence, Oldfield suddenly seemed to be seized with terrible convulsions, and then the car veered violently and shot into the turn, skimming like a huge projectile close to the rail.

"As the front wheels turned, in response to the driver's sudden and tremendous work at the steering wheel, which caused his strange contortions, the rear wheels slid sideways for a distance of forty or fifty feet, throwing up the dirt in a cloud that drove the spectators near the fence hurrying away pell-mell. It was this that caused the whole great crowd to gulp and gasp with a sound that blended into one long moan. Faces of men used to all sorts of daredevil sports blanched, and experienced hands holding watches shook as if with ague. The exhibition was Oldfield's method of making the turn—that was all. He ran wide, and turned in suddenly, instead of trying to hug the pole as closely as possible."

The third event was a ten miles match between a 10 h.p. Franklin and a 10 h.p. Renault, the former proving a winner for a second time in 15m. 15⅕s. Afterwards a fifteen miles match, flying start, for a triangular duel between a representative car of America, France, and Germany, brought out the 80 h.p. Gordon-Bennett Peerless, a 40 h.p. Decauville, and a 60 h.p. Mercedes respectively. The race was very closely contested for the first few miles. The Mercedes, however, showed its superiority, and the cars tailed out in the following order: Mercedes, Decauville, Peerless (the latter being nearly a mile behind the former at the finish); time, 16m. 54⅘s. Of the remaining events, the fifteen miles, flying start, proved the most interesting. This was open to all excepting Oldfield and La Roche, who had previously run off a couple of matches. The competing cars were the 80 h.p. Peerless, 40 h.p. Darracq, 35 h.p. Darracq, 70 h.p. Panhard, and a 40 h.p. Decauville. The Panhard led for about two and a half miles, when it retired through a valve spring giving way. The Peerless gave out very early with its water tanks leaking badly, apparently due to steam pressure developed. Until the fifth mile the 40 h.p. Darracq led the way, when the tyres began to peel in an alarming manner. The driver still stuck to it, but the 35 h.p. Darracq and the Decauville overhauled him, the latter winning in 16m. 39⅘s.

The lawn and grandstand at the Empire City Track. 303 automobiles were parked on the lawn, while the grandstand accommodated over 6,000 spectators

THE 5 h.p. VAUXHALL LIGHT CAR.

A complete Vauxhall two-seated light car.

THIS cleverly designed, cheap, and well-made little car was frequently met with during the recent thousand miles trials, and on all occasions upon which we have had this car under observation it has behaved exceedingly well. The aim of the designer has been to produce a light car propelled by mechanism of the simplest character, controlled in the simplest manner, and we fancy the reader who peruses this illustrated description to the end will agree that he has succeeded in obtaining his objective to a great extent. The car comfortably accommodates two passengers, and allows ample space for baggage beneath a portion of the seat and upon the rear platform. The illustration above, reproduced from a photograph, shows the little car as it takes the road, but to gather an idea of its constructive and propulsive economy it will be necessary to follow the lettered drawings and the explanatory text which accompanies them. Fig. 1 is an elevation of the car, by which it will be seen that the frame is formed by the side panels or members of the body, which are stiffened for such service by sheet steel flitch plates. The motor is a 5 h.p. horizontal, governed, and water-cooled, set with the cylinder breech rearwards, partly under the sloped footboard, and partly under the bonnet, as seen in the chassis plan (fig. 2).

The cylinder has a 4in. bore and 4¾in. stroke, the crankshaft running across the frame and projecting on the near side sufficiently to form an extension for the application of the starting handle. The engine and crank chamber are carried by the two angle iron bearers seen stretching across the frame.

The frame is supported on the axles by spiral springs, which have been adopted with a view to getting the axles right under the angles of the frame, and to obtaining as long a wheelbase as possible. By this arrangement, the centres of steering and driving axles are kept 5ft. 3in. apart. The wheels are prevented from spreading longitudinally by the radius rods $C^1 C^1$ (fig. 1) and the strong central V-shaped casting seen depending from the underside of the frame in the centre.

Any tendency to lateral lurching on the part of the wheels which might be thought likely to occur owing

The Vauxhall car arranged for four seats.

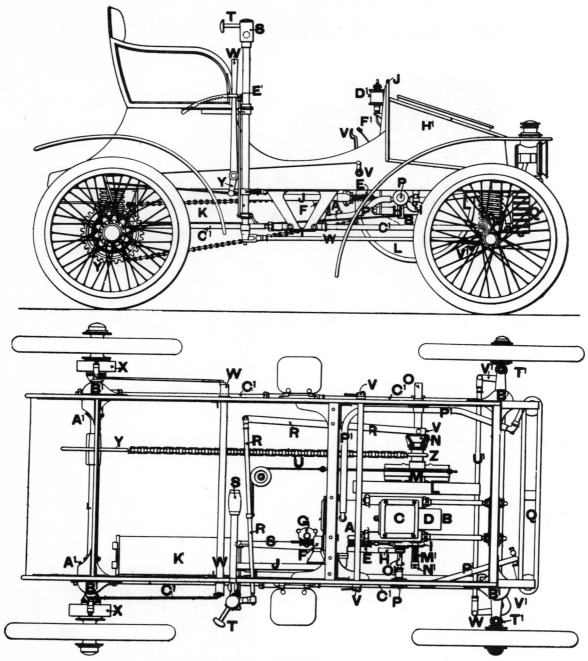

Figs. 1 and 2.—Plan and elevation of the Vauxhall light car.

A, cylinder
B, crank case
C, crank case inspection door
D, crank case cover
E, exhaust valve spring
F, carburetter and inlet valve chamber
    combined in one
G, float feed chamber
H, contact breaker
I, governor
J, exhaust pipe
K, silencer
L, flywheel
M, Crypto gear for low speed
N, clutch actuating device for high speed

O, crankshaft extension for starting
    handle
P, circulating pump
Q, radiator
R R, high speed clutch levers
S, steering tiller
T, combined change speed handle and
    throttle control
U, flexible wire for band brake on Crypto
    gear
V, foot brake
W W, hand brake
X X, brake drums and free-wheel clutches
Y, back sprocket
Z, front driving sprocket

A¹, back axle bearings
B¹ B¹, corner brackets of frame carrying
    top end of springs
C¹ C¹, radius rods to front and back axles
D¹, sight-feed lubricator for whole of
    engine
E¹, advance ignition lever
F¹, accelerator pedal through footboard
H¹, bonnet enclosing the motor
M¹, governor spring
N¹, governor spring adjusting collar
O¹, flexible drive to pump
P¹, water pipes

to the spiral springs is guarded against by strong guides set within the springs and fixed to the frame and axle. These overlap, but do not touch each other, as the springs play up and down. They only bear lightly against the inside of the springs when any tendency to lurching occurs.

The flywheel L (fig. 2) is mounted upon the crankshaft in the centre line of the car, and is, as may be seen, of comparatively large diameter, and of considerable weight, which serves to induce steady and easy running. To the left of the flywheel is found a Crypto gear of the ordinary type, the box M of which serves, in connection with the flywheel L, as the friction clutch when the car is being driven on its inner face with four spring arms, leatherfaced, which, when it is desired to drive on top speed, are forced against the face of the web of the flywheel by means of the actuating device N. This is operated from

Crypto gear, brake, and the high speed clutch friction arms.

The jacket water is cooled by passage through a radiator formed of specially fluted solid drawn brass tube, nested as seen at Q in fig. 1. The circulation is maintained by a small gun-metal positive action pump P, so placed as to be readily accessible from the side of the car. The pump is rotated by a flexible coupling O^1 from the half-speed shaft.

The commutator H (fig. 2) is a simple form of brush make and break, and is actuated by the sparking lever E (fig. 1). M^1, N^1, and I are parts of the governor, which is shown in detail in fig. 4, and hereafter described. The silencer K is fitted with a spring outlet valve at its rear end, the spring of which can be seen through the spokes of the rear wheel on fig. 1. The makers claim that the initial sound which issues from an ordinary silencer is the click of the closing exhaust valve, and if this

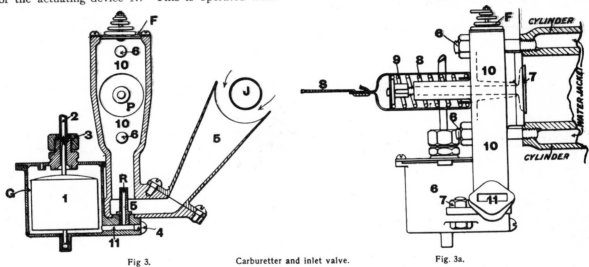

Fig 3.   Carburetter and inlet valve.   Fig. 3a.

J, exhaust pipe
R, petrol jet
G, float feed chamber
F, automatic extra air inlet
S, flexible steel wire to control handle
1, float

2, petrol feed
3, needle valve
4, wash-out screw
5, hot air intake
6 6, studs securing carburetter, etc., to cylinder

7, inlet valve
8, inlet valve spring
9, inlet valve spring compressing stirrup
10 10, mixing chamber
11, petrol passage to jet

the control handle T by means of the connecting rods R R.

In fig. 2 the Crypto gear box M is shown in driving contact with the flywheel L, but when the low speed is required the control handle T is swung rearwards, and the Crypto gear box consequently withdrawn from contact with the flywheel. This movement of the rod R R in a right hand direction applies the strong brake surrounding the Crypto gear, and the drive from the engine then passes through the sun and planet wheels to the sleeve upon which the driving chain wheel Z is mounted, a reduction of three to one being thereby attained. As may be perceived, the drive passes from the chain wheel Z to the sprocket Y on the live axle through the chain shown in fig. 2. It will be understood, therefore, that the drive is direct on top speed without intermediate gearing of any sort, so that the energy exerted by the motor is delivered to the road wheels with as little loss as possible. Suitable adjustments are provided to the

sound is deadened in the silencer the outrushing gases make no noise. We know that this car is particularly quiet on top speed.

The cylinder and crank chamber are lubricated from an adjustable sight-feed lubricator set upon the dashboard. The car is steered by a comfortably placed transverse tiller actuated by the left hand, the right being free to manipulate the single control lever T (fig. 1), the rotation of which throttles the engine, while its radial movement changes speed, as already described. V is a foot pedal applying band brakes to the axle drums X X (fig. 2). Further power may be brought to bear upon these brakes by means of the side hand lever W. These drums and their bands are of unusual width, and are very powerful.

The motor and gear are completely accessible by removal of the bonnet and footboard, and by unscrewing four nuts the forward portion of the crank chamber D can be taken off and the connecting rod and piston withdrawn without disturbing other parts.

Stiff lamp-brackets are provided by the upward extension of the vertical bolts securing the radiator nest in its position on the frame.

The wheels have been built with a small number of large diameter spokes and big hubs, and the amply wide mudguards are kept well clear of both

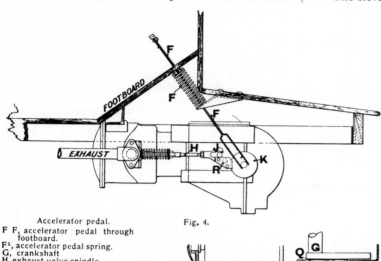

Fig. 4.

Accelerator pedal.

F F, accelerator pedal through footboard.
F¹, accelerator pedal spring.
G, crankshaft
H, exhaust valve spindle.
H¹, knife-edge plate.
J, exhaust valve cam race carrying knife-edge.
K, governor disc, sliding laterally on crankshaft under knife-edge to cut out.
L, governor centrifugal weights.
M, governor spring.
N, sliding collars.
O, half-speed shaft.
P P¹, half-time gear.

Fig. 4a

body and wheels. This has been done in view of the fact that the owner of a small low-priced car of this description is likely to do most of his own cleaning

Figs. 3 and 3a give the details of the simple form of combined carburetter and induction valve, the construction of which is made readily comprehensible by the figure and its references. The engine is throttled by the control of the tension of the induction valve spring, which is rendered stiffer by compression through a pull on the stirrup shown encircling same, by the flexible wire S, which passes up the control lever standard to the control lever T (fig. 1), as shown in detail in fig. 5. F (fig. 3, 3a) is an automatic air inlet valve, which admits extra air in proportion to the speed of the engine. The com-

bined carburetter and inlet valve is secured to the cylinder by the two studs 6, 6, and is held up by them against a ground joint, as shown. The device affords the engine perfect mixture at any speed or load.

The elevation and sectional plan in figs. 4, 4a comprehensively shows the detail of the simple but nevertheless ingenious form of governor employed. The governor balls L fly outward when the engine exceeds the speed for which the governor is set, and pressing upon the disc K force the same outward against the compression of the spring M.

On the outer face of the jaws of the exhaust valve-lifting rod H is set a knife-edged plate H¹, so that when the disc K is thrust outward by the governor, and the exhaust valve is open, the knife edge of H¹ rests upon the periphery of the disc, so that the roller O¹ in the base of the exhaust lifting rod jaw is held clear of the exhaust cam J, and the valve is kept open. When the speed of the engine again becomes normal, the governor allows the disc K to return to its original position, and the knife edge plate H¹ falling against outside it, as shown in the figure, the exhaust valve is again capable of closing.

The governor can be set to operate at any desired engine speed, or can be cut out altogether by the operation of the accelerator pedal F. The collar N (fig. 4a) is loose on the extension of the crankshaft G, and is made with two slots to take the wedge-shaped extremities of the accelerator pedal F F. The further this pedal is depressed, the more the collar N is thrust inwards, and the greater consequently is the compression of the governor spring M. This arrangement is both simple and ingenious, and functions most satisfactorily.

Figs. 5 and 5a are a sectional plan and elevation of the steering tiller and control lever, with its attachments, and can readily be comprehended by means of the lettering and reference. We think we may congratulate the makers of the Vauxhall light car upon having designed and turned out a neat, efficient, and cheap vehicle, which should find many friends.

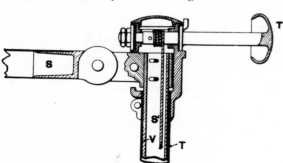

Fig. 5.

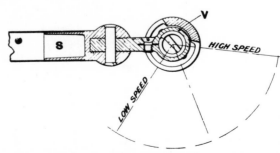

Fig. 5A.

Steering, change speed, and throttle control.

S, steering tiller (hinged to lift up)
S, flexible wire rope to inlet valve

V, internal tube connection to steering gear
T, change speed handle and throttle control

T¹, external tube connection to change speed gear

The Gordon-Bennett Cup and Race.

A HISTORY OF THE CONTEST.

AS comparatively few automobilists recollect the full history of the Gordon-Bennett Cup, or of the series of international races which have taken place in connection with it, we have compiled an account which recapitulates briefly the main features of the struggle for the possession of the coveted trophy, which was first raced for in 1900. The facts we give are all gleaned from the back numbers of "The Autocar," while the engravings are made specially for the article from photographs which were taken at the time the events dealt with happened. Perhaps the most significant phase of the account is found in the interest of the contest, which has increased from year to year, and bids fair to continue to do so, though the conditions will probably be altered, and lower-powered engines used.

The race for the Gordon-Bennett Cup has probably brought few retrospective incidents to the minds of most English people. From the nature of the contest, it did not until a year ago attract much attention in this country, for its interest was very largely minimised by the crushing superiority of the French cars; but when the cup was brought to England the public realised, for the first time, the great value of this trophy, not so much, perhaps, as a means of proving a national supremacy as of encouraging a further interest in the progress of automobilism, which, of course, must do a vast deal of good to the industry itself. Without the Gordon-Bennett Cup, it is probable that we should never have obtained permission to organise a race in the British Isles, or at least the chances of doing so would have been extremely small. As it is, the cup has broken down what appeared to be almost insuperable barriers to racing in any shape or form, and who knows but that this year's race may not be the first of a series of annual races in Ireland, which will do as much good for the sister isle as for the autocar industry? For it must not be forgotten that the automobile movement is destined to do considerable service to Ireland, where the motor vehicle will accomplish more than any amount of legislation, by opening up the country with cheap means of transport, and by attracting an increasing number of tourists of the best class across the St. George's Channel.

Now that the cup has come so prominently to the fore, a short historical sketch of this trophy may be of interest, the more so as there is probably no other branch of sport that can provide a parallel to the strange incidents of the challenge cup contests. They have always narrowly missed being a failure, until it seemed as if a fatality were

Mr. Gordon-Bennett.

The car which won the first Gordon-Bennett race in 1900—a 24 h.p. Panhard driven by Charron

hanging over the trophy, and if a car succeeded in getting through the race it was simply because it had a little less bad luck than the others. There were many things to account for this, such as bad management and the running of experimental and untried cars. In an ordinary race there are so many vehicles competing that the number finishing induces one to overlook the proportion of cars that have dropped out on the road. In an event like the Gordon-Bennett Cup, where each country cannot have more than three cars, the proportion may still be the same, and yet it looks very much greater because only one or two vehicles may terminate the course. At the same time, as manufacturers give special attention to the building of Gordon-Bennett cars, and necessarily send only their best and fastest vehicles, it might have been expected that they would have attained higher speeds than the cars taking part in the open races. If they have not done so, it is due simply to bad luck, for the cars have always attained record speeds during the time they were running, and, as we shall show further on, there is every reason for believing that this era of failure is now at an end, when we shall see the Gordon-Bennett Challenge Cup take the position which it ought to occupy in the calendar of automobile events.

THE AIMS OF THE DONOR OF THE CUP.

It was in 1899 that Mr. James Gordon-Bennett, the great newspaper proprietor and part owner of the Bennett-Mackay Transatlantic cable, had the idea of instituting an international challenge cup on the lines of the America Cup, which has given rise to such splendid struggles in the yachting world. He laid his views before the Automobile Club of France, and stated that his intention was to encourage an international rivalry and provide a means of ascertaining the progress being made in the industry by different countries. The intention was a very laudable one, for it would obviously allow those countries which aspire to supremacy an opportunity of showing what they could do in competition with a country like France, that at present holds the first position in the automobile industry. In the absence of such periodical trials, it was clear that makers of one nationality would be able to live on their reputation when others might be turning out as good or even better vehicles. But with the institution of the challenge cup, manufacturers have to fight to uphold their reputation, while those who claim to build cars equally as good find an excellent opportunity of substantiating their claims. This character of the cup contests was one of the reasons why the first races were a failure. At that moment, no country could pretend to vie with France in the construction of fast cars. Some of the foreign makers entered vehicles that made no show whatever, and for the time being the Gordon-Bennett races were simply a walk-over for the French manufacturers. This obviously could not last indefinitely, for with the progress being made abroad in the building of fast and reliable cars the time was bound to come when the French supremacy would be seriously threatened.

A SINGLE STIPULATION.

The cup was handed over to the Automobile Club of France with the single stipulation that every part of the competing car was to be manufactured in the country it represented. We know what an excellent effect this clause has had in perfecting the manufacture of tyres, coils, and sparking plugs, by showing that the British cars taking part in the earlier races could not rely upon the accessories turned out in this country. As soon as the defect was shown to

The 1901 winner. Girardot on his 24 h.p. Panhard. Photographed at Bordeaux after the race.

Charron—the winner of the first race before the start for the 1901 event. His machine was a 24 h.p. Panhard. From a flashlight photograph.

exist, it was remedied, and nowadays the British maker has no necessity to go abroad for any part of his electrical gear or his tyres. The other regulations for the cup were left to the Automobile Club, who decided that each country should be represented by not more than three cars, that challenges should be sent in by January 1st of each year, and that the course should have a length of at least 500 kilometres. At first it was proposed that the results should be judged by points, the positions of the vehicles being added, and the cup going to the team with the smallest number of points; but this was over-ruled in favour of the trophy being awarded to the winning vehicle. It was also decided that the race should take place in the country holding the cup, or, if this were not possible, it could be held in France. In recognition of the donor's generosity, the club was anxious to call the trophy the Gordon-Bennett Cup, but Mr. Bennett requested that it should be named the International Challenge Cup, and this is the official designation, though the former title is the one by which the trophy is generally known.

THE FIRST RACE FOR THE CUP.

The first race was held in June, 1900, from Paris to Lyons. Challenges had been received from Germany, Belgium, and the United States, and each of these countries sent a car, driven respectively by Herr Eugen, M. Jenatzy, and Mr. Alex. Winton. The cup was defended by three Panhard et Levassor cars, piloted by Charron, Girardot, and Chevalier René de Knyff. At that time, a very strong agitation had been worked up against the speeds of autocars, and in face of this organised opposition the local authorities refused to grant permission to run off the race, so that it was seriously proposed to select a course in Italy. All the competitors were waiting in Paris. After considerable trouble, the Sporting Commission of the French Automobile Club at length obtained the sanction of the authorities, and, thinking it desirable to lose

no time for fear of further complications, the competitors were informed that the start would be given the following day. This did not suit Jenatzy and Eugen, who complained that the notice was too short, and though the German representative was present with his car he refused to start. Jenatzy, however, was prevailed upon to go, though he stated that the car he had was not the one he intended to drive. The race was an extraordinary series of accidents from start to finish. There was no organisation, and the competitors had great difficulty in finding their way. Charron was leading when he struck a drain across the road, and the car flew up, and, fortunately, came down on the four wheels; the rear axle was so badly bent that he decided to give up the race and drive slowly on to Orleans for repairs. While there he was rejoined by Chevalier de Knyff, who told him that he had to give up on account of the change-speed gear breaking, and also brought the news that Girardot had damaged his steering gear and lost his way, that Winton had buckled a wheel and given up, and that Jenatzy was coming along, slowly, pursued by all sorts of ill-luck. Charron thereupon straightened his axle and continued on towards Lyons, covering the distance of 351½ miles in 9h. 9m. Jenatzy lost his way and gave up, and Girardot, who had to repair his steering gear, reached Lyons in 10h. 36m. Thus ended the first race, which, after promising a great international struggle, fizzled out hopelessly.

THE SECOND CUP RACE.

After this experience, the French Automobile Club decided that in future it would be advisable to run off the cup contest at the same time as the annual Paris-Bordeaux race, and this was done in 1901, when the only foreign entry was the celebrated 50 h.p. Napier car, driven by Mr. S. F. Edge. Unfortunately, during the run by road to Paris Mr. Edge had so much trouble with his English tyres that he found it was useless competing with these, and, therefore, he replaced them with French tyres, which, of course, disqualified him for the cup

Levegh on the 50 h.p. Mors. An unsuccessful competitor in 1901.

The 50 h.p. Napier which Mr Edge used in the Paris-Bordeaux race of 1901. This was entered for the Gordon-Bennett section of the race, but had to be withdrawn and run in the open race, as suitable English tyres were not then procurable. The photograph was taken by flashlight before the start from Paris.

competition. He consequently contented himself with taking part in the open race. Thus the only cars competing for the trophy were two 24 h.p. Panhards, driven by Charron and Girardot, and a new 50 h.p. Mors, piloted by Levegh, which was one of the first built with a curved front axle to allow of the engine being placed low down. It was this that proved fatal to Levegh's chances, for the axle does not appear to have given enough clearance from the ground, and when leading at Chateaudun the axle struck an obstacle, and the front part of the car was smashed. Charron then gave up through punctured tyres, and Girardot had so much trouble that he decided to abandon, but on hearing that the others were out of the race he continued the journey, and reached Bordeaux seventh, his average speed being thirty-nine and a half miles an hour. The winner of the race was Fournier, on a Mors of the same type as that driven by Levegh; his average speed was fifty-six and threequarter miles an hour.

THE THIRD RACE—ENGLAND'S VICTORY.

It seemed now as if the cup was likely to remain definitely in the possession of the French at least for a considerable time. No one appeared inclined to challenge for the trophy. Fortunately, at the last moment entries were received from the Automobile Club of Great Britain and Ireland on behalf of the Napier and the Wolseley companies. It was decided again to run the Gordon-Bennett Cup contest concurrently with an open race, and thus it was held at the same time as the Paris-Vienna event, when the cup cars had to run from Paris to Belfort, and from Bregenz to

Innsbruck. The Wolseley elected to start in the open race, so that the only foreign vehicle competing for the cup was the Napier, driven by Mr. S. F. Edge. The French cup cars were the Panhard driven by Chevalier René de Knyff, the Mors by Fournier, and the Charron, Girardot, et Voigt by Girardot. The incidents of the race are still so fresh that it is unnecessary to deal with them here. It will be remembered that Girardot dropped out early in the contest, while Fournier had to give up through a broken shaft, and the only two arriving at Belfort were M. de Knyff and Mr. Edge. The French representative had such a long lead that the race seemed to be over, barring accidents. On the Austrian roads, however, the Panhard was unable to stand the strain of being driven at such high speeds, and on the differential breaking the only cup car left in the race was the Napier, which continued to Innsbruck, and for the first time wrested the trophy from France.

This victory of the Napier car was in every way desirable, because it gave a real international value to the Gordon-Bennett Cup, and, apart from the influence it has had in imparting a high prestige to the British industry, the French naturally considered it a point of honour to get the trophy back again. They accordingly left nothing undone to enable them to triumph in this year's race. The first thing the defeat taught them was the danger of selecting drivers who could run what cars they pleased, and they decided in future to choose the vehicles which were to represent France, leaving the makers themselves to nominate the drivers. This was undoubtedly a wise precaution. The English victory of last year also had another result, in showing foreign countries that the French cars were not invincible, especially on roads that are not so good as those across the Channel; and thus the most powerful cars ever sent out of Germany and the United States were sent over to Ireland for the cup contest, so that the struggle was really one of the giants in the automobile world. The Gordon-Bennett Cup thus became what it was intended to be—a struggle for

The car which won the cup for Great Britain and Ireland in 1902. The 40 h.p. Napier, driven by Edge

An unsuccessful competitor in 1902. The Chevalier Rene de Knyff on his 70 h.p. Panhard. Photographed as he entered the Belfort control well ahead of all other racers in the first section of the contest.

Fournier on the 80 h.p. Mors. The fastest car in the 1902 race. It broke down before the first stage was completed, when making the speediest run of the day.

supremacy among the different manufacturing countries, under conditions that were fair to all. The winning team will always bring credit to its own country, and this credit will be of enormous business value, for it is evident that in a race of this

kind, where everyone is putting forth his whole skill and energy, a decided victory must mean an absolute superiority, always, of course, excluding tyre accidents that may place competitors in a state of inferiority. In fact, they have done so this year.

Mr. Julian W. Orde, Secretary of the A.C.G.B. & I.　　　Mr. Roger W. Wallace, K.C., Chairman of the A.C.G.B. & I.

THE IRISH FORTNIGHT—THE OPENING DAYS AND THE GORDON-BENNETT.

The Winner—Camille Jenatzy.   Second—Chevalier Rene de Knyff.   Third—Henry Farman.

THE DRIVERS OF THE THREE FIRST CUP CARS.

The start, finish, and incidents as seen from Ballyshannon.

THE thousands of people who travelled by train the 35 miles or so separating the chief points of the course from Dublin, starting at 3 a.m. and occupying roughly three hours, must have thought with envy of those fortunate enough to have a car at their disposal for the day. The narrative of various experiences subsequently told may have their humorous side, but we are afraid that the average Britisher is not likely to appreciate Irish humour when it takes the form displayed in the bemuddled mismanagement and disorganisation which characterised the "arrangements" of the Great Southern and Western Railway at King's-bridge for coping with the unusual influx of passengers.

To the Club Headquarters our representative was afforded a seat on one of the M.M.C. 20-h.p. cars driven by Mr. Burgess, starting at 3.35 a.m. from the Shelbourne Hotel, and the run was made through the delightfully fresh and clear morning

Jenatzy, the winner, waiting for the word "go."

air to Ballyshannon House under the hour.   Just a tinge of pink in the sky gave warning of bad weather to follow, which was not belied, as during the day the weather was very fitful, several rushes for shelter from the driving storms and wind having to be made under somewhat uncomfort-able conditions.   Getting away from Dublin, we soon began to overtake cars which had started considerably before us, and the air above the roads by degrees became almost one solid mass of dust in suspension.   The warnings issued by the Club had evidently had their desired effect,

Jenatzy, the winner of the Cup, stopping at the finishing point at 5.36 p.m. He brought his car to a standstill within 30 or 40 yards. He had been driving his car continuously, except for the slight relief given by the controls, since 7.21 a.m.

Jenatzy arriving at the Club Enclosure after covering the first circuit. The car is travelling at about 70 miles an hour.

GORDON-BENNETT CUP RACE RESULTS.

	Official No.	Driver.	Make.	Country.	Net times for each Circuit.							Total.	Average miles per hour.
					1	2	3	4	5	6	7		
					m. s.	h. m. s.	h. m. s.	h. m. s.	h. m. s.	h. m. s.	h. m. s.	h. m. s.	
1	4	C. Jenatzy...	Mercedes ..	Germany ...	48 58	1 1 19	0 49 45	1 1 52	0 53 16	1 1 32	1 2 18	6 39 0	49·25
2	2	R. de Knyff	Panhard ...	France ...	49 47	1 2 31	0 50 57	1 8 16	0 51 40	1 3 39	1 3 50	6 50 40	47·85
3	10	H. Farman	Panhard ...	France ...	47 31	1 10 27	0 49 35	1 5 55	0 50 31	1 2 17	1 5 28	6 51 44	47·72
4	6	Gabriel ...	Mors ...	France ...	53 10	1 0 19	1 2 37	1 4 20	0 51 4	1 13 58	1 6 5	7 11 33	45·33
5	1	S. F. Edge	Napier ...	Gt. Britain	46 23	1 7 3	1 27 59	1 24 59	1 14 35	1 55 21	1 22 28	9 18 48	35·16

Length of Circuits, excluding Controls :—Circuits 1, 3, and 5 = 40 miles each ; Circuits 2, 4, 6, and 7 = 51⅛ miles each.   **Total, 327½ miles.**

for never had livestock before been so cared for in the Emerald Isle. Every donkey, and even a pair of fowls had their custodian, and where the possessions were somewhat more numerous the animals had been carefully put into confinement behind strangely devised fences. Tyre troubles were not for us, but others were less fortunate, and by the time Naas was reached every few hundred yards claimed its victim. The swarms of cyclists wisely took to the paths, as with the almost continuous procession of cars rapidly passing to the course and the intensely dense dust it was hardly prudent for them to keep to the road. At Naas—the scene of the previous day's weighing—the fashions adopted by local beauty in arranging 'kerchiefs and shawls over their heads presented a good deal of similarity to present feminine fashions in motoring headgear, and several of the natives who were jogging along on their carts looked almost as if they had copied the latest confections wherewith to defeat the dust fiend—though mica-masks, needless to say, were not in evidence. In fifteen minutes from Naas, Kilcullen was reached, and there we came first into touch with the course. For a mile or more previously walking parties were passed carrying baskets, many of them having walked from Dublin, probably starting overnight. Then the course itself, with banners flying, and the first Control, at Old Kilcullen Corner, was sighted. Passing on swiftly, the sharp turn before Kilcullen was reached, where the "Westrumite"-treated road gave a brief welcome relief to the fearful dust. A mile further and two stands were passed on the right, followed by the Thomastown stand on the left. A drop down an incline brought us to another stand on the left, another a little further on the right, and we had the Club Grand Stand in view, gay with bunting, to which a few finishing touches were being given. Turning sharp off to the right to the Club Enclosure at Ballyshannon House, we found already about forty cars in front of us ranged round the open garage. The officials were already busy marshalling the cars to their places. In the fields adjoining, tents were dotted about here and there, rendering the adjacent landscape quite picturesque, but everywhere, dust, dust, dust, and still dust. Speed has been immortalised by poets. Who will dare to undertake a like task in respect to that awful demon dust? In the memory of automobilists never had such ghastly objects been seen as those who arrived at the Club enclosure having travelled by road. For the first hour or so Ballyshannon House presented the appearance of a public wash-house, water, however being a scarce commodity. Resource in desperation by some was had to the pool—picturesque but stagnant—at the back of the house. To the uninitiated there were many revelations into the mysteries of feminine attire. Some found out when too late that towels were scarcer still than water. One enterprising and fortunate man who discovered a horse sponge was the envy of the entire company, but in time, as the dust was gradually got rid of, these things were forgotten. In secluded corners breakfast picnicing was going on in every direction, the numerous fallen tree trunks serving as excellent temporary tables. As the cars came tearing along, the sounds of the hooters blended not very harmoniously with the refreshing note of the thrush and other birds singing their morning song, for the day was still young, although most of us had been up many hours. The stand, decked with flags, was reached across the grass, still wet with the heavy dew, in a direct line fronting Ballyshannon House. Officials and others

who had taken train to Kildare at 3 a.m., transferring there to "keears" over a cross country drive of seven miles, were destined to lose what remaining faith remained in them for the responsibility of the dear, delightful, dreamy Irish Railway Companies' methods. Those whose destination was Carlow did not reach that place until about 5.30.

The scene at the starting point, which was about 100 yards on the lower side of the grand stand, was full of life and bustle hours before even the pilot car was dispatched. The peripatetic fruit vendor, as usual, was early on the scene. Some amusing encounters took place between the Irish constabulary and many of the foreigners whose knowledge of English was slight, but when flavoured with a strong Irish brogue, the result can be better imagined than described. Nothing but the natural good humour of the police saved the situation. Well before six the racers had arrived. Numberless cinematograph operators had taken up advantageous positions from which to secure views of the start, whilst the number of general photographers and snapshotters was legion. At 6 sharp all traffic was stopped on the course, and a few moments afterwards Foxhall Keene, on his racing Mercedes, drove up with Mrs. Foxhall Keene on board. A little after 6 ominous clouds began to gather on the horizon, throwing into sharp relief the camp near the Ardscull Moat. At 6.30, to the second, the first "pilot" car—the Star racer, driven by J. Lisle, jun.—started on its course round one of the circuits. At 6.36 Lieut. Mansfield Smith-Cumming on the Wolseley racer, quietly whistling to himself, started his "pilot" on the other circuit. For a considerable distance on either side of the grand stand the road had been carefully prepared with "Westrumite," all the troubles arising from dust being thereby eliminated. This preparation, which hails from Germany, consists of tallow, turpentine, and water, all mixed up together, and is put on by ordinary watering carts. The enclosure was well filled before the start, and a good sprinkling of spectators was on the grand stand before the first car was sent off. A sweet-looking little Irish maiden, wearing a Government badge, was relentlessly turned off the course, to find her road by backways and fields, in spite of her protest that she was His Majesty the King's post-office representative. The suggestion that she might get killed very speedily overcame any of her qualms at having to depart from her daily route. As Edge, who was appointed to start first, took up his position in his car at four minutes to six a volley of clapping greeted him which drew general attention to the imminent starting of the great race. At seven to the second Major Lloyd gave the send-off, the firing of the pistol speedily bringing the few who were not already watching the scene intently up to the nearest point of advantage, and with set and determined face the holder of last year's cup shot under the grand stand at good speed to work up to a splendid pace before the end of the oiled portion of the course was reached, the car disappearing in a cloud of dust over the extreme point of the rising ground on which the start was made. Then came a wait of seven minutes, which seemed four times as long. A shake-hand from a compatriot and the Chevalier de Knyff on the first Panhard was off. He was not as quick to pick up speed as Edge, but fine travelling was made before he was out of sight. Owen on the first American car then wheeled into place so quietly that its exceptional power of making itself heard by means of its exhaust could hardly be thought possible. The pressure of the photographers and others at this time was

A view of the Grand Stand and the Club Enclosure taken the day before the Race. The course, which goes direct **under** the Grand Stand, is situated between two high banks, marked in the photograph by the hedge, just below the **Club Enclosure.**

Charles Jarrott.   Rene de Knyff.   S. F. Edge.

Lieut. Mansfield Smith-Cumming starting on the Wolseley racer as "pilot" round the course at 6.36 a.m.

The Club Enclosure.—Arrival of Earl Dudley, the Lord Lieutenant of Ireland. He is greeting Mr. Roger Wallace and the Hon. John Scott Montagu, M.P. Lieut. Wyndham is facing the Lord Lieutenant, and Baron de Zuylen is standing in the foreground of the picture.

199

keenly felt by the officials, but all round good temper was displayed, and it was a case of give and take. There was a sportsmanlike "God speed" from Jarrott, and the next moment Owen had slipped in his clutch, moving slowly away in strong contrast to the previous competitors. The intervals, although in each case the full seven minutes, seemed to grow shorter as each car came up to the line. It seemed as if No. 3 had hardly got away before the first German Mercedes car was in place. Jenatzy was the driver of No. 4, he receiving a tumultuous send-off from his good-wishers. As with the other competitors, a salvo of applause greeted his departure, which, so far, appeared the best "get-away."

The excitement in the enclosure and stand ran high by this time, and the crowd pressed forward in the enclosure endangering the somewhat feeble wire fencing which separated the eager onlookers from the course.

Following the lead of one observant individual, the occupants of the Grand Stand as each car passed under turned as one man (or woman) and peered through the spaces left between the planks to watch the disappearing racer over the top of the rise as it seemed to plunge head first into a belt of trees. The sight was a very remarkable one.

Jarrott was soon settled comfortably and listening to the last warning words of the starter, and with eyes fixed on his straight path, merely to be turned aside momentarily as a crash on his right announced the collapse of a huge branch of a tree which, being loaded beyond reason with human freight, had taken this drastic method of signifying its objection, Jarrott was on his way, with a splendid start. Gabriel, the hero of Paris-Madrid, then wheeled into place on the Mors car, and at the word "go," surrounded by a halo of exhaust, he literally jumped away and seemed to score the quickest start up to that moment. Mooers, on the wire-bonneted Peerless, with a tiny American flag pinned over his heart, was instantly in place ready for his turn. A turn of the starting handle tested the ignition. Then, as the time drew near, another try and stoppage caused a momentary cloud of anxiety to pass over the American's face. At the word "go," with the pushed assistance of his mechanician, he got away poorly. Two or three seconds lapsed before he was fairly under way, and then, greeted with ringing cheers as his engine settled down to work, he moved slowly away. With a last look over the car for a little final adjustment, Baron de Caters, on the 8th car, another Mercedes, was sent on his round—a grand start. By this time 55 minutes had been consumed, and the turn of the last representative of England came. Stocks, the selected driver, was instantly ready for his share towards endeavouring to ensure that the Cup should remain in the British Islands, and, as far as a look of human determination could indicate, his part in the day's triumph—or the reverse as the case might be—was to be reckoned with. After a rather halting start he made up for loss of time before he reached the top of the rise, and speed was expressed in the bumping of the car as it passed out of sight, the density of dust beyond the oiled portion of the road by this time having considerably abated. Congratulations from all sides were waiting for Henry Farman, on the second of the Panhards, as his engine, impatient to get to work, fired off volleys of explosions. His official number in the race was 10, but his old Paris-Madrid number, 51, was still faintly visible upon the radiator. Then came a second of keen disappointment as his engine stopped. A rush of help, a fresh turn of the handle, and

Farman had disappeared from view, almost before the echoes of the encouraging hurrahs had died away. Rumours of something wrong with Winton's big car caused a sympathetic murmur to pass round the intensely interested onlookers, intensified, as his car, No. 11, was pushed to the side of the starting line where he on one side of the car, and his mechanician on the other, set to work with a will to remedy the evil—ignition troubles. Although Winton declared he could not start, he and his assistant worked on manfully, and a sigh of sympathy was heard from those in the immediate neighbourhood of the car who knew the ill-luck with which he had been visited. By then the word was passed for Foxhall Keene to come forward as the last German representative and the last of the competing cars. He was away—slowly—by 8.17, after a stop and re-start of the engine, losing thereby some 17 or 18 seconds. The starting of the eleven cars altogether occupied 1 hr. 17 mins.

With the disappearance of the last car over the ridge the spectators turned their thoughts to matters of much interest to them, to wit—refreshments. Meanwhile *absolute* clearance of the course was enforced, and it was hardly grasped by the public that Edge in the first car was already in sight on the long straight stretch, finishing up at the Club Enclosure. At 8.23, Edge simply flew past, his front wheels leaving the ground a full half foot at the slightest inequality of the road. But Britain's champion was travelling fast, and it could hardly have been possible for him to hear the ringing cheers which were literally hurled at him as he again disappeared on his round of the Western Circuit, almost, it seemed, before he had been sighted.

And still Winton worked on steadily, his engine coughing huskily at each fresh attempt to start it.

"Car in sight, car in sight," came a stupendous shout, at 8.33¾ a.m., and De Knyff, on his Panhard, was upon us, and was then gone after Edge who, however, had already close on four minutes in hand. Hope for Britain retaining the Cup was strong, especially as De Knyff was not travelling so fast.

And still Winton stood to his guns. An official suggestion that he should change his position from the course to a side road brought from him a reminder that he was "in the race," "on the course," and "doing time," and competitors must pass round him as best they might, as he would have to get round them. Well deserved applause followed Winton's sally, as he had placed his car as near the bank edge as it was possible to force it, and by way of further reply his engine began to cough more vigorously. Nos. 3 and 4—the small Winton and Jenatzy's Mercedes—passed within 30 yards of each other about a quarter of an hour after De Knyff, the Mercedes drawing further upon the small difference dividing them before the pair disappeared in the distance. As they were passing, Winton's stranded car gave forth a continuous volley of explosions, as if urging on its sister car. Possibly encouraged by the efforts of the smaller member of the family, Winton's new "Bullet" at last, at 8.58, answered to the persuasion of his owner, and passed away on the first round to the encouragingly vociferous cheers of the masses, who thus gave vent to their admiration of the American's pluck. Within 3¼ minutes, Jarrott, travelling in grand style, followed up the Winton. A good rest came before the next car was signalled, and then, with the aid of glasses, Gabriel was sighted on the straight, passed at 9.5, and was out of sight under ¾ of a minute, 7 minutes to the bad on Edge's time for the first round. De Caters received the next greeting,

Mr. Edge's No. 1 Napier Car at the starting point. Mr. Edge is standing on the further side of the car in the white coat.
The wire seen above, forming a fence to the Club Enclosure, is the same sort of wire fencing as that through which
Mr. Stocks dashed, when his machine came to grief.

and with calm *sang froid* he waved his arm in courteous acknowledgment of the cheers.   The honour of admission to the contest for the much-coveted Cup is well bestowed upon such men.   Proceedings were immediately afterwards enlivened by the band of the 11th Hussars in the Club Enclosure commencing the first item of a delightful musical programme mapped out for the day.   But music was only of secondary interest on this, the red-letter day of automobilism.   Although it would have pleased the public to have seen Stocks, whose turn it was to come next, Henry Farman, as he sped past for the first round on his Paris-Madrid Panhard, was received with as much enthusiasm as if he had been the first to re-pass the

starting point. Foxhall Keene, well up to time, arrived by 10.30, driving in perfect style.   Edge, from the big circuit, keeping splendid time and travelling without a waver, flashed past at the stroke of 10, having covered the complete circuit in the net time of 1 hour 53 mins. 26 secs.   Six minutes separated De Knyff from Edge on this round.   Mooers appeared for the first time from the start at 10.11, having had ill-luck at Athy. Jenatzy, eight minutes later, had completed his full circuit, in 1 h. 50 m. 17 s. net.   At the time of the cars passing only the gross times were available, and the very uncertainty as to which of the cars were best on net time, although in a measure it detracted from the enthusiastic

Rene de Knyff on his car waiting for the word "go." Major Lindsey Lloyd, the Official Starter, is seen on the left of the
driver with his watch in his hand.

Gabriel on the Mors Car (No. 6) a few moments before his turn to start.

interest of the various supporters of each nation, was at the same time compensated for by the lack of general interest which would have resulted from the knowledge that any particular competitor was a long way ahead. Winton, on the larger car, was timed for the eastern circuit at 10.30, which made his gross time 2 h. 20 m., allowing for the very late start made by him. Taking, however, the time elapsed from his actual start his speed was not such as to make his competition a serious element in the contest. Owen, on the other Winton, after covering the western circuit, had got into the same stretch of road with his "stable companion," a "bunch" looking likely at Kilcullen Corner when in two minutes Gabriel followed close upon his heels. By this time the fact that Stocks was still missing from his first round of the Eastern Circuit, and that Jarrott had not yet finished the double circuit, gave rise to a feeling of regret that Great Britain had only one good string left to her bow, this feeling was emphasised as at this moment a private wire came through from Stradbally to say Jarrott was knocked out, followed about ten minutes later by a cheer of relief when Baron de Caters stopped his car on his next round to impart the gratifying news

that, although Jarrott's car was smashed up, this popular driver had escaped with only trifling injury. Farman, by 11.8, had finished his complete circuit, and sped away, if anything, more speedily than on his first passing. At 11.25 De Knyff came through, commencing his third circuit, and was followed quickly at 11.34 by Keene, and at 11.37 by Jenatzy driving superbly. A few minutes later Lieut. Smith-Cumming, on the pilot car, drove up the course to Ballyshannon, and at a quarter to twelve Earl Dudley, the Lord-Lieutenant, arrived in the enclosure, his presence being announced by the band playing a few bars of the National Anthem. His party included :—Lady Troubridge, sister of the Countess of Dudley; Miss Keyes, General Maxwell, Lord Plunket, the Hon. Cyril Ward, Mr. Fetherstonhaugh, Capt. Cadogan, and Mr. Lionel Earle.

At a few minutes to twelve Edge revived the flagging British hopes by speeding past in magnificent style. If cheers could have given him victory he would have been adjudged the winner forthwith by the mighty ovation which was accorded him. Gabriel, on the Mors, although reported to have broken down, was, apparently, travelling well when he was timed at 6 minutes past 12. Not one

Baron de Caters receiving the good wishes of Mr. Gray Dinsmore upon his taking his place at the line as eighth starter.

THE AUTOMOTOR JOURNAL.

Henry Farman on one of the Panhard Cars (No. 10) getting ready to start.   On the left is Mr. Pembroke, one of the timing officials.   It will be noticed that the old Paris-Madrid number, 51, is still painted on the radiator of his car.

of the least interesting features of the race was the big rush which took place towards the edge of the course from the remotest points of the enclosure and fields adjoining the course as the signal was given that a car was sighted. About midday a thunderstorm threatened, and the announcement at the same time of luncheon caused a general adjournment to the refreshment tents.   An excellent repast put everybody into a more contented state of mind and body, especially as, fortunately, the threatened storm was a false alarm.   Presently, however, the rain started and created an immediate stampede from the Grand Stand and Enclosure.   In the mean-

time the cars were travelling past at short intervals the Mercedes, continuing their steady pace, already indicating one of them as a probable winner of the Cup At 1.15 the rain started in earnest for a short space of time and the surface of the course began very quickly to show the effect.   New interest now in the half-over race was immediately apparent, and speculation rife as to the likely effect the sudden change might have upon the various cars remaining in.   By the half hour, Winton who was still pegging away, passed, Gabriel, Edge, de Caters, and Farman following at intervals in the order named. Keene gave up at Kilcullen, after doing three circuits

Mr. Charles Jarrott before the start being enlightened as to some of the latest arrangements.   The two on his left are M. Rene de Knyff and Baron Henry de Rothschild, respectively.

owing to a broken axle. Soon after 2 the sun shone out once more, and mackintoshes and other unsightly wraps disappeared as if by magic, varied-hued sunshades taking their place, the scene once more presenting a brilliant picture of softly blended colours, only, however, to give place later to a gradually increasing wind which made itself felt particularly on the elevated part of the Grand Stand and threatened destruction to the timekeeper's tent. At 3 o'clock Gabriel finished his fifth circuit, Winton, at 4 minutes past the hour, finishing his third. The drivers still remaining in, steadily persevered with their self-imposed labours, and, watching the bumping and erratic movements of the vehicles as they flew past, one and all marvelled that machinery could hang together under such stress. But the admiration for the men who were able to stand the awful strain of driving the cars for ten or eleven hours on end, relieved only by the short intervals of rest afforded by the controls, was expressed by silent wonder for want of words to convey an adequate appreciation of their endurance. De Caters, at 3.13, passed, followed soon after by Farman, Edge completing his fifth circuit at 3.34. Owen at 3.42 finished his third circuit, and at 3.57 de Knyff started his last and seventh lap, sending his machine along as if he had only just commenced. Jenatzy completed his sixth lap at two minutes past four, and was the second man to start on the last round. Starting with about nine minutes to the good, bar accidents, he looked like lifting the Cup. The other last laps were timed away—Gabriel at 4.43, de Caters 4.51, with Farman a minute after close on his heels, both simply flying over the road, and Edge at 6 o'clock. Owen was again seen at 5.32½ with de Knyff only half a minute behind him finishing his seventh and last round. The cheers had barely died away before the winner of the Cup, Jenatzy, was sighted in the distance, he passing the winning post at 5.36. The first to congratulate him was Mr. Gray Dinsmore, the owner of the car and the representative of America on the International Cup Commission. At 5.49 Winton again passed, followed ten minutes afterwards by Edge completing his sixth round, Gabriel starting his last lap at 6.20. Farman at 6.30 finished his race, and six minutes past 7, with Owen not signalled, the International Commission determined to declare the race over.

This was the result of a meeting held by the Commission having regard to the large difference in time between the leading cars and those which had had ill-luck. At this they had determined that when the first five cars had passed the winning post the race should be declared to be over, and under this decision, J. E. Hutton was despatched later round the course on his big Mercedes with the official notification to the public.

And so the great race had been won and lost—a record race both for starters (twelve) and finishers (five), or seven if allowance be made for the two Winton cars which at the time of closing the race were still running. And although there were many heartburnings at the result, the pluck of the Germans in competing after having had their "giant" creations burned up softened down the feelings of regret that every Englishman must feel at seeing the trophy leave the country.

At 7.7 Hutton, on his Mercedes, arrived from his trip round the eastern circuit, where he had been to notify that the race was over for that portion of the course. He reported that he had found the police already gone, and the road full of cattle and live stock, in high fettle after their enforced confinement during the day. De Caters,

who had broken his axle after touching a bridge at full speed, arrived on another car at 7.15, and at 7.25 Hutton started on his journey round the western circuit with the card, "Race over," displayed back and front. The Lord Lieutenant, in spite of the late hour and the rain storms which came down just before Jenatzy and De Knyff arrived, evinced the great interest which he took in the event by remaining on to the end. And before 8 o'clock a general move was made towards home.

The electrical timing system of Mr. Phillips for the flying mile ending at the Club enclosure, besides being of considerable interest, served a double purpose by giving due notice of the approach of another car when a mile off and preparing everybody to be ready for its reception.

A small coterie of French enthusiasts, headed by the popular journalist, Georges Prades, of L'Auto, had gathered immediately opposite the timing pitch, and during the day by their varying expressions the progress of the race so far as France was concerned was indicated almost as if by a barometer. As the finish of the race approached the excitement grew in intensity, and in many quarters was a source of considerable amusement.

General Impressions and Observations and Incidents at the Inward (Western) Athy Control.

If a man were to become confirmed in the habit of eating breakfasts at 1 o'clock in the morning, there might reasonably be some excuse for his being considered by his friends a fit subject for the Lunacy Commissioners. From a perfectly sane point of view it must indeed be admitted that it is a habit for which but little may be said in recommendation. Truly the laws of Nature demand that a man should go to bed with the sun and rise with the sun. But civilisation has altered all that. A man—a reasonable man, that is—goes to bed some three or four hours after dinner, and rises somewhat about an hour before his appointed breakfast time. But for the confirmed automobilist neither the laws of Nature nor the laws of civilisation have any effect. At least, that is the impression to be derived from the opening days of the great automobile fortnight in Ireland. We were rushed over on Tuesday by the night mail from London, arriving at a perfectly unmentionable hour on Wednesday, after a night in which the gentle nurse had carefully refrained from interfering with the ravelled weariness of our brains. Briefly, we had no sleep on Tuesday night, and we were too much concerned with the proper working of the Gordon-Bennett race to get any sleep during the day on Wednesday. Mere creatures of habit that we are, we went to bed on Wednesday night at our usual hour of 11, and got up the following morning at 1.30, and breakfasted at 2. Some of us, in fact, never went to bed at all, not caring to run the risk of being late for the great race, to such limits does the love of the automobile carry one. The gods might laugh at the freaks and follies of human nature, but "Vive le Sport!"

Undoubtedly from one point of view no better country could have been selected for the "Festival of Speed" than Ireland. For one of the essentials of success in such a carnival is good temper, and to the man with a soul, Ireland and the Irish are a never ending source of amusement and laughter. In such a scheme as the Irish Fortnight, breakdowns and miscarriages of plans were unavoidable, but laughter sweetened our troubles and helped us over the tribulations to which we were subjected. Dublin was crowded, in fact overcrowded. For the nonce the capital of Ireland had become an annexe of the Automobile Club, and the country outside the pale, a racing track at the disposal of its members. Though July will be a memorable month in the history of Ireland—memorable for the passing of the Land Bill and the state visit of the King—all these important matters were forgotten for the time being in the interest and excitement aroused by the opening of *the* fortnight. Although Dublin is by no means

than anybody else, and she undoubtedly succeeded. For, though it must be frankly admitted that the course was not a good one, yet there was never one accident. In spite of all the crowds making holiday—in spite of the roads thronged with people to whom the most ordinary motor car was a revelation—only one boy was knocked down, and, as it was Ireland, it was proved that he fell over his own feet, and that the car never touched him. As one of the

Mr. Alexander Winton, who had trouble with his "carburettor," gave notice he could not start to time. He is seen busily engaged with his chauffeur endeavouring to remedy the fault. The starting line is marked by the post and flag against the bank.

behindhand in the matter of automobilism, yet the wholesale introduction of the automobile world from England, created no little sensation. Outside the Shelbourne Hotel, where the headquarters of the Club had been set up, an enthusiastic crowd collected, staring open-eyed as the various touring cars rolled up. In the country round the course the priests had taken the matter up on behalf of their congregations, and from every pulpit an exhortation had gone forth, begging devout Catholics to avoid

officers of the Royal Irish Constabulary said to me, "We wanted to show everybody that when the Irish Constabulary take over a big order like this, they carry it through without a hitch, and we were determined that there should be no recurrence of the scenes in the Paris-Madrid Race." That they carried out their duties with efficiency and admirable skill is now almost ancient history. But this is a digression.

On Wednesday the gentlemen who were to officiate in various capacities at the race on the morrow were hurried

Mr. Foxhall Keene, the last man to be started, is seen sitting upon the bank on the left of our picture waiting for his call to race, his car, No. 12, one of the Mercedes, being opposite to him.

getting drunk on Thursday, July 2nd. It speaks much for the influence for good that the priests exercise over the people that their wish, thus frankly expressed, was listened to, and was put into force to such an extent that many keepers of drinking shops closed their premises voluntarily. Ireland was on her mettle. She wished to prove to the world that she could manage an automobile race better

down at an early hour to Kildare for rehearsal. "Rehearsal" exactly expressed our experience, for it was all the world like amateur theatricals. Very few of us knew our parts, and the similitude was further heightened by the fact that the manager was late. The weighing in of the cars had taken Mr. Phillips longer than he expected, and therefore we had to lounge about on the roadside for a couple of

The Timekeepers' "pitch." Looking from left to right along the front row at the tables are **Mr. G. Pembroke, Mr. T. H. Woollen, Mr. Swindley, and M. Tampier (the French timekeeper).** Mr. Siddeley is standing between the tables, and Mr. Rees Jeffreys, one of the Club Secretaries, on the left. Behind the left table is Mr. Basil Joy, the Technical Secretary of the Club.

hours, snatching what interest we could from the scene by the passing of Lord Roberts in a motor car and the stream of soldiers coming from the Curragh. Gabriel, too, flashed by, trying his Mors over the course. But at last Mr. Phillips arrived, and having received our badges—rather after the manner of schoolboys receiving their prizes—the serious business commenced. The various head marshals martialled their men, and with the assistance of some touring cars that took the place of the racing cars for the time being, the various controls went through their duties with varying success. Perhaps the majority of us were some-

what hazy as to what we had to do, but we stumbled through the performance to our own satisfaction in time to get a scratch lunch in the town, where beds were being offered for the moderate sum of seven pounds ten a night. Then back we went to Dublin, enthusiasm for the cause and a wild longing for sleep struggling for the mastery in our minds. After a good dinner, some to bed, others to keep a vigil the night through.

At half past one on Thursday morning, Fate, in the person of the "boots," summoned us from dreams and nightmares. It was still quite dark, but we rose without

The Electric-Timing Tent. On the extreme left of the photograph is Mr. R. E. Phillips, the Timekeeper in Chief, who was responsible for the whole of the arrangements. One of the special clocks made for this Race is seen behind Mr. Phillips, and in the centre of the group to the right is Major Lindsey Lloyd, the Official Starter.

The Grand Stand as seen from opposite the timing tent. Waiting for the next car to come round.

grumbling, and scrambled into our clothes by the aid of candle-light.   As was natural there was no little confusion in the hotel.   Dis-organised by want of sleep, it was somewhat difficult to find what we wanted, and my mind will always retain an impression of a certain ardent automobilist wander-ing about the corridors of the hotel with one boot in his hand, vainly trying to keep his temper, and find the re-mainder of the pair.   Most of us had only dined about three hours previously, but we did our best to break even this three-hour fast, as we did not know when we should be able to eat next.   At about two the streets of Dublin had been quiet with the quiet of sleep, but suddenly they seemed to spring into life again, with the panting of automobiles and the rattle of jaunting cars.   All roads lead to Kingsbridge Station, and as we reached the railway the white feet of dawn trod daintily on the blackness of the sky.   But at the station the peace of the early morn was discounted.   We jumped off our cars into a species of pan-demonium.   As far as one was able to discern in the half

Earl Dudley, the Lord Lieutenant of Ireland, on the steps of the Royal Box, watching one of the cars pass under the Grand Stand.

light, the extraordinary passenger traffic was being dealt with in a manner at once novel and completely Irish. The object of the passen-gers — or rather the would - be passengers — was to get into the station, while ap-parently the object of the station officials was to keep them out at all costs.   Seem-ingly it was a sort of up-to-date trial by fire.   Those per-sons who could break their way on to the platform by sheer strength were to be ac-counted worthy of travelling, those who could not were to wait until it pleased the company to let them enter. According to the bills, trains were to be sent off as soon as they were filled, but the word "filled" was allowed a liberal definition.   The race officials had a special re-served carriage, but this was at once invaded by the general public, and we went down to our various destinations in the country packed like sardines. At last we got off, and steamed slowly away.   Our own particular control was at Athy West, and so, about half-past five, we disembarked on Athy Station.   So far our la-bours had been purely physical. We had got ourselves into the neighbourhood of duties by good luck and a little honest pushing. But now another task lay before us. We had to find our control. It was useless to ask any of the native population of the little grey town. They did not know, and we had to set out on an exploring expedition. Fortune was good to us, for, after a two-mile walk, we came to a red flag stretched across the road, by the side of which were erected two tents. How we came to the conclusion that this was the Athy West Control no man will ever know. Perhaps it was instinct, or just sheer good luck. We had no maps, and nobody told us it was Athy West, but it was—so good are the gods to the innocently reckless. It was then scarcely six o'clock, and the first racing car could not reasonably be expected until after half-past nine, so we had plenty of time to make necessary preparations. From a neighbouring thatched cottage we borrowed a table for the timekeepers, and having marked out the control lines with whitewash on the dusty road, we sat down to wait. And while we waited a happy inspiration entered the mind of one of the assistant marshals—an inspiration which doubtless helped to make this particular control the most efficient and well-worked on the whole course. This heaven-sent idea was briefly this—that as we should undoubtedly be detained at our posts for some sixteen hours it would be as well to make some arrangements relating to the commissariat department. This suggestion was hailed with the applause which it undoubtedly merited, and there and then the assistant marshal in question was commissioned to go to the town and purchase refreshments. This he did, and returned with a man burdened with a basket containing innumerable bottles filled with liquids, varying in strength from Guinness's stout to lemonade. By this simple means the officials of the Athy West Control were kept in the best of tempers the whole day long, and everything worked with a machine-like ease and rapidity.

As we had so long to wait, some of us went over the fields, a matter of half a mile, to Athy East Control, through which the cars were due to pass some ninety minutes earlier. Here we learnt that Winton, in going round the course before the commencement of the race to heat his engines, had had what might have been rather a bad accident. For just inside this control there was a very nasty corner, which he had failed to negotiate properly, and ran his machine in consequence into a stone wall. We had not long to wait before a constable stationed at the top of the road signalled the approach of the first car. A little whisper of excitement passed through the expectant crowd, Suddenly on the top of the incline Edge's green Napier appeared, and before we could quite realise his speed he had drawn up between the two white lines. It was then six minutes to eight, and he had done the thirty-seven odd miles from the start at the rate of sixty miles an hour. Rapidly swallowing a sponge cake and a few strawberries, he followed his pilot cyclist. And here may well be noticed a certain fact. The rules of the race set down that no competitor was to travel at the rate of more than about fourteen miles an hour through the control, and add further with a touch of unconscious diabolical humour, that any competitor over-running or bustling a pilot cyclist would be immediately disqualified—a compensation which, it is fair to say, the deceased cyclist would be the last to appreciate. But this rule as to speed was never observed, and every car that I saw travelling through the control was going at a speed of quite twenty miles an hour. The enthusiasm of the pilots

put them to a lot of unnecessary exertion in trying to keep well ahead. After Edge came De Knyff, three minutes behind the cup-holder's time. As yet the race had not warmed into excitement, in spite of the pace. But a new interest was aroused by the arrival of Owen on the Winton. Scarcely had he drawn up outside the control than the cry went up that another car was coming. Hurriedly the pilot jumped on to his cycle and Owen got away, just in time to allow Jenatzy to enter. As to whether Jenatzy should have been allowed to precede Owen through the control was a moot point which nobody at the East Control seemed prepared to determine. But now as the time was getting on we had to scramble back through the cornfields to our own control, to spread the good news that Edge was doing splendidly and going strong.

While yet there was time we fed, lying at our ease on the grass at the side of the road or sitting on an adjacent heap of flints. But time and the automobilist wait for no man, and we had to drop our food in a hurry shortly after half-past nine, for a constable was wildly signalling the approach of a car, and above the green trees in the distance rose a cloud of dust. Now our own duties had commenced, and we rushed to our places with alacrity, and with a precision which did great credit to the organising capacity of the head marshal. There was no disorder and no confusion, and we were perfectly prepared as Edge bounced up the top of the hill and swept down on us. Still he was well up to time, and he sat in his car, calm and cool, smiling and chatting courteously. Indeed he might have been taking a trip round the country in a donkey cart, instead of speeding over a difficult and dangerous course at something like sixty miles an hour. His coolness and good nature throughout the whole of the race—in good fortune and out of it—proved him to be a thorough type of the best English sportsman. As he moved away we cheered him lustily, speeding him on with good wishes for his final triumph. Once more comes De Knyff, black-bearded and solemn, the patriarch of the car. As he dashes up, the Panhard men, unfamiliar figures in their blue French workmen's clothes, who are lined up outside the control with the representatives of the other manufacturers whose cars are competing, with everything ready for a breakdown, rush into the road and hysterically wave cans of water and cases of petrol and lubricating oil. "Petrol," shouts his chauffeur, and as he is whirled by a can of petrol is hurled into the car. Viciously the chauffeur seizes it and stabs it with a steel blade, making a vent so that it will pour the quicker into the tank. We look closely at this strange figure, for rumour has it that it is his last race. "No man," he is reported to have said, "should race after he has reached the age of twenty-three or twenty-four." He himself paradoxically is over forty. Solemnly he replies to the innumerable questions of his friends, who are far more excited than he. He has made up his lost time, and has gained fifteen seconds on Edge. The Frenchmen are deliriously happy, and shout wildly after him as he speeds towards the town. After the lapse of half an hour his pilot cyclist returns with a long face. De Knyff, it seems, reached the exit before Edge, who had stopped his engines, had got away. He arrived, in fact, in time to see Edge being pushed across the line. Immediately, De Knyff lodged a protest. "We allow that on the Continent; but you make your own rules here, and I shall have to report the fact that you have been pushed over the line." From the same source, we also hear that Edge got away from the control,

De Knyff on No. 2 Car (Panhard) passing the Club Enclosure at the finish of his first circuit. Winton is seen in the distance still trying to start his car.

but broke down a few yards out, and was passed by De Knyff while sticking in a ditch. This is the beginning of many strange rumours. I think that we killed all the competitors one by one in the course of the day—so many and so various were the rumours that seemed to originate from nowhere in particular, but were most industriously circulated and most industriously believed. Perhaps it was the Celtic imagination that was at fault, but certain it is that Edge never stuck in a ditch outside the exit of the Athy controls, and neither was he passed by De Knyff at that point. But the "news" cast a shadow over us all. For our sympathies are with Edge. As to the exact effect of these rumours on the Press I am unable to say. But I know I overheard an Irishman informing a representative of the fourth estate, who was taking down "facts" industriously in his note book, that Edge was dead, his chauffeur disabled for life, while De Knyff was lying a mangled corpse on the highway amidst the wreckage of his Panhard. As

the Press had calmly monopolised our official tents, there may be some excuse for the giving of this information. At 9.58, Jenatzy, the demon of automobilism, skids thirty-two yards into the control with his back wheels locked. Owen, the American, ought to have arrived, but he has not come. But his fate we do not consider while Jenatzy is in the control, for truth to tell, the German occupies all our attention. He is the most fascinating of the competitors. There is some strange sympathetic likeness between the man and his car. As the Mercedes stands there, its mighty engines panting and straining impotently, while a blue flame flashes from its exhaust, it seems a veritable extract from hell. And Jenatzy fits the Mercedes. The other drivers who have passed us were calm, but he is excited—wildly so—and his language when we inform him of his time allowance is in keeping. To be at rest appears to be for him an almost unbearable physical torture; his face is covered with oil and grease and dust, through

One of the most exciting events of the Race. Just at the beginning of the Club Enclosure on the first round, Jenatzy travelling at a terrific speed caught up Owen on the small Winton Car, and was within 30 yards of him. The feeling of excitement rose to an enormous pitch as the two cars were seen to disappear over the ridge in the distance, neck and neck.

which his sunburnt complexion stands out ; his red moustache and little red beard add the necessary finishing touch to a figure that seems to be the incarnation of the delirium of speed.

Then comes Owen, his Winton an absolute furnace, and after him Gabriel, the little boyish-looking Frenchman with the black moustache. I have in vain searched my vocabulary for a word that represents the speed and rush of a racing automobile, and I have come to the conclusion that the English language does not yet contain the proper epithet. It would have to be coined. It should be some grand wonderful onomatopæic word, in which the strength, the panting roar, the effect that it has on the mind of some almost cruel physical torture, the sense of terrific, inhuman speed, is all represented. Possibly it may be simply an illusion, but it seemed to me, watching Gabriel as he reached the top of an incline and began his descent, that the Mors travelled quite twenty yards in the air with all four wheels off the ground. For less than a second his terrific momentum seemed to have carried him like a projectile through the air. From Gabriel we get a hasty word that Jarrott is lying dying in a ditch, his car smashed to pieces, and his chauffeur badly hurt. He speeds away leaving us in despair. The star of England seems to have set. According to many-tongued rumour, only Stocks is left alive, and we have seen nothing of him as yet. We begin to believe that before the race is over all the competitors will be killed, and that Ireland in years to come will be known as the hecatomb of automobilists. But the arrival of De Caters at 10.34 dispels the rumour as regards Jarrott. The young Belgian, with his finely-cut aristocratic face, who, in spite of his wealth, lives the life of an ordinary chauffeur, and is rarely seen clad in anything except oilskins, had seen and passed Jarrott. His car was smashed to pieces, and both he and his chauffeur were slightly hurt. How did he know, we asked ? He had stopped to ask him if he could be of any assistance. Such humane courtesy deserves to be recorded in the annals of automobilism. Like all the other competitors he wished to win. The eagerness and frenzy of the race must have been in his blood, but all the same he lost many minutes in order to help the Englishman. It was a kindly action—the action of a sportsman and a gentleman—and when he passed the grand stand and again stopped to report the fact that Jarrott was all right, he was cheered long and loudly. Miss Jarrott was in the stand, and on hearing the rumour that her brother was killed she had fainted. To her the news must have been a great relief. Baron de Caters deserved that cheer.

As far as we are concerned, with the passing of Farman and Foxhall-Keene, the first round is over. Stocks never reaches us, and Mooers, on the Peerless, rushes through the control at full speed, refusing to take any account of our signals to stop. The second round commences at 12.42 with the arrival of De Knyff, and we know for certain —for we were getting somewhat wary of rumours—that something has happened to Edge. Six minutes later the fiery Jenatzy arrives, rapidly gaining the lead. Then, at 1.1, comes Winton on his first round, his car almost red hot, with a long strip of aluminium hanging from below. He is very much out of the race, and his young son, a boy of about fourteen, who is watching from our control, looks very gloomy, and "calculates that he'll give his father beans when he gets home." Then, at last, at 1.15, comes Edge—not dead or injured—but as cheerful and

calm as ever. He has had trouble with his tyres, in fact, it is fair to estimate that had he had tyres suitable to his car, the cup would still be in the possession of England. We start him off again on his third round with another encouraging cheer, though we realise secretly that his chances are gone. So the race goes on, twice more the competitors passing us, and soon we decide among ourselves that the chances of victory lie all in favour of the Germans, with some hope, perhaps, for the Frenchman Gabriel. For ourselves we sit down and eat miscellaneous meals and talk, while the weather changes from thunder to rain and from rain to a young hurricane. At the third round De Knyff and Jenatzy still stick close together, with the German car, however, always gaining. Edge keeps running, although all his chances have vanished. At the fourth round De Knyff comes in at 5.11 and Jenatzy at 5.14, while the gallant De Caters breaks down two miles outside our control. Gabriel rushes in at 5.58, and Farman some ten minutes later. Then we have a long wait of an hour and twenty minutes, for we do not know how many competitors there may be still left, and we have to remain at our control until the last has passed. We amuse ourselves with the villagers, who, in picturesque rags, have come to see what is going on. We throw pennies to the boys to scramble for, and the road becomes a seething mass of rags and bare legs. At last, at 7.27, the cry comes down the road that another car is coming. The highway is cleared of the children, and Edge—still cheerful—rolls in. When he, too, disappears, we know that the great race is over, and, deciding that it is no good waiting for the official notification, which might have kept us from our beds for another three hours, we pack up our traps and rush bodily for the station.

The long day is over. The sun which we saw rise has set as we disentangle ourselves into cars at Kingsbridge Station. It is dark, and the streets are crowded with expectant throngs awaiting the return of the cars. But we care for none of these things. Our minds are centred on a good dinner and a bed. We throw ourselves into the dining-room of the hotel and eat. And then to bed with brains so weary that we can hardly undress. Sleep falls suddenly upon us as soon as our heads touch the pillow, and blots out all recollections of the first day of the great Carnival of Speed.

From the end of the Athy Controls.

Stationed at the exit of the Athy Controls, where the cars were again re-started on the nine-mile stretch towards Kilcullen, which led them back to the starting and finishing point, a very good opportunity was afforded for keeping more or less in touch with the events of the day, for noting the condition of the competing cars seven times during the race, and for gleaning interesting information from the drivers. One of the Dunlop Tyres Company's tents was pitched at this spot, and the Continental Tyre Company was also stationed here. Supplies of Pratt's Motor Spirit, and the Vacuum Oil Company's Lubricating Oil were available, and the Napier Company had a station too. The large tubs of water placed on a bank of broken stones stretching along the roadside were a very prominent feature of the scene, the water being used both for filling up the tanks on the cars, and also for pouring over the tyres as the racers shot out from the control. Buckets and cans of all descriptions were handy, and there was quite a small army of men ready for any emergency. One of the amusements during the day was

De Knyff, on the Panhard, on the third circuit just before sweeping past under the Grand Stand.

to watch some of these men who had been waiting in readiness, two on each side of the road, and all armed with buckets of water, attempting to throw the contents over the heated tyres, as the cars sped past. The bulk of the water often missed its mark completely, but usually the driving wheels got the desired wetting. Cases and cans containing motor spirit, and smaller ones full of lubricating oil, were also laid out in readiness upon the heap of stones, the wooden cases serving as excellent seats for those present between the frequent moments of interest when a racer was either approaching or awaiting the signal to go. A sign-board and a few " parts " indicated that this was one of the Napier stations also.

At about 8 o'clock considerable surprise was occasioned by the sound of cheering in the village, and of a distant hooter, for it was not supposed that the large Napier would arrive until 15 or 20 minutes later. The pilot cycle, followed by this car, however, made their appearance over the crown of the railway bridge, the journey round the Eastern Circuit from the starting point having been made in

remarkably short time by Edge. It was seen that rags had been bound over the filling tube through which the water is poured into the cooler, and that steam was issuing through them. The stream of steam and hot water had apparently made the run uncommonly unpleasant for the holder of the Cup and his cousin. The engine was very hot, the cause of the trouble being that the belt driving the fan had come off. Apart from the question of tyres, this belt, as much as anything, accounted for the loss of the Cup, for, although it was repeatedly replaced and tightened, it would not stay on for long. At the end of about 14 minutes the word was given to go, and the car shot out of the control at a tremendous pace. A minute or two prior to this, the Chevalier De Knyff had arrived on his Panhard, and just before he left, Mr. Owen was escorted up by his pilot cyclist. Almost at the same instant that De Knyff left, Monsieur Jenatzy arrived. It was almost exactly at 8.30 that Jarrott put in his first and only appearance, the unfortunate accident shortly after occurring to his car whilst traversing the Western Circuit.

In the Athy Control.—Mr. Charles Jarrott smilingly waiting his time to start off again.

When he came in Jenatzy was still in the control, and before Jarrott left, Gabriel was there. From 8 o'clock until about ten minutes to nine, six of the cars had therefore put in an appearance, and been sent forward on their way, and during this time there was not a moment when one or more were not standing in the road near us. A slight diversion was caused by a somewhat animated discussion occasioned by Gabriel wishing to refix a light sheet metal casing which had shaken loose in the front of his car. The whole point at issue was a fine one, and showed how difficult it is to draw any hard and fast line between an "adjustment" and a "repair."

The method adopted for timing the cars in control appeared to work admirably. The pilot cyclist, behind whom the racer travelled from one end of the control to the other, brought with him a stop-watch in a neat wooden box, and this on his arrival he handed over to the presiding officer, subsequently taking it back with him to the other end. The accuracy of the records was thus ensured, and, as we have said, the system seemed to work out perfectly.

The Baron de Caters ran up about four minutes after Gabriel's departure, followed ten minutes later by Farman, and another fifteen minutes afterwards by Foxhall Keene. The scene was thus one of great animation until 9.30, when the last-mentioned was again started off. Speculation was then rife as to what had happened to Stocks, Mooers, and Winton, all of whom ought to have put in an earlier appearance. It was not for some time that we heard of Stocks' accident, and it was not until after ten o'clock that Mooers and Winton got there, the former having had trouble with his gearing, and the latter having failed to make a start for a considerable time. When Winton did arrive he was evidently losing water fast, and there was a considerable amount of steaming. It seems that Stocks had come to grief at the Ballymoon Corner where the right road turns off at a very sharp angle, and there was a wire fence across the straight-on road. De Knyff had already run through the fence, but had backed out without injury, and the fence had been put up again. When, however, Stocks charged it, one of the posts caught his near front wheel, sharply turning the car round, and completely breaking the wheel to pieces. The car then dashed into the bank throwing the occupants violently out. Very little later in the day, however, Stocks appeared at Athy, and was none the worse for his *contretemps* when we saw him there. The wire fence was afterwards removed entirely, the corner being so deceptive.

It was only twelve minutes after Foxhall Keene's departure that Edge again ran up, having completed the Western Circuit in less than an hour and a half. The car was then steaming badly and the engine frightfully hot, so much so that it was by no means easy to re-start it. The car did not, however, stay more than its allotted time in the control, and shot off to make its second journey round the smaller circuit, De Knyff coming up just as Edge was leaving. Edge and his cousin had pushed the car out of the control, and other assistance was given when it was outside—some talk of disqualification being indulged in by the "enemy" in consequence. De Knyff was despatched at the end of about eight minutes, and a couple of minutes later—10 o'clock—Mooers came up. In spite of the troubles he had had with his low gear, he seemed to be enjoying himself thoroughly, and was soon on his way again. Jenatzy turned up at about three minutes past ten, and it was just after he

left that Winton came up. His 8-cylinder engine appeared to run very smoothly, but it was evident that the mixing valve (which on his cars replaces the ordinary carburettor) required very careful handling. When the engine is running and the car is at rest there is very little vibration—in fact, hardly any movement is to be seen. He was only kept about two minutes before the word was given to go. Starting, however, is not a strong point on his car, for the low gear not only appeared to slip considerably, but the speed attained with it seemed to be insufficient to enable the high gear to be introduced with any degree of certainty, although the pace becomes high when once the engine succeeds in picking up speed on the direct-through-drive. In comparison with the Mercedes cars, which got away with remarkable readiness, and with the large Napier, which proved itself to be no less satisfactory in this respect when running properly, the performance of all the American cars was decidedly second-rate.

Winton had hardly left the control before Owen came through, having traversed the larger circuit in about an hour and 38 minutes. After being kept about six minutes he went off on his way, the start being somewhat like that of the larger Winton in being by no means up to the other racers in point of view of quickness. Just before he left, in came Gabriel, his time for the circuit being a few minutes under the hour and a half. He reported having seen Jarrot injured, and his car smashed to pieces, his description of the wreck leading us to fear that both Jarrott and his mechanician were seriously injured. The radiator in front of his Mors proved itself to be a very effective bird-catcher, for soon after he came up a dead linnet was found firmly wedged between the tubes, and the next time he had captured a sparrow in the same way. After his departure, about fourteen minutes elapsed, and then Baron de Caters arrived, bringing the welcome news that Jarrott was not much hurt, and receiving quite an ovation when it was learned that he had stopped to make enquiries and to see if he could render any assistance, this sportsmanlike action being greatly appreciated by all. We subsequently heard from Jarrott's own lips, through his partner, Mr. Letts, that the steering gear suddenly became useless, and he was unable to move the steering wheel; whether it was a case of a "jam" or of a fracture it is hard to say, but the result was that the car struck the stone walls of a cottage and was badly smashed, Mr. Jarrott and his mechanician fortunately receiving but slight injury.

About six minutes after De Caters had left, Farman again made his appearance, and before Foxhall Keene had completed his run round the Western Circuit, De Knyff, who had been round the Eastern Circuit for the second time, had run in and gone on again. It was while Foxhall Keene's car was standing near us that a crack in the back axle, not far from the near driving wheel, was observed, but this did not deter him from continuing the race. When next he came round, which was at about 12.41, the crack was considerably worse, and although he even then ran on, yet we did not see anything more of him after that.

It was at about 11.15 that De Knyff had left, and about 11.23 when Jenatzy arrived. His car appeared to be running splendidly, and, except for a slight tear on the off-side driver, the tyres were in good condition. The next time he came up it was a few minutes to one, when he filled up with petrol, and at 2.15, when he again appeared, he had evidently realised that he stood an excellent chance of winning the race, for he was keenly excited, and having to get the car outside the control, seized one of the driving wheels and pushed it out alone. After that we saw him again at 3.45, and at 5.19; at the latter time he was only about three minutes behind De Knyff, although he started fourteen minutes later, and had then but a little over nine miles to go—to win.

Now that Jarrott and Stocks were out of the race, the keenest interest was, of course, taken in Edge's performance, and after Jenatzy's departure at 11.28, nearly a quarter of an hour elapsed, during which the chances of retaining the Cup in this country were evidently slipping away fast. However, everybody was glad to see him come in then, and hopes were expressed that he might even yet have the luck—which his pluck and perseverance deserved—of making up for lost time. He was still in front of Gabriel, De Caters, and Farman in point of view of position, if not of time, these three coming up respectively at about 11.53, 12.2, and 12.12.

Gabriel's further appearances during the day were at 1.24, 2.47—when a tyre required re-pumping—and finally at 6.5. His Mors was, on the whole, running well, but the valves on the cylinders appeared to require a certain amount of attention now and again. De Caters, who generally indulged in a few whiffs of a cigarette when he came up, and who left soon after 12, next arrived at about 1.35, then at 2.59, and finally at 4.30. This was his final appearance, because during this run round the Western Circuit his back axle gave way when he was travelling fast, and rendered the car *hors de combat*; he was fortunately able to keep control of the steering until the machine came to rest. The first news that we had of the accident was from his own lips, when he arrived soon after on a non-competing car at Athy. Just as he was leaving the control, at about half-past four, the engine had pulled up and refused to start again, apparently because there was no petrol in the tank; it was soon filled up, and he made off at high speed in his usual skilful manner.

Farman's appearances, after leaving at 12.15, were at about a quarter to two, when he filled up with petrol and water outside the control, and at 3.7, 4.36, and 6.13, water being taken in on the two last occasions. His Panhard, as also that of De Knyff, had been lightened as far as possible on the previous day in order to enable them to pass the scales. Not only were the rubber pipe connections opened up, so as to drain out every drop of water, but aluminium circulating pumps were substituted for those of brass which were fitted; a considerable number of lock nuts, including those for holding the inspection covers down above the valves, were also taken off. It was at about 12.30 that Mooers came up, after completing the Western Circuit for the first time. His front wheel on the off side was badly bent over, as the car had run into a hedge, the tyre coming off when running round a corner having led to the accident. Neither he nor the mechanician were in any way hurt, and after replacing the tyre he came slowly on to Athy. The car was put out of the way by the road side near by, and he spent the rest of the day with us. It was about eleven minutes after his arrival that Foxhall Keene arrived and went on; we afterwards heard that, in consequence of his damaged axle, he had decided to abandon the race when he again reached the starting point. At 11.47 De Knyff appeared after his second trip round the Western Circuit, and, as events showed, he was then about six minutes in front of Jenatzy. After filling up his petrol

tank he continued the course, and was again seen by us at a few minutes past 2, at about 3.41, and at 5.16, running well.

Winton turned up for the second time shortly after 1, and reported having had trouble with a stopped-up pipe; his radiator also showed signs of having been through the grass, but we could not ascertain that any untoward event was responsible for this. He started off just before a quarter past 1, but had some little trouble in starting the engine. His third appearance was at about 2.52, and his fourth soon after half-past 5, after which we did not see him again. Owen's Winton car did not turn up between 10.14 and 3.22; he came along, however, on two subsequent occasions —at 5.13 and at 6.50; at times he appeared to have some difficulty in re-starting the engine.

Edge's times of arrival after 11.42, when he was so anxiously looked out for by us, were at 1.8, 3.19, and 5.40, and he must have passed again soon after we had left the control, which was shortly after seven. His delays were largely due to trouble with tyres, but not to what are generally known as tyre troubles. We believe that he put on no less than seven outer covers, and several of these we saw ourselves. They were apparently none the worse for wear, and it was difficult to distinguish them from new ones. The enormous power exerted by the engine seems to have been too much for them, and it is certainly much to be regretted that time did not permit of the racer being fitted with the 5-inch tyres, which it ought to have had, instead of with these inadequate $3\frac{1}{2}$-inch tyres. The drive of the engine appears to have pulled the covers right out of the rims. It is, of course, impossible to say what would have happened if the cooling system had been satisfactory, and if the tyres had stood out during the whole race, but from the speed at which Edge travelled when everything was working properly, and from the excellent way in which he was able to start off and attain full speed, it is certain that he would have stood a good chance of retaining the Cup for another year, if there had been sufficient time to correct these two sources of trouble. It was, however, a great race, and we believe that the best car won.

At one time a difficulty appeared imminent in regard to the German cars, as a question arose in respect to the tyres being completely manufactured in Germany, but by evidence given before the International Commission they were ultimately passed, as it was proved to their satisfaction that for all the German cars, including the winning car of Jenatzy, the tyres fitted were Clipper-Continental, manufactured in Hanover by the Continental Tyre Company. The importance of this objection cannot be over-estimated, as had the Mercedes cars been compelled to change their tyres at the last moment the result of the race might have been very different.

The Race, as seen from Ardscull Moat.

It was a happy inspiration which originated the Ardscull Camp—the position for seeing the race was admirable, and had the camp arrangements been satisfactory the race would have been seen under the most comfortable and pleasant circumstances. Even as it was, notwithstanding the happy-go-lucky manner in which the campers were provided for, tending, as it did, to create dissatisfaction with things generally, the outing was a fairly enjoyable one.

Our representative at the Moat reached the camp on Wednesday night from Dublin by way of Athy, and found on arriving at the latter place that all decent conveyances had been engaged, so that he and a friend were constrained to make their advent on the scene in a donkey cart. It was not as imposing as the circumstances—and the individuals—deserved, but there was no choice but that or walk, an alternative which was, of course, not to be thought of. And we were in good company, for there were seen people using these conveyances who would scorn to admit it in saner moments.

Bright and early on Thursday morning the camp was astir, and long before any car could be expected to appear, the slope of the Moat facing the road from Athy was crowded with spectators. No better vantage point than the Moat existed for seeing cars approaching. As soon as an advancing car cleared Athy control the cloud of dust gave notice to the Moat campers of its coming, and as it approached speculation was general regarding its identity—

and when the time when it might reasonably have been expected had considerably passed anxiety lest something should have interfered with the race was generally manifested. It was known that the financial question had assumed an acute form, and the possibility of the race being prohibited at the last moment was discussed. Occasionally clouds of dust could be seen rising from the road between Carlow and Athy, and these were at first accepted as evidences of the pilot car's approach, but after one or two disappointments, we agreed to believe in its coming when we should see it leave Athy. As a matter of fact, we did not see the pilot car until the race was half over, when a car with the "pilot" card came rattling, gasping, and snorting from a side road—just to show us, no doubt, that it actually existed, and to prevent disappointment.

View of the course coming up to Ardscull Moat. Rene de Knyff is seen approaching, and, beyond the banner across the road, will be noticed the clouds of dust which have risen from his car up to the point where the roads had been "Westrumited." From there it will be seen the atmosphere is perfectly clear. The straight three-mile road can be seen extending in one long stretch over the hills in the distance.

nationality and the personality of the drivers being two points which received subsidiary attention. But at the Moat the speed of the cars could not be seen, and it was necessary, if one desired to do so, to either pass on towards the finishing point or return somewhat towards Athy, and this many did.

Between six and seven o'clock in the morning the tedium was somewhat relieved by the passing of various contestants—Edge, Stocks, Winton, Owen, &c.—proceeding to the starting point. Then came an official car with a very official gentleman in charge, who issued official instructions in a very official voice to the stewards regarding a drooping banner, and passed on. A long wait followed, the coming of the pilot car supposed to start at 6.30 being anticipated,

Twenty-five minutes past eight a cloud was seen arising about Athy, and the cry went up, "The pilot is coming." The car came up rapidly, and when it came to the oiled portion of the road, about a quarter of a mile away, and was seen to be green, it was recognised as a racer, and as it hurtled up the brae towards the Moat, slowing down for the turn, Edge, notwithstanding his hideous rig, was known, and his welcome was sufficiently hearty. His running at this time was remarkably good, and when the seven minutes starting difference elapsed, and no other car appeared in sight, premature rejoicing was indulged in. The seven minutes were little more than over, however, when another car came in sight, and as it took the turn somewhat widely, the French colour and "No. 2" justified the assumption

Spectators viewing the Race from the Ardscull Moat.

The encampment at the Moat of Ardscull.

that René de Knyff was the driver. And so the cars continued to appear in their order of starting until six had passed, when it was found that the American car—that of Mooers, as it turned out—was out of its place, and expressions of regret were general; and these testimonials of good feeling were still more forcible when Stocks was seen to have missed his turn. Before this, however, Gabriel, whose chances of success were much fancied by the crowd, had passed about 42 minutes behind Edge, and as his starting difference was only 35 minutes it was evident that he was losing ground. But any feeling of elation which this might have engendered was damped when Edge passed a second time, followed in less than six minutes by De Knyff, and when Jenatzy passed about 10.12, only 18 minutes behind the leader, after having a starting difference of 21 minutes, there were ominous head-

shakings. The croakers were still more pronounced in their prophecies of disaster when Jarrott, who had done well in the first half of the course, did not appear in his turn after the second. Cut off from all the world, on something like an island, we had not expected to hear anything of the outside happenings till after the race was over; but evil tidings travel in the air, and there were rumours of accidents to both Stocks and Jarrott, while Edge was said to have been disqualified for having been pushed off from a control. Colour was lent to the latter statement from the fact that Edge's motor was extremely hot, steam having been seen streaming from the escape pipe, as from the safety valve of a locomotive, when he passed the second time, and the suggestion that his pistons may have seized, rendering a start difficult, appeared sufficiently credible. When, therefore, it came to Edge's turn to appear a third

The Kildare Control.—Jenatzy, half a minute before his release for the next stretch.

time, and De Knyff appeared instead about 11.18, most of the interest for the majority of the campers was taken out of the race, and those of us who had from the first recognised that accident would have a strong voice in deciding the result, settled down to witness the struggle between France and Germany. Edge cheered the drooping spirits of the campers by appearing about half an hour behind De Knyff, but it was only too evident that nothing save accident to the leaders would allow him to win. When De Knyff appeared the fourth time, a minute or two before one o'clock, followed within four minutes by Jenatzy, it began to dawn upon us that the probability of the trophy finding a new resting place was considerable; and although the German car had lost ground a little when it came back again, it was still well within its time allowance. The interest in the other cars had by this time largely evaporated. The American cars, notwithstanding the contention of our American contemporary, *Automobile Topics*, that any one of fifteen makers in America could build

coming car might be one of them. We received the first intimation of the German car's success from a yelling howl of applause which went up from a stand down the road, and as Jenatzy swept up and round the Moat within three minutes of the leader we felt satisfied that the Gordon-Bennett trophy would find a resting place for the next year in Germany.

We waited for some time after the last racing car passed to see a car bearing an intimation that the race was over, but like the pilot car it failed to appear. A car passed right enough, which we heard afterwards was intended to carry the intimation, but the card may have fallen off, or like the Dutchman's anchor it may have been left at home. The general impression in the camp was that the best car won, and that next to keeping the trophy, it was well that it should reach new territory; the extremely feeble display of the American cars made it evident that, in the absence of racing roads in the United States, some time must elapse before the trophy may be expected to cross the Atlantic.

Baron Henry de Rothschild takes a welcome rest, after a very early rise, in one of the tents at Ballyshannon.

M. Degrais " on guard."

a car to win the trophy, were seen to be hopelessly behind. Gabriel was losing ground, and although Farman was doing somewhat better, he also was falling behind the leaders. De Caters and Foxhall Keene, on the other two German cars, were out of it, so that by four o'clock it was seen to be a duel between the Panhard and Mercedes cars, driven by De Knyff and Jenatzy. The sixth time of passing, the German car, with an allowance of fourteen minutes, passed within nine minutes of the Frenchman, and at that point it appeared either's race, with a chance in favour of the German to the extent of the time he was ahead; but it was recognised that with sixty miles to go, the slightest accident which would prevent either car going at full speed where the opportunity offered might decide the contest. When, therefore, before De Knyff reached the Moat for the last time a cloud of dust at Athy announced the coming of another car, the interest was very great. If it were Jenatzy then Germany must certainly win, always provided the times in controls were equal, but several other cars were still running and the

The Weighing Up.

On the Wednesday, the day before the race, the formal weighing up of the cars took place in the Market Place at Naas, starting at 11 a.m. An enormous gathering of the public to witness the formalities resulted, and the constabulary had the greatest difficulty at times in keeping the onlookers sufficiently back to enable the officials to carry out their work effectively. Several times they had to be cleared by forcing them back by means of a stout rope, and for a time all was well again, but by degrees, in twos and threes, they managed to slip under and again hem in those working the scales. Good humour, however, pervaded the whole scene, and with glorious sunshine above the day passed off successfully. The day resolved itself into quite a pleasant outing, and for the natives it had more the character of a *fête*. Mr. Lyons Sampson had charge of the weighing arrangements, and with the exception of an objection raised to the accuracy of the scales by Chevalier de Knyff, when it was found that the

The weighing of the cars.—Drastic measures by the constabulary to clear a passage for the cars to get into place. Mr. Edge is at the wheel of his car guiding it on to the weighing machine.

French cars could not get within the limit weight of 1,000 kilos., there was no hitch throughout the proceedings. It took close upon an hour and a half to convince the Frenchmen by demonstration that the scales were accurate to the tenth part of an ounce. In all probability the weighing up under various Continental racing events has never been before so accurately carried through, and hence the astonishment of the Frenchmen at their cars being over weight. It was highly amusing to watch the efforts to bring the weights within the maximum. Cushions and all sorts of odds and ends had to be discarded until at last the cars were passed. The weights as ultimately taken were as follows :—

Car.	Driver.	cwts.	qrs.	lbs.	Car.	Driver.	cwts.	qrs.	lbs.
Mors ...	Gabriel	19	3	0¾	Mercedes	B. de Caters	19	1	24½
Peerless...	Mooers	19	2	17	Mercedes	Keene	19	3	3¾
Winton ...	Winton	19	0	22¼	Winton ..	Owen	19	0	22¼
Napier ...	Edge	19	1	20¾	Panhard	De Knyff	19	3	7¼
Napier ...	Jarrott	19	2	20	Mercedes	Jenatzy ...	19	2	19
Napier ...	Stocks	19	1	1¼	Panhard	Farman ...	19	3	3¾

The maximum weight allowed was 1,000 kilogs., the

Mr. S. F. Edge on his big Napier Car, in the Naas Garage, having his car marked after weighing. Mr. Cecil Edge who again acted as his mechanician is seated on his left.

equivalent of which in English weight was taken to be 19 cwt. 3 qrs. 7 lbs. Subsequent to weighing, the racers retired to the garage yard behind the Town Hall, where the marking was carried through by Lancaster, the Club Engineer, under the vigilant eye of Lieut.-Col. Crompton.

On the Monday evening the Lord-Lieutenant and Countess of Dudley gave a dinner in Dublin in honour of the race, and amongst those who attended at Earl Dudley's invitation were the Duc d'Arion, Baron de Zuylen, Count Sevistorff, Count de Vogne, Baron de Forest, Signor Guinones de Leon, Lord Plunket, Hon. J. Scott Montagu and Lady Cecil Scott Montagu, Sir Thomas and Lady Troubridge, Mr. Gray Dinsmore, Mr. R. C. Wallace, K.C., Mr. Foxhall Keene, Mr. Lionel Earle, and Hon. G. Cadogan and Hon. Cyril Ward, R.N., A.s-D.-C. The guests received the most cordial hospitality, and after each nation's health had been proposed, the National Anthem of the respective countries was played.

The day following the race (Friday), cars, both racing and tourist, were on exhibition at Earlsfort Rink, where a military band played during the afternoon. The building was crowded by a fashionable Dublin throng, and the rink outside, gay with coloured lights, was also utilised for showing the cars. One corner of this had been converted into a temporary washing place for the vehicles by making a bank of sand, inside which, after a time, quite a miniature lake was formed from the washing operations. On the Saturday evening, as a wind-up to the Dublin week, the competitors were entertained at a banquet by the Club at the Shelbourne Hotel.

The only accident to a human being, which could rightly be called an accident, was the unfortunate spill of Mr. Charles Jarrott, two miles outside Stradbally, when travelling at about 75 or 80 miles an hour, without any doubt caused by some slight defect in the steering gear. The gross exaggerations of what took place, which were at first telegraphed to London and all over the world, naturally caused an immense sensation; but, within a few minutes, fortunately, these rumours were contradicted emphatically. Within an hour Mr. Jarrott was calmly smoking a cigarette to all appearance as if nothing had happened. The upset, nevertheless, must have been a great shock, and, when the car, not answering to the steering wheel, plunged into a cottage wall, turning completely over, the steering pillar gave way against Mr. Jarrott's chest. Fortunately, the car, which broke in two in turning a second time, only touched Jarrott very slightly, the one part settling down over Bianchi, his fearless little mechanician. In corroboration of the statement that Jarrott was not seriously injured, on Friday he was holding "court" at the Shelbourne Hotel, and, on the Saturday, was a prominent figure in the Club Enclosure in Phœnix Park, his eyes glistening, as the racing cars speeded past, with envy at not being able to take his part in the trials. In fact, we verily believe that, had his friends not restrained him, it would have taken very little for him to have made a dash for a car.

His recollection of his experiences from the time of the moment of realising that his steering had collapsed were extremely vivid, and were given to ourselves almost word for word, as in the following graphic account which appeared in one of our daily contemporaries some two or three days back:—

"After I had picked myself up," said Jarrott, "my first thought was for my mechanic, who is only a boy. He was lying under a portion of the car, calling for help, and crying that the red hot exhaust pipe was across his body, and was killing him. Injured as I was, I managed to lift the portion of the gear which was lying across him, and shouted to some men who, dazed and scared, were looking on from behind a hedge.

"It seemed an age before I could get them to approach. I suppose they were afraid that the car would blow up. Then, as the boy said he could not get out because he was strapped in, I had to crawl under the car and cut him clear with a knife, imploring him to lie still, and comforting him by saying that the petrol would not catch fire.

"After that I fainted. When I came to I wondered if I were dead. I could see sunshine and nothing else. With the hand I could move I tried to scratch away the blur before my eyes, and found it was a sheet. I looked round and saw that I was lying in a farmyard and by my boy, who was under another sheet. I suppose they had thought us both dead.

"I called out to the boy, who said he thought he was all right. Then a kindly priest nearly choked me by pouring whisky and water down my throat. I struggled up and went into the road, where a policeman stopped me. I said, 'I am a competitor, and have a right to be on the road,' but he replied, 'Your car finished?' 'Not at all,' I said; 'I want to go to my car.'

"I was standing there with the blood streaming down my face, and my clothes torn to ribbons when De Cáters came by. He pulled up short and called out to me. I was so dazed that I could scarcely understand. Then it occurred to me that there was a race, and I asked, 'Are you in the race?' 'Yes,' he answered, so I called out, 'Then get on, man, for goodness sake; get on, I am all right.' Somehow the boy and I got back to Athy, and all that I could think of through the night was that I wanted to repair a tyre."

MR. JARROTT, who has been overwhelmed with telegrams and letters, first of sympathy and then with congratulations, writes to us asking us to convey through the columns of the AUTOMOTOR his thanks to the very large number of his friends who have either written or wired him expressing their sympathy with him in his accident. He continues:—

"So many have I received that it was impossible for me to reply to each individual person, but at the same time I would like to express my gratification at my very lucky escape, and the good wishes from everybody have been a source of considerable consolation to me in one of the biggest disappointments of my life.

"I am getting along very nicely, and hope in the course of two or three days to be quite well again; and I also hear that my boy, Bianchi, is progressing equally favourably.

"The journey over last night (Sunday) shook me up a little, but considering everything, I got through wonderfully well."

Already discussion has started in regard to the location of next year's race. M. Camille Jenatzy, the winner, who is 32 years of age, in an interview stated that he hopes the race will be held in Ireland again. He thinks the Irish people are delightful, although he admits that the course was, he thought, the most dangerous he ever drove on. All German hopes, of course, will be centred on the event taking place within reasonable distance of Berlin, but failing permission being accorded, the Lüneburger Heide, in Hannover, has been suggested, and it is also reported that the Grand Duke of Mecklenburg-Schwerin has offered his territory on which to hold the race failing any other suitable locality.

The Simms Manufacturing Company ask us to point out that the ignition system adopted on the Mercedes cars which won the Gordon-Bennett Irish Race and the Irish Automobile Club's 200 Guinea Challenge Cup is identical with that introduced by them in this country, and so well known here as the Simms-Bosch magneto-electric ignition.

THE SALON DE L'AUTOMOBILE.

Notes at the Great French Show.—I.

MORE brilliant than ever, and more bewildering in its vastness and multiplicity of detail, the Salon de l'Automobile, du Cycle et des Sports was inaugurated in the Grand Palais on Thursday, by President Loubet, with an *éclat* which seems impossible of attainment at kindred English shows. We have no building of such magnificent yet artistic lines; we lack the amazing talent for decorative display which is so conspicuous in the adornment of the Grand Palais itself and of the individual stands; we have no such plethora of native constructors, more than enough to fill a building twice the size without any foreign element whatever; and we have not as yet been favoured with the patronage of the head of the state which is so willingly vouchsafed each year at the Paris Salon. The public interest, too, in the French Show is tremendous. On the opening day it was scarcely possible to move even at

distributed, and the fluctuations throughout the day, it would not be in any way surprising to find the official record of the total amounting to 100,000.

THE SHOW FEVER.

For the avowed *chauffeur* the daily *mise en scène* is one to raise his motoring enthusiasm to fever heat; but even to those as yet outside the pale, who have never revelled in the delights of piloting their own cars, the picturesqueness of the spectacle must be undeniable. Many of the stands are not only works of art in themselves—that of the A. Clément firm is in beautifully wrought iron, and cost £2,000 - but they are profusely decorated with evergreens and flowers, and at dusk become aglow with lights arranged with admirable effect. In themselves the stands would form a *tout ensemble* of extraordinary brilliance, but the splendour of this year's scheme of illumination for the hall has to be

THE HOTCHKISS EXHIBIT.

mid-day; by four o'clock one could only struggle to get out, a process which of itself was alike painful and prolonged. For a whole hour admission was refused to the waiting crowds outside, simply because the huge building was already packed, and the estimates of the attendance ran as high as 200,000 persons. No doubt this was an exaggeration, but taking into account the numerous galleries, the side-halls, and the *sous-sol* into which the public could be

seen to be believed. Certainly it is the most tasteful and entrancing that has ever yet been witnessed at a public exhibition. From the centre of the glass-roof is suspended an inverted cupola of amber-coloured lamps, while others orming strands of gold are carried in close order down all the girders of the great dome with marvellous refulgence resembling the rays of the sun at its zenith. Festoons of lamps, moreover, are carried all round the upper balconies, outlining to splendid advantage the noble proportions of the building. No less than 20,000 lamps are used in this really glorious display, in which, despite its radiance, the chief characteristic is a grateful softness rather than mere garish glitter.

From every point of view the present Salon is the most interesting ever held. The exhibitors are more numerous

CARS OUTSIDE THE GRAND PALAIS.

and more varied; indeed, the complaints which rumbled a year ago are now loud and deep at the process of selection, which has become inevitable. The British representation is for the first time appreciable as to quantity and excellent in quality; how long will it be, one wonders, before it will be as necessary for French buyers to come over to a London automobile show as it now is for Englishmen to go to Paris? In the way of striking novelty there is by no means a super-abundance, but in workmanship and essential details there are undoubted evidences of improvement. It might be said, in fact, that the elimination of weak points is the dominant feature of next season's cars, whatever their individual types of motor; whereas last year we were confronted with a stupendous *volte face* on the part of the French trade in the shape of a wholesale and unoriginal adoption of Mercédès methods.

A MULTITUDE OF ATTRACTIONS.

One must not forget, moreover, in discussing the infinite variety of the Salon, that it includes a very wide aggregation of exhibits in addition to the cars themselves. There is a fine display of motor-boats, including a new Mercédès; the tyre department is astonishingly large to eyes accustomed

PRESIDENT LOUBET INSPECTS THE DARRACQ CARS.

to the limitations of British products in that line; accessories are innumerable; while there are also a *carrosserie* department, an aeronautic section, and one for alcohol, to say nothing of machinery in motion. All these combine to form an array of attractions which captivate the visitor's attention on every hand, and at the end of a week's inspection there would still be new features to examine. Frankly, but for

the crowded state of the hall one would be unwilling to leave the place at all, so many are the fascinations to the expert and the enthusiast alike, while to those who are neither the Dufayel orchestra alone makes no slight appeal, and there are sundry items which catch the eye of even the least curious.

FAMOUS CARS.

The actual Martini car, for example, which ascended the Rochers de Naye is shown upon a facsimile, in wood, of the *crémaillère*, or rack and pinion rail, on which that memorable journey was made. Then, of course, there are various racing cars that have earned laurels during the current year—the " No. 168 " Mors, with the same body on which I saw Gabriel arrive at Bordeaux on the tragic 25th of May; the leviathan 100 h.p. Gobron-Brillié, which swept up all the short distance records of the autumn trials, and the speedy Clément-Bayard, a marvel among light cars. Several firms, too, exhibit models of their motors in half sections, and the De Dion-Bouton mount a huge one on a lofty pedestal, while an Oldsmobile car is shown with a glass-sided body. And by way of gaining the approval of the lady visitors the exhibitors of the Automotrice car have

NOVEL DECORATIONS ON THE F.I.A.T. STAND.

been handing out neat posies of Neapolitan violets, bound with light blue ribbon on which the name of the car is inscribed in gold lettering. Alas for our own insular reserve! Up to Saturday there were but three English ladies who could be persuaded to accept this delicate attention, proffered though it was by Madame Gasté herself; and in one case a British female chose to consider herself insulted, and created a small scene in consequence.—" I suppose that is the English way," said M. Gasté resignedly.

THE NEW FEATURES.

But what of the new features? Will the cars of 1904 present any material change of exterior such as was so suddenly made apparent in those of the present year by the adoption of the square-nosed bonnet, and will any widespread adoption of a detail like the mechanically operated inlet valve set a distinctive mark on the coming types? The answer is in the negative; there is no new departure of a revolutionary kind. In some cases, indeed, one may note a reversal to 1902 methods.

Taking the main details seriatim one may begin with the honeycomb radiator. On the whole, this is more general than last year, although it has been discarded by certain firms. It is now seen in all shapes—octagonal, hexagonal, pentagonal, square, diamond-shaped, and round. The last named seems the best attempt at the solution of a very difficult problem. Cars were beginning to get decidedly elegant through the Mors type of bonnet being multiplied, when suddenly, for mechanical reasons, the fore-front became ugly in the extreme through the adoption of the Mercédès honeycomb. Inasmuch as it is impossible to taper this type of radiator to a point, the only way to modify the bluntness and embody lines of beauty is by introducing curves in lieu of straight lines, and the circle which is seen in the new Hotchkiss is a welcome expedient with much in its favour.

Fans are more variform than last year. In some cases they have no rims and have stronger blades; on the Hotchkiss the latter can be set at any angle so as to vary the amount of draught, and can also be turned completely

spectively, and naturally one looks to see whether either has received the flattery of imitation. The eight-cylinder has not, but the three-cylinder idea has been adopted by the Cottereau, the Argyll, and a couple of other firms. As several six-cylinder motors are on the stocks of English firms—the Napier, Brooke, and Sunbeam, for example—it is also natural to look out for this innovation at the Salon. So far, however, the French trade has nothing to say to it, but a Dutch car, the Spyker, has a six-cylinder car on view.

A new preference was shown last year for the placing of commutators high up and easily accessible, in conjunction with a bevel shaft. It would seem, however, that the system has its disadvantages, probably including that of rattle; at any rate, the method has been abandoned for 1904. Spark gaps, too, which were to the fore a year ago, are seen in merely isolated instances.

The Mors and Renault motors last year had spring clips

THE CHARRON, GIRARDOT, AND VOIGT'S EXHIBIT.

flat. The drive varies considerably, belts broad and narrow, long and short, being used, as well as chains, while in the "C. G. V." a friction pulley on the engine shaft engages with a smaller pulley on the fan shaft.

OTHER FEATURES.

The mechanical inlet valve has apparently come to stay, and is the feature above all others among last year's fashions that has increased its hold on the affections of the makers. Variable lifts, at the driver's option while actually driving, are increasing in favour, though abandoned by the Mercédès people themselves. Magneto ignition appears to stand where it did. In frames the pressed steel pattern is slightly more in evidence, and in the Darracq cars is shaped on novel lines. It is widest in the centre, and the rear portion has a double twist, both inwards and upwards, behind the cross strut, and the tonneau or coupé is thus much higher than the gear-box.

Last year the *clous* of the Salon were the eight-cylinder "C. G. V." and the three-cylinder Panhard motors re-

at the end of their high tension wires, so that any one of them could be instantaneously removed from a sparking plug to test the firing without loss of time. This useful plan is now adopted, in a sense, on the De Diétrich, Peugeot, and Richard-Brasier cars, but instead of the springs being detached they are clipped to a brass rod, of which half is covered with vulcanite, and contact can be made or unmade by a half-turn of the rod. The Panhard method of enclosing the high tension wires in a small cylinder has been pretty generally adopted throughout the Show.

PROTECTING THE MECHANISM.

Several cars this year have taken up the idea instituted by the Décauville in France and the Sunbeam in England of attaching an apron of steel or aluminium beneath the frame, thus protecting the whole of the mechanism from mud or dust. The Peugeot, Germain, Rochet-Schneider and F.I.A.T. are illustrations in point, while the Darracq has partially followed the same idea. If the theories of Colonel

THE MORS STAND.

Amongst other interesting cars shown here was the famous racer, "No. 168," on which Gabriel won the first stage of the Paris-Madrid race this year in such a sensational manner.

THE PANHARD STAND.

A striking and artistic design distinguished this stand, on which a very varied selection of Panhards was staged.

A GENERAL VIEW OF THE SALON.

Crompton and Mr. C. S. Crawley, as enunciated in their recent paper, be correct, this method should go far towards the solution of the dust problem. Complete smoothness below the frame, and an upward tendency towards the rear, were defined as the prime essentials of a dustless car, and all that seems necessary is to affix the apron under the whole frame, and glance it upwards beneath the tonneau, a thing which should not present any difficulty on chain-driven cars, at all events, and could be accomplished even with live axles if the frame were raised as in the new Darracq *chassis*.

THE BRAKEWORK.

Among other noticeable tendencies is the fitting of push pedals instead of the piano type; the employment of internal expanding brakes for the rear sprockets; the casing-in of the rear brake-drums; and the use, in several cases, of compensated rear brakes, the pull being taken from a pivot in the centre of a transverse bar, to receive the ends of which the frame is slotted. Foot brakes are generally improved. On the larger Peugeot cars an extra one is fitted as a stand-by, three pedals being used accordingly in addition to the foot accelerator. The chainless Peugeots have the free ends of the band of the differential brake working on right and left handed worms, with coarse pitch, the object being to remove the strain from the driver's foot. A similar device was shown on the Maurer-Union car at the Crystal Palace. Ball bearings are more in favour than last year. Several cars have five springs instead of four; that is to say, a transverse spring is placed beneath the tonneau in addition to the ordinary quartette that are parallel with the frame length. In the matter of lubrication there is the

the advantage of the industry and the private user alike that so good an accessory has not been confined to one make of car, but made available for all. Lastly, so far as tendencies are concerned, it may be mentioned that the exhaust pipes of several motors are this year made with ribs—not very pronounced, but such as serve to effect some reduction in the heat of the exhaust gases ere they are passed through the silencer.

NEW CARS.

So much for features which are in any way characteristic of the general trend of the Salon. Concerning entirely new cars there is very little to be said. The *début* of the Hotchkiss firm, however, is distinctly interesting, and it may be said at once that they have produced a remarkably smart car, of palpably high class in every detail; indeed, one has hardly a word of criticism to offer save as to the wisdom of making a live axle pattern with so high a power as 35 h.p. The Peugeot firm have made a new departure in their 6½ h.p. single-cylinder and 7 h.p. double-cylinder cars, which are now of the chainless type. Clément cars are no longer entirely chainless, the 18 h.p. pattern being chain-driven. M. Clément's own cars, the Bayard, are chainless except in the largest type, the 27 h.p. For the most part, however, the leading firms retain their last year's nomenclature and types, only the details being subject to minor variation.

Perhaps Colonel Renard's "road train" attracts as much attention as anything. It consists of several vehicles of varying shape, each coupled with universal joint connections, and the whole being drawn by a Darracq car. The carriages are first and second class, with luggage and

THE NAPIER DISPLAY.

usual variety of methods of applying grease, but for oil distribution the Dubrulle lubricator is more widely used than ever. It is not generally known, by the way, that the inventor is the foreman of the Peugeot works, and it is to

delivery vans thrown in, and the idea is not without possibilities of future development for districts ill-served by railways.

The Janvier six-wheeled car is a novelty to French eyes,

but is virtually the adoption of a device illustrated some months ago in THE CAR. The steering wheels are in duplicate, with two axles, two steering rods, etc., and the contention of the inventor is that the arrangement tends to the elimination of side slip. What actual practice may reveal one can only surmise, but the *primâ facie* merit of the device is not obvious, to say the least.

Individual novelties of detail, as apart from those already alluded to, are not very conspicuous. The most interesting are two included on the "C.G.V." machines. One is

tonneau from its pride of place and to substitute a door at each side of the car in lieu of the single door behind. For town work the advantages are obvious; there is less to be said, however, in favour of the innovation for ordinary use. There is an extraordinarily large array, it should be added, of broughams, coupés, limousines, and other types of covered car, from which one may conclude that the makers of petrol-driven vehicles have recognised the formidable rivalry of the electric carriage, and have no intention of being left behind in the provision of cars suitable for urban locomotion.

THE DE DION STAND, WITH LARGE MODEL OF ENGINE ON PILLAR.

an arrangement by which a lamp set in the centre of the front frame is turned concurrently with the steering wheel, so that it always points midway between the two, instead of in a direction parallel to the frame. The advantages and disadvantages of this device are about equally matched. The other novelty is the gearing down of the starting handle. It is placed on one side instead of being coupled directly to the engine shaft, and a pair of unequal cogs effect the transmission from the handle to the motor, with the result that the effort of overcoming the initial compression is somewhat moderated.

Mention must not be omitted of new departures in *carrosseries*. The Panhard stage coach, built for Prince Orloff, is a handsome vehicle of striking proportions, and one only trembles for the fate of the occupants of the upper seat in the event of a bad side slip; the parabola they would describe through space would certainly enlarge their views of the adjoining territory in the shortest possible time. A saloon car shown on the "M.M.C." stand is much admired; like its prototype, the Pullman Mors described in THE CAR a few weeks ago, it is fitted with every conceivable device for luxurious travelling, including a jewel case and a wine bin. It is worthy of note that the sumptuous turn-out was made entirely at Coventry.

OUSTING THE TONNEAU.

An attempt is being made on several hands to oust the

The chief novelty among the accessories is the new type of Alpha lamp, which is not only of great power but is one in which the water supply may be allowed to remain indefinitely. Some very nice touring baskets are shown, moreover, with waterproof coverings laid over the wicker framework.

Amidst so much that is of high quality one can utter but one word of real regret, and that is with regard to the absence of any marked tendency towards the simplification of mechanical details, and the reduction of trouble in the way of attention on the part of the owner. Gear-boxes in many cases are still clamped down by many nuts, without any screw-cap or slide in the centre by which one may quickly add fresh oil. Commutators are still more or less inaccessible on no small number of cars, as well as exposed to mud. Few are the motors which have any arrangement by which a man may know at once whether he has enough oil in his crank chambers, or, what is equally important, whether he has too much and thus fouls his plugs. Many of the four-cylinder engines, moreover, are more complicated than ever, and one famous type is a tangle of pipes and fittings. And finally I may express the hope that something serious will some day be done in the matter of producing a perfect sparking plug.

GAMAGE'S GREAT XMAS BAZAAR.

GLAD TO SEE YOU whether you buy or not.

ADMISSION QUITE FREE.

HUNDREDS OF ACCEPTABLE MOTOR PRESENTS.

HOODS AND VEILS Of Every Description.	THE MOTOR OR CARRIAGE **SKIN FOOT MUFF.** *Made of various good quality Furs.* **Invaluable for Motorists in Cold Weather.**	**FUR OVER BOOTS.** For Ladies & Gentlemen.

Price **7/6.** Carriage 6d.
In High-class Furs, **10/6, 15/6, 21/-, 25/-, 27/6.**
Waterproof Foot Sack, lined Plushette, **15/-**

Please write for Motor Accessory Catalogue, post free.

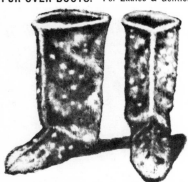

These are made in a variety of Furs, and being fur inside and out are very warm.
Easily slipped on and off Send size of boot when ordering.

In Lynx and Leopard, lined Weenuxk ... } **20/-**
In Wolf and Civet Cat ... ... } per pair.
In Dingo and Leopard, lined Natural Opossum }

A. W. GAMAGE, Ltd., HOLBORN, LONDON, E.C.

Insure Yourself and Car against Accidents
BY TAKING OUT
A "CAR" POLICY
WHICH INCLUDES SUBSCRIPTION TO THIS JOURNAL.

By special arrangement with the Law Accident Insurance Society, Ltd., "THE CAR" is enabled to offer Owners of Private Motor Cars the Insurance Policies as published by the Society at the same Premiums, but including free subscription, as follows :—

For £10 per annum.

(1.) **Accidents to Owner.**—Whilst driving or being driven in, or whilst mounting or dismounting from Insured Car, a sum of £500 in case of Death ; £3 per week during Temporary Total Disablement, limited to 26 weeks any Accident.

(2.) **Damage to Insured Car.**—Accidental Damage through Collision up to £500 in any one year, with a limit of £100 for a single Accident (excluding Fire, Explosion, or Self-ignition, Damage to Rubber Tyres or Lamps, and first £2 10s. of any damage).

Note.—This is **NOT** limited to Collision with a Vehicle.

(3.) **Fire.**—Damage from Fire, Explosion or Self-ignition, up to £200 or value of Car, if of less amount, in any one year.

Note.—Insurance under this heading can be increased up to the full value of the Car at 15s. per cent. on the further amount to be covered.

(4.) **Public Liability (Third Party) Indemnity.**—Claims by the General Public (excluding Passengers) for Personal Injury or Damage to Property, up to £500 in any one year, with a limit of £100 for a single Accident.

(5.) **In addition to the above benefits, a copy of "THE CAR" will be sent weekly post free.**

Indemnity against **Burglary, Larceny** or **Theft** is not included in this Policy, but can be added if desired at 5s. per cent. on value of Car.

For £15 per annum.

(1.) **Accidents to Owner.**—Whilst driving or being driven in, or whilst mounting or dismounting from Insured Car, a sum of £1,000 in case of Death ; £6 per week during Temporary Total Disablement, limited to 26 weeks any one Accident.

(2.) **Accidents to Paid Driver.**—Whilst driving or being driven in or whilst mounting or dismounting from Insured Car, a sum of £100 in case of Death ; £1 per week during Temporary Total Disablement, limited to 26 weeks any one Accident.

(3.) **Damage to Insured Car.**—Accidental Damage through Collision with an object, up to £1,000 in any one year, with a limit of £150 for any one Accident (excluding Fire, Explosion or Self-ignition, Damage to Rubber Tyres or Lamps, and first £2 10s. of any damage).

Note.—This is **NOT** limited to Collision with a Vehicle.

(4.) **Fire.**—Damage from Fire, Explosion or Self-ignition, up to £300 or value of Car, if of less amount, in any one year.

Note.—Insurance under this heading can be increased up to the full value of the Car at 15s. per cent. on the further amount to be covered.

(5.) **Public Liability (Third Party) Indemnity.**—Claims by the General Public (excluding Passengers) for Personal Injury or Damage to Property, up to £1,000 in any one year, with a limit of £200 for a single Accident.

(6.) **In addition to the above benefits, a copy of "THE CAR" will be sent weekly post free.**

Indemnity against **Burglary, Larceny** or **Theft** is not included in this Policy but can be added if desired at 5s. per cent. on value of Car.

IMPORTANT NOTICE.—Particulars of other Policies will be sent on application.

NO RESTRICTIVE CLAUSE AS TO SPEED LIMIT.

A Proposal Form will be sent by applying to the Publisher, "THE CAR Illustrated," 17, Shaftesbury Avenue, London. Immediately it is returned accompanied by a Cheque for the amount of the Premium a Cover Note will be forwarded, giving protection until the Policy is ready.

Remittances should be made payable to "THE CAR—Illustrated, Ltd.," and crossed "Barclay & Co., Ltd."

MOTOR-CAR INSURANCE ON THE CONTINENT CAN NOW BE ARRANGED

Printed for the Proprietors by EYRE AND SPOTTISWOODE, His Majesty's Printers, and published by GEORGE BUTLER MORRIS, Piccadilly Mansions, 17, Shaftesbury Avenue, London. W.—December 9, 1903

Cats
OF THE
GREEK ISLANDS

HANS SILVESTER

THAMES AND HUDSON

Translated from the French *Les Chats du Soleil*
by Emily Lane

British Library Cataloguing-in-Publication Data
A catalogue record for this book is available from the
British Library

ISBN 0-500-01600-3

Printed and bound in Italy

I OUGHT TO BEGIN WITH THE GREEKS, and especially those who live in the Cycladic Islands. They are at the heart of this book. They don't often appear in my photographs, but without them the cats would not survive. The climate allows the islanders to spend much of their life out of doors, and the cats share that Mediterranean habit. Indoors, their living rooms are like museums – full of family mementoes, religious objects, decorative plates, vases round the television and mini-bar. Cats are forbidden to cross the threshold: Greeks allow no pets in their homes, except for their canaries. Yet the cats are true domestic cats, not abandoned or wild, and they have for centuries shared the lives of human beings. The Greek islanders like them without exactly loving them, they care *for* them without exactly caring *about* them; but they totally accept them. Cats are an inseparable part of everyday life: they have always been there, like the wind, the sun, the sea, day and night.

My first stay on Mykonos was in 1982. I was instantly enchanted by the light and the architecture. I photographed some cats, but without really registering the force of their personalities.

A later trip took me to the Cyclades to photograph the islands' dove-cotes. This time I developed a passion for the cats, and we became friends. Subsequently, over three years, I observed them at all hours of the day and night, and through every season, with the utmost patience so as to disturb them as little as possible. To the Greeks I quickly became the fool who runs after the cats. I made them smile, but it was with the greatest kindness that they brought me coffee and cakes and told me stories about their favourite cats during the long hours that I waited for the best moment to take my photographs.

At home, in Provence, we have kept cats for more than thirty years. They are a part of our everyday life. These Provençal cats are similar to the cats of the Greek islands, yet not the same. They are more attached to people and the house; they have lost something of their social instinct; the way they behave between themselves is different, distinctly more individualistic. Our present cat is called Greco. When he chose me as his adoptive father he was a tiny kitten, abandoned in the port of Hydra. Now he's a real tom-cat with plenty of personality, very friendly, very engaging. We have never before had a cat that could purr quite as loud as Greco. (The paw-prints in this book are his.)

Whatever island you visit, Mykonos, Milos, Santorin, Tinos, Syros, Amargos, Folegandros, Sifnos, Paros or Naxos, you will be struck by the vast population of cats. They come in all colours – white, black, grey, ginger, striped, and every conceivable and inconceivable mixture. The Greeks are very generous in feeding them: fishermen throw them their damaged catch, and fishmongers always set aside a portion for them.

In return, the islanders hope to be spared the bother of rats and mice. Indeed, the ancient link between human, cat and rodent still exists in the islands. The more confined the space, the greater the importance of cats as protectors of food and, especially, of seed-corn. And the cat is a powerful ally in the rodent war: an ordinary village cat can easily catch three hundred mice a year, to judge by our own Greco. If you think how quickly mice reproduce, you will realize how important cats are in rural areas. Females are much better hunters than males. Some cats find full-grown rats a problem, but they deal with young rats as easily as with mice. In many countries the development of chemical poisons has radically altered the relationship between people and rodents, and we have quickly forgotten what our ancestors suffered: seed-corn and harvests damaged and lost, disease engendered and spread. But this is still the situation today in many parts of the world, such as India, where it is reckoned that twenty-five per cent of the harvest is lost to rats and mice.

Ships' cargoes were particularly at risk. Supplies were constantly threatened, and to protect them sailors kept cats in the holds of their ships. Cats were as much a part of the equipment as the anchor, the sails and the compass, and it was impossible to register or insure a ship that had no cat aboard. When the great navigators set sail to discover new worlds, they were always accompanied by cats. Without cats to protect their oats, the horses would have starved; without horses, Pizarro would not have conquered the Incas. So cats have played a shaping role in world history. The British Royal Navy provided for the maintenance of cats on warships as late as 1975. (André Malraux provides a striking example of how a lack of cats cost the French the battle of Agincourt in 1415: while the English kept their weapons in cat-patrolled stores, the gut cords of the French crossbows, left unguarded, were gnawed through by rats.

Cats are ill-suited to life on board, which they suffer only under strong coercion, and they care little for travelling. It is thus totally against their own will that they have succeeded in conquering every corner of the globe. One thing is certain, and that is that cats were always ready to jump ship if they had the opportunity, even if it meant swimming ashore: thus it is that these water-hating animals can be found on almost every island in the world.

The inhabitants of the Cyclades are poised between Europe and Asia, and their way of life reflects their dual inheritance. They don't pamper their domestic animals; but neither do they torment them, as happens farther east. People and cats alike live a simple life and know how to be happy in their day-to-day existence. In a port once I saw, painted in large letters on the keel of a fishing boat, the message in English: 'Don't worry, be happy.' Cats retain their independence; their friendship with the human race extends only so far, and it is they who set the limits.

In the industrialized West, domestic animals are often over-indulged, spoiled, and smothered with affection. It is the cats that have adapted best to this new way of life, even if the universe of their urban milieu has become ever more restricted, and alley cats have been transformed into parlour pets. In the old days they might at least have had a garden; now they may not even be able to look out of the window. As an ultimate refinement of domestication, they are de-clawed to protect the furniture.

On the Greek islands, cats lead a very different life. Each lives in his or her own district, where every morning the toms go out for a stroll and mark with a squirt of urine the boundaries of their territory. Within the district, they know every house, garden, roof, shrub, tree and hiding-place. They also know every resident, human or animal. They see a dog at a distance, and know at once how to behave towards that particular creature. People, too, hold no mysteries, and they know to the last detail every shift and nuance in the rhythm of village life: precisely when and in what house leftovers will be put out for them, when the fishermen come back into port – and much else. In the same way, they know who is fond of them, who tolerates them and who hates them, and they adjust their manners accordingly. Their understanding of people is unerring, and their judgment acute. The slightest change in their world is cause for surprise: a new smell, no matter how faint, arouses their curiosity; at an unexpected sound they instantly awake. A rat or a mouse is unlikely to penetrate this world unobserved. When a cat becomes aware of a rodent, her attitude changes instantly. She freezes, and waits for her prey with amazing patience. When the rodent appears, the cat leaps, pins it down with her forepaws, and grips it in her fangs. The subsequent fate of the poor mouse has been vividly described by Jean-Louis Hue (*Le Chat dans tous ses états*): 'The game hots up. Politely, the cat helps her prey to play its part. Standing on her hind legs, she holds it in her forepaws like a mother kangaroo with her baby. Then the pair seem to leave the earth altogether. Paws outstretched, in a whirlwind of excitement, the cat raises her victim up as high as possible before dropping it. What a wonderful game, she thinks, if only the mouse could fly! But it drops down heavily. The cat follows, light as a feather, pacified by her aerial exertions, and for a moment feigns exhaustion, before love of the game spurs her on. Such a charming playmate cannot be allowed to die: the cat tries to revive it by little taps of her paw. Each playful pat is a wounding blow, but heedlessly she goes on, stubbornly trying to coax a response equal to hers in vitality. Death when it comes satisfies the hunter, but disappoints the player.'

Cats form part of the village community, naturally, but they get no more than food from the inhabitants. If anyone speaks to them they purr with delight, and their greatest pleasure is to rub against your legs; only very rarely, however, will they permit themselves to be stroked, hating the crackle of static electricity in their fur. Greeks do not normally give names to their cats, calling them simply *Gata* or *Gatila* (cat or kitty). In some villages, you will find a woman or perhaps a man who is the self-appointed guardian of strays. But if cats become too numerous in any given area their general health declines, epidemics break out, and many die – or a restaurant owner, exasperated by the crowd of cats haunting his terrace, resorts to poison.

Sometimes a really exceptional tom can dominate a whole neighbourhood. He is so strong, so cunning and so handsome that people spoil him, and even greet him in the street. Other toms, awed, keep the peace when he is around. Since he seldom fights he is always in prime condition, and his success with cats on heat is reflected the next spring in the colour of the kittens.

Cats within a neighbourhood know one another extremely well; those on the periphery are familiar, but not intimate associates. A strange cat venturing into an alien neighbourhood is immediately ejected, and a strange dog is greeted by a bristling of fur. Dogs usually know better than to risk confrontation, and instead lurk in hiding-places from which they can see without being seen. Female cats will attack only if their kittens are in danger: their action then is swift, sudden and fearless, and the astonished foe turns tail in terror.

To be really congenial, a neighbourhood needs a ruined house, an old stable or an abandoned courtyard, where wild

passions are consummated and female cats give birth. For a few weeks, it is the gathering place for all the local cats, a secret retreat where their revelry is betrayed only by amorous yowls. (Kittens in the same litter often have different fathers.) Cats have other strong emotions, too, not unlike humans, chief among them jealousy. Unusually disputes are settled among acquaintances in fights of no great moment. In serious fights, however, claws become fearful weapons, blood soon flows, terrible injuries are inflicted, and it is not uncommon for one of the combatants to lose an eye.

Every day, the cats spend hours grooming themselves, licking their fur and using a moistened paw to wash their heads.

In these communities, there are two sorts of marginal citizens. On one side are the privileged individuals who belong to someone. While they are not allowed inside the house, the doorstep is theirs; they are regularly fed, and may even receive extra rations on demand; sometimes they serve as living toys for the children of the family. Fatter and less wild, these cats are easily spotted. They are no less free than the rest, but enjoy much better conditions. At the opposite extreme are those cats who are tramps by temperament and refuse to fit in, scavenging beyond the boundaries of any given neighbourhood. They are the ones that you see first when you land – near the dustbins, on restaurant terraces and haunting the harbour. In fights, they always lose to their more established brethren. Their diet is irregular, feast one moment, famine the next, and nearly always very poor in quality. They are often ill, and they die young.

A cat's position in the social order seems to be established at a very early age. Some kittens are adopted and find homes; most join the neighbourhood group; a few remain solitary outsiders. The social behaviour of cats is complex and difficult to interpret. Each one has its own personality. Because of their strong sense of individuality, cats can never accept a rigid organization, and they do not form packs or groups.

Domestic cats need human beings, and their lives become progressively more difficult the greater the distance that separates them. Cats need not only food but affection. By nature they must purr, and they would rather purr in human company. On some islands I witnessed a genuine harmony between the species that gave equal pleasure to both sides. Cats can manifest through their behaviour just how happy they are.

Cats spend much more time asleep than humans, and their daily rhythm is very different. Their sleep is more like a series of naps. Depending on the season, they rest in the welcome warmth of the winter sun or in cool summer shade. Their naps, somewhere between a dreamy doze and deep sleep, suit them perfectly, and no other animal is as adept at napping; conversely, without these short sleeps cats cannot survive. Cats alternate between sleep and alertness right through the day and night. In the dark they are as deft as during the day, relying on their adaptable eyesight, their memory, and their keen tactile sense.

The more severe and straight-edged the architecture, the less happy the cat. Cats like free forms, changes of level, curves, angles, irregularity, and mixed materials. The white villages of the Cyclades suit them perfectly. Cats live on two levels – on the flat roofs as much as on the ground, using balconies as springboards to sail across the narrow streets. When they need to, they can find good hiding-places from which to observe the rest of the world: it is an environment that suits cats much better than dogs, and here they are at an advantage, able to make themselves heard and to watch any movement near or far. If architects paid more attention to the feelings of cats, we would live in much pleasanter houses. The quality of life depends on urbanism and on architecture. Our ideas of cities went wrong long ago, to the detriment of domestic animals even more than of people. In the Cyclades, cars cannot get into the hearts of villages and towns; the streets, made to the measure of pedestrians and donkeys, are too narrow. And that contributes much to the well-being of cats, dogs and people.

Our domestic cats are descended not from the European wildcat but from the Abyssinian cat, a native of the African deserts. In ancient Egypt cats were sacred and their bodies were preserved by mummification; mistreatment of a cat was a capital offence. Where the cats of the Cyclades came from originally is uncertain, but they must have arrived by boat, a long time ago. Cats are depicted on many ancient Greek vases. Without them, the villages on the islands dotting the Aegean Sea would be different, much less vital, places. The silhouettes of cats against the white houses are as much a part of them as the blue paint on doors and windows.

To live in harmony with their environment and enjoy the pleasures of life – such seems to be their whole *raison d'être*. In this book I have sought to show the quality of life of these island cats; and I have come to understand just how much people and cats have in common, especially when they are happy.